AT THE ABYSS

AT THE ABYSS

AN INSIDER'S HISTORY OF THE COLD WAR

Thomas C. Reed

BALLANTINE BOOKS • NEW YORK

A Presidio Press Book
Published by The Random House Publishing Group
Copyright © 2004 by Thomas C. Reed

All rights reserved under International and Pan-American Copyright Conventions.
Published in the United States by The Random House Publishing Group, a division of
Random House, Inc., New York, and simultaneously in Canada by Random House of
Canada Limited, Toronto.

Presidio Press and colophon are trademarks of Random House, Inc.

www.presidiopress.com

Library of Congress Cataloging-in-Publication Data
is available upon request from the publisher.

ISBN 0-89141-821-0

Book design by Susan Turner

Manufactured in the United States of America

First Edition: March 2004

3 5 7 9 10 8 6 4

*To the Cold Warriors who did their duty, protected their honor, and defended
their countries. They did so with a vengeance, in the service of their own gods,
but they never lost their respect for the fires of hell that would surely follow
any careless act at the edge of the abyss.*

ACKNOWLEDGMENTS

IN THE BEGINNING there was my mother and father, Naomi and Gordon Reed, who tried to instill the values of right and wrong that constitute the foundations of Western civilization. Their guidance channeled my life into an interesting career, supported (and at times opposed) by a host of scientists and soldiers, politicians and presidents. To every one I owe my greatest thanks, but to USAF Col. Jack Dodge, physicist Carl Haussmann, political pro Fred Hafner, and Deputy Defense Secretary Bill Clements I owe much more, for those gentlemen entrusted me with responsibilities that were beyond justification at the time of their granting. Then, in time, my deputies at the Pentagon—John Stenbit in Telecommunications and Jim Plummer in the Air Force—made me look far better than I really was.

When the Cold War ended I was left with a drawer full of mental snapshots. Debbie and Charles Ball, Bill Clark, Harvey Sapolsky, Bob Setrakian, Kiron Skinner, and Mike Wheeler urged the reduction of those souvenirs to written form. At first the stories were inchoate, then they were given shelter by one of the most thoughtful agents ever to police up the literary back alleys of Manhattan. Phyllis Wender of Rosenstone-Wender brought focus, encouragement, and discipline to this wayward scribe; when done she placed the resulting work with Robert Kane, the editor of Presidio Press. That placement might not have happened without the encouragement of Paul Wilderson of the Naval Institute. Bob Kane and his associate, E. J. McCarthy, turned this author's notes into a tightly written story that I hope the reader will enjoy and remember.

In time the Presidio organization was acquired by Ballantine Books, a division of Random House. The talents of new editors, counselors, and publicists—Zach Schisgal, Ron Doering, Laura Goldin, and Colleen Lindsay—were brought to bear. Cover designer Carl Galian, assistant managing editor Crystal Velasquez, copyeditor Peter Weissmann, and their production associates delivered this work to the reader in tangible form.

The tales herein are but the extracts of a thousand lives. I am deeply indebted to all who let me into those lives for a brief moment, to share their triumphs and tragedies. Some were former presidents. George H. W. Bush, a friend of forty years, was kind enough to write the introduction to this book. That is altogether fitting, as he was the instrument of a safe windup to a most dangerous age. Gerald Ford tried, and at times succeeded, in entrusting me with awesome responsibilities; when it was over he took the time to talk about those days. I have known, or at least met, all the Cold War presidents, but those are the two I count as friends.

Others of my respondents were once officers and enlisted men in the mighty armies of the world, scientists in the weapons establishments on both sides, and intelligence operatives whose real names I still do not know. Many a Soviet, from Victor Adamskii to Sergei Zelentsov, risked censure by the shifting tides of an evolving Russia to share their memories. U.S. airmen C. R. Andregg, Ted Cochran, and Jim Stockdale, to whom the war was not "cold" at all, let me into their files and souls to better understand the terrible personal cost of that historic drama. National Security Advisor Bud McFarlane documented the importance of what seemed like mere days at the office to me. Reaganauts Clark, Herrington, Meese, and Nofziger added perspective to my wide-screen view of the fortieth president.

Many an old-timer opened windows into a dim and distant past: Efrem Petoukhov brought wartime Leningrad into grim focus. Andrew Goodpaster shared his perceptions of Eisenhower's thought processes. Arnold Kramish gave names to the opaque shadows only glimpsed in the *Venona* transcripts. Allan Puckett detailed the activities of his seminal Teapot Committee. Vitaly Adushkin showed me his snapshots of life at the Novaya Zemlya nuclear test site. Jack Real told of life as Howard Hughes' last roommate in the drug-clouded resort hotels of Mexico.

Boris Altschuler, Dennis Bonney, Clifford Gaddy, Les Jardine, Tom Jordan, Andrew Marshall, and Harry Rowen all brought sharp scalpels to my postmortem of the Soviet economy.

Two academics had the bureaucratic stamina to pull back the veil of secrecy from hitherto unseen panoramas. Yuri Gaponov, of the Kurchatov Institute in Moscow, convinced MINATOM to hold a conference on the History of the Soviet Atomic Program in Dubna (north of Moscow) in the spring of 1996. Six years later Cargill Hall, of the U.S. National Reconnaissance Office, convinced the U.S. Intelligence Community to convene a seminar on the overflights of "denied territories" by U.S. aircraft during the 1950s. I was fortunate to be a key participant in both.

Research efforts for this book were organized and led by Susan Rice, Ken Alnwick, and P.J. Lenz. Their webs of virtual and real contacts brought substance to my impressions. Richard Childress, Gennady Gorelik, John MacLucas, Michael Warner, and Gus Weiss all granted access to their Cold War files, while Stu Spencer (who never took a note in his life) opened a treasure trove of insight into Ronald Reagan's thoughts at key moments in history.

A variety of photographers (as noted) granted use of their works; Kate Kainu, Phil Schwartzberg, and Elena Ushakova helped with the graphics; Doctors David Anderson and Patrick Coleman kept me alive and able to withstand the rigors of travel to the ruins of the Soviet empire so that I might collect these tales.

Yet at the beginning and the end, it was my family who provided the inspiration and the rewards, for it was to preserve and protect their lives that the Cold War became my war. And when it was time to wind it all up, my dear wife, Kay, was the rock of support, the pillar of good judgment, the finder of Phyllis, and the dear friend who was indispensable to the whole endeavor.

Healdsburg, CA January 2004.

"[We are pushing] mankind toward the abyss of a world nuclear-missile war."
Soviet Chairman Nikita Khrushchev to U.S. President John Kennedy
OCTOBER 24, 1962

CONTENTS

INTRODUCTION   1
George H.W. Bush, 41st President of the U.S.

PROLOGUE   3

1   *Communist Takeovers and Makeovers*   7

2   *The Fifties Unfold*   21

3   *The Paparazzi Pilots*   35

4   *Howard Hughes Supplies the Props*   61

5   *Rockets and Missiles*   69

6   *Sputnik and the Missile Gap*   83

7   *Nuclear Weapons and the Soviet Union*   99

8   *The American Cyberskippers*   113

9   *The Resumption of Nuclear Tests*   132

10   *Getting Started in Vietnam*   142

11   *Winter on the Spanish Coast*   156

12   *Dawn of the Information Age*   170

13   *The Air Force Recovers from Vietnam*   192

14   *Inefficiency Kills—Empires as Well as People*   211

15   *President Reagan Sets Up the Checkmate*   228

16   *Ghost Stories from the Reagan White House*   241

17   *The Queen of Hearts*   258

18   *Cheney, Powell, and the Nuclear Genie*   276

19   *The Closers*   293

20   *The Soviet Solstice*   310

21   *The Heroes*   321

22   *Closing Down*   339

EPILOGUE   347

AT THE ABYSS

INTRODUCTION

George H. W. Bush,

41ST PRESIDENT OF THE UNITED STATES

THE COLD WAR WAS A STRUGGLE for the very soul of mankind. It was a struggle for a way of life defined by freedom on one side and repression on the other. Already I think we have forgotten what a long and arduous struggle it was, and how close to nuclear disaster we came a number of times. The fact that it did not happen is a testimony to the honorable men and women on both sides who kept their cool and did what was right—as they saw it—in times of crisis.

This conflict between the surviving superpowers of World War II began as I came home from that war. In 1948, the year of my graduation from Yale, the Soviets tried to cut off Western access to Berlin. That blockade led to the formation of NATO, was followed by the first Soviet A-bomb test, and turned bloody with the invasion of South Korea. Four decades of nuclear confrontation, proxy wars, and economic privation followed.

I was privileged to be President of the United States when it all came to an end. In the fall of 1989 the satellite states of Eastern Europe began to break free, and mostly peaceful revolutions swept through Poland, Hungary, Czechoslovakia, and Romania. When the Berlin wall fell, we knew the end was near.

It took another two years to close down the empire of Lenin and Stalin. I received that good news in two telephone calls. The first came on December 8, 1991, when Boris Yeltsin called me from a hunting lodge near Brest, in Belarus. Only recently elected President of the Russian Republic, Yeltsin had been meeting with Leonid Kravchuk, President of Ukraine, and Stanislav Shushchevik, President of Belarus. "Today a very important event took place in our country," Yeltsin said. "I wanted to inform you myself before you learned about it from the press." Then he told me the news: the Presidents of Russia, Belarus, and Ukraine had decided to dissolve the Soviet Union.

Two weeks later a second call confirmed that the former Soviet Union would disappear. Mikhail Gorbachev contacted me at Camp David on Christmas morning of 1991. He wished Barbara and me a Merry Christmas, and then he went on to sum up what had happened in his country: the Soviet Union had ceased to exist. He had just been on national TV to confirm the fact, and he had transferred control of Soviet nuclear weapons to the President of Russia. "You can have a very quiet Christmas evening," he said. And so it was over.

It was a very quiet and civilized ending to a tumultuous time in our history.

In the pages that follow, Tom Reed tells the story of the heroic men and women on both sides of the Iron Curtain who fought that Cold War and kept us from plunging into the abyss of nuclear disaster along the way. It is a remarkable story, some details of which I did not know until I first read Tom's manuscript. Some of the stories you will read and some of the people you'll meet will remind you of fictional tales and characters in spy novels. But they are real people, and real happenings, brought out in the open for the first time through Tom's often compelling storytelling. I think you will be surprised to learn about the behind-the-scenes spy games and chessboard diplomacy that made the Cold War an even more dangerous era than most of us realized.

Although I occasionally disagreed with Tom's interpretation of events or judgment of people, I found his view of how the events unfolded fascinating. Through his numerous and diverse jobs in both government and the private sector, Tom enjoyed a unique catbird seat to history and has done us all a great favor by taking the time to record what he saw and heard. I commend what follows to your attention, for it is a remarkable tale of courage, determination, and yes, sometimes luck.

George Bush

PROLOGUE

"Cry 'Havoc' and let slip the dogs of war!"
Julius Caesar, Act III Scene 1
WILLIAM SHAKESPEARE

"The dog did nothing in the nighttime.
That was the curious thing."
Sherlock Holmes in "Silver Blaze"
ARTHUR CONAN DOYLE

The New York Times.

NEW YORK, FRIDAY, DECEMBER 1, 1950.   Times Square, New York 36, N. Y. Telephone LAckawanna 4-1000   FIVE CENTS

PRESIDENT WARNS WE WOULD USE ATOM BOMB IN KOREA, IF NECESSARY; SOVIET VETOES PLEA TO RED CHINA

JOSEPH STALIN may well have been planning to let slip the dogs of war during his final days. Many of his peers thought so. The Soviet Union had achieved nuclear status, and Stalin's scientists were assuring him of a coming thermonuclear capability. In Korea, his Red Chinese allies were at war with and doing well against the United States. His own battle-hardened troops, perhaps the most powerful in the world, were deployed throughout Eastern Europe. World domination, by force of conventional arms, seemed within Stalin's grasp. And then he died. There can be no doubt that Stalin's death in March 1953 was hastened, if not caused, by Lavrenti Beria, Stalin's chief lieutenant for nuclear and security matters.

Only six weeks before that death, a military man, General Dwight Eisenhower, took over as President of the United States. In the remote towns of Sarov (east of Moscow) and Los Alamos (in the New Mexico desert) thermonuclear technology was beginning to bloom.

Thus, in the late winter of 1953, did the global rules of engagement change. The escalating struggle between East and West would now be played out by a new cast of characters, with the most awful weapons of horrible death and mass destruction at their disposal. Would those dogs of nuclear war stay chained to their stakes? At the time, the answer was not at all clear. Those of us in school remember the duck-and-cover exercises and the triple-diamond fallout shelter signs. They were an ominous reminder of what was at stake.

The U.S. and USSR had tested their own atomic bombs; the United States used two in the war against Japan. Chief of the Soviet general staff, Marshal Sokolovsky, viewed such weapons simply as improved artillery. U.S. Secretary of State John Foster Dulles proposed the use of nukes in massive retaliation for any Soviet misdeed. From the time of the East-West confrontations in Berlin and Cuba, to the continuous sorties of armed Strategic Air Command bombers on airborne alert, to miniwars in the Mideast and Asia, to the last-gasp attempted coup in Moscow, things could have gone wrong. Had they, the resulting holocaust would have been beyond comprehension.

Only a few of us, now in our sixties or older, have seen an H-bomb explode. The roar of those huge multimegaton balls of fire, consuming entire islands and persisting for what seemed to be an eternity, cannot be erased from our mind's eye or ear. Hiroshima was only fourteen kilotons. The 9/11 explosions that destroyed the twin towers and a lot of lower Manhattan were the equivalent of a tenth of a kiloton. A single one-megaton (1,000 kiloton) nuclear warhead delivered on the center of Washington, D.C., would have killed virtually every living thing inside the Beltway, the highway that encircles our national capital. A similar fate awaited those inside Moscow's ring road.

In fact, large numbers of U.S. nuclear weapons were targeted at the greater Moscow area during the 1980s, and similar numbers of Soviet weapons surely were aimed at U.S. facilities in Maryland, D.C., and northern Virginia. Those aim points, known as "designated ground zeroes," were but one set of dots on the military planners' maps of America, Russia, Europe, and Asia. The detonation of thousands of such weapons would have killed millions of creatures, large and small, in the blink of an eye. And those would have been the fortunate few. Tens of millions of others, the innocent along with the guilty, would have been forced to endure the fires of hell for a few minutes or a few hours before succumbing to their awful burns or their strange, radiation-induced illnesses.

The Cold War was real, make no mistake about that. It was a fight to the death: at the top, between contending ideologies and national interests; around the globe, with propaganda and money; and in the laboratories and factories with blood, toil, sweat, and tears. In the jungles and deserts it was fought hand-to-hand, with bayonets, napalm, and high-tech weapons of every sort—save one. It was not fought with nuclear weapons.

During the four decades of the Cold War, the wisdom, forbearance, and discipline of professionals on both sides managed to constrain the nuclear horrors. That is the real story of the Cold War. It is the story of the race for supremacy in ballistic missiles, the hitherto untold tales of RB-47 and then U-2 crews flying over the Soviet Union in the fifties looking for signs of surprise attack, and of the ninety-eight nuclear weapons in Cuba, entrusted to Soviet General Pliyev on a most tenuous leash. It is the story of Jim Stockdale in the Tonkin Gulf looking for an attack on U.S. ships that never happened, but which got us started in Vietnam, a bloody war that dragged on for a decade as we eschewed both nuclear weapons and hard decisions. It is the story of two American officers in the ocean's depths who could have fired their nukes but did not, and of the engineers from Leningrad who muzzled the Soviet nuclear dragon because it was the right thing to do.

It is the story of U.S. efforts to keep control of its nuclear weapons in the NATO countries via the archaic short-wave cemetery net as those nations—our allies—perpetuated their centuries-old quarrels among themselves. It is the story of smart weapons, stealthy bombers, and cruise missiles, all built to offset ballooning Soviet nuclear firepower, as Leonid Brezhnev's last orgy of military spending spread a dark cloud over the free world. It is the story of economics and White House politics on a grand scale; how Eisenhower understood that in the long run American economic power would decide the game; how Reagan thirty years later decided to use that power to topple what he dubbed the "evil empire"; how the closers, Bush and Gorbachev, wound it all down without a nuclear shot being fired.

During all those years, the dogs of nuclear war did nothing. The four decades that followed the death of Stalin, the coming of Eisenhower, and the birth of thermonuclear technology came to be known as the Cold War, not World War III, not the holocaust, and not the War from Hell. That is the curious thing.

CHAPTER 1

Communist Takeovers
and Makeovers

WHY WAS THERE A COLD WAR? Fear. Fear of what "they" would do to "us" if they took over.

Citizens of the Western democracies watched in horror as one ancien régime after another fell to Marxist ideology, fearing the slaughter and suffocation that inevitably followed those takeovers. They did not want such horrors visited on themselves or their children. To the east, in the fact-free Soviet empire, the government generated a fear of capitalist imperialism. It invoked the horrors of World War II, horrors that we westerners can never comprehend. On a personal level, Soviet citizens came to fear the obligations and risks that logically follow individual freedom.

To me, there was the immediate fear of the war in Korea. In 1951, I was about to graduate from high school, so events there began to get my attention. A war started on the Korean peninsula during the previous summer; President Truman had threatened to use the A-bomb to protect American forces there. By the spring of 1951 that war had stagnated into a mindless meat grinder. No one was winning, but it was clear to us high school seniors, primary draft bait, that we could be the big losers. Our silent generation reacted to that war differently than did our children when faced with Vietnam, but the underlying feelings were the same: something was terribly wrong, our government did not know what it was doing, and we were being set up to pay the price. In the shadows stood some greater conflict, a fundamental struggle between good and evil only dimly perceived.

In a speech to the U.S. Congress that spring, on the occasion of his recall from command of the UN forces in Korea, General Douglas MacArthur spoke words that resonated with the righteous weariness of the Old Testament. He praised the men he had left behind in Korea, then spoke of the challenges ahead: "Once war is forced upon us, there is no other alternative than to apply every available means to bring it to a swift end. War's very objective is victory, not prolonged indecision." He was speaking of Korea, but he just as well could have been laying out the markers for the forty years to come.

WHITTAKER CHAMBERS EXPLAINS IT TO THE FREE WORLD

In the spring of 1952, Whittaker Chambers's book *Witness* was published.★ It was the defining work for many of my generation, certainly for the cold warriors then taking up arms. In a preface to its republication in 1987, columnist Robert Novak describes how, as a twenty-two-year-old Army lieutenant, it changed his worldview, and how, over the ensuing thirty-four years, he found a large fraternity of like-minded leaders whose lives were similarly impacted.

Witness is an unforgettable book in part because Chambers was a talented writer. In 1928, as a freelancer, Chambers came to national literary attention with his translation of *Bambi*, by the Austrian novelist Felix Salten, into beautiful English. That book became a best-seller, then a Disney movie, and created a demand for his talents. In due course Chambers went to work for *Time* magazine, starting out as a book reviewer in 1939. He was an immediate success, and by 1944 was

---

★ Whittaker Chambers. *Witness*. Random House, republished by Regnery Gateway, 1987.

in charge of the foreign news department. From that vantage point he illuminated the foolishness of Yalta and the disintegration of China. He explained the meaning of "Iron Curtain" and "Cold War," terms new to the American lexicon in the late 1940s. Henry Luce, publisher of *Time*, described Chambers as, "the best writer *Time* ever employed." My acquaintances there agree.

In addition to its beautiful literary form, however, *Witness* is a book of immense historical substance. It documents Chambers's life as a student at Columbia University in the early 1920s, as a recruit to communism in 1925, his selection in 1929 for "Special Tasks" by the Soviet intelligence service, and his promotion to management of the Ware espionage group in the United States in 1934. The book then tracks his disenchantment with communism as Stalin began to kill off competitors in the purges of 1937-38. The denouement was Chambers's defection and flight into hiding on April 15, 1938.

In 1939, Chambers began his work for *Time*, hoping the visibility of that job also would give him protection from kidnapping or assassination. But this also was a time of sudden national interest in communist activity. The Nazi-Soviet Pact of August and the subsequent bilateral invasions of Poland made the Communist party an instrumentality of a potential enemy. On September 2, 1939, Chambers told a part of his tale to Adolph Berle, a U.S. government official.

With the German invasion of the Soviet Union and the attack on Pearl Harbor in 1941, the U.S. government lost interest in communist underground activity. Overnight, the Soviet Union had become an ally, but from the minarets of *Time*, Chambers kept calling attention to that nation's dubious geopolitical aims and its moral rot.

With the breakdown of the end-of-war Yalta accords, the new Republican Congress of 1946 decided to take a serious look into the matter of communist influence on U.S. policy during the Truman administration. In August 1948 the House Committee on Un-American Activities called Whittaker Chambers as a witness, based on his revelations to Adolph Berle almost a decade earlier. At those hearings, Chambers revealed his prewar membership in the Communist party, his break with communism, and the identities of individuals prominent in the U.S. government who were still active in the Communist party. State Department official Alger Hiss was the name of greatest interest to the committee, and he was called to testify. Hiss denied ever having transmitted government documents to Whittaker Chambers, and denied even meeting with Chambers after January 1, 1937.

At first only one young congressman, Richard Nixon, believed Chambers, but within eighteen months Nixon's persistence led to Hiss's January 20, 1950, conviction on two counts of perjury. Hiss served a forty-four month term in federal prison. The *Venona* transcripts,★ released in 1997 and identifying Hiss via his code name Ales, and the postwar testimony of defecting Soviet code clerk Igor Gouzenko, remove any doubt about Hiss's guilt.

In the spring of 1950, after Hiss's conviction and sentencing, Chambers wrote two chapters of what was to become *Witness*. The book was published in May 1952, becoming the ninth best-selling book of the year. His twenty page foreword, in the form of a letter to his children, describes the seductive appeal of communist theory and the horrifying consequences of its reality. In those pages, Chambers tries to answer the questions: What is communism? Why do men become communists, why do they continue to be communists? Why do some break with it and some go on? He identifies communism as a call to change the world, to dispense with God and to enthrone man as the supreme being.

My definition is more prosaic. To me, communism is a nice theory on how to meet noble human goals, but in reality it relies on terror to make it work, and even with the full application of terror, the system does not deliver. Communist states always have dictators because the concentration of economic power means the concentration of all power. Such power corrupts; the dictatorship of the proletariat never withers away. The people lose their freedoms because communism denies the existence of a soul, of a conscience able to judge right from wrong, or of any authority higher than the state.

Chambers explained what communism gave to its adherents: "A reason to live and a reason to die." Then he tells why, despite all its appeal, people cease to be communists. He used the words of a young girl who explained, with some embarrassment in the 1930s, why her father, a staunch Communist party member, had become an implacable anticommunist. "One night, in Moscow, he heard screams."

★ Robert Louis Benson and Michael Warner (eds.). *Venona*. Central Intelligence Agency—Center for the Study of Intelligence, 1996. These are the transcripts of Soviet messages from the U.S. embassy and consulates back to Moscow during and immediately after World War II. The Soviet codes were broken in the late 1940s, leading to the arrest of their nuclear spies in the U.S., among others.

Chambers went on to write:

> *What communist has not heard those screams? They come from husbands torn forever from their wives in midnight arrests. They come, muffled, from the execution cellars of the secret police, from the torture chambers of the Lubyanka, from all the citadels of terror now stretching from Berlin to Canton. They come from those freight cars loaded with men, women, and children, the enemies of the communist state, locked in, packed in, left on remote sidings to freeze to death at night in the Russian winter. They come from minds driven mad by the horrors of mass starvation ordered and enforced as a policy of the communist state. They come from the starved skeletons, worked to death or flogged to death (as an example to others) in the freezing filth of sub-Arctic labor camps. They come from children whose parents are suddenly, inexplicably, taken away from them— parents they will never see again.*

Of course, not all Communist party members heard those screams. Nor did many of the Soviet rank and file hear them, for their government was very good at muffling those screams, at jamming the internal systems of communication, leaving the Soviet word as the only word. For that reason, the Communist Party of the Soviet Union (CPSU) held onto power for over seventy years, and for a while it seemed that power might envelop us all.

Witness left a lasting impression on me not only because of the quality of its writing and the description of the screams. Chambers's most compelling observation was that "in this century [it] will be decided for generations [to come] whether all mankind is to become communist, or whether the whole world is to become free . . . It is our fate to live upon that turning point in history."

It was my fate to participate in that transformation, to watch and help as the hinges of fate swung shut on the communist horror. Forty years later, when the Cold War was over, I had a chance to talk to some of those who had screamed.

THE COMING OF THE GULAGS

In 1917 the communists took power in St. Petersburg by intrigue and mob rule, not by popular vote nor the consent of the people. There was not, and never has been, any legitimizing event leading up to their seizure of power. A civil war ensued that took four years to put down. Assassinations of political competitors was one tool of the Red Terror, but the most long-lasting and terrible instrumentality of the mob was the Glavnoe Upravlenie Legerei (Main Camp Administration), soon to be known by its acronym, the Gulag. These concentration camps were built, according to Anne Applebaum, to safeguard the Soviet Republic from class enemies by means of isolation. In the process, they extracted free labor from the healthy while killing off the undesirables.

Construction of the Gulag started in 1919; by 1920, eighty-four camps, holding 50,000 prisoners, were up and running. Their commandants were pioneers in horror. They developed a system of food allocation that disposed of the unproductive. They optimized their tortures and perfected procedures for the murder of the uncooperative. By 1922, when Lenin successfully imposed his will on a new Union of Soviet Socialist Republics, there were over three hundred such camps in operation, "home" to nearly a quarter million prisoners, known as "zeks."

Lenin died in 1924, and in the ensuing four years Joseph Stalin seized and consolidated his power as General Secretary of the CPSU. In the process, Gulags metastasized throughout the new Soviet Union. Close to five hundred Gulags processed over eighteen million souls through their portals during Stalin's thirty years in power. Millions more never made it to the camps, dying in railroad cars and ships' holds en route to their fate. Another six million offending citizens were simply exiled from their homes in the cities to the forests and deserts of Siberia and Kazakhstan.

FAMINE IN THE UKRAINE: TEN MILLION DEAD

One of Stalin's targets in his consolidation of power was Russia's neighbor and sometimes possession, Ukraine, a country not interested in the Bolshevik revolution. The peasants there wanted to keep running their farms as they had for generations, making Ukraine and the Caucasus the breadbasket of Europe. Such activity was not compatible with communist theory, so in 1930, Stalin imposed collectivization on those Ukrainian farms. The peasants would not cooperate. They fought back with guns, axes, and knives. They slaughtered their cattle rather than turn them over to the state. Stalin decided to starve the peasants out, imposing grain production quotas that the peasants could not possibly meet. For two years he decreed the confiscation of all food and the destruction of all crops.

Elena Yakimenko lived in Armanir, in the northern Caucasus. She reported that to effect this famine, the Komsomol, or communist youth, made twice daily calls on every farm and farmer. They would walk in teams through the maize crop, knocking it over as they went. They would prod soft spots in the ground with metal rods, looking for hidden food. In the afternoon, after the farmers had raised up the bruised crop, the Komsomol teams would come back to trample it again. Any food found in homes was confiscated. She confirmed that by 1933 most of the men were dead or had disappeared, transported to the Gulags. Their families were being wiped out where they lived. By 1933 the authorities were removing an average of 250 corpses per day from the Kharkov train station alone, lost souls trying to escape the horrors of the government-imposed famine.

Elena's neighbors to the east had lost both parents and four of their six children to the famine. The two surviving children sold their farmhouse to a well-connected apparatchik at the mill for a sack of flour. Then they disappeared. To the west lived a mother with three children. One evening she produced four potatoes from a secret stash, boiling them for dinner. One child stepped away from the table for a moment and another reached for the unguarded potato. The mother responded with a tap on the offender's forehead with a wooden spoon. The child was so weak that he fell over, dead. Without missing a beat, the surviving two children asked that he not be buried but that his remains be cooked.

Recent post-Soviet literature now estimates the death toll among the Ukrainian and northern Caucasus peasantry during these Stalin-directed famine years to be around ten million, one-fourth of the people living there. Today the terror is gone, but the legacy of incompetence remains. The government still owns the land. Ukraine is a net importer of food.

STALIN'S GHOSTS: TWENTY MILLION DEAD

The struggle in Russia itself was far worse. At every turn "counter-revolutionaries" and "saboteurs" were identified and tortured until they "confessed" and implicated others—who were then sucked into the same maw of Soviet terror. There was a voracious need for slave labor to build the canals and dams of the new Soviet Union. Slaves built the nuclear facilities that fueled the Soviet military machine while slowly killing those who operated them. There was an unquenchable need for labor in Siberia, people to dig mines, denude forests, and suck oil from the bowels of the earth. On top of all that, there were arbitrary "execution quotas," assigned to local officials for no reason other than to keep the people in line.

In February 1956 the first authoritative glimpses of these horrors were revealed to the *nomenklatura*★ of the Soviet Union. Stalin had been dead for three years, Nikita Khrushchev had consolidated power as Stalin's successor, and at the Twentieth Party Congress, Khrushchev began to reveal the excesses of Stalin's rule. Rumors of that speech percolated into the Western press within a month, and on June 5, 1956, the *New York Times* was able to publish the full text. The headlines told the story: KHRUSHCHEV TALK ON STALIN BARES DETAILS OF RULE BASED ON TERROR. The first screams were now out there, reliably reported to anyone who would listen. I was a few days from college graduation, and I certainly heard their echoes.

A generation later I met the relatives of some of those Russians who had screamed. I talked to those who had watched the infrastructure of the Soviet empire being built by zeks. I heard firsthand stories from those who had been exiled for no reason other than a friendship with a misfit. Historians in Russia and the West are now trying to come to terms with the scope of this Soviet cruelty. Reliable records are hard to come by, but today's Russian textbooks count the casualties during these years at twenty million dead, with another forty million imprisoned or shipped off to labor camps. *The Black Book of Communism,* a scholarly work by six authors from as many different respected research institutes, published in Paris in 1997, confirms these numbers.

It was not only the uncooperative masses who were victimized. The Soviet nation as an institution paid a terrible price. In the 1930s, Stalin directed the arrest and execution of most senior officers in the Red Army. Starting with Marshall Mikhail Tukhachevsky, by all accounts a true military genius, Stalin killed off all possible contenders for power. The cost of this folly first became evident in November 1939, when the remnants of the Red Army were unable to prevail over the troops

---

★ Literally, the "list of names," *i.e.,* the establishment of the CPSU and thus the USSR, the insiders who ran the country and benefited from the perks.

of tiny Finland in a minor border dispute. It took mighty Russia five months to defeat the Finns. The final bill came due two years later when the well-oiled Nazi war machine invaded and rolled over the rabble trying to defend Belarus, the Baltic States, Ukraine, and much of western Russia. A year of time and an ocean of blood were required before the Soviet Union could field a new and capable officer corps.

MAO'S GHOSTS: ANOTHER THIRTY MILLION DIE IN THE GREAT LEAP FORWARD

Professor Sang-chen "Sam" Tu was born in Kashing, fifty miles southwest of Shanghai, in 1928. During World War II he managed to get a university education, but in 1948, as China's civil war closed in, he left for the United States. Sam pursued graduate studies in electrical engineering at Cornell, and during the 1955-56 school year, as my thesis adviser, he oversaw my work on a very primitive analog computer. During the summer that followed, Sam Tu heeded the call of the mother country to return home, to help build the new China. He got there just in time for the Great Leap Forward.

Mao Tse-tung announced this bizarre economic plan in January 1958. The intent was to vastly increase the production of food, steel, and infrastructure, all perceived to be the sinews of a modern state. Communes were established, and everyone was to build a backyard blast furnace. The results were disastrous. The peasants could only melt down their scythes to make their steel quotas, leaving the grain to rot in the fields. By 1959 millions were starving. The government started "antigrain concealment drives," just like those in Ukraine in the thirties.

The Tu family, living in Beijing, knew little of all this, and they suffered not at all. In fact, they were the beneficiaries, members of the elite with special cards that allowed them to shop at special well-stocked stores in the city. It was their relatives in the countryside who paid the price. The Great Leap Forward went on for three years. By 1961, China's rural society was near collapse.

Twenty-five years later the U.S. Department of Agriculture concluded that during the Great Leap Forward wheat yields had fallen by 41 percent, oil seed production by 64 percent, and textiles by 50 percent. The pig population had dropped 49 percent, and the population of all draft animals seems to have fallen in half as well.

The Great Leap Forward was finally stopped in 1961 by Liu Shao-qi, president of the country and Mao's heir-apparent. By then, tens of millions of peasants had died. In 1984, Dr. Judith Bannister estimated the casualties at "30 million excess deaths during 1958-61." In 1988, *Contemporary Chinese Population* concluded that "out of a population of 500 million, there were 19.5 million deaths in the countryside," a quarter of whom appear to have been "useless" peasant girls who were allowed to starve or were killed by their parents. Other recent books published in China lump deaths and reductions of births together at around forty million during this period.

In 1966, Mao tried to stage a comeback with a new orgy of ideology known as the Cultural Revolution. In part this was to be a reignition of revolutionary fervor, but Mao's main motive seems to have been political revenge. He wanted to reclaim the power lost in 1961 and to punish those who had usurped it. The Cultural Revolution was to be an upheaval of the intellectual community, enfranchising students and fools to operate as "Red Guards," attacking and destroying those who had limited Mao's power and ended the famine.

Liu Shao-qi was one of its first victims, but the Tu family took their hits too. Sam was not harmed physically, since his Institute for Automation was responsible for the control systems of China's embryonic missile and space programs, and the first Chinese satellite launch was only four years away. But Sam was subject to the ridicule and harassment imposed on all "intellectuals." His family was not so lucky. His mathematician wife, Mary, was sent to a commune in Hubei Province, and their four sons were scattered to other hopelessly inefficient state farms.

In the cities during those years, the Red Guards set out to destroy the very heritage of China. Communist party officials organized orgies of cannibalism to prove their ideological ardor. During the decade that ended with Mao's death, the Chinese killing machine again took the lives of millions. *The Black Book of Communism* estimates total Chinese deaths due to Mao's ideology, from his accession to power in 1949 to his death in 1976, at between 45 and 72 million people.

I crossed paths with Sam Tu in 1998 when he returned to the United States for a family reunion. Sam and Mary confirmed that it all happened. China's weapons and space programs were successful, and continue to be, but the Great Leap Forward and the Cultural Revolution were disasters. Their boys put history as only the young can do: "It was crazy. The last ten years of Mao were really bad. Everyone's life became worse. Mao was nuts."

THE LESSER DICTATORS—JUST AS BLOODY

KIM IL SUNG, trained as a communist in prewar Moscow, was installed as the puppet dictator of North Korea when that peninsula was partitioned at the end of World War II. But within a few years he had eliminated all political competition. By the spring of 1949 he had a clear plan for the reunification of Korea under his control.

At 4:00 A.M. on Sunday, June 25, the North Korean army invaded the South. Within two months they had nearly cleared the peninsula of defenders. The North Korean political cadres, following in the wake of the army, were killing local anticommunist officials and the landlord classes at an appalling rate. The U.S. Marine landing at Inchon changed that, cutting off the North Koreans from their supplies and annihilating their reserves. As the invaders fled northward, they executed all the anticommunist political figures they could find. In the village of Hamhung alone, three hundred men and women were killed. The more valuable prisoners were taken to the North Korean capital, Pyongyang, but that was no refuge: they were executed as U.S. troops approached.

With this rout in process, Kim Il Sung called for help. The Chinese responded, and so did the United States—with the threat of nuclear weapons. The battles raged for three years. By the time the armistice was signed, on July 27, 1953, three million Koreans had died, along with a million Chinese. The North Korean regime, a last relic of Stalinist government, killed another million of its own people in pursuit of its ideology. Kim's son remains in power today, his people starving while he dreams of dealing in nuclear terror.

NICOLAE CEAUSESCU came to power in Romania in 1965 as the heir to the first postwar communist dictator. The state police, known as the Securitate, were already in place, but Ceausescu empowered them to decimate the country. Prewar Bucharest was glorious, but with the arrival of Ceausescu, the beautiful city villas and ancient town squares were flattened to make room for Stalinist apartment buildings. The economy collapsed. The use of low-grade coal added pollution to the already darkened streets while Ceausescu amassed a personal fortune. Unused presidential houses littered the countryside. His personal office in the presidential palace occupied an acre of floor space. He wore a new suit of clothes every day, pretested to detect any signs of radiation and then burned after that day's use. There is no accurate count of the deaths incurred by this regime, but the violence of the December 1989 revolution that overthrew and executed Ceausescu and his second in command—his wife—speaks volumes. A decade later the Romanian economy is still shrinking.

In Cuba, FIDEL CASTRO came to power by means of revolution, deposing a corrupt dictator on New Year's Day 1959. At that time the economy of Cuba was about on a par with the state of Florida. Castro created a one-party socialist state, imprisoning and killing his political opponents, creating collective farms, nationalizing all industry, and otherwise wrecking the economy.

In 1962 the Soviet government attempted to use Cuba as a missile base, with the planned installation of SS-5 intermediate range (2,800 nautical mile) rockets on Cuban soil. American discovery of this operation led to the Cuban missile crisis during the very tense week of October 24–28. Incredibly, on October 26, 1962, Castro asked Khrushchev for a preemptive nuclear strike on the United States. Khrushchev thoughtfully declined.

As the Cold War drew to a close, Cuba lost its economic dole from the Soviet Union. By the year 2000 the once-equal economies of Florida and Cuba had diverged sharply. Florida's per capita output now exceeds that of still-socialist Cuba by a factor of more than three.

The NORTH VIETNAMESE ARMY overran Saigon on April 30, 1975. Thousands of the Republic of Vietnam's leaders were executed, and others fled the country. The 400,000 government officials, military officers, and friends of the U.S. who were left behind were dispatched to reeducation camps where many spent the rest of their days. *The Black Book of Communism* charges the communists with a million deaths in their struggle for power in Vietnam.

When POL POT came to power in Cambodia in 1975, his Khmer Rouge emptied the cities. The civil war and the ensuing slaughter in the killing fields claimed between 1.3 and 2.3 million lives out of a population of only eight million. Thousands of those victims, the middle class "parasite intellectuals," were photographed and then tortured to death in a former *lycée* in Phnom Penh that became known as the Tuol Sleng prison. Vann Nath heard the screams there, night and day. He is one of only seven survivors of that torture house: fourteen thousand other souls perished there. Nath avoided their fate only because he was an artist, chosen to portray dictator Pol Pot for the masses.

I visited Tuol Sleng in 1994. The ghastly cells, the drowning tanks, the electroshock apparatus, the racks and shackles, are all still there, along with the sad photos of those who passed through that hell.

In all of these places and times, from Russia in 1917 to Cambodia in 1975, the story was the same. Communism was but a concept, a set of advertising slogans, designed to secure absolute power for the well-organized few. Lenin made his plans clear in 1918. The Soviet world order could be achieved only "by subjecting the will of thousands to the will of one."

As Lord Acton warned, absolute power corrupts its holders absolutely. Communist leaders achieved and clung to power by means of terror, and once in power, they destroyed their societies in an attempt to build new ones. The sad thing is that all of those sacrifices were for naught. Those hopelessly inefficient societies could not possibly deliver on the economic promises of their masters. Some, like the Soviet empire, sank from view, leaving behind a detritus we have yet to unscramble. Others, like Cuba and North Korea, remain as relics of lost civilizations. They are the modern day equivalents of the overgrown temples at Angkor Wat, but with their leaders very much alive, dreaming of nuclear revenge.

EMBARKATION

Some of these horrors were still in the future when I returned for my sophomore year at Cornell in the fall of 1952. I had listened as General Eisenhower and young Senator Nixon were nominated to lead us out of the Korean morass. That seemed like a step in the right direction. Late night talks with fellow students Carol and Bob Wray brought the words of Whittaker Chambers into sharp focus. We talked about duty-honor-country and about the mess in Korea. Upon my return to school, I enrolled in the Reserve Officer's Training Corps, which would lead, in time, to a commission in the U.S. Air Force.

I did well in college, spent my summers in less intellectual pursuits—such as working in the oilfields of west Texas—but I watched the communist empire continue to grow. Something about the siege and fall of

Dien Bien Phu, in May 1954, in a faraway place called Vietnam, seemed spooky. I read the last dispatches from that lost outpost and wondered what it must have been like to be overrun. Why were those Frenchmen there? And what were we supposed to do about their demise? I did not know that even then some American pilots were being killed there or that some officials of the American government were proposing the use of nuclear weapons to "save" Dien Bien Phu.

Classmates interested in the frontiers of technology were talking about the aircraft industries in southern California. One showed me an ad in the *Cornell Engineer*. It charted the employment growth of a firm called Ramo-Wooldridge in Los Angeles. The ad did not explain what Ramo-Wooldridge did exactly, but the gossip was "missiles." I applied for and got a temporary job there, awaiting the call to active duty in the U.S. Air Force. It was an easy choice, as southern California seemed the promised land.

In June 1956, I graduated at the top of my engineering class and as the cadet commander of the Reserve Officers' Training Corps. I received my lieutenant's gold bars, returned my first salute (cost: one dollar to the sergeant making that first salute), married, and headed off to California. I was ready to play my role in Whittaker Chambers's turning point of history.

CHAPTER 2

The Fifties Unfold

GIANTS DRESSED THE WORLD'S STAGE. At least that's the way it looked to me from the ivy-covered portals of Cornell in the 1950s. During those years, Eisenhower made his entrance, Stalin made his exit, and Khrushchev postured. It was a great show, although we could not see the ropes and pulleys, the levers of power that would let these men change the world. But they did, for once they had taken over, Eisenhower and Khrushchev changed the rules of engagement by which the Cold War would be fought. It all started with some mysterious goings-on at Stalin's Nearer Dacha.

STALIN CHECKS OUT

Joseph Stalin's winter of 1952–53 was rife with conspiracy. First of all, he was growing senile. At age seventy-three, he was forgetful of names and confused about events. By a series of ongoing purges he had reduced his inner circle to just four: Georgi Malenkov, Lavrenti Beria, Nikita Khrushchev, and Nikolai Bulganin. He was probably preparing another purge to replace those four.

Khrushchev's memoirs confirm that Stalin feared Beria most of all: "The practical means for achieving Stalin's goals were all in Beria's hands. . . . If Beria could eliminate anyone, then Beria could eliminate those of his own choosing. . . . Stalin feared that Beria would choose [Stalin himself] for elimination." Secondly, there is some evidence that Stalin was planning to complete his career with a final apocalyptic World War III. In a conversation with Andrei Vyshinsky in the presence of others on February 7, 1953, Stalin is alleged to have said: "If the imperialist gentlemen feel like going to war, there is no more suitable moment for us than this." A retired military hero had been elected President of the United States. Stalin's paranoia was growing.

Let us add the H-bomb dimension to this story, a hypothesis that seems reasonable to me and to my colleague John Nuckolls, a former director of the Lawrence Livermore National Laboratory. In August 1949 the Soviets detonated their first A-bomb. From conversations with Yuli Khariton, scientific director of Arzamas-16 (the Soviet equivalent of Los Alamos), we now know that first Soviet bomb was an exact copy of the U.S. "Fat Man," dropped on Nagasaki during August 1945 to end World War II. Both U.S. and Soviet editions of Fat Man gave yields of twenty kilotons. The Soviet explosion, years earlier than expected by the West, was the product of Klaus Fuchs's and Ted Hall's espionage at Los Alamos. Our Russian peers, as well as the *Venona* transcripts, confirmed the role of the Rosenbergs and others as couriers for this valuable information.

The U.S. responded to the troubling events of 1949, including this Soviet test, by starting work on H-bomb technology. These latter monsters are as different from A-bombs as the sun is from the moon. A-bombs get their energy from the fission, or splitting, of uranium or plutonium nuclei. H-bombs use the energy from an A-bomb to light different thermonuclear fires, releasing energy when two hydrogen nuclei fuse to make helium. Thermonuclear reactions are the source of the sun's energy, and they produce energy that is typically a hundred times that of an A-bomb. The technology to achieve such a yield is also a hundred times more complicated.

On November 1, 1952, the U.S. detonated the world's first thermonuclear. It was known as the Mike device, and it gave a ten megaton yield—five hundred Nagasakis—which vaporized a good bit of Eniwetok Atoll in the Pacific. At that time, the Soviets were only thinking about H-bombs. They had detonated a home-designed A-bomb, a significant improvement over Fat Man, but an H-bomb was beyond their understanding.

Stalin was a man who made it his business to know a lot about things that affected his personal security. He paid close attention to the matter of nuclear explosions, and he seemed to know about them even before official messengers brought him the news. At Potsdam, in July 1945, President Truman took Stalin aside the day after the first, secret U.S. A-bomb test in New Mexico to tell him about the super weapon. Stalin already knew. Lavrenti Beria was in charge of the Soviet nuclear weapons program as well as its intelligence service. Yet when Beria called Stalin from Semipalatinsk early on the morning of August 29, 1949, to report the successful first Soviet test, again Stalin already knew. He had informants everywhere. As to the events of November 1952, however, our Russian scientific colleagues try to paint a different version of Stalin's network. They maintain that neither they nor Stalin had any idea of the size or significance of the U.S. Mike test in the Pacific. Some claim that while they had collected radioactive fallout samples, a technician washed them down a drain and lost them. Others, to this day, deny that U.S. press reports of the monster shot made any impression in the Soviet Union.

Nuckolls and I doubt this Soviet claim of perceptory impairment. Consider, for instance, the firsthand information from one of Soviet academician Isaak Kikoin's associates about his unique diagnostic tools. In 1952, when Kikoin was a department head at what is now the Kurchatov Institute in Moscow, he was in charge of research on isotopic separation, the difficult but essential process of separating bomb-usable U-235 from the far more prevalent but nearly useless U-238.

In 1952 the Soviet scientific community was aware that the United States was at work on an H-bomb and that test preparations were under way in the Pacific. In anticipation of the U.S. test shot, Kikoin built an acoustic sensor with which to detect that test. This was a unique idea, as nuclear tests had previously been detected by seismic sensors—listening for earthquakelike shock waves reverberating through the earth's core—not sound waves in the atmosphere. He hung the device in his office at what was then called Laboratory Number 2. On the evening of October 31–November 1, 1952, this instrument recorded a significant signal. Because it was nighttime, Kikoin was not there. In the morning, when he saw the paper tape, he concluded that while that signal might indicate an American test, it also could be a disturbance caused by someone bumping the instrument. Kikoin calculated that if it were a real signal from a real test, a second wave, traversing the globe in the other direction, would arrive at midafternoon the following day. At the predicted moment there was another signal.

On a secure KGB telephone line, Kikoin called Efim Slavsky, the minister of Medium Machine Building, as the nuclear weapons ministry was then known. Kikoin was questioned and requestioned on the reliability of his findings and threatened with great bodily harm if he were wrong. Kikoin stuck to his guns to the end of the conversation. Thereafter one must assume Slavsky proceeded to Stalin's office to advise the dictator of this development.

Consider, as well, the reaction of the British and French, with whom the United States did not share nuclear secrets in 1952. Both countries now confirm that, from their own instruments, they promptly deduced what had gone on at Eniwetok in November 1952.

Nuckolls and I believe that when Stalin heard about the huge American test explosion, he summoned his nuclear weapons and intelligence chief, fellow Georgian Lavrenti Beria, for an explanation. The latter was unable to provide one. We hypothecate a grim exchange: Stalin's hard questions, Beria's admissions of ignorance, Stalin's recounting of history—all previous KGB chiefs had been executed by their successors.

Yet on December 2, 1952, a full month *after* the Mike shot, Beria prepared an "all is well" memorandum to his scientific deputies, Kurchatov in Moscow and Khariton at Arzamas-16. In this memo, Beria states that "according to some information we have obtained, the U.S. is working on a Sloyka-type device." In fact, Sloyka was a dead-end Sakharov design, not a true H-bomb. The device, formally named RDS-6s, was scheduled to be tested shortly afterward, but it never went into production. Thus, in that December 2 memo, Beria was telling his underlings that the American Mike test represented nothing new. This must have been the position he was taking with Stalin at the same time; we doubt Stalin believed him.

In addition, RDS-6s was not ready for testing as planned. At the end of 1952, Beria had already agreed to one postponement of its test; the shot date was moved to March 1953. But RDS-6s was not fired then either. Stalin knew of these missed deadlines, and they must have added to his aggravation with Beria. By the end of 1952 he and Beria were like two scorpions in a bottle. Both were men of enormous power, no scruples, and extreme cruelty. Both were the epitome of evil. And both knew that each would not tolerate the other's survival much longer.

Beria may well have decided to strike first, to knock off Stalin before Stalin got him, before the postponed test of RDS-6s displayed the inadequacy of the Soviet thermonuclear program and/or before Stalin could start World War III. The details of what happened during that last week of Stalin's life emerge from the notes taken at a reunion of his death-bed guards held on March 5, 1977, and from a more recent examination of Soviet archives by Vladimir Naumov and Jonathan Brent.

On Saturday night, February 28, 1953, the Politburo Four—Malenkov, Beria, Khrushchev, and Bulganin—watched a movie at the Kremlin. Then they were driven out to Stalin's Nearer Dacha, located in Kuntsevo, about ten miles west of Red Square. They remained there until 4:00 A.M. Sunday, March 1, dining and consuming large quantities of Madzhari, a light Georgian wine. During that gathering, Beria apparently added an extra ingredient to Stalin's wineglass—a hefty, or repeated, dose of warfarin, which is a tasteless and odorless blood thinner that can induce severe intestinal hemorrhaging. Fittingly, in large doses it is used to kill rats.

When Stalin's four guests left, the leader allegedly told a guard named Khrustalev: "I am going to bed. I shan't be wanting you, you can go to bed too. . . ." Stalin had *never* given an order like that before. He expected at least two armed guards on duty at all times. But Khrustalev was the only one to hear this supposed order. He passed it on to the watch commander, who promptly and happily dismissed the other guards for the evening, leaving only Khrustalev on duty—as the warfarin did its work.

At 10:00 A.M. that Sunday morning, the guards reassembled in the dacha kitchen. They observed no activity from Stalin's quarters. At 6:00 P.M. one guard saw a light go on, confirming that things must be all right and thus it would be unwise to enter. By 10:00 P.M., however, when there was still no movement inside, guard Lozgachev was elected by his peers to enter Stalin's quarters. He found Stalin on the floor, conscious but mostly paralyzed, with one arm raised in the air. Lozgachev assumed a stroke had felled the Soviet leader; a broken pocket watch on the floor had stopped at 6:30, suggesting that Stalin had lain there for three and a half hours, unattended. Lozgachev called the other guards, who entered the suite along with the housekeeper. The four of them lifted Stalin onto a sofa and then put in calls to Beria and Malenkov. They first connected with Malenkov, but he referred the matter to Beria, who called back a half hour later to tell the guards, "Don't tell anybody about Comrade Stalin's illness." No medical help was requested. Five hours later, at 3:00 A.M. on Monday, March 2, Beria and Malenkov showed up at the dacha. The guards told them the whole story. Beria said, "Don't cause a panic, don't bother us. And don't disturb Comrade Stalin." The two then left, again leaving Stalin without any medical help. At 8:00 A.M., Khrushchev made his first appearance at the dacha, and at 8:30 A.M. the doctors finally arrived, fourteen hours after the dictator's collapse to the dacha floor.

At 9:50 P.M. on Thursday, March 5, four days after the alleged "stroke," Dr. A. L. Myasnikov pronounced Stalin dead of a cerebral hemorrhage. But a first draft of the autopsy report, only recently unearthed, describes a major stomach hemorrhage as the most likely cause of Stalin's death. During his death throes, on March 4, the attending physicians noted that Stalin was vomiting blood. As usual, the Soviet News Agency *Tass* misinformed the world, announcing that Stalin had died in his Kremlin apartment.

Beria was there at the Nearer Dacha at the time of death. According to Stalin's daughter, Svetlana, Beria "called out in a loud and undisguisedly triumphant voice, 'Khrustalev, the car!' " Note that Khrustalev was the one called, and Beria was the first to leave. And it was Khrustalev who was on hand for the embalming of Stalin's remains. Strangely, he fell ill and died shortly afterward.

Stalin's remains were embalmed by the special laboratory at the Lenin Mausoleum. They were interred next to the body of Lenin in the red marble mausoleum that protrudes out from the Kremlin's walls and into Red Square. Stalin was to be immortalized, buried in his uniform with shoulder boards, buttons, and hero's stars made of gold. Later that spring Beria said to Molotov: "I took him out."

On June 26, 1953, three months after Stalin's death, Lavrenti Beria came to a meeting of the Presidium of the Council of Ministers with a scheme to accumulate more power. Khrushchev and Malenkov had other plans. By prearrangement, Minister of Defense General Georgi Zhukov and a handful of his army (not KGB) troops were waiting in an adjacent room. On a signal from Khrushchev, they stormed in to arrest Beria. He was taken to an army prison and nominally charged with planning to overthrow the Soviet government. Counts against him went back to his dealings with Hitler in 1941.* The real issue, however,

---

* During the summer of 1941, as the Soviets reeled in retreat in the face of German advances on Moscow, Beria met with intermediaries of the Nazi government to explore terms for a truce or separate peace.

was the survival of Khrushchev, Malenkov, and the other Politburo members. After a pro-forma trial, Beria was shot, on December 23, at the headquarters of the Moscow Military District. His execution was not entrusted to an underling. It was carried out by a three-star general, Pavel Batitsky, as Beria pleaded for his life.

Georgi Malenkov fared better. After attempting an abortive coup against Khrushchev in 1957, Malenkov was consigned to manage a power station in remote Kazakhstan. Nikolai Bulganin was promoted to Premier for a while, until he was of no further use to Khrushchev. He was dismissed into comfortable retirement in 1958. Khrushchev was the one left standing. With the real power in his hands, he installed himself as General Secretary of the CPSU and eventually as premier as well.

NIKITA KHRUSHCHEV REBURIES STALIN, AND STALIN'S APPROACH TO THE COLD WAR

By mid-February 1956, Khrushchev felt secure enough in his position to open the Pandora's box of Stalinist history. He convened the Twentieth Communist Party Congress, not a trivial undertaking in itself. The prior nineteenth congress had been Stalin's swan song, held in October 1952 as a vehicle to restructure the Politburo and to purge some old-timers. Khrushchev's closing address to the twentieth congress was four hours long, delivered in secrecy and at night on the twenty-fourth and twenty-fifth of February. In that speech he began to reveal and condemn the brutality of the Stalin years. He described Stalin as "sickly and suspicious . . . a flawed leader," incompetent in his anticipation of and in dealing with the German invasion of 1941. He referred to Stalin as "a pathological criminal, guilty of administrative violence, mass repression, and terror." He called the system itself the "cult of the individual."

The Soviet leadership tried to control distribution of the anti-Stalin speech, issuing it only to the *nomenklatura* and key military officers, but the word got out. Rumors appeared in the Western press within a month. A text broke in late spring and was publicly reprinted on June 5, 1956. With that, a new era in Soviet history began. The irrational brutality of the Stalin era was replaced with a still mindless bureaucracy that continued to rely on terror to keep itself in power, but with Khrushchev's address, things began to open up.

Before the speech, Khrushchev had shifted military policy away from Stalin's reliance on the massed power of the Red Army, preferring the muscle afforded by thermonuclear weapons and their supporting rockets. Eisenhower adopted a similar new look in the United States. Khrushchev shifted his state's emphasis from the promotion of armed might to his hopes for a burgeoning economy based on technology. Today, when Russians are asked, "When were the golden years of the Soviet Union?" most will cite the Khrushchev speech in 1956 or the launch of Sputnik a year later. Most younger Russians welcomed the move away from military posturing. They looked forward to challenging the United States in the more productive arenas of technology and economic progress.

KHRUSHCHEV—THE MAN

I never spoke with Nikita Khrushchev, but my father did. In 1959, Eisenhower invited Khrushchev to visit the United States, the first Soviet leader ever to do so. His September visit started in New York with an impressive performance at the UN. Khrushchev promoted nuclear disarmament, asked for better U.S.-USSR relations, and forecast a Soviet economy surpassing that of the United States. In 1956, Khrushchev had expressed these latter thoughts more bluntly. "We will bury you," he said then. He also had accepted an invitation from the New York Economic Club. My father was part of the club's host committee. He found Khrushchev to be a brittle, ill-informed, and doctrinaire peasant, devoid of the charm one usually expects from a visiting head of government. He thought that much of Khrushchev's rigidity, however, came from the shock he felt at being exposed to a free and prosperous society so at odds with the picture painted by Soviet propaganda.

My father's initial impressions were dominated by what he saw. When he entered Khrushchev's hotel suite, the man was barefoot and in shirtsleeves, sporting a pistol in a holster around his chest. After some confrontational capitalist-communist exchanges, he dressed and readied himself to go downstairs. Only the soothing words of his security aide convinced Khrushchev to leave his pistol on the table as he left the room.

This habit of Soviet leaders remaining personally armed when visiting outside the USSR was reconfirmed during the Brezhnev years. A film clip of that aging dictator shows him handing his pistol to an aide as they board their Aeroflot plane for home.

Once Khrushchev and his party arrived in San Francisco a week later, the security detail was a little more relaxed. Perhaps they had developed a greater confidence in the U.S. Secret Service and FBI men that surrounded him like a blanket. Or perhaps they adjusted to Western lifestyles. Whatever the reason, once Khrushchev began his speech to the World Affairs Council in San Francisco, his security detail slipped into camaraderie with the locals and then into alcoholic oblivion.

By 1961, Khrushchev felt confident enough to complete the de-Stalinization of the Soviet Union by moving Stalin's remains—at night and in great secrecy—to a lesser grave outside the Kremlin wall. He did it, fittingly, on Halloween. On October 31, 1961, the militia cleared Red Square and closed off all entrances. Without fanfare, Stalin's body was removed from the mausoleum, the environmental systems were switched off, and the gold buttons and stars were replaced with brass. At 10:00 P.M. the survivors of the Communist party leadership arrived. None of Stalin's relatives were present. The remains of Joseph Stalin were moved to a simple grave outside the Kremlin's walls and covered with dirt.

IN THE UNITED STATES, EISENHOWER TAKES OVER

Dwight David Eisenhower was elected President in November 1952. The war in Korea was grinding on; Alger Hiss had been convicted of perjury after testifying falsely to Congress about his communist espionage activities; there were clouds of scandal hanging over Truman's White House. After twenty years of continuous Democratic administration, many voters felt it was time for a change. Eisenhower's election was not a repudiation of Roosevelt's New Deal. Rather, it was a demand to end the Korean War honorably and to rearm the country, morally and militarily, for the challenges that lay ahead.

General Eisenhower was the hero of the Normandy invasion and the defeat of Nazi Germany. He went on to serve as Chief of Staff of the U.S. Army, then as the first Supreme Allied Commander in Europe upon the creation of NATO.* He returned to the United States to serve as the president of Columbia University, and soon afterward responded to a political draft. Eisenhower was seen as a centrist who could win the Republican nomination, then pull the country together

---

* The North Atlantic Treaty Organization was an alliance of the U.S., Canada, and ten West European nations when started in 1949. Its purpose was to present a unified front to the threat of Soviet postwar expansion.

to win the presidency itself in November 1952. He carried thirty-nine of the forty-eight states, with 55 percent of the popular vote. His coat-tails were modest but adequate. Republicans also gained control of both houses of Congress for the first time in a quarter century. They won the House by three votes, and achieved a 48-48 tie in the Senate. With Vice-President Nixon's tie-breaking vote, that was enough for the Republicans to prevail. The Truman-to-Eisenhower transition was cold in the extreme. The formal ceremonies on January 20, 1953, were devoid of any oral communication or other indications of warmth between the two men.

Eisenhower made good on his promise to go to Korea, to look into the situation there and end the war honorably and promptly. Employing some visible and some veiled threats to the communist government of China, and benefiting from the recent changes in Moscow, the new President achieved a cease-fire along a line not too dissimilar from the prewar boundary between North and South Korea. The cease-fire was signed on July 27, 1953. The Cold War could cool off. The conflict would turn to other battlefields.

Upon Stalin's death, the new President began a full review of the U.S. defense posture. Since the start of the Cold War, "containment" had been the policy set forth by Truman. It was to be supported by a massive U.S. military buildup across the board. Eisenhower was not sure the economy could or should carry that burden. He wondered how the passing of Stalin and the coming of the thermonuclear age should refocus America's defense posture.

The initial thinking was done by about forty of the new government's leaders. The Secretaries of State and Defense, the Director of Central Intelligence, and the Joint Chiefs of Staff, along with their second- and third-tier deputies, plus a few wise men from earlier times, gathered for five weeks of discussion, off and on, at the stiflingly hot National War College in Washington, D.C. The advisers broke into three teams. The first, led by George Kennan, was to review the containment option—waiting the communists out. A second, led by Major General James McCormick, was to explore the possibility of drawing lines on the globe, with the threat of massive nuclear retaliation should the Soviets cross those lines. The third, led by General Andrew Good-paster, was to consider the rollback option. Should the United States try for a "win" during the Eisenhower years?

Some ideas sank without a trace. Others seemed to make sense. By midsummer each team had reached some conclusions. They prepared briefings, and each was allocated an hour and a half to present their conclusions to the Commander in Chief. That meeting occurred in the White House solarium during July 1953. After listening to the discussions, Eisenhower took the floor for forty-five minutes to review what he had heard. He displayed a marvelous grasp of the details and brought his wartime and NATO experiences to bear.

His first conclusion: containment of the Soviet Union was the only sensible alternative. An immediate victory was not in the cards, and trying for one could unleash a nuclear holocaust. Second, during the containment years to come it would be important to understand what was going on inside the Soviet Union. Eisenhower wanted transparency. That meant an active and high-tech approach to penetrating and circumventing the Iron Curtain. He was concerned about the possibility of surprise attack, now that the Soviets had nuclear weapons. He also wanted to make sound decisions about the allocation of U.S. resources.

As a result of that meeting, Eisenhower instituted a long range plan to modernize the armed forces. It was a modernization based on technology and on the new thermonuclear weapons. In the collection of intelligence, he wanted overhead photography, signals intelligence from a variety of platforms, and new surveillance radars. Armed with the facts, he believed he would be able to strike the right balance between rebuilding the military and protecting America's powerful economy, since the latter was the engine that ultimately would tip the balance at the end of the containment game. Soviet leaders failed to understand that economic fact of life. With that mistake, they condemned the USSR to a forty-year death spiral into bankruptcy and defeat.

One of Eisenhower's first steps was to augment the use of Air Force and Navy aircraft in top-secret overflights of both the territorial waters and the heartland of the Soviet Union and China. Although each flight was a risky violation of the target nation's sovereignty, Eisenhower thought the flights were essential. They were executed only after a careful weighing of the pros and cons of each one. In time, those inquisitive U.S. fliers were joined by their brethren under the sea. Specially equipped submarines, some with detachable underwater minisubs, patrolled the edges of the Soviet empire. Some deployed ELINT★ antennae, others took pictures through periscopes, and still others deployed underwater crews to tap into the Soviet undersea telecom cables. As a result of those sailors' and airmen's courage and skills, the United States

---

★ Electronic Intelligence: sensors looking for radar or navigation signals, missile telemetry, or voice channels.

got its first glimpse of Soviet strengths and weaknesses. It would be half a century before some of these men would tell their story. Others did not live to do so.

General Goodpaster, often Eisenhower's chief-of-staff, recently summarized the meaning of the Eisenhower intelligence programs:

> *Ike knew that a strong and healthy economy was more than important; it was the key to the ultimate success of the West. America's economic power had provided the margin of victory in World War II. Ike did not want the U.S. to become an armed camp. He wanted to spend enough, on the right things, but not too much, especially not on huge land armies. Overflights of the Soviet Union helped him avoid unnecessary expenditures. They gave Ike confidence in the adequacy of the U.S. deterrent.*

MY FIRST STOP: EDWARDS AIR FORCE BASE

As a newly commissioned officer in the U.S. Air Force, my first duty station was at Edwards Air Force Base in the Mojave Desert northeast of Los Angeles. It was a marvelous time to be there, for Edwards was the Air Force Flight Test Center, home of the boys with the "right stuff." Chuck Yeager was there. So was Ivan Kinchloe and a host of others. They were handsome, athletic, and incredibly bright human beings, scornful of the rules other than those they had learned the hard way in the skies over Korea. They flew to the ragged edge of their aircraft's performance—and sometimes a little beyond.

Edwards was the home of amazing technology, such as the first Atlas missiles brought to the rocket stands for engine tests. It also was to be the home of one of the silliest airborne ideas ever—a 300-ton nuclear-powered bomber. This aircraft, known as Weapon System 125A, was to cruise the borders of the Soviet Union like an airborne submarine: always on patrol, immune to surprise attack, and ready to go to war at a moment's notice. There were just a few problems. The first was this behemoth's size—substantially larger than the B-52s then entering the Air Force inventory. Another was the limited number of missions any given crew could fly before reaching their maximum lifetime radiation dose. And at the heart of the concept was the prospect of dozens of such hot reactors roaming the skies while awaiting their inevitable crash.

I was put to work scoping the real estate needed for a safe engine run-up by this aircraft. It soon became clear that we would need much of San Bernardino and Kern counties, even by the comparatively lax safety standards of the 1950s, just for the flight test program In the operational world, every engine start could be an environmental disaster. Fortunately, cooler heads prevailed. By the end of the decade, WS-125A had been cancelled, but only after fifteen years of engineering and a billion dollars of expense. The good news was that the new successes, such as the U-2s, were soon to arrive at Edwards. Their presence was denied, and they flew mostly at night, but the young technical officers like myself prepared their way and were dazzled when they did arrive.

WHERE DID THEY ALL GO?

In 1956, Eisenhower was reelected to the American presidency by an even bigger margin than his first victory—58 percent of the vote and forty-one states. His party lost control of Congress, however, and in time his Vice-President would be unable to hold the White House for the Republicans. Nixon's 1960 loss was due, in part, to his hesitation to run on the Eisenhower coattails, and in part to his reluctance to abuse his inside knowledge of Soviet weakness.

In the go-go sixties and the crisis-laden seventies, Eisenhower was viewed as a nice old man who presided over a wonderful postwar boom in a detached sort of way. At the end of the century, however, historians are coming to appreciate his genius. Eisenhower knew exactly what he was doing. Instead of supporting his old comrades with huge land armies, he turned to the new thermonuclear technology. He beat the Soviets at their own long range rocket game, proposed modest defense budgets, and then unleashed the American economy to play its defining role in winning the Cold War. And through it all he had enough self-confidence to keep his intelligence coups to himself. He died at Walter Reed Hospital outside Washington, D.C., on March 28, 1968. He and his wife Mamie were buried at Abilene, Kansas.

With the events of 1960, Nikita Khrushchev shifted to a policy of confrontation. His follow-up visit to the UN, on October 12, 1960, was the occasion of unbridled abuse, table-thumping, and shoe-pounding on the lectern. It was but prologue to his even more confrontational approach to John Kennedy. Khrushchev's antics made his peers in the Politburo nervous. He was removed from power in 1964, gracefully, with his skin intact and with time to dictate his memoirs. He died of old age in Moscow on September 11, 1971. His remains are buried in the Novodevichi Cemetery outside Moscow.

I completed my tour as an engineering officer at Edwards Air Force Base in the summer of 1957, with orders to return to Los Angeles. It would be there that the struggle for the high ground of technology would be fought by some of the brightest scientific minds in America.

CHAPTER 3

The Paparazzi Pilots

SURPRISE ATTACK IS A REAL WAKE-UP CALL; a society so disturbed had best open its eyes. At no time was that more true than when the North Korean communist state, suddenly and unexpectedly, invaded its free southern neighbor on Sunday morning, June 25, 1950. Their invasion was preapproved and supported by the Soviet Union, heating up the Cold War to a bloodred intensity. The United States responded militarily, thereby saving South Korea's sovereignty, but it did much more than that. In 1950 the Air Force and Navy began serious overflights of "denied territories" far beyond Korea with photo and electronic reconnaissance aircraft. These missions became known as the Sensitive Intelligence, or SENSINT, program. They were flown only with the specific prior approval of the President, and they suffered no losses until the Powers shootdown of May 1, 1960.

In contrast, the PARPRO—or Peacetime Airborne Reconnaissance Program—consisted of regular flights around the periphery of the Soviet empire, China, and North Korea, authorized by theater commanders.

These intelligence-gathering forays were legal, since they remained outside the sovereign territory of others, but the communist states took great offense. They often tried to decoy the Americans into their territory, and upon occasion the PARPRO aircraft were shot down even when over international waters. My college roommate, a Navy pilot, survived such an attack. During the period 1950–91, well over a hundred U.S. crew members were lost on such flights.

The first targets for the more confrontational SENSINT flights were the Korean battlefields, North and South. Then came North Korea's patrons: the People's Republic of China, Manchuria, and eventually the maritime provinces of the Soviet Union. Those missions had some rationale under international law, since the U.S. was acting under a UN mandate in its protection of South Korea, and those territories were "co-belligerents" of the North Korean aggressor.

When the Chinese communists joined the fight, to reinforce the North and to push south, the Western allies feared that a simultaneous invasion of Europe was imminent, perhaps even a global assault. Nuclear weapons were on the table. The UK intervened, offering to participate in reconnaissance overflights of the Soviet Union itself, to alleviate fears of a surprise attack, in exchange for American nuclear calm.

Eisenhower's inauguration brought the local conflict in Korea to an end; the struggle moved to the world stage. The first rumbles of the thermonuclear age could be heard. Long range bombers were beginning to appear in the Soviet Union. Tupolev's Tu-4, a copy of America's wartime, piston-engined B-29, already was deployed, but in 1953 hints of an all-jet Myasichev M-4 "Bison" bomber began to appear. On one-way missions these aircraft could deliver Stalin's new atomic weapons to U.S. soil.

The Soviet system was secretive in the extreme. It had already authorized one surprise attack, on South Korea. Eisenhower was worried about another. To stay abreast of force deployments behind the Iron Curtain, Eisenhower continued to authorize overflights of the Soviet Union. Initially they were to be conducted by reconnaissance versions of operational aircraft then on hand, mostly RB-45s, RB-47s and RB-57s. To cover future bets, he authorized the development of aircraft specially designed for long range operations over denied territory, the U-2, and in time, the SR-71. For the benefit of the next generation of American leaders, he initiated work on reconnaissance satellites. The first of these, Corona, finally flew two successful missions just as Eisenhower was leaving office.

The aerial overflights of the Soviet Union had no justification in international law. They were espionage, pure and simple. If intercepted and shot down, those aircrews were dead ducks. But a handful of interesting and courageous men flew them anyway, to snap fleeting photos of the unwilling, then to head for the border. They were the airborne equivalent of the paparazzi, the photographers who stalk the cafés of Paris and Rome snapping photos of celebrities and others who prefer not to be exposed, then dashing for cover before bodyguards can grab them. These young American pilots of the fifties were the paparazzi of the skies.

It was not until February 2001 that they were allowed to assemble with my peers and me, to tell their once-secret stories and to show the photos they had brought home fifty years before. They referred to themselves as the "*Mad* generation." The silent generation had come before, and the boomers were but twinkles in these airmen's eyes. Their *Mad* generation was the here and now, named after the humor magazine of that name and time. Its protagonist was Alfred E. Neumann. His motto was: "What, me worry?" As these men set off for Mukden, Baikonur, and Mys Shmidta, I can hear the aircraft commander completing his checklist with a "What, me worry?" before starting the takeoff roll.

IN THE BEGINNING

Government officials often ignore the hard facts of life; brave young men then have to pay the price. Korea was no exception. When war broke out there, the U.S. Air Force had to look to World War II aircraft—P-51 Mustangs and B-29 bombers—along with a few F-80 jets, to fight for control of the skies. The F-80 Shooting Star was a first attempt to marry jet propulsion to a conventional airframe. The aircraft was underpowered and had little high-altitude capability. There was no wing sweep and it had no ejection seat to accommodate a bailout at jet speeds. The result was a not very good fighter plane, no match for the Soviet MiG-15s, but it was the best we had. A few F-80s were equipped with cameras, to become RF-80As, and one, piloted by First Lieutenant Bryce Poe, flew over the Soviet's Kurile Islands in 1949–50 in an early search for Soviet Tu-4 bomber bases.

In time, help was forthcoming. By December 1950 the first squadron of North American F-86 Sabrejets made it to Korea. They were the greatest, with swept wings for agility and speed, six .50 caliber machine guns for armament, and the new J-47 engine for power. The F-86s dominated the skies over Korea, achieving a 10:1 kill ratio over their Soviet-built MiG opponents. At the time, it wasn't clear who was flying those MiGs, but there were some interesting indicators. As the conflict wore on, American pilots learned to head for the Yellow Sea when in trouble. The MiGs would seldom follow over open waters. The surmise, later confirmed, was that those aircraft were piloted by Russians. Their shoot-down, where the U.S. Navy could recover them, would constitute clear proof of direct Soviet involvement in the war. Dogfights in MiG Alley often were brief because some MiGs did not carry a full load of fuel. Too much fuel might allow those aircraft, if piloted by North Koreans, to continue their practice of defecting to the South.

A few F-86s were outfitted as reconnaissance aircraft. The replacement of armament with cameras was an obvious step. Painting guns onto the fuselage to fool attacking MiGs probably was less useful, but it was done. The main security for those aircraft was three accompanying, fully armed F-86s. This flight of four was led to the photo target by the RF-86. If attacked, it would relinquish command to the second element leader and the sortie would turn into a full-fledged dogfight with the usual result—two or three MiGs shot down.

At first, the RF-86 pilots, like Captain Mele Vojvodich, were honored that the very best hotshot fighter pilots wanted to fly escort, but in time they noticed that these flights were returning with few reconnaissance photos. The reason: the RF-86s were being used as bait. They drew the MiGs up for a fight; then the hotshots, the McConnells, Jabaras, and Risners, could take command and run up their kills.

By the summer of 1952, Captain Vojvodich preferred to fly with just a wingman, but his most memorable flight, on March 27, 1953, was flown alone. His wingman returned to Seoul's Kimpo Air Base with mechanical difficulties. Vojvodich decided to continue with his mission into Manchuria by himself. He was now flying an RF-86F, equipped with stiffer wings and four wing tanks, giving him plenty of range—about 1,650 nautical miles. On that day in March, he needed every one of them.

Vojvodich made it to Harbin, took some pictures, then turned south to take in the airfields around Mukden, now known as Shenyang. Approaching Mukden at 50,000 feet★ and Mach 0.9, he was overtaken by

---

★ The F-86E had a rated service ceiling of 42,000 feet, but when flown clean, *i.e.,* with no external tanks, it could reach 50,000 feet and higher.

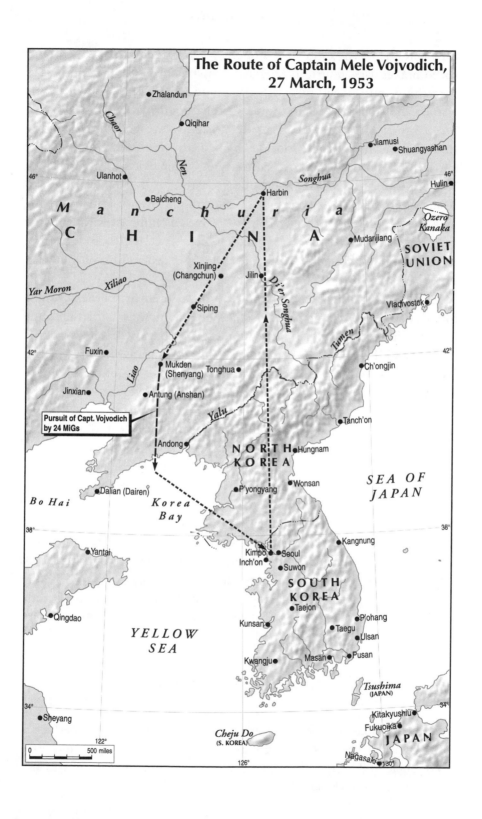

The Route of Captain Mele Vojvodich, 27 March, 1953

Zhalandun

Qiqihar

Chaor

Nen

Jiamusi

Shuangyashan

46°

Ulanhot

Songhua

Hulin

Baicheng

Harbin

46°

M a n c h u r i a

Mudanjiang

*Ozero
Kanaka*

C H I N A

**SOVIET
UNION**

Xinjing
(Changchun)

Jilin

D'er Songhua

Siping

Vladivostok

Xiliao

Yar Moron

42°

Liao

Fuxin

42°

Mukden
(Shenyang)

Tonghua

Ch'ongjin

Tumen

Jinxian

Antung (Anshan)

Yalu

| Pursuit of Capt. Vojvodich
| by 24 MiGs |

Andong

**N O R T H
K O R E A**

Tanch'on

Hungnam

Bo Hai

Dalian (Dairen)

*Korea
Bay*

P'yongyang

Wonsan

**SEA OF
JAPAN**

38°

38°

Yantai

Kangnung

Kimpo   Seoul
Inch'on

Suwon

**SOUTH
KOREA**

Qingdao

Taejon

P'ohang

*YELLOW
SEA*

Kunsan

Taegu

Ulsan

Masan   Pusan

Kwangju

Tsushima
(JAPAN)

34°

34°

Sheyang

Kitakyushiu

122°

Fukuoika

J A P A N

0   500 miles

Cheju Do
(S. KOREA)

Nagasaki

126°   130°

four MiG-15s. They just flew along, in formation, then popped their speed brakes for a return to Mukden. Vojvodich should have suspected something, but his visitors seemed to be unarmed, probably out on a training mission. About ten minutes later the grown-ups showed up—twenty-four MiG-15s, fully armed. Not good. Vojvodich finished up his snapshots, then turned south. His pursuers were a few thousand feet above him and there were no Americans within 500 miles. Vojvodich rolled, dove, did a split-S, and boomed through the sound barrier, to Mach 1.05. The MiGs were out of control, all twenty-four fishtailing and firing their cannons like crazy. The good thing about a dogfight with twenty-four bad guys, Vojvodich now says, is that only one of them can get on your tail at any one time. The rest are shooting at each other.

By the time Vojvodich got to Antung, a town in southern China now known as Anshan, he was on the deck, flying down the flight line of a Chinese fighter base. The Chinese must have wondered about a single F-86, booming along a hundred feet overhead, with two dozen MiGs in hot pursuit. He headed for the Yellow Sea, thinking the Navy might rescue him there and knowing his pursuers would lose interest. That worked. He turned toward Kimpo and called the tower to ask for a flameout approach, only to be told he was number six in the flameout pattern. He had been in the air for over three hours, but made it home. His engine did not flame out until he was taxiing on the ramp. Reconnaissance pilots live that way. They have a saying: "The only time you have too much fuel is when you're on fire."

It turns out that Vojvodich brought home the crown jewels. The United States was concerned about the Russians and Chinese bringing Ilyushin-28 bombers into the theater, aircraft capable of attacking U.S. bases in Japan. Vojvodich's photos showed that they had arrived. The major powers exchanged warnings, Vojvodich was awarded the Distinguished Service Cross, and the Korean War never escalated to Japan. That summer it was brought to a close.

THE BRITS GIVE US CABBAGE RAVINE

During the darkest days in Korea, in early December 1950—before Mele Vojvodich's F-86 ever got there—the whole show could have gone nuclear. The British helped us keep our cool, and in the bargain, they showed us Cabbage Ravine. It happened this way:

Korea had been a seesaw battle. On October 25, 1950, the first units of the Red Chinese army showed up at the village of Onjong. They began to slow the U.S. advance through North Korea until November 26, when their full-scale onslaught began. U.S. leaders feared the Chinese offensive was but one piece of a global communist assault, a diversion to facilitate the long-feared Soviet invasion of Western Europe. A surprise attack on the U.S. itself might be in the works. In response, the Truman White House, probably at the urging of General MacArthur, the UN commander in Korea, was giving serious thought to the use of nuclear weapons in Asia. "No military option is ruled out," the President said. The intent was to disrupt the flow of Chinese troops and supplies across the Yalu River and into Korea. A bonus would be to send a clear message to the Soviets: "Don't!"

By early December 1950 over half of the Americans responding to a Gallup poll thought World War III had already begun. Our European allies were alarmed over the possibility of nuclear escalation into their backyard. The Soviets had first tested an A–bomb fifteen months before and were now thought to have a modest inventory of those weapons. At the end of November, Clement Atlee, prime minister of the UK, met with his French counterpart to discuss this crisis. Then, on December 3, he flew to Washington to meet with Truman.

Any written agreements reached during that visit have yet to see the light of day, but it appears the results of those Atlee-Truman discussions were twofold: a stabilization of the nuclear crisis, and an opening of the overflight window into the western Soviet Union as a hedge against the feared surprise attack. Specifically:

1. On December 9, 1950, Truman announced there would be no use of American nuclear weapons in or around Korea without prior consultation with the British.

2. On December 16, Truman declared a National Emergency in the U.S., a declaration that activated a broad spectrum of major alerts, reserve call-ups, force movements, and resource expenditures. The President's declaration was a signal that he would deal with the crisis by conventional, not nuclear, means.

3. The British government agreed to join in the overflights of denied territory. In the spring of 1951 the RAF formed a Special Duty Flight to train for operating modified U.S. RB-45C Tornado bombers over the Soviet Union. These

aircraft were painted with Royal Air Force colors at Sculthorpe RAFB and flown under the command of RAF Squadron Leader John Crampton.

To this day the British Government has not declassified the activities of the Special Duty Flight, so the record of what happened next is not clear, but the United States did recover in Korea, there was no Soviet invasion of Europe, and the Brits did give us our first look at Cabbage Ravine.

The first British overflights of denied territories took place on the night of March 21, 1952, when three RB-45Cs, sporting RAF colors, took off from Sculthorpe. One flew a zigzag course to the east, then north, to inspect Soviet facilities in the Baltic states. Intelligence collection was done by radarscope, given that the flights were conducted at night. The take-home product was photography of those radarscope images, an excellent portrait of 126 different intelligence targets. Not the least of these were the air defenses U.S. bombers would encounter on any first run into the Soviet Union. The second British aircraft jinked east, to fly across Poland and then circumnavigate Byelorussia. The airfields around Minsk, the infrastructure supporting the poised armored divisions of the Red Army, and a variety of other targets were imaged in detail. The third aircraft flew a similarly erratic course to the south, for the longest tour of all: Germany, Czechoslovakia, and then the armaments centers of Ukraine all the way to the Russian border at Kharkov.

The Soviet air defenses went crazy, but they could not find the Tornadoes in the dark. The erratic courses of the intruders had been deliberately chosen to trigger as many Soviet ground radars as possible, but the Soviet interceptors in the air were not equipped with airborne radar. All three British aircraft returned to Sculthorpe safely. The take, both from the intruders' scopes as well as from the observing British and U.S. ELINT platforms, was of immeasurable value. It assured the allies that no surprise was in the offing, and it facilitated planning for future ingress past Soviet defenses.

The success of those missions emboldened the British to continue. The Special Duty Flight trained to concert pitch in the autumn of 1952, but their December overflights were cancelled for political reasons. They got another chance in April 1954 when the Special Duty Flight struck again, covering much the same territory as it had in 1952.

In the meantime, however, another RAF aircraft gave the allies their first daytime, overhead view of Kapustin Yar.

There had been intelligence reports of unusual activity a few miles to the east of Stalingrad. Radio intercepts and other indicators suggested a rocket test range in active use there. Eisenhower wanted the facts as soon as possible, for the construction of a rocket test range would confirm the reports from repatriated German scientists that a serious Soviet rocket program was under way. The base was called Kapustin Yar—"Cabbage Ravine" in Russian—and it was thought to be at the center of an embryonic Soviet rocket program. The Brits agreed to take a look during daylight hours, when photography was possible, but when intercepting MiGs could be lethal.

On or about August 27, 1953, a single RAF Canberra, similar to the U.S. RB-57, made a solo dash for those crown jewels of the Soviet military establishment. The mission was flown in broad daylight from Giebelstadt in West Germany and tracked by Soviet radar immediately upon takeoff. The Soviets made a chaotic attempt to get at it, but the Canberra had been stripped of all extra weight and was able to fly unscathed at 46,000 to 48,000 feet across East Germany and past Kiev. Over Kharkov, misguided Soviet fighter pilots started firing at each other. Over Stalingrad, they did better, using pop-up maneuvers to get in a few hits just as the Canberra was photographing the Kapustin Yar test range. The British aircraft survived the attack, turned south, and followed the Volga River to the Caspian Sea and a safe landing in Iran.

The photographic results were blurred because of aircraft vibration while under attack, but the pilots saw the target and were able to report. It was left for other fliers in future years, especially the new U-2, to keep track of what was going on at Kapustin Yar, but that flight in August 1953 rang the bells. Back home, Eisenhower's Defense Department assembled a group of technical wise men—to be known as the Teapot Committee—to settle on a response. If not for a few brave British fliers, the missile gap might really have come to pass.

IT WAS, AFTER ALL, A BAND OF BROTHERS

As part of the Soviet May Day parade in 1954, the mysterious Myasichev-4 jet bomber made its first appearance in the skies over

Moscow. That was the final straw. The U.S. intelligence community asked SAC to ready a sortie of RB-47s to look for deployed M-4s around the Kola Peninsula in northern Russia. Eight such reconnaissance aircraft had already been relocated to Fairford in the UK, while their eight accompanying KC-97 tankers were stationed at Mildenhall. After some deliberation, Eisenhower approved their use.

In broad daylight on May 6, 1954, six RB-47s made a practice, or decoy, run from Fairford to the coast of Norway, west of Stavanger, the standard refueling rendezvous point. There, the RB-47s tanked up before heading north along the Norwegian coast. All flights were conducted in complete radio silence. Bomber/tanker rendezvous were accomplished by beacons on the tankers. The aircraft flew to the northern tip of Norway and its border with the USSR, broke into separate trajectories for reconnaissance over international waters off the Soviet coast, then returned to Fairford. They hoped they had been noticed by the Soviets.

On May 8 a similar package was planned. In the predawn darkness, nonflying crews did the preflight checks of the aircraft while the crews of the six mission aircraft received their final route and weather briefing. Then Colonel Joe Preston, the B-47 wing commander, asked one crew—Major Vance Heavilin and Captains Hal Austin and Carl Holt—to step into another room. Two colonels from SAC headquarters were there, one from Intelligence and another from Operations. Colonel Preston left the room while the officers from headquarters laid it out: "One aircraft—yours—is to fly over the Soviet Union."

There was no heroic speech, no call for volunteers. The colonels made it clear that Austin, Heavilin, and Holt had been selected for the mission because they were the best. Protecting the U.S. was their job; they were expected to do it, and they did, no questions asked. There followed an Emergency War Operation briefing. Aircraft commander Austin, copilot Carl Holt, and navigator/electronic systems operator Vance Heavilin were to take off as part of a standard six RB-47 package. After refueling, three of those aircraft were to continue north along the Norwegian coast, as they had two days before. This time, however, upon reaching a point along the northwest coast of Norway, all three aircraft were to turn east, flying to a point about a hundred miles north of Murmansk. When off Murmansk, two of the aircraft were to turn around and head for home. Austin's RB-47 was to turn south, fly across the Kola Peninsula and northwestern Russia, photograph nine suspect airfields, then escape with a dash back to the West,

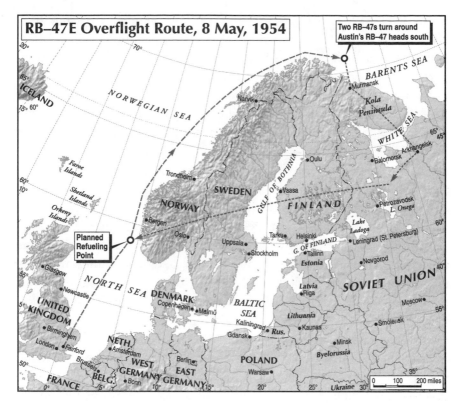

RB–47E Overflight Route, 8 May, 1954

Two RB–47s turn around
Austin's RB–47 heads south

Planned
Refueling
Point

across Finland, Sweden, and Norway. The colonels unrolled a strip map of the nine airfields, starting at Murmansk. They provided comments about the photos they wanted. "Cameras on here, off there." They furnished some bogus maps, for use if the crew went down, and a "blood chit" of gold coins and other survival equipment—nice, but useless. The only sure path to survival was to stay aloft.

The crew was briefed on the air order of battle. They were advised that Soviet radar was primitive and probably could not see them at 40,000 feet. The only interceptors on duty would be MiG-15s, aircraft that could neither reach nor catch the B-47s, cruising as they would at over 500 mph and 40,000 feet. The new MiG-17s were not yet deployed in adequate numbers to pose a threat from the northern bases. Austin and crew were to rendezvous with their tanker, outbound and if needed on returning, at designated times in the usual box off Stavanger. The crew was to discuss this mission with no one, ever. Their fellow-RB-47 crews were not aware of this plan. Upon their return to Fairford, a ground crew would meet their plane, unload the cameras, and be gone. The three officers could then enjoy a good dinner and a sound night's sleep. At least, that was the plan.

At 7:00 A.M., UK time, all six aircraft were off. They met their KC-97 tankers off Stavanger; the RB-47s then continued north. In the late morning three aircraft reached their turn point off the northwest corner of the Scandinavian coast, then turned east and proceeded to a point a hundred miles north of Murmansk. Then the excitement began. The two unbriefed RB-47s did a 180-degree turn, but aircraft commander Austin turned only 90 degrees and headed south. Major Jimmy Valentine, aircraft commander of the adjacent RB-47, was horrified, as his fellow pilot seemingly had gone berserk. Austin and crew were headed into Russia and could trigger World War III. Heated debate ensued within Valentine's aircraft. Should they break radio silence, call Austin to ask what he was doing? Should they call their home base at Fairford to report a rogue crew? SAC discipline prevailed. Valentine and his accompanying RB-47 were told to return home, and they would do so. Austin undoubtedly had his own orders. The two confused RB-47s disappeared over the western horizon in silence; Austin, Heavilin, and Holt headed south.

At noon they crossed the Russian coast at an altitude of 40,000 feet and a speed of over 500 mph. Within minutes they found their first and second targets, airfields near Murmansk. Click, click. The next stop was to be Arkhangelsk, but twenty minutes into the Soviet Union the first nine MiG-15s appeared, coming up from the left rear and below. They could not make it to altitude, but the fact that they showed up so quickly meant Austin and crew were being tracked by radar; so much for that piece of intelligence. To make matters worse, the RB-47 was now putting out heavy contrails. On to targets three and four.

There, they encountered more MiGs, closing in at their altitude. The MiGs did not make any firing passes, but the fact that they could reach that altitude meant Austin and his crew now were dealing with MiG-17s, not MiG 15s; more erroneous intelligence. The Americans photographed target number five, then things got worse. Another flight of MiG-17s showed up, firing live rounds. Every sixth round was a tracer, but at that altitude the MiG-17s were unstable. They could not get a bead on the RB-47, and so the Americans pressed on unscathed.

Austin had photographed target number six and was beginning a sweeping 45-degree turn to the left when it happened. More MiGs came in from the left rear, blazing away. Each made a single pass, and one of them got lucky. A 23 millimeter cannon shell scored a direct hit on Austin's left wing, about eight feet from where it joined the fuselage. The shell exploded, tearing a hole in the flap and putting fragments into the RB-47's forward main, self-sealing fuel tank. The damaged tank did not leak and did not catch fire, but the wing and fuselage now had some sizable holes creating serious drag. Even worse, the incoming shell hit the communications electronics. The intercom, essential in a B-47 because the crew was seated in line rather than side by side, was gone. They could not easily communicate with each other without the intercom. On that May 8 flight, messages had to be passed from pilot to copilot by navigator Heavilin. It appeared the radio might not work either.

Once it became clear that the MiG-17s were playing for keeps, co-pilot Holt was told to turn his seat around, to start operating the 20mm cannon in the tail of the RB-47, to deal with the incoming raiders. This was a terrible piece of equipment; radar gunsight and cannon would not work together. Holt only got off a few rounds before the whole kluge quit, but that was enough. The MiGs stayed out of the RB-47's 45-degree tail cone, which made it tough for the interceptors to get in another good shot.

On they went, dodging MiGs and taking snapshots of the local scenery. Over target number seven another flight of six MiGs appeared. They made passes but avoided the B-47's tail cone and thus fired without effect. On to Onega and target eight without incident, then number nine near the Finnish border, where one last flight of MiGs rose to greet them. One MiG pilot was instructed by his ground controller to ram the RB-47 if he could not shoot it down. Soviet pilots effected such collisions during World War II, but during the Cold War the designated suicide pilot often developed a mechanical malfunction that precluded further engagement.

Austin's RB-47 entered Finnish airspace, but the chase continued. The RB-47 corkscrewed through the sky with MiGs in hot pursuit. That scene is hard to imagine today, when we think of big bombers as cross-country airliners, but the B-47 was more agile than its pursuers. As the first all-jet bomber, it was designed to outmaneuver an intercepting fighter at its operating altitude.

The Swedish press later reported strange contrails and gunfire over their country, but everyone denied any knowledge of the events. Soon the chase was over, but not the problems. Austin's dodging and turning and the increased drag from the torn wing combined to put his aircraft almost an hour behind schedule and on the wrong side of the fuel consumption curve. The clash between duty and reality began.

Copilot Holt was watching the fuel gauges, and they were not telling a good story. In its ballet through the skies, his aircraft had used up an extra hour's worth of fuel. Stavanger was the designated emergency landing field, but setting down there in a SAC bomber, to say nothing of an RB-47 carrying several cameras loaded with film exposed over the Soviet Union, could provoke a major international crisis. Even so, Holt was urging an immediate landing while there was still enough fuel to operate the on-board equipment and lower the landing gear. To do otherwise could only result in an unpleasant if not fatal ditching in the frigid North Sea.

Austin had a different view. He'd been told to bring the cameras and their contents back to Fairford, and Holt agreed that without a good film return, it would be hard to prove where the boys had been. The RB-47 continued to fly westward at 43,000 feet and 480 mph, the optimum corner of the fuel economy envelope. The minutes ticked by; the engines kept running. Once out of the Soviet Union, Austin felt it acceptable to turn on his radio, to see if it worked and to attempt an emergency message to the UK.

Back at Mildenhall, gloom pervaded the ready room of the tanker squadron. Austin's RB-47 had failed to call for a refueling rendezvous. There had been ominous radio traffic between MiGs and their ground controllers over Russia. Now nothing. The standby tanker crew feared the worst as they sat in the gathering dusk, listening to nothing but static on emergency Channel 13. Then Jim Rigley heard it. A syllable, a phrase, badly broken up. Nothing more. But Rigley knew that voice. It was Hal Austin's! The message was unintelligible but the voice unmistakable. He knew that if Austin was trying to broadcast, he must be alive and still in the air. If that were true, he had little fuel, and that's what tankers were for.

Major Rigley jumped to his feet, summoned his crew, ran to his KC-97 and cranked it up. He called the tower for clearance to take off, which was denied until incoming traffic had been cleared. Too bad. While the traffic dodged, Rigley rolled, took off, and headed north at full power. The tower's screamed threats of court-martial receded into the distance.

Austin continued to head west, now well out over the North Sea. Holt was sweating blood. The fuel gauges were barely wiggling. And then they saw it—Rigley's tanker. Austin dropped his aircraft to refueling altitude, down and under the KC-97. The difference between the maximum speed of a KC-97 and the stall speed of an RB-47 is only nine miles per hour—no room for error. The boom operator was ready with a "wet boom," fuel in it, pumps on, dangerous as hell. Thunk, they connected. The JP-4 began to flow, the gauges came to life. Holt began to breathe again.

The landing at Fairford was uneventful, but the plane was isolated the minute it came to a stop. Austin's crew chief looked up in horror at the one-foot-diameter hole in the wing of his once beautiful aircraft. As Austin opened the RB-47's canopy, he gave a one-word explanation: "Birds." The three crewmen could sit there quietly, listening to their engines spool down amidst an ebbing flood of adrenaline, because they and their buddies in the tanker knew that "we few, we happy few, we band of brothers" had pulled it off.

Colonel Preston collected Austin, Heavilin, and Holt and swept them away before they could say a word to their gathering colleagues. Two civilians removed the exposed film from the cameras and were never seen again. The flight crew were taken to brief the U.S. ambassador in London, then to Omaha to tell their story to General LeMay. They had never before set foot in either place. The general listened, had a few scornful comments about Soviet fighter pilots, praise for his boys, and then dismissed them. "Talk to no one," he said. "All of this never happened."

That's the way it stayed for more than forty years. Only in 2001, when we all met in Washington, did Austin and Holt★ get to see the photos from their trip, now unclassified and mounted on poster board as part of a glorious thank you to those to whom duty, honor, and country had become second nature.

It turns that out the nine airfields in northwestern Russia were virtually devoid of M-4s—another Khrushchev bluff. Those photos and others from later U-2 flights confirmed that there was no "bomber gap." On the other hand, they showed far more MiG-17s than expected. The President could sleep more soundly—the United States need not spend much money on bomber defense—but it had better produce something that could outfly those MiG-17s.

HOME RUN

Not every RB-47 crew could return to the leafy comforts of rural England. Some were based in Thule, Greenland, a SAC base on Danish

---

★ Vance Heavilin could not make the reunion; he had died in 1998.

territory 690 miles (10 degrees) *north* of the Arctic Circle. When viewed from space, Thule appears ideally suited for its strategic coverage of the northern approaches to the Soviet Union. But airmen do not live in space. They must live in barracks near their flight line. They must eat and sleep, care for and operate their aircraft, from real bases in the real world.

It hardly gets much more real than at Thule. Temperatures hover around 35 degrees below zero. Howling winds blow the snow up to a condition where one cannot see one's hand in front of his face. To survive, the airmen and their crews live *inside* railroad refrigerator cars. There is one Eskimo village thirty-nine miles to the south. Boys being boys, the Air Force painted large orange numbers on the back of its hefty parkas, to better identify those traded to the Eskimo girls during the long winter nights.

During the 1950s B–47s and their tankers operated out of Thule. Today it's B–52s, E–4s and other tankers that pass through, but the mission is much the same. Thule remains a front-line base for the U.S. Air Combat Command.

In the spring of 1956 a series of RB–47 reconnaissance flights staged out of Thule to investigate the air defenses of the Soviet Union along its northern border. The U.S. was looking not only at Soviet bomber bases, but for air defense radars, interceptor bases, and all other defenses that might impede the ingress of the Strategic Air Command. This operation was known as *Home Run*, a grand finale flown in daylight on May 6 and 7.

A flight of six RB–47s, both photographic and ELINT versions, undertook a massive penetration of the northern defenses of the Soviet Union. They flew in formation across Siberia, then exited the Soviet Union at the Bering Strait. The operation came off without a hitch. The aircraft flew in from Thule, past the North Pole, and down into Siberia, making landfall at Ambarchik. From there they flew eastward across Siberia at 40,000 feet and full power, exiting the Soviet Union at Anadyr for a landing at Eielson AFB near Fairbanks, Alaska. No interceptors rose to meet them. There was little indication that they had been noticed. Along the way they photographed ground facilities and listened to the electronic signatures of dozens of Soviet bases.

When *Home Run* was over, the United States had concrete assurances that the northern approaches to the Soviet Union were poorly defended. Our nuclear strategic deterrent could penetrate the northern

Soviet border, if it had to, with little attrition along the way. One more argument for a hair-trigger nuclear posture had been laid to rest, at least for the remainder of the fifties.

THE MISFORTUNE OF LIEUTENANT SAFRONOV

The use of then-available combat aircraft was only an interim solution to Eisenhower's initial intelligence dilemma. In the summer of 1954, in the aftermath of the first sightings of the new Soviet M-4 bomber, and of H-bomb tests on both sides, Eisenhower created what was initially known as the Surprise Attack Panel. It was led by MIT president James Killian, and in time its name was changed to the Technical Capabilities Panel. This group was to advise Eisenhower on the role technology might play in strengthening the U.S. military posture and in precluding surprise attack. The individuals involved formed and re-formed into various panels and subcommittees, including Edwin Land's Intelligence Panel. Inventor of Polaroid photography and a true genius, Land displayed unusual military foresight in a letter to the President on November 5, 1954. The letter was the report of his panel's work. It covered a range of topics but had two specific, and secret, annexes. One recommended the development of a light, single engine reconnaissance aircraft, capable of flying for long distances at extremely high altitudes, with enough payload to carry sophisticated camera systems. The other annex called for the development of satellites, a recommendation made three years before the launch of Sputnik.

Despite objections by the Air Force, which was committed to a heavier, twin engine reconnaissance design, the President authorized the CIA to proceed with the development of a most remarkable and different airplane. Originally created in the mind of Lockheed's Kelly Johnson, this plane was to cruise at 70,000 feet, far above the reach of Soviet fighters or their early surface-to-air missiles. It was to have a range of 3,000 miles, enough to traverse the Soviet heartland, and carry a 700-pound payload. The new aircraft became known as the U-2. The development of this frail, large-winged, single engine sailplane was authorized by the Eisenhower administration within a month of receiving Edwin Land's report. Work started in December 1954. The first test aircraft was completed at Lockheed's Burbank "Skunk Works" only seven months later.

Eisenhower wanted the Cold War to be free of surprises. At his first summit meeting with Nikita Khrushchev, in Geneva in July 1955, Eisenhower proposed an "Open Skies" policy, a plan to allow overflights of each nation's territory by aircraft from the other side. Such flights would be scheduled and regulated in advance. Khrushchev adamantly opposed the plan. Given his resistance, Ike moved full steam ahead with the U-2 program.

The plane first flew at a remote Nevada test site in August 1955, a month after Ike's return from Geneva. After ten months of development, training, and testing, the U-2 and its crews were ready for deployment. The first detachment of a half-dozen planes and pilots was to operate from Lakenheath Royal Air Force Base in the UK, but the so-called Frogman Episode★ gave the Brits cold feet. The Germans were more hospitable, so Detachment A deployed to Wiesbaden the following month. The first three operational U-2 flights took place over Eastern Europe; then the show began for real.

As I left Cornell University in the summer of 1956, operational U-2s first traversed the Soviet Union. On the Fourth of July, Harvey Stockman flew his U-2 over Minsk, Leningrad, and the Baltic States. On the following day, Carmine Vito's U-2 took him right over Red Square. He went on to inspect the rocket facilities around Moscow and the airfield at Ramenskoye, home to new Soviet experimental aircraft. Those flights were classic Eisenhower. Unlike Khrushchev's hollow boasts and bogus parades, Eisenhower quietly, without a lot of fanfare, rolled American power right down the main streets of the Soviet Union.†

In ensuing years, hundreds of U-2 missions were flown by U.S. and British pilots, although with growing concern. In the autumn of 1956, U-2s overflew Suez and the eastern Mediterranean during the crises and invasions there. Then attention turned to Syria, Iraq, the Caspian Sea states, and the oil complex at Baku. On August 5, 1957 a U-2

★ In June 1956, Nikita Khrushchev paid a call on the UK, making his visit aboard a Soviet cruiser. A legendary British frogman, Lionel Crabb, disappeared while conducting an underwater surveillance of that ship. His body washed ashore fourteen months later, minus head and hands.

† And, it turns out, their radar screens as well. Eisenhower had been assured that while Soviet radars could track azimuth and range, they could not track high altitude vehicles. Thus the U-2s were supposed to be invisible. Not so. The Soviets tracked those first two flights and were outraged, but did not know how to complain without exposing the shortcoming of their own air defenses.

found the Baikonur Cosmodrome★ just two weeks before the first successful Soviet R-7 (SS-6) flight from that new launch facility. U-2s collected bomb debris from the Soviet atmospheric nuclear tests of 1958.
They overflew Indonesia during its civil war, and they looked for PRC
troop buildups during their bombardment of Quemoy and Matsu.
Finding none, the U.S. was able to assure Taiwanese leaders that no invasion was in the offing.

But the U-2s were not operating in secret. Despite early CIA assurances to the contrary, about half the flights were tracked by Soviet
radar. In an effort to escape this coverage, U-2 flights began to originate outside of Germany. Early radar coverage to the Soviet south was
not as sophisticated nor complete as along the European border. Even
so, the U-2s were becoming an endangered species. The Soviets were
deploying new SA-2 (S-75 in Soviet nomenclature) surface-to-air missiles, capable of reaching U-2 altitudes. They were developing new
zoom-and-climb tactics for their interceptors, and equipping those interceptors with new K-5 air-to-air missiles.

On April 9, 1960, in the face of this growing threat but with no
alternative means of intelligence collection available, U-2 pilot Bob Ericson took off from Peshewar, Pakistan, with a flight plan that would take
him on a tour of key Soviet nuclear and missile facilities throughout
Kazakhstan. Soviet radars detected him as soon as he entered their airspace, and the entire country went on alert. Four MiG-19s rose to greet
him over Andizhan. The vectoring by their ground controller was
good, but the MiGs could only climb to 52,500 feet—three miles under Ericson's U-2.

As he approached the nuclear test site at Semipalatinsk, four new
Sukhoi-9 interceptors were ready and on alert. They had practiced the
new zoom-and-climb maneuvers. With the assistance of booster rockets, they had achieved altitudes of 65,000 feet, enough to put them
within firing range of the U-2. But fortunately (for Ericson), Murphy
may have been a Russian. The Soviet bureaucracy took too long to approve the takeoff and landing plans for those interceptors. Ericson was
long gone by the time they were airborne. His next target was the embryonic ABM missile launch facilities at Sary Shagan, on the shore of
Lake Baikal. New SA-2 surface-to-air missiles were positioned there in

---

★ Given the more accurate name Tyuratam, after the nearest rail spur to a
pre–World War II rock quarry, by CIA analyst Dino Brugoni.

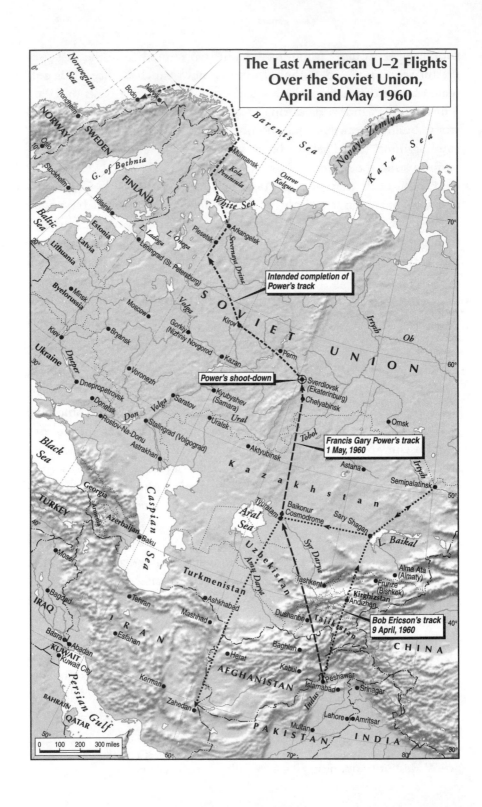

**The Last American U–2 Flights
Over the Soviet Union,
April and May 1960**

Intended completion of
Power's track

Power's shoot-down

Francis Gary Power's track
1 May, 1960

Bob Ericson's track
9 April, 1960

0   100   200   300 miles

anticipation of an overflight, but on April 9 those missiles were off their launch rails for training. Ericson's last target was the Baikonur spaceport near Tyuratam. Again he was expected, but inexperienced ground controllers botched the intercept. Two MiG-19s and two Su–9s were scrambled in vain. One MiG crashed on return to its base, killing its pilot. Ericson's overflight of Tyuratam made the whole trip worthwhile. He brought home photos of a new launch complex, solid evidence that a second generation Soviet ICBM—the R–16 (SS-7)—was being readied for flight test.

Ericson flew on, heading for then-friendly Iran, but the Soviets remained in dogged pursuit. Two more MiG-19s were scrambled and told to follow him into Iranian airspace, to attack when he began his letdown and to ram him if they could not shoot him down. Fortunately, Ericson's landing site was at Zahedan, 500 miles inside Iran, too far for the MiGs' limited range. They gave up and went home. Ericson landed uneventfully and in time for lunch.

Khrushchev was furious. A number of Soviet officers were fired, if not imprisoned. The cry so familiar to American baseball fans went up throughout the Soviet government: "Wait till next time!"

"Next time" came on May 1, 1960, and the pilot was Francis Gary Powers. The stakes were high, as the U.S. intelligence community was desperate for a look at the Soviets' new operational R–7 launch facilities at Plesetsk. The new American Corona satellite continued to fail its flight tests. Getting a look at Plesetsk would require an across-the-country U-2 flight with recovery in Norway. All earlier flights had been horseshoe tracks, in and out across the same border. Powers took off at dawn, also from Peshewar. He climbed to 70,000 feet, then turned north and headed across the Soviet Union, intending to land at Bodo, Norway. With the first radar return, the Soviet Union again went on full alert. The Politburo convened. All air traffic in the country was grounded so that every radar could concentrate on Powers. Interceptors rose to meet him; he saw their contrails, but they could not get to him.

At Tyuratam, Powers flew around the SA-2 engagement radii. His cameras clicked away as he flew northwest over his assigned targets near Chelyabinsk. More Sukhoi-9 interceptors. But when he got to Sverdlovsk, the once and future Yekaterinburg, his luck ran out. Unknown to U.S. intelligence, a battery of SA-2s had just been deployed around Sverdlovsk. A barrage of SA-2s brought Powers down. Subsequent Soviet analysis of the debris confirmed that they did not get a direct hit.

An explosion to the rear and below the U-2 blew off its tail, forcing it into an inverted flat spin.

The wings came off, but Powers kept his wits about him. The spinning fuselage forced his knees under the instrument panel, assuring a double amputation if he was not careful evacuating the aircraft. Thus, before throwing the camera destruct switches, Powers popped open his canopy. The lack of atmosphere at that altitude sucked him out of the plane, and he could no longer reach the switches that would have destroyed his cameras and their associated propaganda value. Still tethered to the cartwheeling wreckage by his oxygen supply tube, Powers was satisfied that he'd done all he could. He broke free of his oxygen umbilical and soon afterward passed out, regaining consciousness only when a barometric switch deployed his parachute at about 15,000 feet.

Powers landed safely, was captured, and put on trial in Moscow. He subsequently spent two years in a Soviet prison, until traded for Soviet spy Rudolf Abel★ in February 1962. Each spy was released at opposite ends of the Glienicker Bridge, then an empty and haunted span linking West Berlin to Potsdam in East Germany. It was a scene worthy of John LeCarré.

Most Americans my age remember the Powers shootdown, but it turns out we knew only half the story. As Powers proceeded north through the Soviet heartland, the Soviets made one effort after another to bring him down. SA-2s at Tyuratam and Su-9s at Chelyabinsk met with no success. One Su-9 pilot got close to Powers's altitude. He was given the usual shoot-or-ram instructions, and, as usual during the Cold War, he suddenly developed radar trouble that dictated an abort. As Powers approached Sverdlovsk, a flight of MiG-19s took off from

---

★ Born Vilyam Genrikhovich Fisher, to Russian revolutionary refugee parents in the UK in 1903, Abel returned to the USSR in 1921, served in army communications, and was sent to the U.S. in 1947 with a bogus passport. Once in the U.S., Fisher became "Emil Robert Goldfus," an illegal who operated spy networks, most notably the "Volunteer" net of Los Alamos scientists. In 1957 one of Fisher's agents defected. Though warned by Moscow, Fisher did not move fast enough. He was arrested in New York City on June 21, 1957. Confessing to espionage, he gave as his "real" name Rudolf Ivanovich Abel, a deceased KGB colleague. Fisher/Abel was sentenced to thirty years, and started serving that time at the Atlanta Penitentiary until traded for Powers in 1962.

Abel/Fisher returned to a hero's welcome in Moscow, then oblivion. He lived out his days as a KGB pensioner, hanging around the office with a chair but no desk. His remains lie in Moscow's Donskoy Monastery alongside those of other departed KGB luminaries.

Koltsovo. They could not get to him, but they were told to keep on the U-2's track.

Over Sverdlovsk, the SA-2s got lucky; the MiGs did not. A shower of U-2 debris enveloped the trailing fighter aircraft. A confused battery commander, Major Voronov, unable to differentiate between friend and foe, fired repeatedly at the confusing radar returns. And the MiG-19s, flying at 40,000 feet, were perfect targets. The flight leader, Captain Boris Ayvazayan, escaped, but his wingman, Senior Lieutenant Sergei Safronov, was not so lucky. He took a direct hit. Safronov was able to eject but was dead when he hit the ground. In later years, Powers confirmed that he saw another chute as he was floating down, but with no live pilot attached. In their obsession with the U-2, the Soviets had killed one of their own. "That's life in the Red Army," my Russian sources said.

Powers was killed seventeen years later in a helicopter crash, flying as a traffic reporter over the freeways of Los Angeles. He was buried with honors at Arlington National Cemetery and was awarded the Distinguished Flying Cross posthumously by the U.S. Air Force.

CORONA

The second piece of advice from Edwin Land's 1954 Intelligence Panel had to do with satellites. That farsighted group of scientists saw worlds of opportunity in space, although their early advice had as much to do with policy as with technology. The Land panel recommended that the U.S. develop and launch an instrumented scientific satellite in order to establish a precedent: freedom of space, the legal right to overfly the sovereign territory of others if done by orbiting satellites outside the atmosphere. Some of the satellite systems now deployed return high-resolution images of earthly activity in near-real time. Other infrared-sensing satellites look for bursts of thermal activity. When such signals are found, their signatures—duration, intensity, and spectrum—are compared to a known data base in order to differentiate volcanos from the exhaust plumes of rockets on the rise.

Electronic intelligence or "ELINT" satellites constantly listen in on us earthlings below, to our cell phones, microwave towers, and portable radios. Other ELINT satellites look for radar signals or the telltale bursts of electromagnetic energy from a nuclear detonation.

In 1954 all of this was but a vision in Edwin Land's mind. The U.S.

Air Force took the first step with Weapon System 117L, a charter to develop a family of imagery, ELINT, and infrared collection satellites. The job was assigned to the Air Force Ballistic Missile Division in July 1956. The need for such a system was becoming urgent. The allegedly invisible U-2 turned out to be easily tracked. It was continuing to work the hot spots of the world, but its days were numbered. Something that could fly higher and faster—a satellite—would have to take its place.

In the aftermath of the Sputnik launch in October 1957, President Eisenhower requested a review of the intelligence satellite situation. In March 1958, WS-117L was split into compartments and disappeared into the black world of covert funding, code words, and joint Air Force–CIA management. One of its cloaks was called Talent-Keyhole.★ The imagery satellite was given a number (initially KH-1), a code name (Corona), and a cover story (biomedical research). The initial satellite system was to be launched atop a Thor IRBM with an Agena rocket as its second stage. The vehicle's public name: Discoverer.

Corona was to take photographs from space utilizing sophisticated stabilization techniques and a 24-inch focal length camera. The images were to be stored on film negatives that would be wound into a capsule, then returned to earth. After deceleration, the recovery capsule would deploy a parachute; a C-119 military aircraft was to snare it during descent. If the aircraft missed, the capsule would be recovered from the ocean's surface by helicopters and divers stationed aboard nearby ships. To achieve the necessary polar orbit, the launch would be from Vandenberg Air Force Base in California; recovery would take place off the coast of Hawaii. This new and restructured CIA–Air Force project was approved for development in April 1958. The design was frozen two months later. Operations were expected by mid-1959, but that's not the way things turned out. At the dawn of the space age, the operation of spacecraft and recovery of their payloads were complicated matters.

A first test firing of the Discoverer system was attempted in January 1959. Separation rockets fired prematurely and the test was postponed. The first launch occurred on February 28. No radio signals were received from the departing spacecraft; it probably crashed near the South Pole. The year that followed brought a tedious succession of bimonthly

---

★ "Talent" was the original codeword for aircraft-collected imagery, i.e., the U-2. When satellites were added, so was the phrase "Keyhole." Imaging satellites were given Keyhole numbers, i.e., KH-1, KH-2, etc.

misfires and failures in orbit. As Discoverer 8 suffered a camera and parachute failure, the Soviets launched their first operational R-7 ICBM from their new Plesetsk rocket base.

In the United States, concern was shifting to panic. On February 4, 1960, Discoverer 9 failed to achieve orbit. As an alternative, the administration had hoped to place its bets on a new reconnaissance aircraft, the A-12, later to be known as the SR-71. In time, that aircraft would achieve speeds over 2,100 mph at altitudes over 85,000 feet, but in 1970 it was just another program behind schedule. Eisenhower had no choice but to authorize another round of U-2 flights. They were to start on February 5, 1960.

Two weeks later, Discoverer 10 was destroyed by the range safety officer. Two months later and a week after Bob Ericson's precarious U-2 flight, Discoverer 11 was launched. It achieved orbit, the cameras operated properly, the film fed into the capsule—and then the capsule's spin rockets exploded. The U.S. desperately needed a look at that new Soviet facility at Plesetsk; another U-2 flight was the only possibility. Powers took off on his ill-fated mission on May 1.

Two months later the dreary saga of Corona continued. Discoverer 12 failed to achieve orbit. With the shootdown of Powers, the intelligence community had gone blind. Then, in early August, Discoverer 13 made it into orbit; a test recovery capsule ejected and reentered the earth's atmosphere. It missed its impact area by over 500 miles, but ships deployed around Hawaii made it to the splash point in time to recover the floating capsule. For the first time in history, man had put an object into orbit and then recovered it. We had beaten the Soviet launch and recovery of a much larger, dog-carrying Sputnik V by nine days. The capsule was brought to the White House, where the President posed with the American flag contained within it for an election-year photo-op.

A week later a fully operational Corona satellite, Discoverer 14, did the job right. It carried a functioning camera and a twenty-pound load of film, used to photograph real targets of great interest to the United States. The film transferred into the capsule, a recovery sequence was effected on the seventeenth orbit, and the capsule was recovered by air snatch, as intended. Corona went on to image all the Soviet ballistic missile complexes, putting the lie to any fears and claims of the so-called "missile gap."

Severodvinsk, the primary Soviet SLBM submarine facility, was first detected by Corona. That enabled the U.S. to track the production of such boats. Corona went on to track the Soviet fleet, to inventory their aircraft, and to watch the construction of ABM sites around Moscow. Corona mapped the location of all fixed Soviet SAM sites, allowing SAC planners to avoid them when laying out ingress and egress routes for U.S. bombers. In time, Corona would fly 145 successful missions over more than a decade, mapping 750 million square miles of territory. It stabilized the Cold War and put the paparazzi pilots out to a well-earned retirement.

RETURN TO SENDER

With the coming of the sixties, Corona and its descendants took over the heavy lifting. Reconnaissance of the Soviet heartland was left to the spacecraft, beyond the reach of MiGs and SAMs. The U-2s and their brethren would continue to fly over Cuba, Iraq, and Bosnia, but flights over the USSR were out of the question. Yet some questions did remain.

Over a hundred reconnaissance pilots who had flown the more legal PARPRO missions around the Soviet periphery had been shot down. Some were thought to have made it safely to earth, never to be heard from again. The sixties became the seventies and the wind-up of Vietnam. Then came the eighties, and the collapse of the Soviet empire. With the nineties, it was all over. The American embassy in Moscow began to advertise—by radio, newspaper, handbill, and word of mouth—for any news of those missing pilots. The embassy got an inquiry from a village near Vladivostok. Vasily Saiko was looking for an address; the embassy responded. A month later Mary Dunham Nichols, the widow of a reconnaissance pilot long gone, found a small package with a Russian postmark in her mailbox. It contained her husband's Annapolis ring. Only that and nothing more.

CHAPTER 4

Howard Hughes Supplies the Props

I NEVER MET HOWARD HUGHES—few people did—but I knew him as an icon. To us young, male, snowbound, easterners about to graduate from engineering schools in the fifties, Howard Hughes was the personification of Los Angeles. A man of both inherited wealth and creative genius, Hughes was making movies, building airplanes, running an airline, dating movie stars, and organizing the future. He was doing all that in a place where it never snowed, gas cost twenty-five cents a gallon, houses cost $20,000, and you could park anywhere. What follows is a story about a few people who did know Howard Hughes, about the miraculous technology he spawned as casually as a bull plays at pasture, and about the resulting industrial climate that blossomed in post–World War II southern California, when the technology of instant nuclear warfare took shape in the United States.

THE YOUNG TEXAN

Howard Robard Hughes Jr. was born in Houston, Texas, on December 24, 1905, the only son of a talented inventor, the man who founded the Hughes Tool Company. The senior Hughes's contribution, the source of his great fortune, was the rotary rock drilling tool, an odd-looking conical instrument with multiple and hardened cutting edges mounted on rotating subassemblies. Rights to the Hughes tool were protected throughout the industrialized world by a solid wall of patents.

The younger Hughes's mother died when the boy was sixteen, and death claimed his father two years later. With the help of a court order, Hughes took full control of the company on his nineteenth birthday. He did not meddle in the company's operations, preferring to leave them as both a monument to his father and as a cash cow to fund his own more diverse interests. He picked good people to run the place, and he displayed an immediate understanding of the business by continuing to lease, not sell, rock bits to Hughes's customers. These leases included the services of an on-site engineer to recommend the right tool as different formations were encountered at each well. Those men built personal relationships with drilling contractors that withstood the expiration of patents. In the mid-1950s the Hughes Tool Co. still controlled half the world's market for drilling tools, earning profits of over $300 million, in year-2000 dollars. Young Howard Hughes owned it all.

In the fall of 1925, having installed management that he trusted, and blessed with one million of today's dollars in *daily* cash flow, Howard Hughes departed for southern California. On arrival in Los Angeles, he hired CPA Noah Dietrich to serve as his financial adviser. Hughes then set about doing what he wanted to do: making movies and airplanes. During the ensuing twenty years, Hughes produced one hit movie after another, acquired a pilot's license, and set world speed records in aircraft of his own design. During World War II his airplane company developed a flying boat, helicopters, and reconnaissance aircraft, all unique. Some were lethal to their crews; none were produced in volume. This was a time when many of the established aircraft manufacturers, then headquartered in Cleveland or Dayton, were opening new facilities in southern California, where the pleasant, rain-free weather facilitated construction, the outdoor assembly of aircraft, and the flight of those new planes. When the war was over, Hughes Aircraft was an innovative but chaotically run spinoff of Hughes Tool, set in the heart of that new landscape.

THE POSTWAR YEARS AND MIDLIFE CRISES

The postwar chaos of 1946 produced two milestones in Hughes's life. One was his attempt to pilot his new F-11 Navy reconnaissance plane on its first flight on July 7. It crashed just short of the Los Angeles Country Club golf course. He suffered broken ribs, heart and lung damage, and third-degree burns. Doctors administered morphine to ease what were thought to be his last moments, but Hughes pulled through. On leaving the hospital he demanded increasing doses of morphine, in time cut back to codeine, but it was the beginning of a drug addiction that stuck with him to the end of his life.

The second milestone came a few months before the F-11 crash, when Si Ramo, a young scientist from General Electric in Schenectady, New York, came to call. His visit had been organized by the staff at Hughes Aircraft, eager for some competent leadership. Ramo already had a national reputation in the field of electricity and magnetism. Within a few years he would coauthor a textbook on those subjects, one that became a standard for young engineers. Hughes Aircraft had grown to be a rich man's plaything, building racing planes and unflyable behemoths like the Spruce Goose.★ The staff wanted Hughes Aircraft to become a world-class participant in the postwar technical boom. They thought Ramo could pull it off.

For his part, Ramo was looking for an opportunity to build a large military electronics business. After graduating from Cal Tech in 1936 he went to work on radars for GE in Schenectady. He felt that World War II had lifted the U.S. to a higher technological plateau, that there was room for new firms in the military electronics field. The wartime industrial giants had left that playing field to pursue the postwar consumer products market. The weather in California was an attraction,

---

★ An immense flying boat whose structure was made entirely of wood to avoid the use of wartime-scare aluminum. It had eight engines and was intended to carry 750 passengers across oceans. With the end of World War II the government ceased funding its development, but in 1947 Howard Hughes flew the aircraft himself, for a distance of one mile across Long Beach harbor, to prove that it would fly.

but it was the intellectual climate that closed the deal. Stanford, Cal Tech, and the University of California at Berkeley were always on any list of the top ten scientific schools in the nation. Theodore Von Karman, head of the Aeronautics Department at Cal Tech, was in a class by himself. And on a more fundamental level, California was a new society. Everyone was from somewhere else, so there were no established customs and taboos to worry about.

Ramo wanted to create his own company, but he knew that his kind of electronics giant could not be started in a garage. The U.S. Army Air Corps had money to spend, and Wright Field, its research and development center in Dayton, Ohio, made it clear that it would fund good, new, high-tech firms. The United States could not and would not abandon its lead in technology. Ramo saw in Hughes Aircraft a company running out of control. He wanted to take it over, to start within it a new electronics division that in time would outstrip the airplane-oriented parent. For his part, Hughes had come to understand the importance of communications and navigation in the operation of his global airline, TWA.

These two men met and had a meeting of the minds. Ramo now thinks Hughes's amiability reflected the freebie nature of the deal. Mellon Bank would fully finance the new electronics division once Ramo had in hand a cost-plus-fixed-fee contract from Wright Field. Hughes would not have to part with any serious cash, just floor space and office support. With that, the new Hughes Aircraft Company was born. Since Ramo's project did not involve airplanes, Hughes had little further interest in whatever Ramo was doing. The two men did not meet again until it became clear, seven years later, that Ramo and several of his associates were getting ready to leave the Hughes nest. During those seven years, Hughes Aircraft moved to the forefront of military electronics. The "Aircraft" part of the company's name became a misnomer.

RAMO AND WOOLDRIDGE

One of Ramo's first recruits was a man he had known since their graduate student days at Cal Tech. Dean Wooldridge had "one of the greatest technical minds" Ramo ever knew. Wooldridge helped Ramo with his homework at Cal Tech. They double-dated, but after graduation they parted ways, heading east to pursue their own careers wherever they could find work in those prewar, Depression years. Wooldridge went to Bell Labs, Ramo to General Electric. But when Wooldridge heard that Ramo had been recruited by the Hughes staff to build a new electronics business, he asked to join the new firm. Ramo was delighted, and the technical partnership of Ramo and Wooldridge was born.

These men and their expanding pool of technical wizards designed and developed the nation's first airborne fire-control system. It became the standard for every interceptor in the U.S. Air Force. Ramo and Wooldridge were there at Hughes when the transistor was invented at Wooldridge's alma mater, Bell Labs, and they were the leaders in its exploitation for military purposes. They recruited the brightest and the best, men like Allen Puckett, who helped develop the Falcon air-to-air missile, guided by an active radar located in the missile itself. Later, in the wake of Sputnik, it was Puckett who promoted the technology for the first synchronous communication satellite. Puckett went on to become president, then chairman and CEO, of Hughes Aircraft, although he never actually met Howard Hughes. Other future stars included Harper North, an early expert in those new semiconductors. He built the first solid state diodes at Hughes and in time headed up Pacific Semiconductors. In the mid-fifties, at Hughes, Ted Maiman built the first crystal to resonate microwaves. He called it a "maser." Subsequent light-resonating devices, descended from the Maiman device, became known as lasers. Henry Singleton worked in the Hughes Research Lab on new digital computers. In time, he left Hughes to join Litton, then started his own company, a firm that became Teledyne. Milt Mohr worked computers at Hughes too. He started Quotron. Jim Fletcher was recruited early on to do electronic theory and analysis at Hughes. Two decades later he was administrator of NASA. Rube Mettler left Hughes for a short stint at the Department of Defense. He would eventually become chairman and CEO of TRW.

Tex Thornton was an early Hughes recruit. Thornton and Ramo wanted Hughes to acquire a small manufacturer of vacuum pumps, a firm owned by an ailing Charles Litton, but Hughes would not hear of it. He never parted with cash to buy a business, and there was no Hughes stock to use in acquisitions. When Hughes Aircraft began to disintegrate in 1953–54, Thornton left Hughes to seize the Litton opportunity himself. With the backing of investment bankers, he bought the little manufacturer and turned it into Litton Industries, one of the first of the electronics conglomerates. Litton's subsidiaries went on to blaze new trails in radar tubes, printed circuits, and small computers.

Surrounding Hughes, and eventually its spinoffs, were a plethora of small specialty electronics and aerospace shops. When the Korean War broke out in 1950, the market for military electronics exploded. Howard Hughes's Los Angeles became the Silicon Valley of the early postwar years. In 1954, when Ramo and Wooldridge left Hughes Aircraft, its revenues were approaching $1 billion per year, in 2000 dollars. It had become bigger than the parent tool company.

LOS ANGELES IN THE MID-FIFTIES

Los Angeles was very different in those days. In 1955 only 2.25 million people lived in that county. The surrounding counties—Orange, Riverside, San Bernardino, and Ventura—were virtually empty, home to orange growers and ranchers, but not much else. The bicycle shops of Dayton and the auto parts manufacturers of Cleveland provided fertile ground for the Wright Brothers, but serious flying required better weather. In the thirties the airplane manufacturers began to open up their shops in Los Angeles, Santa Monica, and San Diego. Then came World War II.

Military thinkers with foresight understood the importance of airpower, but Hitler's use of dive bombers in the Spanish Civil War and Churchill's victory in the Battle of Britain made it clear that control of the skies was essential to victory, even survival, on the ground. The Allies needed airplanes—lots of them. The U.S. government began to contract with airplane manufacturers for quantities and delivery schedules incomprehensible to the conventionally minded. As the tides of war began to turn, components for military aircraft were being assembled in the open fields along Wilshire Boulevard. When finished, these pieces were loaded onto trucks or towed along the highway to the Douglas plant in Santa Monica. From there they emerged as combat-ready aircraft. By V-E day (victory in Europe, May 8, 1945) Los Angeles was the aircraft capital of the United States.

By the mid-fifties Howard Hughes was king of this mountain. The Hughes Aircraft Company had reinvented itself, creating and dominating the world of airborne electronics. The Pentagon was spending more on electronics than on ships or guns, but Howard Hughes, the man, was being left behind. He began to protect his privacy in a manner that was extreme but understandable, given the scope of his assets and the progress of his hearing problems, both physical and professional.

All was not well at Hughes Aircraft. New opportunities were knocking, but Hughes was deaf to their rhythm. In June 1953 the new Eisenhower administration began its review of all U.S. guided missile programs. Howard Hughes could not be part of those reviews because he protected his privacy to the point of paranoia. For instance, he would not submit to the fingerprinting necessary to gain a Secret clearance. As the postwar years unfolded, Hughes had to be excused from, or could not be admitted to, meetings with the military that were defining the future of his company. Nor would Hughes let Ramo and Wooldridge run Hughes Aircraft in a way that was acceptable either to them or to Hughes's principal customer, the U.S. Air Force. In the autumn of 1953, Ramo and Wooldridge decided to leave Hughes to form their own company.

The U.S. Air Force wanted Ramo's full and undivided attention on the ballistic missile program. They did not want him distracted by radar, computers, corporate development, or anything else. Wooldridge's calm and less aggressive personality made him a better "Mr. Outside," more acceptable to bankers, investors, and the officers of the Air Force. So Ramo assumed the title of Executive Vice-President of the new company, and with it full oversight of the Guided Missile Research Division. The more intellectual and less driven Wooldridge became president of Ramo-Wooldridge. The new company was financed by Thompson Products, an old-line automotive manufacturer based in Cleveland. Within days of leaving Hughes, Ramo-Wooldridge was selected to oversee the conceptual design of the U.S. Air Force's family of ballistic missiles.

Ramo and Wooldridge's departure from Hughes was the beginning of a major explosion that scattered technical talent all over the Los Angeles basin. As a patriotic American, Hughes might have been pleased with all of this, but he certainly did not profit personally. Talent was fleeing his control in droves.

Now, a half a century later, it is hard to get an accurate picture of the reclusive Hughes. His friends from the aviation industry, men like Jack Real of Lockheed, would come to describe Hughes as smart, self-educated, and fully informed on subjects he thought were important; that is, aviation. He was very tight with money but personally generous to a fault. These friends, and other employees who never actually met the man, all agree that Hughes Aircraft was the defining postwar incubator of the military electronics industry. Others, like Si Ramo, had disagreements with Hughes. They describe him as eccentric, uneducated, uninformed, out of touch, and impossible to work for. The same things

were also said about Hughes's knowledge of the electronics business—
that he tolerated it because it was a good investment, though the business did not interest him personally, nor did its executives, whom he
did not care to meet. Like the blind men and the elephant, people were
describing different parts of the same man. But whoever he was, there
can be no doubt that Howard Hughes was a giant of the fifties, setting
the stage for what was to come.

Ramo and Wooldridge were enormously successful. Their colleagues,
the Hughes alumni, enjoyed similar prosperity. At the end of the fifties,
Ramo-Wooldridge merged with its financial backer, Thompson Products. Their names have been reduced to initials now: TRW. Hughes
himself became a drug-clouded recluse, moving from one overseas re-
doubt to another until his death, on April 5, 1976, while en route home
to Houston.

I worked briefly in Los Angeles for Ramo-Wooldridge while awaiting entry into the U.S. Air Force. When called to active duty, I first
served at Edwards Air Force Base, learning how to salute and to wear
the uniform. Then, in July 1957, I was reassigned to the Air Force Ballistic Missile Division in Los Angeles. The Soviet launch of Sputnik was
only three months away, although we did not know it at the time. That
launch was a complete surprise, a declaration of technological war by
the Soviet Union. What I did know was that as a young lieutenant I
was headed for the front trenches of the Cold War, to serve under brilliant leadership, and I knew it would be interesting.

CHAPTER 5

Rockets and Missiles

IT WAS NOT THE TINTINNABULATION of Poe's silver bells, with their tin-kle, tinkle, tinkle in the icy air of night. Rather, it was the clangor and the clamor of the brazen bells, the alarum bells, that heralded the 1950s for most thoughtful Americans.

The first Soviet A-bomb test (in August 1949), the communist takeover of China (in October 1949), and the outbreak of the Korean War (in June 1950) combined to focus American attention. Something was seriously wrong. The Cold War was no longer just a European concern, a geopolitical struggle an ocean away. A direct nuclear attack on the United States was now possible. The communist flood was enslaving, if not killing, millions of new subjects in Asia. American GIs and pilots were dying in an attempt to stem that tide. The lessons began to sink in; the U.S. itself was in mortal peril. Yet the most dangerous part of this threat was hidden from view. It lay in the minds of the two hundred German rocket scientists then working at the Eighty-eighth Scientific Research Institute, north of Moscow, in the Soviet Union.

During the fifties and sixties intelligent men and women on both sides of the Iron Curtain would give their all, sometimes their lives, in the battle for the high ground of space. They did so in the service of masters in whom they believed. On the Soviet side that meant the Politburo, a group of aging men whose monopoly on information allowed them to hide their corrupt, inefficient, and murderous ways. But then, that's how those Soviet scientists saw us: capable, hardworking Americans in thrall to *our* capitalist-exploiter bosses. To the American people, the race for space was a matter of political, if not physical, life and death. As Wellington said after the battle of Waterloo: "It was a damn close-run thing."

It all began in Peenemunde, a small German town on the Baltic Sea, directly north of Berlin and well inside what was to become—for forty-five years—the German Democratic Republic, also known as East Germany. There, the German rocket program of World War II got its start. In October 1942 the German scientists working at Peenemunde first fired an experimental V-2 guided ballistic rocket downrange, across the Baltic, for a distance of 120 miles. By September 1944 the Nazis were able to introduce that weapon into combat; 3,745 were fired at the West. One-third were targeted at London, the rest at the ports and cities of Belgium. The V-2s were neither accurate—the average miss distance was four miles—nor reliable. Only half of the rockets launched ever reached their targets. But with their use, the world entered the rocket age.

When the war ended, rocketry was not an alien concept to the Soviets. The first mathematical analysis of liquid propellant rockets and orbital mechanics had been done by Konstantin Tsiolkovskii, a Russian, in 1895. During World War II, Soviet spies watched German wartime rocket experiments. When the Red Army arrived in Peenemunde and its administrative headquarters at Bleicherode, a hundred miles southwest of Berlin, it knew what to look for. The scientific search party was led by a recently minted colonel, released from the Gulags of Kolyma and Magadan only a year before. Sergei Pavlovich Korolev was a rocket and space fanatic. By correspondence from the Gulag (not all that unusual), he had convinced Stalin of the possibility of "rocket airplanes." The boss turned him loose and, within a year, dispatched him to Germany.

A few months after the war's end the Soviets began to "recruit" German custodians of that V-2 rocket technology. Initially they were housed at a new Soviet facility known as Nordhausen, located on the grounds of the Peenemunde center. Then, in early 1947, hordes of people, crates of papers, and boxcars of hardware, including fifty fully-assembled V-2s, headed east to the research center at Boltshevo, a suburb north of Moscow. It would become the future home of Soviet rocket science.*

During this time, the United States had other priorities. Its armies reached neither Peenemunde nor Bleicherode, but Wernher von Braun, the German chief of rocket research, and some of his associates, did flee from there into U.S. arms. It was not until December 1945 that the U.S. government began the formal resettlement of those 130 German rocket scientists. They arrived in the United States as guests of an army and a government with little serious interest in rocket weapons.

A few years later the German guest scientists captive in Russia began to return home. Upon their release, they told Western intelligence services about the growth of serious rocket design bureaus in the Soviet Union. Those institutes were exploiting the German V-2 capability and were training young Russian scientists to pursue that technology. Once those design bureaus were fully Russified, the Germans were told they could leave. The fact that they were sent home instead of shot is one of the many enigmas of the Cold War.

At the same time, a British communications intelligence team, posing as archaeologists while traveling through Iran, monitored the early Soviet V-2 flights across the border. Then a high level Soviet defector brought out firsthand details of the Soviet program. There were indications of a huge Soviet rocket engine, a device producing over 250,000 pounds of thrust with another factor of two in the offing. That came as a surprise. American industry was thinking about a 220-ton, seven-engine U.S. monster rocket to be known as Atlas, but only 120,000 pounds of thrust was the design goal for each engine. What was going on over there?

A NEW LOOK

A new administration came to power in Washington in 1953, and President Eisenhower ordered a major review of all departments. Examination of the Defense Department was entrusted to a young man

---

* Today it is known as *Energia,* or more formally, the Joint Stock Company Academician S. P. Korolov Rocket-Space Corporation Energia.

named Nelson Rockefeller. The Rockefeller committee found a need to strengthen military research and development. In its April report, the committee proposed eliminating the World War II era Munitions and R&D boards, replacing them with Assistant Secretaries of Defense authorized to make decisions and allocate money. Congress agreed. Fiscal restraint was the primary objective of that move, but the result was to entrust power to individuals who would push the technological envelope.

There had been no such dithering in Russia. By 1953 the launching of captured V-2 rockets and then their Soviet R-1 copies had been going on for five years. The U.S. intelligence agencies were beginning to take notice.

The Air Force was studying the implications of America's first thermonuclear test, in late 1952. Professor John von Neumann, a leading light of Princeton's Institute for Advanced Study, assumed the chairmanship of a nuclear weapons panel for the Air Force Scientific Advisory Board. Meeting in Los Alamos during June 1953, the von Neumann panel concluded that a thermonuclear warhead would be possible for U.S. ballistic missiles. They thought a yield of at least half a megaton might be coaxed out of a 3,000-pound warhead. Three months later the Air Force Special Weapons Center, tracking the design work at Los Alamos, cut that weight estimate in half, to 1,500 pounds.★

Then, on August 12, 1953, came the first Soviet H-bomb test. We know now that the RDS-6s weighed 10,000 pounds and gave a yield of 400 kilotons. In the mind of its designer, it confirmed the possibility of a megaton-size weapon. That yield would be large enough to compensate for the few-mile miss distance inherent in any first-generation Soviet rocket's guidance system.†

Back then, the U.S. knew only that the Soviets were very confident. On August 8, 1953, during a major public speech to the Supreme Soviet, Georgi Malenkov forecast an immediate end to the brief U.S. H-bomb monopoly. He may have been willing to go out on this limb because the Soviet security services had recently acquired intelligence on a similar U.S. approach to an operational H-bomb. Whatever it was

---

★ These warhead yields are detailed in Jacob Neufeld's *Ballistic Missiles*, an Air Force history office publication.

† The Soviets use the term "rocket" to describe what we call a "ballistic missile." Hereafter I will use "rocket" or "missile" when referring to Soviet or U.S. weapons systems, respectively.

that gave Malenkov the courage to forecast the historic Soviet shot, U.S. sensors picked it up right on schedule.

In November 1953, the designer of that Soviet device, Andrei Sakharov, was called to a meeting of the Soviet Politburo to discuss the RDS-6s. The Soviet leadership directed the development on an improved, hopefully one megaton, version of the RDS-6s, and the engineers at the Eighty-eighth Scientific Research Institute were ordered to design and build a rocket to deliver that 10,000-pound warhead to the American continent, 5,500 nautical miles away. Thus, 10,000 pounds became the standard Soviet payload, a decision that accounts for the size of all Soviet rockets even today.

It turns that out the RDS-6s was a dead-end design. Conceptually, it "fizzled out," in Sakharov's words, "replaced by something quite different." A new and more compact weapon, the RDS-37, delivered 1.6 megatons on its first test in November 1955, but by then the Soviets were already committed to huge, five-ton payloads.

A young man, Trevor Gardner, was watching all this for Eisenhower's Secretary of Defense. Though only thirty-seven at the time, Gardner had a wealth of technical experience gained at Cal Tech, General Electric, Goodyear, and his own electronics company, Hycon. Secretary of the Air Force Harold Talbott recruited Gardner to serve as his special assistant for R&D. (The job matured into Assistant Secretary of the Air Force when authorized by Congress.) As a result of the Rockefeller report, Secretary of Defense Wilson asked Talbott to look into all the U.S. guided missile programs. In the summer of 1953, Talbott told Trevor Gardner to go do it.

THE TEAPOT COMMITTEE

In 1953 the armed services were awash in missile programs. The Air Force, for instance, had air-to-air projects, a variety of surface-to-air antiaircraft missiles, and two air-breathing strategic missiles, Snark and Navaho, neither of which were on schedule or within budget. And there were paper studies of Atlas, a monster intercontinental ballistic missile. Snark and Navaho, having wings and looking like airplanes, enjoyed Air Force funding at a level seventeen times that of the original Atlas program.

Trevor Gardner served as chairman of a committee to sort through this duplication. In October, however, he reempaneled von Neumann to form a second committee to look specifically at the Air Force strategic missile programs. It would be known by its code name, the Teapot Committee, a group that made technological history. With their uncanny technical *and* managerial foresight, that committee showed America how to pull its chestnuts out of the fire, just in the nick of time.

The Teapot Committee was composed of the brightest and best from the academic and industrial world.★ Si Ramo and Dean Wooldridge had just left Hughes Aircraft to form Ramo-Wooldridge, and Gardner immediately contracted with them to support and administer the committee's work. Gardner and Ramo had known each other from their prewar days together at General Electric in Schenectady. By today's standards, that procurement decision—to hire the two-day-old Ramo-Wooldridge Corporation—was pretty cozy and rather informal, but time was of the essence. Calling on friends who are known commodities may not be fair, but it's the quickest and surest way to build a good organization fast. Knowledgeable scientists were hard to find then, and the Soviet momentum was scary. To serve as the Teapot Committee's military representative, Gardner chose a young colonel, Bernard Schriever. At the time, Schriever had the bureaucratic-sounding title of Assistant to the Deputy Chief of Staff for Development Planning, but that moniker was misleading.

"Bennie" Schriever had earned an engineering degree from Texas A&M in 1931. He then joined the Air Corps and earned his wings, but in those Depression years military pay was a sometime thing. Upon occasion, Schriever flew as a commercial pilot, but in 1938 he was posted to Wright Field in Ohio as a test pilot. In 1942 he earned a master's degree in mechanical engineering from Stanford, then went off to the war in the Pacific. He flew thirty-eight combat missions in B-17s. By war's end, at age thirty-four, Schriever had risen to the rank of colonel while serving as Deputy Chief of Staff for Logistics of the Fifth Air Force. Schriever understood technology; not only what was then current, but what the future might hold. After the war, he was given a se-

---

★ John von Neumann of Princeton's Institute for Advanced Study served as chairman. The members were: Clark Millikan, Charles Lauritsen, and Louis Dunn of Cal Tech; Henrik Bode, Bell Labs; Allen Puckett, Hughes Aircraft; George Kistiakowski, Harvard; Jerome Wiesner, MIT; Lawrence Hyland, Bendix; and Simon Ramo and Dean Wooldridge, previously of Hughes Aircraft but now on their own.

ries of Pentagon jobs that involved anticipating technical possibilities open to the Air Force. In 1953 he was selected for promotion to brigadier general and posted to the Teapot Committee.

During that same year, the American technological giant was coming to life. At Los Alamos, Carson Mark, head of that laboratory's theoretical division, was converting the November 1952 thermonuclear experiment, code named "Mike," into a real H-bomb design. His teams of design engineers were working with the new computers to better understand the energy flow and burn within a thermonuclear device. To make it go, they settled on the use of new materials not yet in production. Device designs were completed by mid-1953. Only the lack of necessary materials held up the tests of these new designs for half a year. Ben Diven was the designer of one new device to be tested as *Bravo;* Harold Agnew was the designer of another, to be known as *Romeo.* Both devices were scheduled for testing in 1954's Operation *Castle.*

At the Ames Laboratory in California, Dr. Harvey Julian Allen was doing calculations on the physics of hypersonic vehicles reentering the atmosphere. Delivering a warhead by rocket to the far side of earth requires velocities over 20,000 miles per hour. The question was: upon reentry into the atmosphere, where was that energy to go? He showed that such energy is partitioned between skin friction heating of the reentering vehicle and shock wave heating of the atmosphere as the reentry vehicle speeds through. He also showed that with proper design, less than 1 percent of the vehicle's kinetic energy would go into skin heating. The other 99 percent could be made to go into ionizing the atmospheric gasses around the vehicle, leaving behind the fiery tail usually associated with "shooting stars"—meteorties entering the atmosphere. He concluded that a reentry vehicle could be designed to deliver Agnew's warhead or, in time, U.S. astronauts, safely back to earth.

In Cambridge, an MIT professor, C. Stark "Doc" Draper, devised a way to use the gyroscopes developed for gunsights in World War II to guide aircraft (and eventually missiles) over long distances. These new gadgets used what came to be known as "inertial guidance," because they relied on their own internal measurement of acceleration to calculate net velocity in each of three orthogonal coordinate systems. Knowing where it started, and with an accurate clock keeping time, such a guidance system would know exactly where it was without any further outside-world data.

During the early 1950s Doc Draper built several such experimental systems, and during the last week of January 1953 he installed one, his new SPIRE (space inertial reference equipment) in the bomb bay of a B-29. On February 8 he rode with the system as it flew that plane from Bedford, Massachusetts, to Los Angeles. The control of the aircraft was completely automatic; the crew's only jobs were to keep the engines running and to adjust altitude. (Mountains posed hazards that SPIRE could not see.) The nonstop flight took 12.5 hours. Upon arrival in Los Angeles, the SPIRE system missed the L.A. airport by only nine miles. Draper was flying to Los Angeles to attend a top secret symposium at RAND on self-contained navigation systems. The results of his test flight stole the show. His follow-on work with SPIRE Junior opened the eyes of the Teapot Committee. It was clear that intercontinental missiles could be self-contained weapons, arriving at their targets with reasonable accuracy without any outside radio or stellar input of any sort.

In February 1954 the Teapot Committee rendered its report. It was a bombshell to those cleared to read it. In part that was because the credentials of the chairman and his committee were unassailable, and in part because they forecast a serious Soviet missile threat to the United States. The Teapot Committee report did *not* call for an immediate flood of new money. Instead it said a practical American intercontinental ballistic missile (ICBM) would be feasible within six to eight years, but only if a radical reorganization of the ICBM program was accomplished. Rather than pouring money into the existing Atlas program—a 220-ton missile with seven engines, needed to deliver an 8,000-pound warhead to the other side of the world—the committee recommended taking a year to do a weapons system study, to define a more realistic Atlas along the following lines:

1. Warhead: Plan on a 1,500 (not 8,000) pound warhead with a yield in the megaton range. This would drastically reduce the size of the missile. Details were to be reviewed in light of the upcoming *Castle* nuclear test series then getting under way in the Pacific.

2. Reentry vehicle: Do away with the requirement for high-speed (Mach 6) approach to the target. Reentry heating considerations would not allow that. Mach 1 would be good enough.

3. Guidance: Strive for the use of self-contained inertial guidance, and be content with a two to three mile average miss distance,★ not the 1,500 feet called for in the then-current Atlas specifications. With a megaton warhead, that would be close enough.

4. Engines: Use the technology under development for Atlas as well as the other strategic missiles (Navaho), and expand the construction of test stands to support that work.

5. Basing: Get realistic about the need for reduced vulnerability to nuclear attack, a higher rate of fire, and a faster response time. These requirements would make the missile design more difficult, but they were necessary if U.S. missiles were to strike the nuclear facilities of any attacker on a timely basis.

These technical guidelines were impressive, but they paled in comparison to the proposed revolutionary management scheme. The Teapot Committee felt that the usual armed services procurement regulations, the unending layers of review authority, could not deal with this crisis. They concluded that the Atlas program "must be relieved of excessive detailed regulation by existing government agencies." While subsequent committees would spell out the details, the Teapot Committee wanted a direct line of authority from the Pentagon to the new Atlas development agency. That would be the Western Development Division (WDD), to be organized in Los Angeles, where the technical talent lay, the products of Howard Hughes's unintentional incubator. Brigadier General Bernard Schriever would be the WDD's commander.

The Teapot Committee also had little faith in the Air Force/civil servant development laboratories. Those institutions had been in charge of Atlas since the end of World War II, and not much had happened. The committee wanted "the overall technical direction [of the Atlas program] to be in the hands of an unusually competent group of scientists and engineers . . ."

The Air Force's first choice to do this work was the Bell Telephone Laboratories, which at the time was the nation's preeminent commercial

---

★ The correct technical term is "circular error probable" (CEP), defined as the radius of a circle within which half the shots or weapons would hit. "Average miss distance" is easier to understand, however.

electronics organization; the transistor was invented there. Bell Labs declined the honor, as did Cal Tech's Jet Propulsion Laboratory. The Air Force then turned to the fledgling Ramo-Wooldridge Corporation, technical advisers to the Teapot Committee, directing and authorizing them to build an organization from scratch, to hire the brightest and best scientists, engineers, and managers at whatever cost and with the greatest urgency.

In March 1954 the *Castle* nuclear test series started in the Pacific. *Bravo* was fired on March 1. It provided an enormous exclamation point to the Teapot Committee's report. The first U.S. thermonuclear test, in November 1952, had been an experiment two stories tall and weighing 82 tons. It produced a yield of ten megatons, but was hardly portable. On March 1, things changed.

The *Bravo* device weighed only twelve tons. It was expected to yield six megatons, but the designers had neglected to consider the proclivity of a certain isotope to breed more neutrons. When the shot went off, *Bravo* gave a yield of fifteen megatons, a thousand Hiroshimas and more than twice what was expected. Fallout from its unexpectedly large yield also became a bad omen for the Japanese fishing boat *Lucky Dragon*. *Bravo* was a wake-up call to the other superpowers as well.

The United States was not yet sharing nuclear design data with the British, but our allies were keenly interested in what we were doing. The Brits had joined the nuclear club two years before but were still struggling with the thermonuclear puzzle. In subsequent conversations with British nuclear historians, I learned of two British aircraft lost in the process of collecting fallout debris from the *Castle* shots.

The Soviets were equally interested, but their scientists did not know how to ask the right questions. Memoranda from Yuli Khariton, chief scientist of the Soviet nuclear weapons program, tasked Soviet intelligence collectors at the time in the wrong direction. It was only after *Bravo* that the Soviet designers realized the possibilities. A portable, multimegaton thermonuclear device *could* be built. They went back to their drawing boards and intelligence files. Within a few months they came up with the right answer: radiation implosion.★

Also in March 1954, a second thermonuclear shot gave eleven megatons, again several times the expected yield. Within three months these devices were weaponized and the U.S. had a portable H-bomb, ready

---

★ Where radiation energy from the primary, not kinetic energy or neutrons, is used to implode a thermonuclear secondary stage.

for deployment aboard the B-36 bomber. In July of that year Schriever formally received his orders to take charge of the new ICBM program. Ramo-Wooldridge already was hired to start work on systems engineering studies. But within nine months of the Teapot Committee's report, contracts were being let for a very different ICBM.

ATLAS, TITAN, AND THOR

The new Atlas was to weigh only 120 tons, compared to the 220 tons originally planned, since it needed to carry only a 1,500-pound warhead. Tests in 1956 and 1958 would show how much yield would emerge from that weight, but there was confidence that the Atomic Energy Commission labs could reach at least a megaton. A conservative engine and staging plan was adopted. Two booster engines, delivering 135,000 pounds thrust each, would be jettisoned after two minutes of flight, while a third sustainer engine, delivering 60,000 pounds of thrust, would continue to burn until shut down by the guidance system. Thus, there would be no need to light a second-stage engine in space, which no one knew how to do. Atlas became known as a one-and-a-half-stage missile. The first round of Atlas missiles were to be radio controlled, and a miss distance of two nautical miles was deemed acceptable. The reentry vehicle would be a blunt heat sink design. The resulting weapon system was to be operational in 1959.

These decisions were made in an atmosphere of crisis because Moscow's Eighty-eighth Scientific Research Center was on a roll. On May 16, 1954, just as the U.S. system studies were getting under way, the Soviet Union fired an R-5★ rocket 630 miles downrange from Kapustin Yar. The race was on in earnest; the United States was in second place. Allowing the Soviets to have a monopoly on operational ballistic missiles would have a disastrous effect on the "correlation of forces" all around the world. It would negate the U.S. Strategic Air Command's deterrent, and thus could embolden the Red Army, or its proxies, to

---

★ In U.S. terminology, the SS-3, a single-stage, liquid-fueled rocket designed by the Soviets. As described in *Russia's Arms Catalog, Volume IV* as well as by now-retired officers of the SRF, the R-5, when deployed, was capable of delivering a single 300 KT warhead to a range of about 750 miles, i.e., the distance from East Germany to Paris or London, with an average miss distance of about two miles. Its first launch, apparently unobserved by the U.S., took place on April 2, 1953.

move as it wished. It was thought that a forced reunification of Germany on Soviet terms could be next.

To hedge its bets, the Western Development Division was authorized to proceed with a second generation ICBM, the Titan missile. This weapon system would be a true two-stage design, using more sophisticated liquid fuels. It would use inertial (self-contained) guidance and would work toward the use of higher speed, ablative reentry vehicles. Titan was to become operational in 1962, based in more secure, faster launching silos.

In mid-1955, the new U.S. FPS-17 intelligence radar, located at Diyarbakir, Turkey, came on line. It could not see the Soviet rocket launches from Kapustin Yar or anyplace else, but it could see the top of the rockets' flight path—the apogee. This confirmed each flight, and thus the seriousness of the Soviet rocket program. It also allowed the calculation of launch and impact points, which in turn could cue various other reconnaissance assets. The overflying RB-47s and U-2s (described in Chapter 3) could be told where to look for launch facilities. To guard against any "missile gap," the WDD also was authorized to start work on a single-stage Intermediate Range Ballistic Missile based on Atlas and Titan technology and components. The IRBM Thor would be based around the periphery of the Soviet Union, just as the early B-47 bombers had been assigned before the advent of the longer range B-52s.

On December 27, 1955, the Air Force contracted for the development of Thor. The target operational date was to be 1958. Colonel Edward N. Hall, previously in charge of WDD's propulsion division, was put in charge. He had just received the Robert A. Goddard award for his contributions to liquid rocket technology in the United States. A young engineer, Rube Mettler, formerly with Hughes but more recently a Pentagon consultant, became Ramo-Wooldridge's systems engineer.

Thor first tried to fly just one year later, in January 1957. It rose less than a foot off its launch ring, then suffered engine failure, settling back to earth in a newsworthy ball of fire. With the fuel system redesigned, the second launch seemed to be going well until the range safety officer blew it up for the wrong reason. He thought the missile was headed for Tampa, not the open ocean. Thor finally made it downrange eight months later, but even then it was a bird without a nest.

At the beginning of the Eisenhower years the UK had wanted an IRBM stationed on its soil, and the U.S. assumed that other NATO allies would welcome the overseas basing of Thor as well. But they did not. The stumbling blocks were nuclear secrets and control of the "button." Negotiations with the UK dragged on longer than the experimental flight test program. By the summer of 1957, Colonel Hall was sent to the UK to expedite Thor's deployment in the face of some very ambiguous U.S.–UK agreements.

Aside from the policy questions surrounding nuclear control, there was the problem of money. American fiscal ingenuity played a role in finding an answer then, just as it did three decades later with Iran-Contra. In 1957, England's apple crop had failed. Tobacco, usually imported from Turkey, was also in short supply. American farmers were happy to take up the slack. The transatlantic spread in apple and tobacco prices as determined by supply (in the United States) and demand (in the UK) provided an opportunity for arbitrage. Imaginative U.S. fiscal officers in London skimmed the apple and tobacco import market to finance the deployment of Thor in the UK.

Money was a problem everywhere. The Washington political community was beginning to tire of *all* missile program costs. In addition to the Air Force program, the Army/German team at Redstone was working on another IRBM, known as Jupiter. The Navy received authority to develop still a third IRBM, to be known as Polaris. This latter effort would feature a solid fuel missile carried aboard and fired from a submerged nuclear-powered submarine. Such a ship could remain hidden at sea for months at a time. The Air Force program alone was about to exceed $1 billion per year in the fiscal year beginning in July 1957, over $6 billion, in 2000 dollars. Cutbacks began. Control of Congress had shifted to Eisenhower's political opponents, budget constraint was in the air, and the bureaucrats' unending complaint about the "uncontrolled" management of WDD were all taking their toll. By the beginning of the new fiscal year, on July 1, 1957, a "poor man's program" was put in place by the new Deputy Secretary of Defense, Donald Quarles. To live within these constraints, missile operational target dates were slipped by a year.

At that time, Thor had no home, and its flight tests had produced spotty results. Even worse, Atlas had not flown at all. The first Atlas test flight, on June 11, 1957, resulted in an engine failure ten seconds after liftoff. The exploding missile was on newsreels everywhere. Pictures of General Schriever and then Ramo and Wooldridge were on the covers of the April 13 and 29 issues of *Time* magazine. In Washington that usually means a major political purge is under way.

While the Air Force program managers were growing frustrated and discouraged, their leaders were just plain worried. NSA was continuing to intercept communications from rocket test ranges in the Soviet Union, but now those signals seemed to be coming from facilities far beyond those connected with the Kapustin Yar range. They were also collecting telemetry from rockets launched from Kapustin Yar, but that data was unintelligible. Then, in August 1957, a shocking piece of new evidence, the final piece of the puzzle, came into view. A U-2 overflew, and an alert photo interpreter identified a huge new Soviet launch facility near the village of Tyuratam in remote Kazakhstan. The Soviets were up to something big.

CHAPTER 6

Sputnik and the Missile Gap

I DEPARTED EDWARDS AIR FORCE BASE and joined the newly renamed Air Force Ballistic Missile Division (BMD) in June 1957. The atmosphere there was heavy, for the Scylla of the U-2 photos from Tyuratam stared at the Charybdis of the poor man's budget across the narrows of history. For me, as a young officer, it was a heady time. The senior officers welcomed me with open arms. For the most part they were veterans of World War II; few were eminent scientists. They were cut from the same cloth as our leader, General Schriever. From the general on down, the officers in Los Angeles were honest, dedicated, and intelligent men, but their engineering skills were perfunctory. They welcomed me, a graduate from a strong engineering university, newly bedecked with academic honors. They had confidence in their Ramo-Wooldridge technical advisers, but there were some areas, such as the internals of nuclear weapons, where Ramo-Wooldridge was not allowed to tread. My new boss, Colonel Jack Dodge, had asked that I be assigned to his armament (reentry vehicle) division at BMD.

It was summer, the beginning of a new fiscal year. Los Angeles was awash with technical innovation and opportunity, but in Washington the poor man's program was the order of the day. It had induced an unwarranted lethargy in the leadership of our nation's ballistic missile program, but things did not stay that way for long. On August 21, after three unsuccessful tries (reported nowhere in the Western press), the Soviets launched the world's first ICBM. It was an R-7 rocket★ fired eastward from the newly discovered facility near Tyuratam across much of the Soviet land mass. The Soviet name for the launch complex, as noted earlier, was Baikonur Cosmodrome. The R-7 impacted on the Kamchatka peninsula, 3,500 miles downrange, near the Pacific coast. Most of this historic flight was tracked by our new radar at Diyarbakir, Turkey.

The differing Soviet and Western attitudes toward range safety are a stark reminder of the differences between our competing values and systems of government. The United States launches its long range missiles and spacecraft out over the Atlantic and Pacific Oceans. Every Western nation has taken a similar precaution. Even the Nazis launched their first V-1s and V-2s eastward from Peenemunde over the Baltic Sea. In fact, the U.S. once flirted with the idea of an "operational base launch," a test of a Minuteman missile to be fired from a true operational base in Wyoming. While the target would have been Kwajelein Island in the Pacific, the first-stage booster was expected to fall into the redwood forests of northern California. I was given the job of explaining this bizarre concept to the representative of the First Congressional District of California, home of those remote redwoods and the proposed impact point for those crashing first stages. The shrieking and carrying on was understandable. The congressman mobilized the entire California delegation. The Pentagon and White House were besieged with objections. The operational base launch was cancelled, never to be heard from again.

But that's not the way it worked in the Soviet Union. The citizens there had no voice in their government. They had no channel for complaint. Their lives and personal safety were subservient to the interests of the state. The Soviet launch sites were built well inland, where the

---

★ SS-6 in U.S. terminology, a 280-ton monster, comparable in size to Atlas as originally conceived. To lift off, it required five engines with four rocket chambers each for a total of twenty propulsion units, all operating at full thrust.

military wished to have them, sited away from the prying eyes of Western intelligence. (Or so the generals thought.) Test ranges crossed the Asian land mass. Jettisoned boosters and launch misfires were allowed to crash down on hapless peasants. Farms, villages, and livestock herds suffered "collateral damage" without objection.

Some traits of human nature are immutable, however. Kids will be kids, and young officers like to live on the edge. Some have a saying: "If you're not living on the edge, you're taking up too much space." My friends from the Soviet Strategic Rocket Force, now retired, tell of partying at night downrange from Kapustin Yar, watching the launch fireworks, but driving like mad to avoid the falling upper stages when their apparent impact point seemed too close for comfort. A large-caliber form of Russian roulette, I suppose.

Back in the U.S., we again tried to fly another Atlas during September 1957. In ghastly counterpoint to the Soviet R-7 success, an engine turbo pump failed again after only a few seconds of flight. Things were looking bleak, but we hadn't seen anything yet. On Friday afternoon, October 4, 1957, the Soviets used their R-7 booster to launch an artificial satellite into earth orbit. The device, called Sputnik, circled the earth every ninety-six minutes. It emitted a regular "beep" and was visible in the night sky, a new, moving star.

America went into stunned analysis over the weekend. By Monday the United States was awash in fearful headlines; the Ballistic Missile Division was dealing with a dozen "what if" questions. The months that followed saw unparalleled changes in American society. The education system was revamped to promote science and engineering. Missile programs were granted immediate budget increases. Recriminations and concern were everywhere. And with this awakening the brightest minds of the American scientific community began to work their magic.

Nowhere was this talent more productively focused than in the most secret Telemetry and Beacon Analysis Committee (TABAC) assembled in the immediate aftermath of Sputnik. This group of youngsters★ was

---

★ Including Bud Wheelon of Ramo-Wooldridge, Carl Duckett of Redstone Arsenal, Eb Rechtin of Jet Propulsion Laboratory, and Bill Perry of Sylvania's Electronic Defense Lab. All were barely thirty years old at the time, and all went on to illustrious careers in the service of U.S. national security. From 1977 to 1981, Bill Perry served as director of Defense Research and Engineering. In that capacity, he oversaw the introduction of smart weapons and stealth into the U.S. military inventory. From 1993 to 1997, Perry served as U.S. Secretary of Defense.

given the job of looking into the mysterious Soviet telemetry signals. When they started work, the NSA tapes seemed like those huge jigsaw puzzles often found at summer resorts. Everyone just sat down at a corner and started assembling pieces. The group soon came to understand the modulation scheme used to transmit those signals. Then they were able to assign meaning to each of the forty-eight channels (engine pressure, guidance signals, acceleration, engine cutoff, etc.). Lastly, they calibrated all this data, giving it some absolute numerical values, by reading the telemetry transmitters at liftoff. When their work was done, TABAC had thrown open a huge window into the inner workings of the Soviet military machine. For the next two decades the U.S. knew as much about every Soviet rocket launch as the Politburo did.

In the more visible world, operational R-5 rockets rolled through Red Square as part of the Soviet revolutionary celebrations of November 7, 1957. There could no longer be any doubt that the United States and the Soviet Union were engaged in a serious race. Two years later the R-5s would become the world's first ballistic missiles operationally deployed with nuclear warheads. Khrushchev's public posturing and threats made clear the consequences of losing that race. But shortly after that parade in Red Square, on December 17, 1957, the tide began to turn. The U.S. Atlas finally achieved a successful flight, impacting 600 miles downrange. No separation of booster from sustainer engines was attempted, but Atlas had flown.

MINUTEMAN

These struggles to produce the Atlas family of missiles were just a reaction to the Soviet challenge. In time an operational missile would be produced, but Atlas was not an initiative. That responsibility—the job of putting the United States into the role of missile leadership—fell to Colonel Ed Hall.

Hall was born to Barney and Rose Holtzberg in New York City on August 4, 1914. He attended the College of the City of New York, graduating in 1936 with a B.S. in engineering and, a year later, with a professional degree in chemical engineering. In 1936 he and his younger brother simplified their last name to Hall, as many of our ancestors had upon arrival in the New World. At that time, New York City, and especially CCNY, were hotbeds of Depression-spawned Marxist activism. Julius Rosenberg was a classmate of Ed Hall's.

As the clouds of war blew across Europe in 1939, Hall enlisted in the Army Air Corps as a mechanic. Pearl Harbor instantly brought the gold bars of a second lieutenant in the Army Reserves and a transfer to Greenland. From there he went to England, where he met and married Edith Shawcross, to France as the allies swept across Europe, then back to England to serve in technical intelligence. For all of those years, as enlisted man and officer, Hall suffered the slings and arrows of incompetent leadership. At least, that's how he sees it today. He feels he was made to work for a procession of unqualified nonengineers, people put in charge of complex technical projects that he had to execute. By the closing days of the war he was in charge of repairs to battle-damaged aircraft returning to England. His trademark was a swarm of mobile service teams, not a bureaucratic central depot. He was doing whatever it took to get those planes back into combat.

At war's end, Hall was assigned to technical intelligence, overseen by "worthless stockbrokers," as he puts it. He applied for a regular commission and was turned down. He then applied to Cal Tech, hoping to earn a Ph.D. in engineering, but other Air Force assignments cut that short. He was awarded an M.S. in 1948, returned to Europe for two years, then was assigned to the Air Force's research and development center at Wright-Patterson Air Force Base in Ohio. Again he started work as somebody's assistant, this time as the assistant chief of the rocket and ramjet engine group. He worked at Wright-Patterson for four years, until 1954, when he was tapped by General Schriever to join the latter's new Western Development Division as chief of the propulsion division. For once, Ed Hall was unequivocally in charge of something, overseeing the development of the liquid-fueled engines for Atlas.

But he knew there was a better way. During his years at Wright-Patterson, and then during the year he oversaw the Atlas engine work, he had been thinking and learning about solid propellants. The Atlas engines were powered by difficult-to-handle liquid fuels and oxidizers. Those missiles had to be filled with such chemicals right before firing, a dangerous procedure that consumed much valuable time. He knew that a missile with solid propellants would change all that. Premixed pastes could be poured into a tube, allowed to harden, then lit off years later as part of the launch process. The ideas were simple, like Fourth of July fireworks, but the practical chemistry was daunting. Even so, Hall wanted to pursue solid propellants as part of any second-generation missile.

Upon his return from the UK, Hall asked Schriever for the authority to start work on a solid-propellant, multistage missile system. Schriever demurred, but he did allow Hall to conduct a study of what such a missile might look like. It was the job Hall most wanted, for in time he would define the next generation ICBM, the missile that would establish U.S. missile supremacy at an affordable cost. His study became known as the Advanced Missile System, a three-stage solid propellant rocket designed to carry a fractional megaton warhead to ranges of 8,500 miles with a quarter mile average miss distance. In addition to technology, he understood costs, and the role of those costs in actually deploying a meaningful weapon system. He envisioned a cheap missile: a bargain at a million dollars each, inexpensive to operate in unattended, underground silos. The U.S. could afford thousands; he envisioned an impossible-to-target force of 4,000 missiles deployed by 1965.

These studies proceeded quietly until the post-Sputnik events of October 1957. That month, Hall found himself in Washington, engaged in debate with the Navy about the merits of their proposed solid propellant IRBM. His comments focused on what could be done if the technology envelope were pushed. Hall's boss, Colonel Charles Terhune, thought Air Force Vice-Chief of Staff Curtis LeMay ought to hear what Hall had to say. These two, accompanied by General Schriever, gave General LeMay a rundown. Never happy with the complexity of Atlas and Thor, LeMay reacted favorably. The quick-firing, underground-based Minuteman was his kind of bird.

Being a man of action, LeMay led the threesome down one Pentagon flight of stairs to the office of the Secretary of Defense. LeMay asked Hall to repeat his story to Neil McElroy, with regular reinforcement by LeMay. The Secretary of Defense was impressed, both with the technology outlined by Hall and by its endorsement from LeMay. On the spot, McElroy said $50 million would be made available to kick off this advanced missile system and that the Air Force should proceed to develop it without delay.

PROJECT Q

With $50 million in his pocket, directly granted by the Secretary of Defense, Ed Hall went home to start work on this system. He decided to call it Project Q. It was a strange name with an even stranger history.

During his first three years at the Western Development Division, Ed Hall had grown bitter about the role of Ramo-Wooldridge in the

U.S. ballistic missile program. He saw that firm as yet another example of the blind leading the visionaries. He felt that the Air Force had the technical talent to design and develop new missiles, that it did *not* need to hire a bunch of high-priced outsiders to do systems engineering studies and provide technical direction. Hall himself certainly constituted Exhibit A. Some officers, such as himself, were fully qualified and on the cutting edge of missile technology. But on the larger scale, most observers then (and most historians now) agreed with the Teapot Committee's recommendation: get ICBM development away from the Air Force bureaucracy. Ed Hall did not agree, and as his years at WDD unfolded, his feelings intensified. He felt the Ramo-Wooldridge engineers would view the modestly improved technology reflected in Titan I as the definitive next-generation ICBM. Hall knew better. His advanced missile system would make the difference.

To keep it out of Ramo-Wooldridge's sight, he decided to give the advanced missile project an innocuous name. Only when the Ramo-Wooldridge engineers surfaced in their opposition would he blow them out of the water. He likened his plan—invisibility before deploying the overwhelming power of his arguments—to the Q-boats of World War I. Thus the name.

As a resident of Great Britain during World War II, Ed Hall had read about the British "Q-boats." The problem in World War I had been German submarines surfacing to attack British coastal shipping with deck guns during the early phases of the war. One solution, first proposed by First Sea Lord Winston Churchill, was to outfit some tramp steamers with serious firepower, to be hidden inside crates on deck that could be quickly disassembled. These Q-boats lured the Germans to the surface at close range before dropping their disguises to open fire. The Q-boats were very effective.

During February 1958, the Q missile system was fully funded, granted program office status, and given a real name: Minuteman. On March 5 these historic events were written up in *Time* magazine. While *Time* credited Schriever with ballistic missile leadership, it gave the full credit for Minuteman to Hall, describing him as a "day-after-tomorrow kind of officer."

At that time, I was a special assistant to the armaments chief, Colonel Dodge; he assigned me to the new Minuteman account. I became the technical project officer for its reentry vehicle. With the growing success of the Atlas and Thor flight test programs in 1958, with the approval of the next-generation Titan ICBM, and with the pending nuclear weapons tests in the Pacific that summer, the U.S. ballistic missile program was turning the corner. Atlas would maintain parity with the Soviets, Thor would preclude any missile gap, and Minuteman would put the United States into a position of leadership. The Soviets had made their point with Sputnik, and the U.S. was not home free, but the Soviets were now stuck trying to boost 10,000-pound warheads across intercontinental distances with dangerous liquid fuels. Their flight test program was not going well.

There were just two oddities that bothered me then, and they still do. The first was Colonel Hall himself. He had a chip on his shoulder where he should have been wearing his colonel's eagles with aplomb, and he was tape-recording the weekly Minuteman program meetings. He said it was to assure that no one would go back on his commitments to the program, but in 1958, tape recording was not a simple thing. It involved tape-to-tape reels. And *any* recording of those highly classified discussions was contrary to security policy. In discussions forty-five years later, General Schriever was outraged to hear of such activity.

The second puzzle was the set of political constraints that would follow the *Hardtack* nuclear test series, to be conducted in the Pacific during the summer of 1958. The leadership of the U.S. and the USSR had agreed to a moratorium on nuclear tests, to be effective on October 31, 1958. This "agreement" was not a treaty. Rather, it was a pair of unilateral declarations to the effect that henceforth nether side would conduct nuclear tests anywhere; underground, in the atmosphere, in space, or wherever. This scheme was referred to by some as a "gentlemen's agreement," illustrating by that name alone the folly of such an undertaking. A "gentlemen's agreement" with a nuclear-armed dictatorship, totally lacking legitimacy, led by murderers, few of whom could be called gentlemen? Absurd. Yet the moratorium had the potential of stopping the Minuteman warhead development in its tracks.

Colonel Hall's studies indicated the possibility of a much simpler, cheaper, smaller, and more reliable ICBM than Atlas, but it could only carry a warhead half the size of Atlas's. What warhead would that be? How could it be developed without a nuclear test? Now that the Cold War is over, nuclear testing can be viewed in a different light, but testing moratoria and bans always have serious consequences. They incur costs still not well understood. The development and deployment of Minuteman saved U.S. taxpayers hundreds of billions of dollars. Would those savings have been possible if the Soviets had not unilaterally resumed nuclear testing in 1961? Such treaties are important, and they can be beneficial to mankind, but their terms and conditions need to reflect fiscal and technical reality.

THE NUCLEAR GENIE

This problem first came into focus for me in February 1958, when I flew to Albuquerque with Colonel Dodge for my first exposure to the world of nuclear weapons. Unlike engines, guidance, and reentry physics, warhead technology was off limits to contractors, including most Ramo-Wooldridge employees. It was an Air Force/AEC preserve. Albuquerque was the central node of the U.S. nuclear weapons establishment. It was the administrative headquarters for the Los Alamos design laboratory, and it was the home of Sandia, the organization responsible for the safety, arming, and firing components of nuclear weapons.

Our meetings were held at the Sandia Corporation offices. To gain admission, I had received not only a top secret clearance but an AEC "Q" as well. I was impressed by the security procedures, dazzled by the technical competence of the scientists and engineers from the weapons program, and overawed by the responsibilities heading my way. Sandia had a museum. Most hush-hush institutions in the United States and Russia have such secret rooms, filled with cutaway models of everything from their first experiments to the currently deployed hardware. My first visit there was mind-bending. At our business meetings, we discussed the technical details of integrating warheads into reentry vehicles, but I had glimpsed the nuclear genie. It would never let me go.

When we returned to Los Angeles, Colonel Dodge opened his personal safe to let me have a look at his weapons notebook. It was marked "Top Secret—Restricted Data." I do not remember its formal name, but it was printed on pink paper, and it contained cross-sectional drawings, dimensions, and design details of every U.S. nuclear device tested. It was the Nieman-Marcus catalog of the military-industrial complex. The responsibility for leading the Air Force and Pentagon through the Minuteman warhead options was being placed squarely in my lap.

In March 1958 a formal "Phase I" warhead feasibility study meeting was held in our Los Angeles offices. Representatives from the two U.S. nuclear weapons labs, Los Alamos and Livermore, were there. It was on that occasion that I first met Jack Rosengren, a physicist not much older than I. He had proceeded through the conventional physics apprenticeship: a Ph.D. from UC Berkeley, a stint teaching at MIT, and a brief tour through the aerospace industry. He was recruited to the Lawrence Livermore staff in 1957 by Harold Brown to design thermonuclear experiments, devices, and weapons. Rosengren was tall, thin, handsome, quiet, witty, and smart; all substance and no flash. Underlying that substance were core values of integrity and good judgment, nice to find in people dealing with nuclear weapons.

The most critical problem facing Livermore's A (thermonuclear) Division was the Polaris warhead program. Edward Teller promised the Navy a strategic warhead yield within a very portable weight package, and the Navy went out onto the Polaris limb in reliance on those promises, but their fulfillment within A Division might best be described as problematic. Interesting experiments during the summer of 1956 showed promise, but the nation's primary deterrent was awaiting substantive results. In 1957, Rosengren was put in charge of the Polaris warhead design team. In the spring of 1958 a test was scheduled in the Pacific. It would show if Rosengren's calm leadership had paid off.

At the same time, the definitive struggle broke out over Ramo-Wooldridge's future role in Minuteman. They wanted to act as the prime or integrating contractor for the system; the Air Force, or at least Colonel Hall, was dead set against that. By summer, Boeing had been selected as the assembly and test contractor. The other guidance, reentry vehicle, and engine contractors also had been selected—and Hall was reassigned. In August 1958, Ed Hall was sent off to France to help the French with the development of their own IRBM, to be known as the Diamant missile. A year later, upon completion of the minimum twenty years needed for retirement, he called it quits. He retired to an engineer's life in the corporate world and then to another twenty years of complete retirement.

What happened, and why? Today, forty-five years later, Schriever and Hall each have nothing but undisguised scorn for the other. The same is true of Ramo and Hall. In his memoirs, Hall makes the highly unlikely claim that he never even talked to Rube Mettler, R-W's systems engineer for Thor and Minuteman. Mettler recalls Hall's role as peripheral, at best, a creative mind that laid out ideas but was uninvolved in the hard work of implementation. Hall's inability to get along with people is the generally cited reason for his departure from Los Angeles, but were there more reasons than that? What were the missing pieces that Schriever and Mettler never saw? I'll touch upon this again shortly.

GETTING A DECISION AND LEAVING TOWN

The *Hardtack* nuclear test series during the summer of 1958 produced a cornucopia of good news. After preliminary tests in 1956, the selected approach to an Atlas and Thor warhead gave a yield in the megaton range. Los Alamos did its job. The Navy's Polaris warhead, designed by Livermore's Jack Rosengren, tested equally well. And then there was another quite small and unique Livermore device that gave twice the yield expected. So far so good, but the question now was, what warhead to use for Minuteman?

Such yield factors of two, along with parallel improvements in accuracy, could have a significant impact on SAC's ability to attack and destroy Soviet hardened targets: command posts, communications nodes, submarine pens, and weapon storage bunkers. How were we to make that decision in the absence of nuclear testing? Should the Air Force planners opt for surety? Should they select a weapon that had been tested in 1958 and call it quits? If so, the Polaris warhead was the leading candidate. Or should they reach for another factor of two, opting for a scale-up of the 1958 experiment? Such a design should be straightforward, but nuclear devices are full of surprises, and our country would be betting its life on their reliability.

By the end of 1958 this undecided Minuteman warhead question was controlling the entire program. Without a decision on warhead size, weight, and configuration, the rest of the missile design remained in flux. My job was to reach my own conclusions, make some recommendations, then get a decision from the Secretary of Defense if necessary.

At the end of January 1959, I first visited the University of California's Lawrence Livermore Laboratory. The quiet, self-assured competence of the people there was impressive. In March, Jack Rosengren, now the designer for the Minuteman warhead, visited me in Los Angeles. He reflected a growing confidence in the scale-up of the 1958 experiments, a confidence that came, in part, from a new relationship with the British Atomic Weapons Research Establishment. As part of the testing moratorium, the U.S. and UK governments had agreed that it would be a good idea for both countries to review each other's weapons designs.

In August, I was sent to Washington to brief representatives of the Secretary of Defense on the Minuteman warhead options: an expensive, high-yield, but untested warhead; another design tested at half that yield; or a lightweight device with a tested yield down by another factor of two, but enabling the global reach first envisioned by Colonel Hall. It was decision time.

The conversations were as arduous as the entire year's studies. The stakes were immense. On the first of September, however, the answer was forthcoming: go for the higher yield, build in every possible margin of safety regardless of cost, and check the design with Los Alamos and the Brits. As a result, Minuteman missile design could proceed. The trilogy of Atlas (for immediate defense), Thor (as a "missile gap" hedge), and Minuteman (the long-term deterrent) could go forward.

Now I could think about new challenges and perhaps some peace and quiet. My first child, a daughter, had just been born; it was time for a more stable life. My exposure to the Livermore Lab in general and Jack Rosengren in particular made that organization my preferred future home. An informal September discussion with the leader of Livermore's A Division led to a job offer two days later. I accepted, with the move set for late November.

QUESTIONS FOR THE END OF AN ERA

1. Was there really a missile gap?

Yes, in our favor. When John Kennedy was sworn in as the 35th President, on January 20, 1961, the Soviet Union had only three huge R-7A ICBMs on alert. They were the only Soviet ICBMs capable of striking the United States. To be fair, there were forty-eight R-5M (SS-3) IRBMs deployed in Eastern Europe (menacing the NATO capitals), and in the Far East (targeting Japan and South Korea). Another thirty R-12 (SS-4) IRBMs were deployed in the peripheral Soviet republics. But there were no Soviet submarine-launched missiles at sea or even close to it.

On the U.S. side, one Atlas was on alert at Vandenberg Air Force Base since January 15, 1958. On the day Kennedy was sworn in, a squadron of six Atlas missiles also was on alert at Francis E. Warren AFB in Wyoming. Offsetting the Soviet IRBMs in Eastern Europe, the

U.S. had four squadrons of fifteen Thor IRBMs each for a total of sixty missiles on alert in the UK. They were able to cover most Soviet targets west of the Urals. The nuclear-powered submarine *George Washington* was on patrol in the Norwegian Sea, with sixteen Polaris missiles aboard capable of reaching the Soviet capital. Minuteman was in train, to be flown successfully on its first firing on February 1, 1961, a week after the Kennedy inauguration. One thousand Minutemen, deployed over the next six years, would stand alert in the central U.S. for the duration of the Cold War. Candidate Kennedy's warning of a coming missile gap was nothing but campaign oratory. Once safely in office, Defense Secretary Robert McNamara looked at the facts and admitted as much.*

Nikita Khrushchev knew he enjoyed no such advantage. During his confrontations with the U.S. in 1960, he boasted that he was going to crank out R–7s "like sausages," but his son, Sergei, then working at a rocket design bureau, knew better. Sergei is now a U.S. citizen, serving on the faculty of Brown University. He is reported to have revealed a 1960 dinner conversation with his father on this subject.

SON: "How can you say we are producing rockets like sausages, Father? We don't have any rockets."

FATHER: "That's all right. We don't have any sausages either."

2. What happened to the Soviet space program?

The Soviet system could not afford spy satellites and trips to the moon at the same time. Just as the U.S. Star Wars initiative threatened to overwhelm the economy of the Soviet Union in the 1980s, the U.S. Apollo program rolled over Soviet space exploration efforts in the 1960s. Yuri Gagarin's first orbit of the earth in 1961 was the apogee of Soviet self-esteem. By 1964, Nikita Khrushchev was forced from Soviet power, with the encouragement of the Red Army. Among other things, the Soviet generals wanted spy satellites; Khrushchev and his rocket guru, Sergei Korolev, insisted on space spectaculars. The Soviet economy and infrastructure could not support both. Brezhnev took over and handed the military-industrial complex the blank check it wanted.

---

* Pentagon news conference, February 16, 1961, as quoted in McNamara's *In Retrospect* (Random House, 1995): "I [have] concluded that if there was a missile gap it was in our favor."

Sergei Korolev, the prophet and mastermind of the Soviet space program, died in January 1966, and with him died Soviet leadership in space. Their moon program involved a super-huge N-1 rocket with thirty engines; it regularly blew up on the launch pad. In the late 1960s, Soviet dreams of a trip to the moon were quietly abandoned in favor of a massive ICBM buildup. By 1970 the Soviet Union had achieved supremacy in some measures of strategic nuclear firepower. Their deployment of massive SS-9 and their replacements, the SS-18 behemoths, endangered the U.S. for the decade to come, but the era of Soviet space leadership was over. Today the Russian rocketeers focus on the heavy lifting. Energia provides the boosters for many international space consortia, but the sophisticated electronics, the controls and on-orbit systems, are left to others in the West.

3. Did the U.S. ever consider the use of nuclear weapons during the Eisenhower years?

Yes, at the beginning and at the end. In 1953, upon assuming office, Eisenhower apparently threatened the use of nuclear weapons in and around Korea if a truce was not forthcoming from the Chinese.

Then, at the end, in April 1959, as Khrushchev was provoking a new Berlin crisis, Secretary of State Dulles created a secret NATO team and war plan known as *Live Oak*. Its purpose was to maintain Western access to Berlin, this time on the ground. His staff had concluded that a 1948-style airlift would not work again. One *Live Oak* option was to force access to Berlin via the East German highways, to be accomplished by an armored division using tactical nuclear weapons if need be.

Fortunately, the East German spymaster, Marcus Wolfe, got wind of these plans during the summer of 1959. An agent inside British military headquarters tipped him off; he passed the news to Khrushchev. Wolfe now says, "*Live Oak* chilled me to the core."

As a result, the Soviet 72nd Engineers Brigade, custodians of the Soviet R-5M missiles in East Germany, were pulled back into Soviet territory. Khrushchev cooled his Berlin rhetoric, resorting instead to construction of the wall three years later.

4. Who was Ed Hall?

Only when the CIA released the *Venona* tapes in 1996 did new light shine on the mysterious conduct of Colonel Ed Hall. During World War II the Soviets regularly transmitted coded messages back to Moscow from New York and Washington. The U.S. Army collected, but at the time could not decode, those messages. When the product finally did become readable, in 1949, it tipped off the FBI as to the wartime espionage activities of the Rosenbergs, Klaus Fuchs, and their associates. It was these transcripts that led to the arrest and conviction of the atomic spies. Still other agents were faceless ghosts, however. The identity of "Perseus," "Mlad," and others remained hidden within the *Venona* transcripts. They lay in the vaults of the U.S. intelligence agencies until the Cold War was over. Then, in 1996, the *Venona* transcripts were published by the CIA's Center for the Study of Intelligence.

With that publication, two persistent journalists, Joe Albright and Marcia Kunstel, took an interest in identifying some of those shadowy figures. With a great deal of legwork, they identified Mlad. They even found him, elderly but alive, in Cambridge, England. They held lengthy interviews with Mlad, now beyond the reach of prosecution since statutes of limitation and the death of most witnesses allowed Mlad a peaceful retirement to the faculty at Cambridge. He taught physics in obscurity until these reporters knocked on his door one evening in 1996.

Fifty years before, however, Mlad was one of the youngest scientists recruited by J. Robert Oppenheimer. He was only eighteen years old when he arrived at Los Alamos in January 1944, but he had already finished the course work for a Ph.D. in physics from Harvard. Mlad was put to work measuring the nuclear properties of enriched uranium. As it became clear that plutonium would not work in a gun-type (Little Boy) bomb, the Los Alamos scientists hit upon the idea of spherical implosion. Mlad developed the instrumentation to confirm that such spherical implosions would work. By the end of 1944, Mlad was the resident genius on such implosion experiments.

He also decided against allowing America to enjoy a nuclear weapons monopoly once the war ended. In October 1944, Mlad arranged for a two-week vacation. He returned to New York, nominally to see his parents, but his key visit was to Amtorg, the Soviet trade agency there. He met with their resident intelligence agent, Sergei Kurnakov, in the latter's apartment. Mlad volunteered his services to the anti-imperialist cause. Given his familiarity with the Los Alamos implosion experiments, Mlad's contribution to the Soviet nuclear weapons program was monumental. With his guidance, the Soviet scientists were saved from many technical dead ends. His couriers for the delivery of information were Morris and Lona Cohen. Their photos today adorn the walls of the KGB museum in Moscow.

Once confronted by Albright and Kunstel, Mlad admitted his espionage efforts. He was proud that he enabled the Soviets to compete in the world of A-bombs. By so doing, he felt that he headed off a postwar American nuclear monopoly that in his eyes could only have led to the global spread of American imperialism. He accepted no Soviet money for his efforts. Albright and Kunstel published their conclusions in 1997 in a book entitled *Bombshell*. In it they reveal Mlad's real name: Ted Hall. He was Colonel Ed Hall's younger and most devoted brother.

Ted attended Harvard at his older brother's insistence. During his interviews with Albright and Kunstel, Ted made clear the source of his early communist orientation. As Albright and Kunstel put it: "The writings of [various radicals] left an imprint on Ted's developing political mind before he was even a teenager. So did the *Communist Manifesto*, which [older brother] Ed brought home from CCNY."

It is all very strange, but it's easy to imagine how a skilled Soviet intelligence officer, posing as a sympathetic friend, could have talked shop with Colonel Hall. Accolades denied him by the U.S. Air Force might have been delivered by these new best friends in exchange for insight into the Minuteman program. Who was Ed Hall? What made him tick? Perhaps we shall never know.

CHAPTER 7

Nuclear Weapons and the Soviet Union

As a boy I remember the respectful shock as we read the headlines: A-BOMB ATTACK ON JAPAN. But the war soon ended, my cousins came home, and A-bombs disappeared from view. Then, four years later, the Soviet Union barged into the nuclear club—uninvited, unexpected, and unannounced. That was a different matter. In high school we debated what the bomb meant, but none of us really understood the depth of that abyss. Nor did we know the names of the kids staring across that canyon from the other side. I do now.★

★ Much of this material was first published by the author, along with Arnold Kramish, in *Physics Today*, November 1996.

THE THREE ESTATES OF THE
SOVIET NUCLEAR EMPIRE

In feudal times society was viewed as three estates functioning under the king's beneficence: the Lords Spiritual, the Lords Temporal, and the Peasants. For all of its modern aspirations, Stalin's world was still feudal. Certainly that was true of his nuclear community. The respect reserved for the clergy in feudal times went to the security services. The nuclear nobility—the designers—lived well and were accorded full honors. And then there were those who did the tough and dirty work, the peasants. Some of the latter were recent graduates in chemistry or physics, receiving serious overdoses of radiation without concern; some were the engineers pursuing one blind alley after another, with no time for the ordered exploration of alternatives; and some were the prisoners and soldiers, building the foundations and infrastructure to support these technological pyramids. Regardless of schooling, the latter were all peasants in Stalin's scheme of things.

Joseph Stalin and Lavrenti Beria were the royalty of this world. While Stalin's spies made him aware of the American atomic project during the war, it was not until Hiroshima that Stalin came to understand the bomb's political implications. Thus awakened, he signed the directive according top national priority to the development of an atomic bomb within two weeks of the Hiroshima attack. Nothing was to be spared in achieving his objective in the shortest possible time. Since Beria was running the Soviet security service at the end of World War II, most of the USSR's knowledge of the Anglo-American bomb program came through him, so it was logical to put Beria in charge of this new program.

It was not a thoughtful program. Milestones were to be achieved by Stalin's birthday or some other arbitrarily chosen date important to Soviet history, not when data would be available or when it would be safe to take action. The result was a pell-mell rush to break the American monopoly, at any cost in terms of lives, resources, or environmental damage. It was, after all, a system of royal decrees.

THE FIRST ESTATE

When I first met Vladimir Barkovsky, in 1996, he was still an elf of a man. At eighty-five, he had a twinkle in his eye and a dry sense of humor. He is now a senior, semiretired spymaster, a high priest of the first estate.

As a young man, Barkovsky was assigned to the offices of the London NKVD, the Soviet security service later known as the KGB. He served throughout World War II as the case officer for technical intelligence. He was part of the chain that collected the British MAUD★ report in the summer of 1941. This seminal document was prepared by the world's leading physicists then residing in the UK. It recognized the feasibility of an atomic bomb and advised the British government to proceed with its development at once. The advice was of great interest in Moscow.

After World War II, Barkovsky returned to the West, this time to New York City, where he was NKVD station chief from 1949 to 1956. He claims he requested the assignment because his wife needed good medical attention, but that was only his cover. This preeminent Soviet expert on nuclear espionage was sent back to break into the American thermonuclear program. Barkovsky's wife was treated at the Sloan-Kettering Institute in New York at the same time that one of his agents, Ted Hall ("Mlad") took up a research assignment there after leaving Los Alamos. Barkovsky did not leave New York until the Soviets fired their first true thermonuclear device in 1955. He likes to talk about the history of Soviet intelligence efforts. From the beginning of the Soviet state, the importation of overseas technology was important, "Taking from abroad with both hands," in Lenin's words.

The word "espionage" is not in Barkovsky's lexicon when he talks about the leakage of allied nuclear secrets to the USSR during the war. His expression is "the united allied scientific effort." He makes the point that Klaus Fuchs, viewed in the West as a master spy, was not a paid agent. Barkovsky describes him as "a hero who did the world a great service."

Fuchs was recruited based on his own perceived need "to short circuit the bureaucracies of allies committed to the defeat of Nazi Germany." In the West, Fuchs is viewed differently, a brilliant German refugee who fled to England with the rise of Hitler, went to work for the British scientific community, and moved on to New York with the British mission to the Manhattan Project in December 1943. From the outbreak of World War II, Fuchs kept his Soviet contacts informed about the British and then U.S. nuclear programs. He was transferred to

---

★ MAUD was not the name of some sinister international organization. It was just a handy code, being the name of Nils Bohr's family nanny.

Los Alamos in August 1944. From there he passed technical information to the Soviet Union on the U.S. A-bomb, and later on early U.S. thinking about an H-bomb. His courier was Harry Gold. Despite his communist affiliations, Fuchs returned to the UK after the war and was "serving" as chief scientist at the British Harwell nuclear research center when arrested and charged with espionage in 1950.

Barkovsky agrees that Soviet intelligence saved time and thus accelerated the first Soviet nuclear test. On the other hand, he makes the point that such information was only useful when fed to technically competent scientists who could correctly interpret the clues being provided. He claims that after the war, Soviet science moved out on its own, that within a dozen years it was fully competitive with the West, and that current capabilities were achieved without the benefit of intelligence beyond that provided by Klaus Fuchs.

This claim is the subject of some contention. The subsequent release of Cold War decryptions has led authors and researchers to look under a variety of rocks. Most investigators agree there were other agents in place, at the U.S. nuclear production facilities such as Hanford and Oak Ridge, as well as at the scientific labs, and that those sources continued to leak information as the United States moved into the thermonuclear age.

Former Soviet agent Anatoly Yatsov was quoted in the October 4, 1992, *Washington Post* to the effect that the FBI succeeded in uncovering "only half, perhaps less than half" of his—Yatsov's—network in the U.S. Yatsov specifically referred to a second spy at Los Alamos, code named "Perseus," who is yet to be publicly identified.★

Whatever his sources, Vladimir Barkovsky conducted his chorus of singers from his podium in New York City, and he did it well. He went on to serve as chairman of the Department of Scientific and Technical Intelligence at the Andropov Institute of Intelligence from 1970 to 1984. He remains a senior adviser to the Russian Foreign Intelligence Service on the matter of new directions in the post–Cold War era.

THE SECOND ESTATE

Victor Adamskii was part of the nuclear nobility. He graduated from Moscow State University in 1949 with an honors degree in physics and

---

★ I believe he is a U.S. national, very much alive, and now living in California.

was immediately detailed to Arzamas-16, the code name for Stalin's nuclear weapons complex in the village of Sarov, 250 miles east of Moscow. Immediately upon his arrival there, Adamskii was immersed in nuclear weapons work, and in time he was assigned to the Sakharov thermonuclear design group. As a young scientist in the 1950s, Adamskii lived well by Soviet standards, but it was a precarious existence. The necks of his superiors had been on the line if the first Soviet nuclear test failed.

In 1992 the leaders of the American nuclear laboratories were invited to visit their counterparts in what had become the Russian Federation. John Nuckolls, by then the Livermore Lab director, was stunned to have Yuli Khariton, the grand old man of the early Soviet nuclear program, openly admit that the first Soviet device was an exact copy of the Nagasaki Fat Man design. The reason could be easily deduced.

Back in 1949, Beria thought that any nuclear test failure would become known immediately to the Americans. In the event of such a failure, both he and Stalin feared an immediate preemptive U.S. nuclear strike on the USSR to stamp out this young nuclear dragon. To assure success, and thus to create an immediate deterrent, the Soviets invested their precious plutonium in an exact copy of the American bomb. Doing so was galling to the young men who had better ideas, but their elders thought it best to succeed first time out. Aside from political considerations, those Soviet scientists knew failure on that first test would have been personally fatal to them. They talk now with some humor about transition meetings held with their seconds-in-command. The senior scientists had to hedge against their own demise, since a failed bomb would be considered a sabotaged bomb, and all those responsible would have been executed.

Igor Kurchatov, director of the Soviet bomb project at the time, tried to protect his scientists. A few weeks before that first test, known as *First Lightning*, Beria asked Kurchatov for a list of the dozen or so people to be held responsible for the success of the shot. Seeing this as the execution list in the event of failure, Kurchatov compiled a list of expendable janitors and drivers, forgetting about the upside of this inquiry. After the success of *First Lightning*, these were the best-fed, best-housed, and most decorated janitors in the history of Arzamas-16.

Two years later the Soviets fired two versions of their own design. They were only half the size and weight of *Fat Man*. Known as RDS-2, they also gave twice the yield and were more economical in their use of precious nuclear materials than the original copy.

THE THIRD ESTATE

Liya Sokhina was a nuclear peasant. Now in her eighties, Sokhina received her physics degree from Voronezh State University in 1948. She promptly reported to work at Mayak (code name: Chelyabinsk-70), southeast of the Soviet Ural Mountains, on June 10 of that year. The plutonium production reactor "A" at Mayak started up on that day. It sat in a pit over a hundred feet deep. Forty-five thousand workers built the reactor, and before that uncounted thousands of prisoners dug the pit and built the surrounding infrastructure to support it. If the prisoners' terms ended while working at Mayak, they were resentenced to longer terms and sent off to Siberia to protect the secret of Mayak. In Sakharov's words, such workers were "resettled in Magadan."

Sokhina's job was to extract plutonium from the Mayak A's fuel rods and to deliver it, in metallic form, to the bomb builders. She was college-educated but fully expendable in this quest for a Soviet bomb. Her first job was to collect plutonium oxide from the rafters at Mayak. It had gotten there as a result of a pyrophoric explosion, and her assignment was to recover it with dust broom and bags but without benefit of mask or gloves. Eighty percent of her colleagues were women; the men were said to be "at the front."

Soviet casualties of World War II left a legacy we Americans will never understand. Men who had simply disappeared in the snows around Moscow or Stalingrad were still thought to be away, "at the front," even though the war was over and the chances of their return were zero.

In 1996, Professor Sokhina told me about the terrible radiation doses and the disregard for the most elemental health and safety precautions. "This was a most dangerous place to be . . . typical radiation doses were 100 rad per year . . . we were constantly breathing radioactive aerosols . . . respiratory diseases were widespread . . . many colleagues died in the fifties . . . the doctors worked heroically . . . but the country depended on us."

Processing efficiencies were equally terrible. Pyrophoric explosions scattered plutonium oxide throughout the building, with the cleanup conditions described above. On the outside, up on the roof, collection and cleanup went on in temperatures of 20 degrees below zero. Most of the plutonium went out in waste or ended up on the ceiling as dust. Only 40 percent of the metallic plutonium made it through fabrication. And yet Sokhina, a survivor who beat the carcinogenic odds, describes those years as unforgettable. "Secrets from the U.S. helped, as did the Smyth Report* but Soviet scientists had to do the hard, dangerous work of actually producing plutonium . . . We all remembered the war which had ended only three years before; we worked with famous scientists; we did our duty."

By 1955, 350,000 people were working in the Soviet nuclear complex. Twenty-nine of them were awarded (some posthumously) the top Stalin prize and the title "Hero of the Soviet Union." The overwhelming majority of the recipients were in the materials production complex. Virtually all were dedicated patriots, aimed in a dangerous direction by their communist government, utterly unable to know if their heroic efforts made any sense, or to protest if they did not.

In 1957 there was an accident of unimaginable scale at Mayak. Several concrete tanks filled with radioactive waste went critical. They blew up, scattering seventy to eighty tons of radioactive debris downwind. A quarter million people in two hundred towns had to be evacuated. In the West we heard nothing.

FIRST LIGHTNING

First Lightning, the code name for the first Soviet A-bomb test, struck at dawn on August 29, 1949. Igor Kurchatov, the Soviet program director, proclaimed success from his bunker forty miles west of Semipalitinsk with the simple word *"Srabotalo"* ("It worked"). That exact replica of *Fat Man* lit up the sky across that northeastern corner of Kazakhstan.

Americans had not expected a Soviet bomb so quickly after World War II. In the 1940s the fledgling Atomic Energy Commission declined to build any detection system to look for such a test. In December 1947 the AEC's General Advisory Committee, chaired by J. Robert Oppenheimer, expressed its "grave doubts that the techniques and the instruments for detection [of Soviet nuclear tests] are available."

Fortunately, the U.S. Air Force, Navy, and America's junior scientists thought otherwise. The Air Force had started equipping its most advanced weather planes—WB-29s based in Alaska—with air scoops and

---

* A report on the U.S. wartime nuclear weapons work, prepared immediately after World War II by Professor Henry Smyth of Princeton University. Many experts felt then, and feel now, that the release of this report was unwise, as it was a road map that proved to be very useful to the early proliferators.

filter paper. That equipment could collect suspicious dust samples at great altitudes. After every flight any radioactive debris that showed up on the filter paper was subjected to analysis. Often there were samples of interest, the products of volcanos and earthquakes spewing forth underground uranium and other rare earths. They were only false alarms, but they gave the airmen some good practice.

The Naval Research Lab in Washington, D.C., believing that any atomic detonation would produce microscopic debris that ultimately must return to earth, began collecting and analyzing rainwater in a large and sophisticated rooftop collector, and other associated facilities around the world began doing the same. Indeed, on September 3, 1949, a WB-29 flying off Russia's Kamchatka peninsula returned with radioactive samples significantly above the false alarm thresholds, and on September 13 the Naval Research Lab detected increased levels of radioactivity in its rain barrel.

Los Alamos, as well as many universities, had the ability to identify and analyze atmospheric debris, but none had the ability to look into the critically important "birthdates" of those isotopic samples. Spontaneous fission goes on all the time in the earth's core, producing a continuous stream of radioactive fission products. In a bomb, however, all of those fission products are born at the same instant. It is only when one knows the birthdates of the isotopes in a sample—whether they are continuous or simultaneous—that the product can be ascertained as a volcano or a bomb. Fortunately, a small firm in Berkeley developed the ability to read such isotopic birthdates. Within a few days of *First Lightning*, the TracerLab Company concluded that the radioactive materials collected by the WB-29 were bomb debris, created in an explosion at dawn on August 29, 1949. On September 22 scientists at the Naval Research Lab came to similar conclusions.

U.S. Secretary of Defense Louis Johnson did not want to hear this news. Another in the long line of establishment elders on both sides of the Cold War who were unqualified for their jobs but who held them by virtue of political connections or coincidence, Johnson's contribution to history was the expedited post–World War II demobilization and disarming of America's armed forces. He did the job so thoroughly that by 1950 the U.S. was barely able to hang on when a new war erupted in Korea. He was fired by President Truman on September 21, 1950, three months after the North Korean invasion of the South, but by then it was too late. Secretary Johnson already had minted thousands of new widows. He was succeeded in office by retired General George

Marshall, the ace reliever in the Roosevelt-Truman national security bullpen.

In September 1949, however, Johnson was still Secretary of Defense. He did not believe the Soviets were capable of developing an A-bomb so soon after the American success. His explanation for the radioactive debris recovered by the WB-29s earlier that month was that a Soviet reactor had blown up. That claim was later elegantly disproved by Berkeley chemist Albert Ghiorso, among others. By analyzing the rainwater collected at the Naval Research Lab, Ghiorso was able to show that it *was* a bomb fueled with plutonium, not uranium, and that the reactor breeding that plutonium had been running for about one year.

Thanks to Ghiorso's detective work, the source of the Soviet bomb's energy and the probable rate of Soviet plutonium production was now understood. Notwithstanding the growing body of evidence, other "wise" men of the American intelligence establishment joined Secretary Johnson with similarly discounted views of the Soviet threat. On September 20, three weeks *after* the Soviet test, the Central Intelligence Agency issued its Top Secret Intelligence Memorandum Number 225. Now declassified, that report opens with the following summary: "The current estimate of the Joint Nuclear Energy Intelligence Committee is that the earliest possible date by which the USSR might be expected to produce an atom bomb is mid-1950 and that the most probable date is mid-1953."

Sorry; it had happened a month before the CIA report was issued. Intelligence Memorandum 225 went on to advise that in the Soviet Union nuclear reactor "production piles are now in the process of design and/or construction," but that none were in operation. Wrong again. The Soviet Mayak A reactor had been turning out plutonium since June of the previous year.

Despite all this pooh-poohing by bureaucrats and politicians, the Atomic Energy Commission assembled a committee of scientists to look into the data. In less than two weeks almost all of the scientific community—or those cleared to know about such things—had come to the same conclusion: it *was* a Soviet bomb. The test was dubbed "Joe-1" by a young AEC staffer, Arnold Kramish. This set the precedent for naming future bombs set off by closed societies: Joe-2, Joe-3, etc., to be followed in time by Mao-1, Mao-2, and so forth. Our British cousins were treated with more respect. Their tests were named GB-1, GB-2, etc., but the French shots brought out the chauvinism in America's heart. They were named after France's most—well, prominent—figure

Brigitte Bardot: BB-1, BB-2, etc. Only with the end of the Cold War and the exchange of test data with the Russians have we been able to confirm our finds and give those devices and tests their correct names.

On September 23, President Truman ignored the rationalizing by the wise men of the Washington establishment. He accepted the findings of his scientists and announced that a Soviet test had, in fact, occurred. This provoked quite a crisis in the Kremlin. Stalin had hoped to keep *First Lightning* a secret until the Soviets had time to assemble a significant inventory of A-bombs. He was afraid, justifiably, of a U.S. preemptive attack on the Soviet Union before it was a serious nuclear power, so his public reaction to Truman's announcement was to lie. He publicly claimed ownership of an A-bomb program that had been producing weapons since 1947.

THE GAC ASSUMES THE OSTRICH POSITION

First Lightning was an enormous shock to the American public in general and to its politicians in particular. Senator Brien McMahon's Joint Committee on Atomic Energy began taking testimony a week after Truman's announcement, and by October the debate was fully joined. To some it was now clear that the United States was in a technological race with the Soviet Union, and the next step would have to be the H-bomb. Atomic bombs, utilizing the energy released by the fission of uranium or plutonium, had achieved yields of tens of kilotons—and killed hundreds of thousands as a result. It was thought that A-bombs could now be used to ignite the fusion energies of the sun, releasing thousands of kilotons of energy as hydrogen atoms fused into helium, as they do on our life-giving star, or as they might do on earth in a life-ending holocaust.

The question of the H-bomb was referred to the General Advisory Committee of the Atomic Energy Commission for comment. These were the nation's nuclear wise men; the committee was chaired by J. Robert Oppenheimer, still director of the laboratory at Los Alamos. After a series of preliminary discussions, the GAC met over the weekend of October 29 and 30, 1949, to reach some conclusions. Their report, on October 30, 1949, recommended several steps to increase the production of special nuclear materials, and they supported studies of the tactical use of A-bombs.

The heart of the report, however, dealt with the proposal to develop "the super," as the H-bomb was coming to be known. "No member of the committee was willing to endorse this proposal," the report said, in part because "there appears to be no experimental approach short of an actual test which will [show] that a given model will or will not work." Naturally. This section of the GAC report concluded that a concerted attack on the problem "might produce a weapon within five years." In fact, the *Mike* device, America's first thermonuclear, was fired just three years later with a yield of over ten megatons. It vaporized an entire island. It did take another two years, however, to deploy the first H-bomb to the armed forces.

The second reason for not proceeding with the super was, on its face, one of size. The report observed that "there is no limit to the explosive power of the bomb itself except that posed by requirements of delivery." In other words, H-bombs could be made infinitely large, and there was no military justification for such yields. Six members of the committee, including Chairman Oppenheimer, went on to sign an addendum that was less scientific and more oratorical in its arguments. "We have been asked by the Commission whether or not they should immediately initiate an all-out effort to develop a weapon [with 1,000 times the yield] of the present atomic bomb. We recommend strongly against such action. . . . In determining not to develop the super bomb we see a unique opportunity of providing by example some limitations on the totality of war . . ."

Two other members of the 1949 GAC, Nobel laureates I. I. Rabi and Enrico Fermi, went even further. In a separate letter, they said: "A weapon like the super is only an advantage when its energy release is [100 to 1,000 times] that of ordinary atomic bombs. . . . No limits exist to the destructiveness of this weapon. . . . The President of the United States [should] tell the American public and the world at large that we think it wrong on fundamental ethical principles to initiate [such] a program. At the same time it would be appropriate to invite the nations of the world to join us in a solemn pledge not to proceed in the development or construction [of H-bombs]." The GAC report of October 30, 1949, was an amazing display of political and technical naiveté. It was not the first time during the Cold War that a distinguished group of scholars would wander far beyond their technical competence to advocate political courses of action. Nor would it be the last. But the miss distance of the 1949 GAC was historic.

Thermonuclear technology led to smaller, not larger weapons

B-17 – 1955
First operational U.S.
H-bomb, megaton class

Fat Man – 1945
First U.S. A-bomb
20 kilotons

W-88 – 1985
Trident II warhead, a
miniature H-bomb,
dozens of times the
yield of Fat Man

Every day Americans entrust their lives to cardiovascular surgeons or to airline pilots. These are intelligent and capable people, but few Americans would entrust the management of their retirement portfolios to them. That calls for a different expertise. Yet during much of the Cold War the musings of Nobel prize-winning scientists seem to have been exempted from this reality check. A mind capable of understanding magnetic resonance or elementary particles, and so accredited by the Nobel trustees in Stockholm, was automatically credited with additional insight into the workings of the Bolshevik mind or the Red Army general staff. It is not clear that is a valid assumption.

In the matter of "providing an example," we now know★ that in June 1948, over a year *before* the 1949 GAC report was written, a thermonuclear group already had been set up at the Soviet FIAN institute under the leadership of Igor Tamm. In May 1949, five months *before* the GAC

★ From witnesses, speaking at the 1996 Dubna conference, as well as from the memoirs of Andrei Sakharov.

writings, the Soviet Council of Ministers approved a formal thermonuclear program. Some Russian weapons historians maintain that Truman's January 31, 1950 announcement provided the incentive for the
Soviets to proceed with their own serious H-bomb project. But Andrei
Sakharov, father of the Soviet H-bomb, writing in his memoirs forty years
later, put it this way: "Any U.S. move toward abandoning or suspending
work on a thermonuclear weapon would have been perceived either as a
cunning, deceitful maneuver or as evidence of stupidity or weakness. In
any case, the Soviet reaction would have been the same: to avoid a possible
trap and to exploit the adversary's folly at the earliest opportunity."

In addition to being bad politicians, the members of GAC 1949 also
were bad engineers. Their claim that H-bombs would only be feasible
if one thousand times the size of Fat Man missed the point. The ultimate result of the U.S. thermonuclear program was miniaturization and
safety, not monster bombs.

The 1949 GAC's standard A-bomb was the Nagasaki Fat Man, a
10,000-pound monster, delivered by a very large and vulnerable bomber
after surviving innumerable safety hazards, from a stockpile in the United
States to its target in Japan. Once delivered to Nagasaki, Fat Man gave a
yield of twenty kilotons.

Thirty years later the Western alliance was still intact. The principal
American deterrent protecting that alliance was its fleet of nuclear-
powered submarines, each carrying sixteen Poseidon missiles. Each of
those missiles, in turn, carried ten warheads with a yield in the kiloton
range. The yield of those Poseidon warheads was not much larger than
that of the Nagasaki Fat Man, but by using thermonuclear technology,
the warhead weighed far less than that early device. In addition, robust
safety and security devices were built into the Poseidon warhead.
Miniaturization and hardening put the American nuclear deterrent at
sea, away from the American mainland and immune to surprise attack.
All this despite the advice of the 1949 GAC.

DECISION TIME

As autumn 1949 turned to winter, debate on the H-bomb proposal
moved from Nobel Prize–winning philosophers to elders in authority,
then ultimately to politicians. The Atomic Energy Commission, influ-
enced by its technical advisers, voted three to two against proceeding with
the H-bomb. On November 19, President Truman asked the Secretaries

of State and Defense and the Chairman of the AEC to come up with some advice. They couldn't, meeting only once to debate the issue. The military was less ambivalent or more realistic. On January 13, 1950, the Joint Chiefs of Staff unanimously supported an H-bomb program.

As the soldiers and statesmen grappled with the issue of the super, the sources of the rapid Soviet nuclear advance were beginning to dawn on the American and British counterintelligence services. As early as September 1949, Los Alamos scientist Klaus Fuchs was suspected of leaking secrets, including early thermonuclear concepts, to the Soviets. At the end of January 1950 he confessed.

Truman's State, Defense, and AEC advisers came to see Truman on January 31, aware of the impending Fuchs arrest. They were prepared to deliver their divided advice, but Truman cut the debate short. He relied on his instincts and common sense. "What the hell are we waiting for? Let's get on with it." That afternoon he issued a statement approving "work on all forms of atomic weapons including the so-called hydrogen or super-bomb." Some authors think he had already come to that conclusion when making budget decisions during the previous fall. By whatever chain of events, the race for nuclear supremacy was now in the hands of young American and Soviet patriots, doing their jobs as best they could.

CHAPTER 8

The American Cyberskippers

DECADES AGO I CAME TO KNOW and respect my Russian nuclear colleagues, from their radiochemical signatures if not their names, so when the Cold War was over it was rewarding to meet them in person, to dine together and heave a sigh of collective relief. My familiarity with American nuclear weapons covers those same years, as I worked at the University of California's Livermore Radiation Laboratory during the time of the Cold War's last atmospheric tests.

The Livermore Lab was the brainchild of Edward Teller, its birth one consequence of the Teller-Oppenheimer struggle over the merits and feasibility of an H-bomb. For a decade Teller felt that an H-bomb, replicating the sun's fire on earth, could be built, but until the winter of 1950-51 the details escaped him. Then, in March 1951, he and Stan Ulam published a paper through classified channels that articulated the solution.

Within fourteen months the U.S. Atomic Energy Commission asked the university to open a new weapons laboratory. It was to compete intellectually with Los Alamos, for in the eyes of many in Washington, that older institution had been infected with Oppenheimer's 1949 view of H-bombs—that in all probability they wouldn't work, and even if they could be made to work, they would cost too much in terms of money, talent, and tritium. Besides, they would be too heavy to deliver, and our efforts to build them would only spur the Soviets on to a similar H-bomb program, so we should not work on them in the first place.

The U.S. government, including the President of the United States, thought otherwise. This new laboratory was to be an offshoot of E. O. Lawrence's Berkeley Radiation Laboratory. It would be located on a World War II naval air station just outside Livermore, thirty miles east of Berkeley. On July 1, 1952, the university accepted its new responsibility, adding Livermore to its portfolio of preeminent physics institutes. In September 1952 the Livermore Lab opened its doors. Herbert York became its first director; Edward Teller was its éminence grise.

HIS EMINENCE

Edward, as he has always been known at Livermore, saw things differently from most of us. During World War II, Edward Teller fled his native Hungary to become a bright young theoretical physicist at Los Alamos. From the summer of 1943, almost immediately upon his arrival at that wartime scientific nerve center, he left his stamp of genius on America's nuclear weapons program. He arrived in hopes of pursuing thermonuclear technology in parallel with the difficult enough challenge of uranium fission weapons. He was disappointed. The wartime focus at Los Alamos was on immediately achievable, practical results: an A-bomb that could be fielded within a year or two.

At the time of Teller's arrival, the favored solution to A-bomb design was the rapid assembly of two pieces of fissionable material, fast enough that they would go critical before the nuclear energy released could blow them apart. Enclosed guns firing uranium projectiles at each other was the envisioned solution. It was this approach that was used in Little Boy, the bomb dropped on Hiroshima on August 6, 1945, and it was the approach taken by the Soviets at their Moscow Laboratory Number 2 until they gained access to the secrets of Los Alamos. This gun-type assembly was a terribly inefficient use of U-235, and it would not work at all with the new reactor-bred metal, plutonium.

Teller's earliest contribution to this program was his reflection on the compressibility of all matter, in particular, metals. One does not ordinarily think of iron as being compressible, like a gas, but in June 1943, Teller discussed this question with the great mathematician and fellow Hungarian refugee at Los Alamos, John von Neumann. They noted that at the center of the earth, where pressures are about five million atmospheres (75 million psi) there are indications that the earth's iron core is compressed by something like 20 to 30 percent. The same effect might be achieved in a weapon by the convergence of shock waves driven by high explosives. Von Neumann had been studying this convergence of shock waves as a possible means of destroying German submarine pens, and one of his contributions to the A-bomb project was the development of high explosive lenses that would better focus these shock waves at the core of the weapon. Might the metals at the core be compressible?

Another scientist at Los Alamos, Seth Neddermeyer, had suggested the use of spherical implosions as a means of rapidly assembling a critical mass. Could these effects be combined? The scientific team at Los Alamos soon came to understand that with reasonable spherical convergence, explosive-driven shock waves would create pressures on the order of ten million atmospheres at the center of a metal ball. They further calculated that such pressures would significantly increase the density of the heavy metals known as "actinides." The most prominent actinide is plutonium. Since critical mass depends on density, and since the rate of increase of criticality runs much faster with spherical convergence, the scientific team at Los Alamos had just hit upon the secret of the modern A-bomb: spherical implosion of a fissionable pit using carefully designed high explosive lenses. With that discovery, the bomb program was reoriented into two parts. The use of U-235 in Little Boy was continued, but spherically imploded balls of plutonium became the basis of the Trinity device, the Nagasaki bomb, the U.S. postwar nuclear inventory—and the Soviet A-bomb as well.

With the end of the war Edward Teller's mind turned to other new challenges. In later years Eugene Wigner, another prominent Hungarian physicist, would describe Teller as "the most imaginative person I have ever met." This gift of unclouded vision regularly led Teller to urge U.S. pursuit of technology that did not yet exist. His mind looked carefully into the physics of any given challenge. Once satisfied that a proposed scheme or plan was not contrary to the laws of physics, Teller would put his name and prestige on the line most forcefully, assuring all who would listen (and some who did not wish to listen) that this thing could be done. The time, practical engineering, and resources required to bring these insights to fruition seldom concerned Teller. He became bored with the details that could be worked out by other, lesser minds. To his dying day he probably did not have a clear idea of how the intricate components of U.S. H-bombs really work. Such things were engineering details to him, although most of us designers think of them as mind-boggling physics and materials challenges. I worked for Teller in the 1960s, and I thought he was a man of vision; others thought he was nuts.

As World War II ended, Teller refocused his vision onto the thermonuclear challenge. In 1946, Los Alamos convened a conference on the super. It was a gathering of distinguished physicists, including Teller and Klaus Fuchs, to consider whether thermonuclear reactions could be achieved on earth. They sketched out some ideas, but the war was over; most of those present wanted to turn their attention to other things. Then, on August 29, 1949, with the first Soviet A-bomb test, priorities changed. Teller urged a full-scale U.S. H-bomb program on any who would listen, and on January 31, 1950, President Truman authorized the development of such weapons.

It is one thing to implode a ball of plutonium to get a critical mass and thus a few kilotons of explosive yield. It is quite another to achieve the temperatures, pressures, and densities found at the center of the sun in order to start fusing hydrogen nuclei into helium. Teller's initial scheme for achieving these conditions was simply to light a tube of thermonuclear fuel at one end, using an adjacent A-bomb as the "match" or igniter. The name "super" became attached to this particular geometry, and Teller promoted it heavily in early 1950. But life turned out not to be so simple. Within a few months of Truman's approval to proceed with the program, cooler heads—John von Neumann and his associates—undertook some serious machine calculations of the super configuration, using the new digital computers available at Princeton. They concluded that the Teller approach would not work. Later calculations show otherwise, but at the time, the von Neumann findings caused a serious political setback.

The results of these calculations troubled Teller deeply. He had been instrumental in pushing the U.S. government into an H-bomb program, but it was not until the winter of 1950-51, a full year after President Truman's go-ahead, that Teller finally hit upon the idea of using the radiation field from an adjacent primary to implode, compress, and light the thermonuclear fuel. In March 1951 he and Stanislaus Ulam published their paper. Twenty months later a device based on their concept, and yielding ten megatons, blew away much of Elugelab Island at the Eniwetok atoll.

Teller's next intellectual leap occurred in the summer of 1956, when the U.S. Navy was thinking about pulling together the technology of nuclear-powered submarines and ballistic missiles to create a new, invulnerable deterrent. The Navy called a conference at the Nobska lighthouse facility at Woods Hole, Massachusetts, to discuss all sorts of nuclear and missile technologies. At that time, U.S. intercontinental missiles were undergoing their first flight tests. The Atlas ICBM was a monster. The Soviet R-7, booster for Sputnik, was even bigger. The thought of putting a useful ballistic missile into a submarine seemed ludicrous, but the game was worth the candle. Missiles on submarines would be invulnerable to surprise attack; the nuclear deterrent would be stable in times of crisis.

The size of a missile would be determined by the size of its warhead. On August 12, 1953, the Soviets fired their first H-bomb, known as RDS-6s. As they reported at Dubna, in 1996, that device weighed five tons and gave a yield of 400 kilotons, only 15 to 20 percent of which came from thermonuclear fusion. American technology was a little better, but the first Atlas was designed to deliver a similar five-ton payload. Then, at Nobska, Teller asked the rhetorical question: Why use 1958 technology in a 1965 warhead? He promised that his new Livermore Laboratory could produce a megaton-yield device in a package suitable for delivery by a 30,000 pound rocket. (The Soviet R-7 rocket weighed over 600,000 pounds, twenty times the Teller goal.)

The other weapons experts in attendance were astonished. His companion from Livermore, Johnny Foster, was appalled. No one had a clear idea of how to accomplish such a thing, but Teller had that feel for physics that his peers lacked. The inventive minds at Livermore made good on his promise. Four years later the first Polaris submarine went on combat patrol, armed with a Livermore-designed warhead with a yield substantially greater than the Soviet RDS-6s but weighing very much less. Edward Teller was vindicated; thermonuclear technology had miniaturized warheads.

A quarter century later came Teller's third leap. He had been thinking about intercepting incoming missile warheads since the late 1950s. By 1982 he shared President Reagan's desire for some sort of defensive system. Teller's solution was the X-ray laser, and early experiments had shown some limited success. The idea was to identify attacking missiles as they lifted off, to then fire a specially designed nuclear device in space, focusing the X-ray energy coming out of that device onto the attacking missile half a world away. These ideas were destined to play a significant role in President Reagan's Strategic Defense Initiative, the trump card in that President's end game versus the Soviet Union, even though he chose not to pursue Teller's specific solution.

New ideas were the Teller trademark, and from its inception his new laboratory at Livermore was to work on such potential breakthroughs. In practice, however, it nearly choked on these new ideas. Livermore's first A-bomb prototype, certainly an unconventional design, was tested, as the Ruth event, in Nevada on March 31, 1953. It was a total disaster, with the shot tower left standing. Livermore's first thermonuclear, fired as the Koon event at Bikini on April 6, 1954, was similarly unsuccessful. The university leadership understood that in good science some experiments must fail, but the Ruth and Koon shots did inject a note of reality into the new institute's life. To rescue the laboratory from this wilderness, and to guide its recovery to the sunny uplit highlands of success, the university turned to two very young men: Harold Brown, still in his twenties, and John Foster, then thirty-two.

THE AMERICAN WITH SAFETY ON HIS MIND

Johnny Foster was a teenage radar technician during World War II. He came home from the war, got his B.S. at McGill, then joined the growing firmament of physics stars at the University of California at Berkeley, working in Nobel Prize–winner E. O. Lawrence's Radiation Laboratory. Foster was awarded his Ph.D. in 1952 and immediately thereafter joined in the formation of the new Livermore Laboratory. During that summer, in the wake of the early Soviet nuclear tests and the ongoing Korean War, American thermonuclear leadership was the nation's top priority. It was akin to the moon-landing program of the sixties. The country needed a success, and Foster appreciated the opportunity. His technical contributions were substantial from the very beginning, but the force of his personality put Livermore on the map.

In 1956, Foster accompanied Teller to the Navy's future technology conference at Woods Hole, described above. On July 20, Teller spoke at length. His words astounded all who heard him in that pre-Sputnik era of 1956. Teller foresaw a Navy "which essentially consists of nuclear submarines." He described Soviet progress in nuclear weapons as "really disquieting." He saw little military usefulness in multimegaton H-bombs, but he did see an urgent need for a solid-fueled, intermediate-range ballistic missile that could be carried on and fired from a submerged nuclear-powered submarine. As a payload for such a missile, Teller foresaw (or promised) a megaton-class H-bomb, no larger than a small trunk. That was an enormous leap of faith, since the megaton weapons first tested in the Pacific only two years before were the size and weight of railroad cars.

The "customers" in Teller's audience—that is, the Navy officers—were ecstatic. The "competitors"—the scientists from Los Alamos—were dubious. Johnny Foster from Livermore was startled. Neither he, nor Harold Brown, nor anyone else at Livermore had any clear idea of how to fulfill Teller's pledge, but they went to work. Five months later, as a result of that meeting and its follow-up studies, Secretary of Defense Charles Wilson initiated the Polaris Submarine Launched Ballistic Missile program. Within a year Foster and his associates created a new approach to the design of primaries, the A-bombs that start the thermonuclear explosions. A version we will call *Birdie* was fired successfully in the late 1950s as the primary for the Teller-promised warhead. The product of an insightful mind, a dedicated organization, and a sophisticated high-explosive test facility, *Birdie* was a great breakthrough in many ways. High yield, low weight, and materials efficiency were important, but Foster had another objective in mind.

On an early trip to the Armed Forces Special Weapons Center in Albuquerque, Foster saw a military technician testing the detonators of an early Mark-7 A-bomb with live electrical probes. Mindful of his wartime experiences with the troops, he began to worry. The United States had some very rigid rules and regulations for the care of nuclear weapons, but what if one of those probes had too much voltage? What if somebody dropped one of these things? What if the aircraft carrying one crashed, or burned on the ground? What if a U.S. nuclear storage site in Europe was overrun by bad guys? What if an American officer just lost it and tried to fire his weapon?

There was little interest in these "what ifs" right after World War II. Back then, it was tough enough just getting A-bombs to go off when you wanted them to. In 1950, however, the Korean War broke out and the United States began to change its custodial procedures. A-bombs were released from secure AEC bunkers in New Mexico, to be dispersed and forward deployed with Air Force units around the world. Soon thereafter the accidents started, five of them in 1950 alone. By "accident" I mean a nuclear weapon leaving its aircraft unintentionally, the high explosive inside going off, or a weapon splitting open with radioactive material being dispersed. In fact, there has *never* been an accidental nuclear detonation of a U.S. weapon, nor has there ever been *any* nuclear yield as a result of an accident involving a U.S. weapon.

As a result of the accidents of 1950, people began to think about the unique challenges of nuclear safety. On one hand, a nuclear weapon must be absolutely reliable. When the President decides that our nation's security is so imperiled that nukes must be used, there can be no doubt that they will in fact work as designed. On the other hand, an occasional accidental nuclear explosion is simply out of the question. There can be nothing less than absolute safety (protection against accidental detonation) and security (protection against unauthorized detonation). Yet these design objectives of reliability and safety conflict. At the heart of the problem is the high explosive.

A-bombs work when a charge of high explosive implodes pieces of plutonium or uranium into a supercritical mass, doing so quickly before the multiplying chain reactions can blow the assembly apart. Designers want to use the most powerful explosives, delivering the most energy per unit weight, to minimize the payload the military must carry to target. Such "racehorse" high explosives tend to be temperamental. If dropped or set on fire, they can go off, and such assemblies may not be "one point safe"; that is, if ignition occurs at any one point due to ground impact or a flying fragment, a nuclear yield might result.

As a young physicist reflecting on the accidents of the 1950s, and after seeing the soldier testing the Mark-7 detonators, Foster got serious about safety, feeling it should be designed into weapons, not left to the guards. He started to discuss this problem with the Armed Forces Special Weapons Project, the military agency responsible for nuclear custody. No interest: "Our rules and procedures work just fine." He thought of some internal design solutions, but they were not of interest to the then-director of Livermore: "Not good physics. It's a Sandia problem." The Sandia Laboratories are the part of the weapons complex that makes the fusing and firing sets. Foster started conversations there but soon ran up against the reliability wall. Sandia was managed by Western Electric, at the time the nation's principal supplier of telephone equipment. Sandia knew all about the reliability of switches. Their engineers were appalled at the thought of putting switches, intended to work without fail for decades, inside metal cans to be welded shut.

But time was working in Foster's favor. In 1956 he was appointed to run B Division, the part of Livermore that designs atomic bombs and primaries for thermonuclear bombs. By 1958 he had designed safety into his *Birdie* device. He thought it would be one point safe, but with his increased stature, Foster now began to cajole his physics and electronics associates into other safety measures.

Some were smart electronics, like putting an electronic map inside the bomb case, thus precluding an arming sequence unless the weapon is outside U.S. boundaries. Another solution was the introduction of insensitive high explosive, a material with less bang per pound, but immune to detonation by flying fragments or fires. A third approach became known as "permissive action links," or PALs. These are a family of devices and circuits that preclude a nuclear weapon from arming itself unless some outside information is inserted, information held only by the President and his designated successors.

In 1961, after earlier directors Herb York and Harold Brown had departed Livermore to serve in the Pentagon, Foster became director of the Lawrence Livermore Laboratory. He pursued all of these approaches to safety. They came to fruition in early 1962.

On September 1, 1961, the Soviet Union unilaterally and with a big bang breached the nuclear testing moratorium in effect since 1958. President Kennedy immediately authorized the resumption of underground testing, and in early 1962 approved an atmospheric test series in the Pacific, to be known as Operation Dominic. On March 23, 1962, Kennedy came to visit the Berkeley lab, to tell the physicists of his decisions and to deliver a pep talk. Kennedy would stand behind the weaponeers and take the political heat, but he expected a lot of hard and productive work in exchange. At that meeting, Foster got to show Kennedy one of his prototype PAL devices. The President liked the concept and soon afterward directed its orderly introduction into all U.S. nuclear weapon systems.

Since 1980 there have been no nuclear accidents of any sort in the U.S. inventory. *Birdie* technology is the basis for all Livermore-designed weapons and most Los Alamos weapons in the stockpile.

THE WEST POINTER

Carl Haussmann was a graduate of the U.S. Military Academy at West Point. He entered the Academy during World War II, mindful of the slaughter of innocents that can occur when their governments do not tend to their basic responsibilities. He graduated from West Point in 1946, now mindful of and comfortable with his commitment to duty, honor, and country. The Army recognized young Haussmann's talents, sending him on to earn a graduate degree in physics from Penn State and earmarking him for responsibilities in the new atomic Army. He was sent to a six-month nuclear weapons course at the Special Weapons Center in Albuquerque, spent a few weeks at Los Alamos, then was sent off to babysit nuclear weapons in the U.S. stockpile. In the early 1950s the United States had only a few hundred atomic bombs. Their assembly was complicated, and they were stored in the disassembled mode for reasons of safety. But Lieutenant Haussmann's quiet life did not last long. A West Point classmate already was involved in the very secret Project Matterhorn at Princeton.

With President Truman's 1950 decision to proceed with the H-bomb, John Wheeler, a preeminent physicist in the wartime A-bomb project, was asked to oversee the thermonuclear burn calculations for the new weapons. He accepted, but he would not return to Los Alamos to do that work, so the AEC set up a laboratory around him at his then-current academic home, Princeton University. Thus the Matterhorn complex was born, and by the fall of 1951, Wheeler had attracted some bright young stars to its galaxy. Carl Haussmann was one of them. A secondary reason for locating the new lab at Princeton was the proximity of the Sperry Rand Univac facility in nearby Philadelphia. Calculating the conditions for successful thermonuclear ignition are quite complex, and unlike Johnny Foster's *Birdie*, H-bombs cannot be designed by small-scale experiment. Only *gedanken*, or thought-experiments, are possible, and they require extensive computational support.

In 1951 it became possible to do these calculations on the new computers under development in Philadelphia. In Moscow it was being done by acres of ladies punching desk calculators. America's brand-new Univac computers used vacuum tubes rather that mechanical relays. As they were being assembled, Carl Haussmann and the Matterhorn staff were writing the computational codes to make them run. There was no time even to move the machines off the factory floor for shipment to Princeton. The Univac machines that helped design the first H-bomb could remember only a few kilobits of information, and they could process it with clock speeds of only a few hundred instructions per second. It would have taken ten thousand Univacs to compete with a single Cray I machine twenty years later, but they did the job. The Mike device worked; the thermonuclear era began.

After that, Matterhorn's bomb work began to close down. Much of it was taken over by the new lab at Livermore. Those remaining at Princeton turned their attention to the possibilities of controlled thermonuclear reactions as a source of commercial energy. In 1953, Haussmann resigned from the Army and moved to the new laboratory at Livermore. He brought with him the Matterhorn computer codes and a sense of urgency. All around the world challenges to democracy were growing more worrisome. In March 1953 he began work on Harold Brown's thermonuclear team. He ran calculations for Brown on Livermore's new IBM 701 computer, the first fully electronic machine. It ran twelve times faster than Univac. In the summer of 1954, Haussmann spent time in the Pacific during the nuclear tests there. At home he pushed for the development and acquisition of still bigger and faster computers. He started to do design work on the new machines, and within a few years became Brown's deputy leader of A Division. At the time, both men were still in their twenties. By the spring of 1958, Haussmann was working on his end of Teller's bargain with the Navy, preparing several alternative devices for test during the summer.

At the same time, the wise men in Washington came up with another in a long chain of "good ideas." This one was to be the "gentlemen's agreement" described in earlier chapters. The Soviet Union promised to discontinue all nuclear testing, without verification or enforcement. To most of us, the phrase "trusting the Russians" was an oxymoron; to the wise men it seemed like a good idea, a "step toward peace." This moratorium was to start at midnight on October 31, 1958.

Haussmann thought about the devices planned for test before then. He felt the lab could do better, that it must do better in the face of the coming moratorium. During April 1958 a new approach took shape, and during the first week of May, Haussmann, Brown, and a handful of others started work on a new approach to thermonuclears. Working feverishly with the new all-transistorized IBM 709 computers, the Haussmann group, their supporting engineers, and their machinists conceived, gestated, and delivered a brand-new device in only twelve weeks.

When their device was tested in the Pacific it gave twice the expected yield. When Harold Brown moved on to management of the whole laboratory in 1959, Haussmann became the leader of A Division. His major challenge was to exploit the new technology, but without the benefit of nuclear tests. His role in my life was to be at the right place, at the right time, to invite me to join A Division.

THE FARM BOY FROM ILLINOIS

John Nuckolls's love of explosives may have been hereditary. His father was an explosives expert who worked for the Underwriter's Laboratory. He had attended nuclear physics courses at the University of Chicago and built a library on that subject that would entrance his son. On the Illinois farm where the Nuckolls family lived, young John entertained himself with those books in the evening. In 1948, as a high school junior, he entered the Westinghouse Science Talent Search. Having read the 1945 Smyth Report, *Atomic Energy for Military Purposes*, his entry in the contest was an H-bomb design. It wasn't very good and would not have worked, but even then that put him on a par with Edward Teller; in 1948, Teller had not figured out how to build an H-bomb either.

At Wheaton College, in Illinois, Nuckolls majored in physics. He became known as "Atom Bomb Nuckolls." He built rockets too, not all of which worked. One launch failure caused shrapnel to hit his shoulder. The faculty was proud of him, although they considered him "unusual." In 1953, Nuckolls graduated from Wheaton and entered graduate school in the physics department of Columbia University. It was a prestigious department, with some of the brightest minds of nuclear physics on the faculty, such as I. I. Rabi, who was awarded the Nobel Prize for physics in 1944 for his prewar work on magnetic resonance. Rabi had spent the early war years at MIT developing radar, then moved to Los Alamos. After the war, he came to Columbia to build a world-class physics department. During that time, he was appointed to the General Advisory Committee of the Atomic Energy Commission, with service as its chairman starting in 1953. He opposed development of the H-bomb in 1949. Robert Serber was another of the Columbia stars. He was a wartime veteran of Los Alamos, author of *The Los Alamos Primer*, a then-secret booklet printed in April 1943 to supplement his orientation lectures on nuclear matters to the new arrivals. When the war was over, Serber joined the exodus to Columbia. In time he served as president of the American Physical Society. He also had opposed development of the H-bomb.

These men may have been famous, but they were too rigid for Nuckolls. Within a year of entering Columbia, he was locked in serious battles with his elders over the matter of quantum mechanics, a theory he found insufficient to explain the results of some of the classic physics experiments. He agreed with Einstein: "God does not play dice." As a boy, Nuckolls had read of Hitler's atrocities. Now, in the 1950s, he was hearing about similar horrors in Stalin's Gulags and Mao's communes. He was alarmed by the first Soviet nuclear test but took comfort in the American responses. In the distance he heard (figuratively) the rumble of H-bombs going off in the Pacific. He felt it was time to take action, not to argue further with the Columbia faculty.

In February 1955, Nuckolls saw a recruiting advertisement for the University of California's new Livermore Laboratory. Following its early exploits with great interest, he applied, hoping to find a home more tolerant (and appreciative) of his creative talents. At his interview with the Livermore recruiter, Nuckolls was asked if he "liked to calculate." The implication was mechanical adding machines with shift registers. Livermore offered Nuckolls a job. In June 1955 he called it quits at Columbia, accepted a master's degree, and headed west, joining the enormous technoimmigration into California that was remaking that state. The result was a boom that no one then understood, but it was enormously good fun. Those bright young men and women of the fifties left behind what they felt to be the intellectual dust bowl of postwar America to head for the promised land. When he got there, Nuckolls was on the first team, finally designing real H-bombs.

He went to work for another genius and another recent Columbia graduate. Harold Brown had received his Ph.D. in physics there in 1950, at the age of twenty-one, and started work at Livermore shortly thereafter. Now, at the ripe old age of twenty-eight, Brown was running the thermonuclear design division. He became the director of Livermore in 1960, then went on to an illustrious career in Washington. He became President Kennedy's Director of Defense Research and Engineering, President Johnson's Secretary of the Air Force, and President Carter's Secretary of Defense. But in the summer of 1955, Brown needed a helper to run design calculations.

As real computers began to appear, Nuckolls began to develop codes to run on them. He developed an early one-dimensional hydrodynamic code and, in response to Sputnik, an early code to calculate satellite orbits and to predict their decay. Harold Brown was drawn to those with imagination and intellectual curiosity. He asked Nuckolls to critique the Van Dorn cannon. In response to the Soviet launch of Sputnik, a University of California professor named Van Dorn had come up with a bizarre scheme: a nuclear detonation that might drive a thousand-ton payload up a one mile tunnel and out into orbit. It never got off the ground.

Three years after Nuckolls's arrival at Livermore, the U.S. entered into the ill-considered nuclear testing moratorium. Haussmann and others were caught up in the intricate physics of weapons design and their associated engineering problems—how to meet Teller's full commitment to the Navy without further tests—but Nuckolls was thinking about the fundamentals. To him the basic question was how to compress thermonuclear fuel to high densities. When the Soviet Union unilaterally, and by total surprise, broke the moratorium on September 1, 1961, Nuckolls's mind was a fertile source of new ideas.

WHAT SORT OF PERSON IS A BOMB DESIGNER?

At Arzamas-16, in the Soviet Union, and at Los Alamos in the United States, the design of nuclear weapons started out as a top-down process. The leaders were serious, senior people with world-class reputations as physicists. They spent their lives measuring nuclear cross sections or developing equations of state.★ Under their guidance, mathematicians use such equations of state to calculate implosions or use cross sections to calculate the burn efficiency of thermonuclear fuel. Only at the bottom of this pyramid would one find the designers, often designated "engineers," who actually laid out the designs of things to be built based on these scholarly calculations.

The Lawrence Livermore Laboratory was different. When it was founded in 1952, large-scale computers also were being born. These new machines would allow imaginative leaders like Brown and Haussmann to reallocate the skills of the scientific staff. The theoreticians and mathematicians were put to work building computer codes, not bombs. Their mathematical recipes would calculate and graphically display the inner workings of a thermonuclear device. These codes had names like Proteus, Egg, Coronet, and Ghoti. The latter was pronounced "fish," taken from an observation by George Bernard Shaw that the English language can be mystical: *Gh* as in "enough," *o* as in "women," and *ti* as in "nation." The targets of this joke were the computer operators. The codes were user-friendly, at least by the standards of the 1960s. A thermonuclear device designer needed only input geometry and some initial conditions. The codes and the computers would calculate the

---

★ The Boyle's Law some of us learned in high school, relating the pressure and volume of a confined gas, is a simple equation of state.

consequences, the flow of energy or matter over time. In that world, time is measured in nanoseconds, not minutes, since a thermonuclear capsule will complete its implosion and burn within a few hundred nanoseconds. There are a billion nanoseconds in a heartbeat.

Assigning the best physics and mathematics minds to the creation of computer codes led to the creation of a new class of "user" physicist at Livermore. Creative young men and women now could bring their talents to bear on new design concepts without going through all of the equations. Their elders had set them free. These young people with the energy to try new ideas—youngsters lacking the "experience" to "know" that certain things could not be done—set about doing them. They became known as "designers." They had inquiring minds, a creative flair, a good feel for hydrodynamics, and an adequate understanding of the other physical phenomena that take place in a thermonuclear device. They had graduate degrees of some sort in physics, but they were not potential Nobel laureates. They were practical, focused, driven, and creative people.

Rather than calling them "designers," John Nuckolls likes the word "explorers." Like Columbus, these people boarded ships built by others to look for new worlds. The explorers of five centuries ago, Columbus and Magellan, needed to understand how the wind would fill their sails, how moving ballast could destabilize their ships, and how to read instruments like barometers, sextants, compasses, and clocks. But they did not need to know how the clocks and barometers worked. Their job was to find new worlds. To get there, they needed good boats plus vision, courage, and stamina. Those explorers of the sixteenth century boarded their ships (today we would say "entered their data") and set sail across unknown waters ("uncharted cyberspace") to seek new worlds.

In the mid-twentieth century the nuclear designers/explorers could cast their eyes to the far horizons of technology. They could sail wherever they wanted aboard their computational cyberships, asking "what if" in ways the old-time physicists could only dream about. How lucky I was, at the age of twenty-seven, to be given command of one of those cyberships.

COMING INTO SAN FRANCISCO

As 1959 began to unfold, I was still stationed at the Air Force Ballistic Missile Division in Los Angeles. I became an expert on missile reentry vehicles, but with my first trip to Albuquerque, I was becoming our expert on nuclear weapons as well. I was granted the clearances needed to understand the difficult choice that lay ahead for the Minuteman program office and ultimately the U.S. Air Force: Should we design our new systems with tested and known nuclear warheads, or should we gamble on a scale-up of the new technology for twice the yield? The payoff from a doubled yield could be significant. A better assurance that those early, less accurate missiles could destroy their intended targets could in turn cut the size of the needed missile force. That would have a significant impact on the defense budget. There also were tradeoffs in weight, diameter, and center of gravity—all important to the aerodynamicists. There were issues of maintainability, reliability, and cost. And then there was the ultimate bet-your-country issue. Will they work?

It became a fascinating niche. Once I understood the technology, once I had read the top secret files, I would spend much of early 1959 explaining these issues to the program managers, briefing the Office of the Secretary of Defense, and meeting with our British cousins to compare notes. Best of all, my charter as BMD's warhead expert regularly took me to the heart of the American nuclear weapons complex, the laboratories at Livermore, Los Alamos, and Sandia.

My first trip to Livermore occurred on January 27, 1959. Four of us, military officers and our technical advisers, went there to talk about both Titan and Minuteman warheads. The visit lit up my life, for on that day the name "Livermore" took on substance. The easy informality of a university environment, the intellectual firepower seated around the table, the hearty disdain for any claims not based on provable fact, the evident power of the new transistor-driven computers—all combined to make me want more.

Or was it the Irish coffee at the Buena Vista? Nuclear weapons are serious things, but let's be honest, one cannot write about a young lieutenant's first exposure to San Francisco in the fifties and stay serious. Cheap food? The Spaghetti Factory. Nocturnal coffee? The Vesuvio in North Beach, with "beatnik costumes" (shaggy wigs) to help young officers fit in. Music? The Hungry i, the Purple Onion, and best of all, the Red Garter, where young officers en route to the Pacific could stop in, uniforms on, to sing their service hymns along with the banjo band. The night air of San Francisco and the daytime brilliance of Livermore captured my heart, like the song says.

In September the Secretary of Defense made the hard choices in se-

lecting a warhead for Minuteman. These events set my mind to thinking about the future. During one fall visit to Livermore it all came together. I was seated next to Carl Haussmann, the new A Division
leader. I mentioned the end of my obligated tour at BMD; two days
later he was on the phone with a job offer. Not just any job, but a
chance to come do design work with the big boys in Livermore's A Division. I couldn't have been happier. I finished my work at BMD; on
November 15, 1959, I departed Los Angeles and headed north. Starting
serious work at Livermore after the holidays, I was assigned to the
group that had designed the wonder experiment of 1958, the shot that
had given twice the calculated yield for no apparent reason. After a
short course on thermonuclears, learned from written memoranda in
the files, I was put to work.

I was to recalculate the performance of the device using the new
two-dimensional codes and the all-transistorized IBM 709s. It would
be an attempt to replicate that astonishing yield as well as all the other
observables: transit time, radiochemistry, and electromagnetic signals.
Calculating the two-dimensional transfer of energy, neutrons, and hydrodynamic forces from the primary had been barely feasible with the
1958 codes. Now things were different. We could develop a first-class
computational model of what went on in that device during the few
nanoseconds of its active life.

I spent January 1960 collecting data on exactly what was shot and
what was observed. In February, I laid out the geometry in what is
known as a LaGrangian grid, suitable for computation. The process was
done by hand, onto input sheets, which were then transferred to punch
cards. In March the Brits came to town to take a look at my calculations to offer some advice. The two-dimensional radiation and hydrodynamic calculations were to be run on the new IBM 709 machines.
Each run would take a day and a half of computer time, so they were
scheduled for weekends, when shorter production runs were out of the
way. In April the first runs started and I was exposed to the twenty-
four-hour life of a weapons lab. The designers knew they should drop
in every few hours to see if their calculations were running smoothly or
to make repairs if they were not, and so I did. During May we calculated the flow of neutrons out of an exploding primary using a Monte
Carlo type code and megadoses of computer time. I then inserted those
results back into the basic model for another 2-D calculation. It ran for
thirty-eight hours on a 709 available over the weekend at Newport

Beach. By late May we had good solid calculations on how matter and energy emerged from the primary and impacted the secondary. Now it was time for two-dimensional implosion calculations.

June was dedicated to writing the input for the 2-D hydrodynamic code. More hours on the 709, but while it was running I also was becoming a serious player in the warhead design world. In mid-June there was a review of possible new Minuteman warheads. Livermore, Los Alamos, and the British Atomic Weapons Research Establishment people were there. So were the careful thinkers from RAND and a knowledgeable chairman, Mike May, later to become lab director. This review put me on the same podium as my earlier hero, Jack Rosengren. He talked about the Minuteman program; I reported on the efforts to understand the surprise test of 1958. It was a serious, major-league oral exam. I seem to have survived, in the process earning accreditation among my peers.

By the end of June the hydro implosion calculations were complete. It was time to calculate the burn of the thermonuclear fuel. There was a wonderful new machine for this work, IBM's 7090, still another order of magnitude faster than the 709s they replaced. The 7090 would only run for ten to fifteen minutes before crashing, but those were impressive minutes. A month was consumed in getting the burn code to run on the 7090 and then in doing my calculations, but by the end of the month they were done. The calculated results were beginning to match the observed values.

In the fall of 1960, I was a speaker at A Division seminars, at the Naval Ordnance Lab, and at other nuclear weapons forums, explaining my findings. An assistant, Dobree Adams, helped with final computations and wrote up the results. Another assistant helped in the design of spin-offs for other military systems. The calculations were essentially complete; they had taken almost a year of manual inputs, computer time, laborious hand-plotting of results, and recycling to recover from mistakes. Today those calculations would take only a few minutes on the lab's mainframe computer, less than an hour on a stand-alone PC anywhere in the world.

In March 1961, I signed off on a final report. The bottom line: with the correct initial conditions, opacities, cross sections, and mixing, one could correctly reproduce the observables if one used the new, two-dimensional codes to calculate events during those nanoseconds of the device's active life. I gave a full seminar to the laboratory, and a week later my bosses reported a flood of compliments from our peers.

My mind was no longer on 1958, however. In January 1961, as I was assembling a final report on that device, it came to me. Certain things had happened that made it work surprisingly well; they could be used on a whole new family of devices. Those insights led to a flurry of calculations, a few papers, some conversations with John Nuckolls, and a new device name. Let's call it *Oso*. During April the verbs in my memoranda on this concept shifted from "should" to "will" work.

On May 4, 1961, A Division held a seminar on prospects for the high compression of thermonuclear fuel. There were two speakers. One was future director John Nuckolls; his topic was "Wild Ideas." I was the other speaker; my topic was *Oso*. The problem was that any such new design would require nuclear testing. No such testing was allowed in the spring of 1961, nor was there any prospect of tests in the future. Thus there was no prospect of trying any of this out.

As a further distraction, the Kennedy years had begun. In his campaign and in his inaugural remarks a few months before, the new President had offered vistas of a New Frontier. In that spirit, it seemed time to move on to other scientific worlds still open to experiment. I turned to work on magnetohydrodynamic generators (don't ask) at the Avco Everett Research Laboratory near Boston. My family was from New England, so it seemed like a good idea. I wrote up a final report on *Oso*, signed on as a continuing consultant to Livermore, and moved East. What a ridiculous idea that was.

CHAPTER 9

The Resumption of Nuclear Tests

ON AUGUST 31, 1962, two months after my move to Boston, Premier Nikita Khrushchev announced the imminent resumption of atmospheric nuclear testing by the Soviet Union, thus unilaterally ending the three year moratorium on such tests. The U.S. was taken by surprise, as it often was by Soviet perfidy. Our nuclear talent was scattered, our facilities neglected or abandoned. Getting our act together again would entail another exhausting, competitive scramble.

THE SOVIETS SHOOT FIRST

The cavalier attitude of the Soviet Union toward a nuclear "gentlemen's agreement" should have been evident from the very beginning of the moratorium. At midnight on October 31, 1958, all nuclear tests were to end. On the U.S. side, there was one shot still scheduled for October 31. It was a safety test in the best interests of everyone, but during the night the Nevada weather closed in. The test director called off the shot. The deadline came, and nuclear testing was over for the United States.

The Soviets viewed things differently. On October 31, 1958, two of their important missile-launched tests had yet to be conducted. On November 1 and again on November 3 they fired anyway, launching missiles with nuclear warheads aboard from the Kapustin Yar proving ground. The warheads detonated downrange, each with yields of ten kilotons. So much for the gentlemen's agreement on days one and three.

Three years later, when Khrushchev announced his intention to resume nuclear testing, it was hardly a casual decision. On July 10 he summoned the leaders of the Soviet nuclear weapons program to a meeting in the Kremlin's Oval Hall. He told them that nuclear testing would resume on September 1, with an announcement the day before. While that July 10 meeting constituted his final approval, there can be no doubt that weapons design, fabrication, and test planning had been underway for years.

- During the sixty-five days that followed, from September 1 through November 4, the Soviets conducted fifty-nine shots at two test sites (Semipalatinsk and Novya Zemlya) plus four missile launches, with live warheads aboard, from Kapustin Yar.

- During that same period, they conducted their first ever underground test, at Semipalatinsk on October 11.

- They conducted their first missile-borne live firing from Novya Zemlya.

- On October 27 they fired two space shots, timed for virtually simultaneous detonation.

- Their tests included that nation's first in the multimegaton category, including a fifty megaton burst that set a world record.

Even more disconcerting than the intensity of this test series was the radiochemistry of the bomb debris wafting across the Soviet borders and the electromagnetic signals given off by the tests. Atmospheric testing of nuclear devices is not a good idea. The merits of testing anywhere may be debated on policy grounds, but there can be no doubt that any nuclear event, be it test or accident, that releases irradiated materials into the atmosphere is bad for all of us. The venting of small amounts of short-lived isotopes may be harmless compared to the background radiation we all receive from the sun every day; the fallout from a few nuclear tests over a desert may be insignificant when compared to the increase in solar radiation many people accept willingly when they move from a coastal city, such as New York, to a mountain retreat, such as Denver; but such activities do have an impact on our environment. That is why containment vessels are built around nuclear power plants, and why the nuclear states agreed, in 1963, to ban any further testing of nuclear devices in the atmosphere.

However, in terms of the Cold War, atmospheric testing provided an important insight into the weapons programs of the closed Soviet society. We first learned that the Soviets had tested a nuclear device, and we learned what it was made of, solely on the basis of bomb debris analysis; we calculated the efficiency of Joe-1, and we noted its similarity to the first U.S. A-bomb. In the decade that followed, the technology of radiochemistry underwent significant improvement. The U.S. flew diagnostic aircraft, equipped with all sorts of filters and other instruments, around the edges of clouds thrown up by our own tests.

If one knew the makeup of a device beforehand, such radiochemical sampling could be helpful to the designer in diagnosing its operation. But collecting debris from Soviet tests was even more enlightening. Think of it as sampling the smoke from your neighbor's chimney. The amount of unburned carbon coming out, the presence of sap or other materials, tells you whether he's burning firewood or coal, whether he's operating a large foundry or just staying warm, and whether his fire is well-tended or simply part of the interior decor. The U.S. got very good at flying around the edges of the Soviet Union, China, and other emerging nuclear states, sniffing for evidence of a test. The results gave us a clear view of the disasters awaiting if any of us made a mistake.

In addition to radiochemistry, the United States deployed a network of acoustic sensors around the world to listen for the sound waves emanating from huge explosions. The results could confirm the location, date, and approximate yield of any nuclear test. In the 1950s we also deployed electronic sensors to detect the electromagnetic pulse given off by any nuclear event. At first we just looked for the signal, again to determine the date, place, and size of its source. In time, however, we began to look for pulses within that signal. These could evidence two-stage tests, prima facie evidence of an H-bomb. The time interval between these pulses or spikes would indicate the size and nature of the secondary or thermonuclear explosion.

All of this technology was brought to bear when the Soviets announced the resumption of nuclear testing. The collected debris indicated a degree of design sophistication and test readiness far above what had been seen before. The American acoustic sensors confirmed the size and scope of the test series, but the evidence from the radiochemical and electronic sensors was frightening.

As reported by Charles J. V. Murphy in *Life* magazine, there were higher than expected amounts of transuranic elements in the bomb debris. That confirmed a new generation of two-stage, fission-fusion-fission devices. Longer than expected primary-secondary interval times, gleaned from electromagnetic signals, indicated a new approach to secondary ignition. That, in turn, meant an increase in efficiency, more yield per unit weight, and thus a more threatening missile capability.

The Soviets were testing a whole new generation of weapons. And they were investigating the effects of one detonation on another in space; that is, the ability of a defending warhead to disable or destroy an incoming weapon. It was confirmation of a new antiballistic missile system that would soon ring Moscow.

When I talked with the designers of those devices a generation later, the scientists involved denied any long range scheme to defraud the United States. The July 10, 1962, Kremlin meeting was the first confirmation they had of a resumption of atmospheric nuclear testing. On the other hand, they admitted that they were just kids at the time. They did not know what was in the mind of the Politburo or their lab directors when the moratorium was started in 1958. They pointed out that in the Soviet system there were no alternative jobs. People could not leave Arzamas 16 to pursue academic or commercial work. One did what he was told, and those Soviet nuclear scientists were told to keep on designing. Some said that their environment relaxed for a few months after the 1958 moratorium started, but by the beginning of 1960 the pressure was back on. No Soviet laboratories were closed and no test ranges were abandoned after the 1958 halt, as was the case in the U.S. While there is no unequivocal proof, most American experts agree that planning for the Soviet test series of 1962 had to be at least two years in the making.

I was at Livermore on that fateful September 1, 1962, having returned to do some consulting with those still working on *Oso*. Within a day, the Kennedy administration authorized the resumption of underground tests in Nevada. But there was a great deal of hand-wringing in Washington about atmospheric tests. I gave some directions to my former assistants regarding *Oso* and agreed with A Division leader Carl Hauss-mann that I would try to be more helpful if atmospheric testing was resumed.

OPERATION DOMINIC

On October 17 an A Division physicist called to say that atmospheric testing was now being scheduled in the Pacific, though always subject to presidential reconsideration. On November 6, 1961, Edward Teller called the Avco-Everett Research lab director, Arthur Kantrowitz, to urge my release. The latter had been a Teller graduate student, and that call did it. In November, I returned to Livermore to assume responsibility for the design of an *Oso* device for testing in the Pacific during the following summer as part of Operation Dominic.

Oso was not a major program, and in the grand sweep of nuclear history, my contributions were not all that significant. The cybership *Oso* sailed too close to the black holes of uncertainty ever to be seen again, although some of the ideas involved came to fruition in other warhead designs a few years later. I relate here the events of 1961–62 only to give the reader a view of the incredible Livermore system.

Designing an item for test is quite different from doing paper studies. At an early meeting, I discovered that Teller had thought about my *Oso* approach earlier but couldn't figure out how to make it work; how nice. Several younger physicists were returned to my team, but far more impressive was the enthusiastic support I received from the older scientists designated to serve under my direction.

George Maenchen, an expert on one of the hydrodynamic codes, became my assistant designer. Victor Karpenko, a fabulously talented engineer, was to build this device. Dick Adelmann was to make all the test arrangements, tend to logistics, and pay the bills. I was twenty-eight, and all of these gentlemen were substantially older, yet they followed me through the labyrinth of a nuclear design with an enthusiasm that characterized the glories of Livermore.

Computer time was indispensable to good design. My souvenirs of that spring show that John Nuckolls and I gobbled up almost all the available time. Detailed calculation of *Oso* with better tools showed that it would not work as planned. New IBM machines were being installed as we labored, meaning cables and men in suits everywhere.

On March 23, John Kennedy showed up. He understood the difficulties we faced and came to Berkeley to express his support. He and his key defense advisers first met with the leadership of the Los Alamos, Livermore, and Berkeley laboratories to exchange views on the importance of the upcoming U.S. tests. Then he met with a roomful of designers, engineers, and technicians, the men and women who were working around the clock for six months and who now had to move out to tropical, remote stations to carry out the tests. He gave a pep talk that still rings in the ears of those who were there. He pledged to take the political heat. Our obligation was to deliver the technology. Finally there was his appearance at UC stadium, where 80,000 people crowded the field, filled every seat, and stood in every aisle to glimpse the Kennedy magic. And he delivered. The people there, and all who heard him on radio and TV, felt that he was talking to them, about their country and the perils it faced.

Meanwhile, back at the lab, the days grew longer and the time remaining until the shot would take place grew shorter. By May the pressure was on to tell the logisticians the dimensions of my device so they could plan its carriage to target. We drove the engineers to the brink of insanity, partly by designing things that couldn't be built—foam supports with zero density or plating one molecule thick—and by refusing to commit to a design freeze.

On May 24 there was a major *Oso* design review in the conference center. I had charts and wrote all over three panels of blackboard. My plans seemed to draw enthusiastic support, so when the meeting was over, engineer Karpenko asked if this was what I wanted built. I said, "Sure," but in my heart I meant no. I planned to return to my office and the computers to tweak the design one more time. No such luck. Karpenko pulled out a pocket camera, photographed every chart and chalk mark, and thanked me profusely. We had just executed a design freeze.

The action shifted to Oak Ridge, where components were being conjured by Merlins of the machine shops. No design was too complicated, no tolerance too tight, no deadline too short for those artists. Whatever the designer wanted, he got, but in the process the glories of the AEC system—absolute control by and accountability of the designer—began to get scary. I was out there all alone.

I traveled to Oak Ridge to inspect some parts, returned to Livermore to give some talks about the shot, then returned to Oak Ridge for assembly of the secondary components. At first they just looked like so many pieces of dark brown metal, but Yakov Zeldovich, an elder of the second Soviet nuclear estate, knew better. When he saw similar pieces of uranium and plutonium, he could not help but feel that a multitude of human lives had been compressed into each gram: those of the prisoners who worked the mines, the technicians who inhaled the dust, and then the potential victims, if any of that metal ever went critical.

My next stop was Travis Air Force Base, to watch the primary being mated to the main device. Then off to Hawaii. At the Barber's Point airfield on Oahu, I watched *Oso* being unloaded from its C-124 and inserted into the bomb bay of a B-52. Then I was off to Hickham Field and the flight to Christmas Island, base camp for the Dominic test series of 1962.

That spot was hardly a resort. It is not the Christmas Island located in the Indian Ocean with an extinct volcano and some residents, but an atoll, also known as Kiritimati, located in the Gilbert Islands, on the equator. The Tarawa battleground of World War II fame is the best known of the Gilberts. The United States had abandoned its Pacific test facilities as the moratorium wore on, but our British friends were less foolish, letting us make use of their outpost, inhospitable as it was. (In fact, Christmas Island, or Kiritimati, was the base camp, home for diagnostics, not the test site itself. The devices were dropped from aircraft a suitable distance away.) The Brits used Kiritimati to test their first H-bombs in 1957. The island is seventeen miles long and fourteen feet high. Everyone lived and ate in tents. There was no air-conditioning other than in the instrumentation trailers. Swimming was only possible in the morning, when the troops would throw grenades inside the chain-link underwater fence, killing off any sharks that had snuck in during the night. Entertainment was movies, the mess hall, and a bar known as the Snake Pit. There was little consumption of alcohol except in postshot celebration or remorse. I recall seeing no women on the island.

Nuclear tests are best conducted at dawn. This allows good photographic coverage of the expanding fireball, important to the diagnostics. A few moments later the skies start to lighten, allowing the diagnostic airplanes to see the cloud they are supposed to sample. We tend to get carried away by the physics, but the scope of the entire test operation was staggering. Just one small component of the test task force was Patrol Squadron 872. That Navy organization, which flew P-3s to collect radiochemical samples, consisted of over fifty officers and 250 enlisted men who operated ten aircraft out of Barber's Point in Hawaii for the entire summer.

I awoke early on the morning of the shot, in part out of nervousness and in part because of the droning of the countdown director, "Mahatma," running through his checklist over the loudspeakers. At 6:00 A.M., I climbed up "the hill," a sandpile a few feet high, to get my coffee and doughnuts, and to watch. The B-52 started practice runs at 5:30 A.M. The drop took place at 6:30 A.M. at a spot seventeen miles away. It took sixty-six seconds from drop to bang, but it seemed like there was time to review the whole program, if not my whole life, as those seconds dragged by. They felt like sixty-six years. Then the unforgettable. Even though we were wearing black goggles, and even though the yield was much lower than expected, the sky was filled with light. When all seemed dark, we removed those goggles, only to be blinded all over again. The ball of fire was white, then took on incredible colors—yellows and purples fascinating the mind's eye.

For that shot, and for others that week, the loudspeaker tried to warn of the approaching shock wave, but the greenhorns always forget about it. When the blast wave arrived, two minutes after the flash, coffee flew everywhere. Several fellows were knocked over. Emotionally, I was too, for there's nothing in the human experience that in any way relates to the detonation of a nuclear device on the distant horizon, no matter how "small" or how far away. I cannot image what it would be like to be any closer.

There's the light, a brightness that simply does not stop. People talk about a flash, but a thermonuclear detonation is not a flashbulb event. The sun starts to burn on earth; darkness seems never to return. There are the colors—purples and other hallucinogenic hues that confirm Shakespeare's observation about the next world: "What dreams may come when we have shuffled off this mortal coil must give us pause." There's the heat. It makes no sense to the brain, because the explosion being observed is almost over the horizon, as far away as Baltimore is from Washington. Yet the first flash gives way to an oppressive, lingering heat whose persistence becomes unnerving. And then there's the all-enveloping roar of the savage beast unleashed. As noted earlier, it takes a while, several minutes, for sound waves to get from detonation point to observer, assuming that observer is a lucky, peacetime scientist. So much else happened that the senses are numb. The first shock wave is not a crack or a pop, as one hears from a gun fired far away. It is the opening of a roar encompassing the senses, seeming to continue forever. I saw only a few such events, none of them an act of war. The rest of you have no idea how lucky you are to have missed this experience in the real world.

LIVERMORE IN THE REARVIEW MIRROR

The decision by the Livermore Laboratory's founders to invest their money in computers and to invest the talents of their brightest physicists and mathematicians in code development gave Livermore its distinctive character from the day the lab was born. The 1950s generation there became the designers of most warheads for the strategic weapon systems fielded in the 1960s. Those, in turn, changed the map of American deterrence.

They also drew the attention of the Chinese intelligence services. The secrets apparently stolen from Los Alamos by Chinese agents during the 1990s were, for the most part, not drawings—they were computer codes, the software that would allow Chinese cyberskippers to explore the far reaches of thermonuclear technology on their own.

The thermonuclear division at Livermore was once led by Harold Brown, then Carl Haussmann, and then by Jack Rosengren. John Nuckolls and I worked there. I was only a rookie in that lineup, but that group constitutes an interesting sample. We did our best creative work in our late twenties and early thirties. Some of us went on to play important management roles at the laboratory. In time, Brown and Nuckolls became directors, Haussmann and Rosengren associate directors. Some went on to important national security jobs in Washington. Brown and I served as Secretaries of the Air Force. Brown became a Secretary of Defense; I became a Special Assistant to a President. Rosengren made good on Teller's IOU to the Navy. By the summer of 1962 he had brought a new sense of order to the Polaris warhead program. Rosengren went on to become the Scientific Deputy Director of the Defense Nuclear Agency. Nuckolls led the way in the use of lasers, rather than A-bombs, to implode small pellets of thermonuclear fuel.

The National Ignition Facility now under construction at Livermore will focus 192 laser beams, 500 square feet of laser power, with a brief power level of a billion megawatts, on a capsule of thermonuclear fuel. When the National Ignition Facility starts operation, Nuckolls's concepts will have replaced A-bomb primaries with 192 lasers.

Less than half of these five designers ever earned a Ph.D. in physics or any other discipline. Nuckolls, Haussmann, and I went to graduate school and acquired master's degrees along the way, but we were too impatient to settle into the academic system.

We were fortunate that other more learned men and women gave us the ships to sail through cyberspace. It was a marvelous division of labor. We were lucky to be able to undo the damage done by the wise men, those visually challenged intelligence counselors, dreamy Nobel laureates, Soviet-trusting cabinet officials, and rigid bureaucrats. Those who led the United States into the sixties and the unpoliced moratorium should have been as suspicious of their Soviet competitors as we foot soldiers were, but that was not always the case.

When atmospheric testing ended in 1963, the U.S. once again had recovered. The world was safer from the airborne junk once deposited on them, but one more window into the closed Soviet society slammed shut. We would never again be able to glimpse the inner working of a Soviet nuclear weapon.

While I have many memories of those years, one week is indelibly etched into my mind. It began on that hot evening in June 1962 when I pulled into an earth-berm building on a remote corner of Travis Air Force Base in California. It was there that the *Oso* components were assembled and the final product was loaded onto a C-124, for shipment to Hawaii and mating with its B-52 host. I last saw *Oso* seventeen miles off Christmas Island in the Pacific. It disappeared in a flash, then a psychedelic sphere of many colors, that I will never forget. Twenty-eight-year-old kids do not get to do that very often.

CHAPTER 10

Getting Started in Vietnam

IN THE SIXTIES, while some of my generation were forging the weapons of nuclear war, others were paying a terrible price for our not using them. The choices were not easy. Throughout the Cold War a quick shot of nuclear firepower, an armed sortie that might antagonize another nuclear power, or a violation of long-honored diplomatic principles was often the proposed cure for a geopolitical headache somewhere in the third world. Cooler heads always prevailed, but nowhere was the price of forbearance more painful than on the peninsula hanging down from the southern edge of China.

A SHORT HISTORY OF VIETNAM

As Generals Grant and Lee were settling American accounts at Appomattox a century and a half ago, French explorers were sailing into the harbors of then-independent Vietnam. By 1883 the French bombarded enough ports and overran enough provincial capitals to declare the Union of Indochina a colony. That arrangement continued, without the consent of the governed, until World War II, when Japan occupied French Indochina. Ho Chi Minh was a leader in the resistance at the time. When the war ended, the Chinese occupied the northern part of the country and the Brits the south, until the French could reassert colonial control.

The U.S. government supported French claims to the repossession of postwar Vietnam for reasons having nothing to do with that colony's best interests and everything to do with the precarious condition of postwar France. The westward expansion of the Soviet empire was devouring Hungary, Czechoslovakia, and the eastern part of Germany. The U.S. wished to stop that red tide before it reached the English Channel. The "loss" of Vietnam, or so the American government thought, would do serious damage to the prestige of noncommunist French leaders in Paris. They lost it anyway. In 1945, Ho Chi Minh declared Vietnam to be an independent nation, thus beginning a decade of insurrections and jungle warfare that culminated at a remote French fort in the northeast corner of that land.

The siege of Dien Bien Phu, in the spring of 1954, was reported extensively in the U.S. press. As a college student, I wondered what it must be like to be surrounded and cut off, deep in the jungle, by a native force determined to kill you. In one of those strange twists of history, it was American artillery that crushed the French defenders. The 155 millimeter howitzers bombarding the fort into submission were given to the Vietminh by their Chinese allies. Those weapons had been captured, in turn, from the Americans in Korea as they retreated from the surprise Chinese onslaught three years before.

The French asked the Eisenhower administration for help in the defense of the Dien Bien Phu, and some American officials* wanted to play the nuclear card. It was the opening deal in a dangerous game, as Vietnam could have become a confrontation between four nuclear powers: France, China, the U.S., and the USSR. As the fifties gave way to the sixties and seventies, any of a dozen incidents might have esca-

---

* By some accounts, Secretary of State John Foster Dulles advocated the release of two nuclear weapons to the French for their use in defense of the fort. Others attribute an advocacy of direct use to members of the Joint Chiefs of Staff. There is no evidence that such proposals received a serious hearing at the White House.

lated out of control. A noncombatant freighter, for instance, flying the colors of an opposing nuclear superpower, could have hit a mine.

That was a distinct possibility in May 1972 when Nixon finally initiated the mining of Haiphong harbor. Soviet and Chinese freighters regularly plied those waters as they brought war supplies into North Vietnam. Or the capture of a reconnaissance vehicle might have set things off. The North Korean capture of the USS Pueblo during the Tet offensive of January 1968 could have done it. That U.S. intelligence ship was seized *in* international waters and escorted into a North Korean port. The U.S. mobilized reserves; the crew was held captive for eleven months; a serious confrontation was only narrowly avoided. In reacting to such an event, an inexperienced watch officer might have selected the wrong initial response. Escalation would have started. As it was, the wheels of fate ground more slowly in Vietnam.

The U.S. did reinforce Dien Bien Phu with C-119 transport aircraft, mechanics, and crews. James McGovern and Wallace Buford, piloting aircraft into and out of that enclave, were the first Americans killed in Vietnamese combat. Other aircraft flew supply missions into Da Nang and Hanoi, and when the siege of Dien Bien Phu was over, American C-124s evacuated wounded French troops to the United States for treatment. Accepting defeat, the French agreed to a partition of Indochina. On October 9, 1954, they abandoned Vietnam north of the 17th parallel. In the ensuing bloodbath—a replay of communist takeovers throughout the twentieth century—thousands of anticommunists in the North were executed; millions of refugees fled to the South.

Fearing a domino effect in southeast Asia, the U.S. picked up the fallen French banner. A few military advisers were sent to assist the government of South Vietnam, then hundreds, then a thousand. By the end of 1962 there were 11,300 U.S. military personnel in Vietnam. Some of my Air Force contemporaries were there, flying B-26s in support of the South Vietnamese ground forces. Nominally, the Americans were "instructors." Before taking off, the U.S. pilot and his navigator would pick up a third crew member—any South Vietnamese airman would do—as the nominal "trainee." His job was to die with his American hosts, if shot down, so as to preserve the fiction of the Americans being only "advisers."

Lyndon Johnson assumed the U.S. presidency on November 22, 1963, after the assassination of John Kennedy. The growing threat to South Vietnam was high on his list of problems. By May 1964 the CIA was predicting the imminent collapse of that nation. Johnson faced several questions. Should he commit major U.S. forces to that fight after his hoped-for reelection in November 1964? How should he conduct himself during the summer of 1964, before that election, to appear firm but not warlike? How could he gain the support of the American people for a further involvement in Vietnam?

Some generals and conservative politicians were not helpful. General Curtis LeMay's proposed solution was to "tell them [the North Vietnamese] that they've got to draw in their horns and stop their aggression, or we're going to bomb them back into the Stone Age." Ronald Reagan, at the time a Hollywood personality campaigning for Barry Goldwater, said, "It's silly to talk about how many years we will have to spend in the jungles of Vietnam when we could pave the whole country and put parking stripes on it and still be home by Christmas." Senator Goldwater put it even more bluntly: "I could have ended the war in a month. I could have made North Vietnam look like a mud puddle."

As it was, President Johnson chose delay and obfuscation, a deviousness that would be his undoing, but in the process he and his successor, Richard Nixon, declined the temptations of a quick nuclear fix or a risky confrontation with a nuclear superpower. If there was one individual designated to pay the price of that forbearance, it was Jim Stockdale.

THE GUNS OF AUGUST—ONCE MORE

James Stockdale was an Annapolis midshipman, graduating in 1946. He spent three years at sea on a destroyer, then entered flight training at Pensacola. He earned his wings in 1950, became a test pilot in 1953, went to survival school in the mountains above San Diego, then went back to sea as a naval aviator. In February 1964 he assumed command of Carrier Air Group 16, a group of several hundred men and seventy-five aircraft with a variety of missions—air superiority, ground attack, and reconnaissance among them. CAG-16 was assigned to the aircraft carrier *Oriskany*. In April 1964, Stockdale, the *Oriskany*, and CAG-16 headed off to the South China Sea.

By the summer of 1964 the CIA could hear a death rattle in the throat of South Vietnam. There were fundamental problems in the countryside; one proposed solution was to carry the war into the North. Since 1961 the CIA had been sending armed patrol boats north of the 17th parallel to insert agents and to conduct psychological warfare. A full-scale invasion was out of the question, but attacks on coastal radars, gun emplacements, and the interdiction of enemy movements at sea all seemed feasible. U.S. Army Special Forces, U.S. Navy SEALs, and the South Vietnamese Coastal Security Service would do the work.

In January 1964, in support of these operations, the CIA implemented OP 34A, a scheme to run high-speed gunships into the harbors of North Vietnam. These 75-ton PTF (Patrol Torpedo Fast) boats were known as "Nasties," and they earned that name. Eighty feet long, powered by two British-built Napier Deltic diesel engines delivering 3,100 horsepower each, the mahogany-hulled boats were capable of making 43 knots during their run-in to their targets. They mounted a potpourri of weapons: a 40mm cannon (range three miles), an 81mm mortar, two 20mm cannon, a .50 caliber machine gun, and various small arms. The boats were built in Norway and were usually skippered by Norwegian mercenaries. The crews were nominally South Vietnamese, but naval officers on duty at the time had no doubt that U.S. SEALs were often aboard.

The Nasties used in OP 34A were based near Da Nang. Typically, they would leave port in the late afternoon, "plaster their targets" around midnight, then return to port at dawn. During the last week of July 1964 crew members aboard the U.S. destroyer *Maddox* remember seeing two Nasties pass by, rooster tails high, as they raced for home. They had exchanged fire with the shore batteries at Hon Me, a fortified island near the North Vietnamese coast, taking casualties aboard their own ships in the process. OP 34A was not some rogue operation. The leaked *Pentagon Papers* make it clear that these patrols were presidentially approved and that the CIA kept both Pentagon and White House fully apprised.

By the end of July 1964 the North Vietnamese were organizing to deal with the Nasties. They improved their warning and shore defenses, and they organized a counterforce of high speed (45 to 50 knot) Russian-built torpedo boats (P-4s) and slower Chinese-built smallboys, known as Swatows. The latter could not keep up with the PTs, nor were they heavily armed, but they were good communication platforms and support ships. They provided the radio link back to their primary base at Port Wallut, an inlet north of the harbor at Haiphong.

Into this seaborne stew the U.S. Navy was directed to insert regular U.S. destroyer sorties. Known as DeSoto patrols, these ships were to stay in international waters, as defined by the United States,★ but they

---

★ Three miles offshore, rather than the more commonly accepted twelve miles.

were to make their presence felt up and down the coast of North Vietnam; that is, in the Gulf of Tonkin. It would be logical for the North Vietnamese to assume the DeSoto patrols were operating in support of the Nasties, but in fact the latter were operated by the CIA under the control of MACV, the Military Assistance Command Vietnam. The U.S. Navy controlled the destroyers, with little communication between the two organizations.

On the morning of August 2 a flotilla of six North Vietnamese boats was seen proceeding down the coast in the direction of the *Maddox*. The latter was operating not far off Hon Me Island. This train of three PT boats, two Swatows, and a small tanker disappeared behind Hon Me; the PTs then reemerged, in broad daylight, to begin their run at the *Maddox*. At the time, Commander Stockdale, by then flying off the USS *Ticonderoga*, was already in the air. His four F-8 Crusaders were engaged in training maneuvers when they were told to switch to strike control and proceed 300 miles north in search of the *Maddox* and its attackers. When they arrived at the scene, they found three North Vietnamese boats, in formation abreast, making 45 to 50 knots in pursuit of the *Maddox*. The latter was making 30 to 32 knots, forcing the PTs into a tail chase that would give *Maddox* the most time for its longer-range guns to bear on the attackers.

Stockdale's Crusaders dove on the PTs from 37,000 feet. As they passed through 10,000 feet, they saw all three boats launch two torpedoes each. None of the six tin fish seemed to be steering a steady course, so they did not pose much of a threat to the *Maddox*. Her skipper, John Herrick, turned right to further avoid the torpedoes and to head toward the *Ticonderoga*. Meanwhile, the Crusaders attacked the PTs with Zuni rockets and 23mm cannon fire, severely damaging and inflicting casualties on all three. The engagement ended by mid-afternoon.

There was no doubt that a U.S. ship had been attacked in international waters by North Vietnamese vessels. On the other hand, it would have been logical for the North Vietnamese to view the Nasties—boats that had been shooting up their home port facilities—and the *Maddox* as part of the same task force.

In light of the attack on the *Maddox*, another destroyer, the *Turner Joy*, was ordered into the Gulf of Tonkin to join the patrol. The aircraft carrier *Constellation*, along with its supporting battle group, was directed toward the gulf as well, to reinforce the *Ticonderoga*.

THE EVENTS OF AUGUST 4, 1964

The U.S. government was now suspicious of any North Vietnamese naval activity. Or was it looking for an excuse? On August 4 we intercepted a message from the North Vietnamese at Port Wallut. It directed another attack by North Vietnamese patrol boats. But on what? Where? The U.S. assumed the objective was a return engagement with the *Maddox*. But was it? Or was their target to be the fleet of Nasties operating in that same area?

Word was flashed to the *Ticonderoga*, then to Stockdale. As he readied for takeoff, his wingman developed engine trouble, so Stockdale requested permission to go it alone. Flying alone, at night, is contrary to Navy regulations, but he was the best. The skipper, Captain Hutch Cooper, approved the launch, and Stockdale was off into the night. He was to look for intruders. He heard the *Maddox* and *Turner Joy* exchange radio messages about targets in the water north of them. Within minutes Stockdale was there. Even though it was the dead of night, the wakes of those two destroyers "stood out like spotlights," as Stockdale puts it now.

The entire Gulf of Tonkin was awash in bioluminescence during that hot summer month. Storms or schools of fish will make tropical water sparkle, but on the night of August 4 the wakes of the destroyers were visible from miles away. When Stockdale arrived over those ships, he could read the notes on his knee pad by the reflected light of those wakes. As he closed on the *Maddox* and *Turner Joy*, he could see they were firing. But at what? He dropped down to skim the waves at an altitude of a few hundred feet, but he saw nothing. The five-inch shells from the destroyers were sending up water spouts all around him. From one close call he got salt spray on his windshield, but there were no attacking PTs. Their wakes would have lit up the gulf like beacons, but aside from the U.S. destroyers, the sea was dark. Stockdale crossed back and forth, all around the destroyers, to make sure. He did not want to leave the scene any sooner than absolutely necessary, for if the destroyers were under attack, it was up to him, and him alone, to protect them. If they were not under attack, he was the only eyewitness to that fact. And that was the fact. No North Vietnamese PT boats attacked the *Maddox* or the *Turner Joy* on the night of August 4.

Now dangerously short of fuel, Stockdale nursed his F-8 back to the *Ticonderoga*. The skipper offered to send up a refueling aircraft. "Thanks, no," was the reply. "I don't have enough fuel even for that. I'll just do it right the first time."

The landing signal officer who would orchestrate the landing from on deck was an old friend and flying chum, Tim Hubbard. "You're looking good, Skipper," he said. "Keep coming down and catch that wire."

Stockdale saw the meatball★ and caught the only hook that stood between him and the icy deep. Five minutes later he was in the ready room, warm and dry, the butt of laughter by his buddies. He had been on a flight to nowhere. Stockdale, through the *Ticonderoga's* skipper, sent an "All is Quiet" message to the National Military Command Center in Washington, then turned in for a good night's sleep. But not for long.

A PREORDAINED RESPONSE

At 9:20 A.M., Washington time, on August 4—9:20 P.M. aboard the *Ticonderoga*, just as Stockdale was taking off on his first search for intruders—the White House situation room learned that North Vietnam had authorized a raid of some sort, on something, by its Swatow and PT boats. The President talked to his Secretary of Defense on the secure phone, asking McNamara how long it would take to retaliate if such a raid had in fact occurred. The Joint Chiefs responded that aircraft from the *Ticonderoga* and *Constellation* could strike targets in North Vietnam by 6:00 P.M. that evening, Washington time. Soon afterward, the White House press office notified the TV networks of a pending presidential statement, to be released in time for their 7:00 P.M. news shows. This advisory was issued even though there had been no attacks on the *Maddox* or *Turner Joy*, nor had any retaliatory raid been approved.

Later that night, Stockdale was put in charge of planning and leading one retaliatory strike, by aircraft from the *Ticonderoga*, against the POL facilities at Vinh. That city of 44,000, on the coast of North Vietnam, was home to about one-third of North Vietnam's total inventory of petroleum supplies. The raid was beautifully planned, utilizing sixteen aircraft armed with bombs, rockets, and cannon. None of the aircraft were armed with defensive munitions with which to fend off MiG

★ The orange ball that turns red or green if the approaching pilot is too low or high.

interceptors, as Stockdale was counting on surprise to get his men in and out safely. "This raid is a replay of Pearl Harbor," he told his pilots. So it came as a great shock as they left their ready room to be told that a half hour before, in Washington, President Johnson had told the public of the raids still being planned.

The logistics of mounting the proposed strikes delayed their execution until well past the TV deadlines back home. Johnson grew anxious as 7:00 P.M. came and went. When he missed the 11:00 P.M. news, also the deadline for the major East Coast newspapers, he vented his anger to McNamara: "Bob, I'm exposed here! I've got to make my speech right now." At 11:36 P.M., East Coast time, President Johnson took to the air. He announced the strikes still in the planning process aboard the *Ticonderoga* and another carrier, the *Constellation*, now also at the mouth of the Gulf of Tonkin. The President had blown Stockdale's element of surprise. His aircraft were headed into North Vietnam with no defensive armaments of any kind.

The strike on Vinh was executed with only ninety seconds spent over the target. A similar raid, from the *Constellation*, bombarded naval facilities at Ben Thuy, Quang Khe, Hon Me, and Hon Gai. There was mayhem below, but the U.S. also suffered casualties in the skies. Lieutenant Richard C. Sather, aboard an A-1 dive bomber, was killed by antiaircraft fire. Lieutenant Everett Alvarez, flying an A-4 Skyhawk, was shot down but survived. He became the first airborne POW in the war against North Vietnam, spending eight and a half dreadful years in captivity.

It is hard to tell whether President Johnson's premature announcement tipped off the antiaircraft gunners along the coast of North Vietnam, but it is clear that Johnson attached a higher priority to his own image and poll ratings than he did to the safety of his warriors overseas. And there was no doubt in Jim Stockdale's mind, as he looked down at the huge fireballs where the coastal town of Vinh once stood, that the U.S. involvement in Vietnam was irretrievably on.

THE GULF OF TONKIN RESOLUTION

To make the new war legal, a Congressional resolution was needed. A preliminary draft, giving President Johnson war powers, had been in the works since May 1964, awaiting only the right crisis to give it life. By the time Stockdale was having supper aboard the *Ticonderoga* on the evening of August 4, the Gulf of Tonkin Resolution was on the floor of the House of Representatives, introduced by the Chairman of the House Committee on Foreign Relations with the notation that the President wanted congressional action that same day. Pausing only to hear assurances from Secretary of State Rusk, Secretary of Defense McNamara, and JCS Chairman Wheeler that U.S. ships really had been attacked, the House passed the resolution without a dissenting vote on August 6. It was approved by the U.S. Senate with only two dissenting votes and no debate the following day, August 7. The die was cast.

In November 1964, Lyndon Johnson was elected in his own right to the presidency of the United States. He won in a landslide. At the end of the year, Johnson had the political power and the legal authority to deal with Vietnam as he saw fit.

WITH THE ELECTION OVER, INTO THE QUAGMIRE

On March 8, 1965, 3,500 U.S. Marines waded ashore at Da Nang, South Vietnam. On June 18 the war turned to heavy bombardment with the introduction of B-52s. For the first time, SAC released its nuclear-capable aircraft for other than nuclear operations, even though sortie planning remained a SAC responsibility in Omaha. The B-52s made themselves felt that day with the first of many raids on Viet Cong positions in the south.

On November 14 the first bloody set-piece battle between the opposing armies of the United States and North Vietnam took place in the Ia Drang Valley, with 234 Americans killed, and North Vietnamese casualties probably ten times that. By the end of the year the American public was growing concerned; antiwar rhetoric and demonstrations were starting. There ensued a decade of jungle warfare and aerial bombardment. None of it was conclusive; much was mismanaged. Yet as the American public grew weary of it all, the nuclear option lay quietly on the table.

Some say that a string of Atomic Demolition Munitions were set for deployment along the Chinese-Vietnamese border. Others observed that one nuke, fired from a Polaris boat in the Pacific to impact on Hanoi, would have killed Ho Chi Minh, taken out the entire North Vietnamese government, and paralyzed the logistic support for Viet Cong in the jungle. Either would have sent an unmistakable message to the leaders of the Soviet empire: "We are serious." But it never happened;

the war ground on, consuming the lives of a dozen young Americans every day for ten dreary years.

In the year that followed the events in the Gulf of Tonkin, Stockdale continued to lead his Carrier Air Group off the *Oriskany* into battle over North and South Vietnam. The Navy's responsibilities included Route Package Six, bounded on the north by a thirty-mile buffer, a "no-fly zone" along the Red Chinese border. Giving opposing forces such a sanctuary made no sense to the young American pilots risking their lives every day, but it seemed reasonable to the older officers. They remembered China's 1950 response when U.S. troops approached their border with North Korea. And it made eminent sense to our national leaders, sorting through the evidence of the first Chinese nuclear test during the previous October.

On September 9, 1965, Jim Stockdale's luck ran out. After a lengthy sortie along the coast, looking for targets near Vinh and Tinh Gia, Stockdale found a railroad train worthy of his attention. He and his wingman rolled in for a low level attack when it happened. A 57mm antiaircraft artillery hammered the right side of his plane. With less than 2,000 feet of altitude, Stockdale had only a moment to get out. He did, ejecting and parachuting into eight years of captivity.

The horrors of those years defy the imagination, but through all the rope tortures, beatings, and regular rebreaking of his bones, Stockdale kept his terrible secret: he was the officer who told the American authorities in Washington there had been no attack on the *Maddox* and *Turner Joy*. The North Vietnamese knew there had been no such attack, but right here, in the palms of their hands, was the American who could confirm it. A Stockdale "confession" would have been of immense propaganda value to his captors, but they did not know that Stockdale knew, and he was not about to tell them. For eight long years he kept them in the dark while he lived there himself, with the rats and the filth, in his solitary cell.

LINEBACKER II ENDS IT

Every POW then resident at the Hanoi Hilton now agrees that the morale of the prisoners went through the roof, that their captors turned from surly inquisitors to polite guards, when the B-52s returned to Hanoi. It happened in the middle of December 1972 when President Nixon, wearying of peace negotiations going nowhere, authorized a massive air assault on the Hanoi area. The operation was known as Linebacker II. It was unprecedented in the history of Vietnam; there had been nothing like it since World War II. It was the attack from the air that many military officers had urged years before.

The attacks started on December 18, when 129 B-52s struck Hanoi, accompanied by a hundred tactical aircraft to suppress air defenses, dispense chaff to confuse enemy radar, and provide the essential combat air patrol protection from defending MiGs. The raids continued nightly, with the North Vietnamese opposition wilting in the face of this onslaught.* On December 29 the North signaled its interest in reopening and concluding negotiations in Paris. That was the end of Linebacker II. On January 27 the Paris Peace Accords were signed. Within sixty days 591 American POWs were repatriated to U.S. soil.

Linebacker II was key to ending the war in Vietnam, but it also gave several of us assurances that SAC's nuclear war plans would work if ever needed. A total of 729 B-52 sorties were flown during Linebacker II, with only fifteen aircraft lost, for an attrition rate of about 2 percent. This, despite the fact that the defenders knew exactly when the raids could be expected, from which direction, and in what numbers. They gained this information from Soviet trawlers† stationed off Guam, watching and listening as the B-52s took off. The airmen were furious at the advantage such warning gave the defenders of Hanoi; they wanted to blow those ships out of the water. Cooler heads in Washington, heeding the doctrine of freedom of the seas—secured at great cost by earlier generations—forbade any such action. The sanctity of those trawlers was one of the boundary conditions of the Cold War; it cost real lives in the skies over Hanoi.

COMING HOME

Within two weeks of the Paris Peace Accords, Jim Stockdale was given a clean set of clothes, loaded aboard a bus outside the Hoa Lo prison's

---

* Although "downtown" Hanoi was off limits, as were the levees and much of the civilian infrastructure.

† Actually, Soviet intelligence ships, outfitted with the best in communications electronics as well as fishing nets. They invariably showed up at the scene of every coastal and seaborne activity of interest to the Soviets, be it carrier takeoffs, missile launches, B-52 operations, or underwater searches.

green gate, and driven to the rubble-strewn Gia Lam airstrip. A U.S. Air Force C-141 took him to the Philippines, where his medical recovery began. On February 15 he flew on to Honolulu, then home to San Diego to join his wife Sybil. He recovered reasonably well from his leg and back fractures and lives today in the naval enclave at Coronado in southern California.

On January 17, 1994, Stockdale, his wife, and a few friends returned to Hanoi. He had not seen the place since his 1973 bus trip out. His wife Sybil had never been there. This opportunity to visit came twenty-one years after his earlier departure, as the government of Vietnam negotiated to reopen trade relations with the United States. They opened the door, if they did not roll out the red carpet, to a group of us old military hands whose good words might sway the U.S. Congress in the matter of trade.★

Our group took a modest, shallow-draft boat from Hong Kong to Haiphong. That small harbor had once been the focus of noisy U.S. political debate, then major aerial attacks as it was mined to impede resupply by the Soviet war machine. It was a designated ground zero, had we ever gone to the nuclear option. Now, in 1994, Haiphong had returned to the status of a dowdy third-world backwater, a setting more suitable for a short story by O. Henry than a novel by Tom Clancy.

We were greeted by a dockside banner. Jim Stockdale laughed, but Sybil nearly came apart. WELCOME TO VIETNAM, it said in well-lettered English. The kids holding the sign and the people dockside were curious, friendly, and modestly pro-American. At least they wanted us and our businesses to return under the right conditions. We boarded an antique bus for the forty mile but three hour trip up the Red River to Hanoi. The roads were virtually impassable due to a combination of intense traffic, minimum maintenance, and the suitability of the flat, warm roadbed as a site for drying freshly harvested crops. Upon arrival in Hanoi, we visited the city's central Ho Tay Lake, where the tail section of a downed B-52 still protrudes above the water. The wreckage, put there by the victors after the war, is a historical monument. Then we moved on to the Hoa Lo prison.

Stockdale surveyed the scene but was refused admission by nervous Vietnamese guards. He pointed out a few landmarks to his wife, made a few comments to the gathered Vietnamese reporters, then led a tour

---

★ They did. The U.S. reestablished trade relations with Vietnam in February 1994.

around the periphery of the prison. With the end of that stroll, under a red umbrella, Jim and Sybil Stockdale linked arms, turned, and walked away. The Stockdales could put that war behind them, their honor intact.

A younger generation, lost in space, was not so lucky. Still another 58,000 Americans, their names now engraved on a black marble slab, made payment for our leaders' folly in full.

CHAPTER 11

Winter on the Spanish Coast

ONE JANUARY, DECADES AGO, they all showed up on the beach: men and machines, girls and governments, and weapons of death held on a tenuous leash. A few weeks later they all left to make room for the tourists. A young officer was a little older, the U.S. government had acquired some wisdom, and the season's souvenirs had been equitably distributed. Even King Neptune was treated fairly. He surrendered grudgingly the mortals' trinket, but he was awarded the fruits of their folly in return.

THE AIRPLANE

B-52s are big airplanes, and they are unique. First flown in 1952, the last of 744 B-52s rolled off the production line in 1962. Less than a hundred of these airplanes are still on active duty, now flown by the grandsons of the first B-52 pilots. This eight-engined behemoth was the first all-jet bomber designed for the delivery of atomic and thermonuclear weapons across intercontinental distances. In the early years it served as the backbone of the U.S. nuclear deterrent. Later, some B-52s were detached from nuclear alert for conventional bombing operations in Vietnam, Iraq, and Afghanistan.

The B-52G has an unrefueled combat radius of over 4,000 miles, but with in-flight refueling, that range can be increased significantly. A B-52 loaded with nuclear weapons can take off only with a limited fuel load, but once at altitude, it can cruise with the extra weight of a full load. Unlike propeller-driven planes, jets are more efficient the higher they fly. Just taxiing on the runway will burn almost as much fuel, minute by minute, as cruising at full speed and high altitude. Flying down on the deck, making a full-throttle run at a well-defended target, B-52 fuel consumption goes up by 50 percent. Under those conditions—300 mph at 500 feet above the ground—a B-52G will burn a ton of fuel every four minutes. Four hundred feet per gallon is not great mileage.

A standard Strategic Air Command (SAC) Cold War mission called for three refuelings. The first was to occur early on, when a U.S.-based tanker would connect with its bomber to replace the fuel burned by the bomber on its takeoff and climb to altitude. With early warning, that tanker most likely would have survived any attack on its home base. The second load of fuel was taken on before the B-52's penetration runs into its targets. In the sixties, tankers would rendezvous with their thirsty flock over the Arctic or Spain. These meetings were well out of range of Soviet fighters, surface-to-air missiles, or radar. When the target run was over, the now nearly empty B-52 would climb back to cruising altitude, hoping to rendezvous with a third tanker that had survived the nuclear melee. At least that's how they practiced it.

While a B-52G could make it all the way from its U.S. base to a Soviet target on a one-way mission without refueling, there were three practical reasons for accepting all the complexity of an in-flight rendezvous with tankers. The first was that a surplus of fuel allowed routing flexibility, an approach to the USSR from unexpected quarters at unexpected times. Second, a fully fueled B-52 would be much more likely to penetrate to all of its targets. A copious fuel supply allows it to fly into hostile territory at altitudes of only a few hundred feet at speeds in excess of 300 mph. This would make it hard for enemy radars and SAMs to find it. And last, these refuelings would give the plane a better chance to make it back to a poststrike recovery base. The fact that there would be a tomorrow was an important part of the SAC culture.

Given these considerations, in-flight refueling was, and continues to be, a standard Air Force and Navy practice. It is a dicey procedure. The recipient—be it bomber, fighter, or even helicopter—and tanker must rendezvous at the same speed, flying in exactly the same direction in three-dimensional space, and they must do so within thirty seconds of the specified rendezvous time. The tanker crew must guide the refueling boom into the thirsty aircraft's refueling orifice while both aircraft hurtle through the air at hundreds of miles an hour.

Until 1957 most air-to-air refueling was done from KC-97s, a propeller-driven aircraft known commercially as the Boeing Stratocruiser. In that year, jet-powered KC-135s were introduced into the force. Two years later they entered commercial service as Boeing 707s, but their availability as tankers in 1957 confirmed the Strategic Air Command's position as a truly global nuclear force.

THE AIRCRAFT ON ALERT

Preeminence is never a permanent condition. Sputnik and SS-6 rockets appeared in 1957, and in August of that year the Soviets fired that intercontinental ballistic missile from the Baikonur Cosmodrome to Kamchatka, thousands of miles downrange. Within a few years the Soviets would be able to mount a bolt-out-of-the-blue nuclear attack on the United States. Ballistic missiles fired from the Soviet Union would be able to hit targets half a world away in less than thirty minutes. No U.S. radars then deployed would see them coming. There would be no time for U.S. aircraft to escape.

Faced with this new challenge, the Air Force began construction of its Ballistic Missile Early Warning System (BMEWS), three large radars to be deployed with their associated communications and computers in Alaska, Greenland, and the UK. They were to augment the Distant Early Warning (DEW) Line radars already in place along the Arctic Circle and the Pine Tree radars in mid-Canada. These remote sensors had been designed to look for low-flying aircraft. The new monster BMEWS antennas, the size of football fields, were to spot refrigerator-size objects thousands of miles away in space. At times they would track geese in formation or the moon ascending, but the chances were good that they also would spot the first signs of a Soviet missile attack on the United States. The warnings they would give could alert U.S. bombers and tankers. It would not be the signal to go to war, but it would get those aircraft off the ground, away from a surprise attack. The first of these BMEWS radars became operational at Thule, Greenland, in January 1961.

To utilize this DEW Line warning, the Strategic Air Command put in place a modest ground alert program. By October 1957 SAC had over 10 percent of its bomber force on alert, sitting at the end of runways with bombs loaded and crews standing by, available to launch within fifteen minutes. Appropriate numbers of tankers were on a similar alert status, ready to accompany and support the strike force. By the end of 1960, as the first BMEWS radar went on line and as the Soviet missile threat became real, one third of the U.S. bomber and tanker fleet was on runway alert. At the same time, SAC began to think about the true bolt-out-of-the-blue attack: no warning at all, no radar returns. Unexpected nuclear detonations at SAC bases might be the first sign of trouble. *Airborne* alerts would be the answer.

For two years SAC worked to develop such a system, and by the end of 1959 the procedure was formally put in place: a dozen fully armed B-52s would be in the air at all times, away from their vulnerable bases, ready to go to war. Not only would these aircraft be airborne, they would depart from the United States along planned wartime routes toward the Soviet Union. They would be refueled after takeoff and again before setting out to a specified "go or no-go" line several hundred miles short of the Soviet Union. Upon reaching that imaginary line, if no authenticated order to attack was received from the American President, the bombers would turn around, refuel, and head for home. Their nuclear weapons could not be armed unless the unlocking code was radioed up from the President via the SAC command post. These flights typically would last about twenty-four hours, and prior to their return to base, another bomber would take off to assume the alert duties of the returning craft.

These missions were known as "Chrome Dome flights." There were four routes. Three departed from bases in the central and northern United States and proceeded up over Canada, Alaska, and Greenland. The bombers were to receive their second and third refueling from tankers stationed in Alaska and Greenland. Their no-go lines were over the Arctic. The fourth route originated in the southern United States, crossed the middle Atlantic and Spain, then proceeded to a no-go line over the Mediterranean Sea. Their refueling was supported from bases in Spain.

During the Cuban missile crisis of 1962 those ubiquitous and most unwelcome Soviet trawlers made their appearance in the eastern Mediterranean. Their assignment then was to jam all communications between B-52s and their tankers overhead. The rendezvous then came to rely on accurate timing, visual beacons, and good eyesight. In this way, even minor flare-ups in the Cold War endangered SAC aircrews and their thermonuclear cargos in ways seldom appreciated by the public at large.

TEA-16

As part of this vast nuclear ballet, Captain Charles F. Wendorf started the engines of B-52G Number 256 at dusk on the evening of January 16, 1966. The call sign of this flight was Tea-16. Wendorf was accompanied by an instructor pilot, Major Larry Messinger, a decorated B-29 pilot from World War II and Korea. Earlier that day the ground crews at Seymour Johnson AFB in North Carolina loaded a clip of four Mk-28 thermonuclear bombs aboard Tea-16.

At sundown Wendorf, his crew of five, and his instructor pilot all took off for their Chrome Dome run to the Mediterranean. Outbound, they picked up their first load of fuel. At dawn a KC-135 tanker based at Torrejon, Spain, rose to meet them, to give Tea-16 its final outbound gulp of JP-4. Well short of the go-no-go line, with no instructions to proceed on into the Soviet Union, Wendorf turned his B-52 around.

By mid-morning, Tea-16 returned to the Costa del Sol with an appointment to take on fuel from a tanker, code name Troubadour-14, based at Morón AFB, near Seville. At 10:22 A.M. both aircraft were lined up at 30,500 feet over the town of Palomares, Spain, with an indicated airspeed of 283 knots.

THE BOMB

The Mk-28 H-bomb was America's first production thermonuclear system. It was a system in the sense that the basic nuclear package could be delivered with a variety of add-on noses, fins, and parachutes, depending on the characteristics and tactics of the delivery aircraft. Engineering of this family of bombs started in 1957, after the nuclear test of the prototype weapon in the Pacific during the previous summer. The first operational units, the Mk–28 IN and the Mk–28 EX, were delivered to the stockpile in 1959: IN meant internal carriage, in the bomb bay; EX meant carriage external to the aircraft, on pylons. Safety modifications led to a second (Mod 1) Mk–28, which was introduced in 1960.

While this work was going on in support of tactical aircraft, SAC was considering not only the bolt-out-of-the-blue threat described above, but the dangers of new Soviet ground control radars and new surface-to-air missiles that could reach aircraft flying at high altitudes. Low altitude penetration to Soviet targets would soon become essential. This meant not only a whole new approach to the aircraft's flight plans and profiles described above; it meant a new approach to the ordnance being carried. B–52s would no longer be able to open their bomb bays at 30,000 feet, drop a bomb, then leave with plenty of time to escape before the weapon went off.

On April 17, 1958, the Assistant Secretary of Defense asked the Atomic Energy Commission to develop an Mk–28 bomb which could be released by a B–52 at high speed (over 300 mph) and low altitude (under 500 feet). This would require a drogue chute to slow the bomb down, an energy-absorbing nose and case to protect the weapon inside from ground impact, and a fusing system to detonate the weapon several minutes later, after its mother B–52 had escaped.

The resulting bomb, the Mk–28 RI—Retarded delivery, Internal carriage—weighed over a ton, was eleven feet long and about two feet in diameter, with a yield in the megaton range. When loaded onto a B–52, four of these bombs were carried by a clip, necessary to secure them into the bomb bay and to sequence their release. Delivery and stockpiling of the Mk–28 RI began in June 1960, just as the new G models of the B–52 were entering service and the operational doctrine of airborne alert was being put into practice. These weapons and procedures all were made for each other, but this marriage made in the USA came apart over the coast of Spain on a January morning in 1966.

THE YOUNG HELICOPTER PILOT

Ted Cochran loved airplanes; he had been flying since he was sixteen years old. Upon graduation from the University of Colorado in 1963, he entered the U.S. Air Force as a second lieutenant with hopes of becoming an astronaut, but his flight training at Williams Air Force Base, near Phoenix, exposed him to life in the open cockpit. He opted for helicopter training: no g-suit, no oxygen mask, no positive control. There was just the open door, the wind blowing in, and the appreciative astronauts down below, waiting to be plucked from those rough seas by the chopper above.

Cochran headed off to Stead Air Force Base to learn to fly helicopters. He loved it, graduating in the spring of 1965 as a qualified H-43 pilot. That was a firefighting and crash rescue ship, small, with neither guns nor armor. Space exploration receded from Cochran's mind as he developed visions of fighting fires and saving lives in all sorts of exotic and action-packed places. He liked the rescue slogan: "That others may live," though he did not expect to get shot at. Vietnam was just entering the consciousness of American pilots in 1965. Cochran had only seventy hours of H-43 time. Surely the more experienced pilots would be tapped first for Vietnam.

In the beginning, he was right. Cochran was assigned to K. I. Sawyer Air Force Base, home to a B-52 bomb wing, in northern Michigan. The H-43s were there to support a small tenant squadron of F-101 air defense fighters. F-101s are two-engine aircraft; they seldom got in trouble, so Cochran settled down to the quiet life of searching for lost hunters.

By mid-1965 he was also part of a "510 Alert Team." Ops Plan 510 was an arrangement whereby a pair of helicopters, their crews, and their logistics support would take turns standing alert for one week per month. The idea was to be ready to move, on six hours notice, to some distant crash or disaster site. Vietnam seemed quite far away on that Sunday morning in June 1965 when Cochran was boating on a small lake near the base. Nothing ever happened on Sundays, so he was out fishing, away from the phone, when the real world intruded in the form of a sergeant, shouting from the shoreline: "We're deploying, Lieutenant." There had been some unpleasantness at a place called Pleiku.

There ensued 193 combat rescue missions and credit for forty-two combat saves in the jungles of Vietnam. By the end of that summer of 1965, the college kid with dreams of space had become a war-weary old man of twenty-five. The rescues became more dangerous, the bloodshed worse, the smell of burned corpses unbearable. Then one day his tour was over. Cochran was totally drained, overcome with fear of the "last bullet." He returned to Tan Son Nhut to await a flight home. He lay low in a friend's apartment for three days, then one of those familiar-looking Continental Airlines planes took him home. It was culture shock in reverse. Within a few hours he was back in sunny

California; everyone around him acted as though nothing had ever happened.

Cochran returned to K. I. Sawyer. He visited his family over the Christmas holidays, recovered his belongings, and accepted transfer to another air rescue detachment at Chambley, a NATO dispersed operating base in northeastern France. There, he could forget about Vietnam, enjoy the wine, and finish up his Air Force tour in the bucolic countryside of Lorraine. As he headed for France he began to exhale for the first time in months, but as his transport entered French airspace, Captain Wendorf was starting the engines of Tea-16.

THE TOWN

San Javier was a sleepy resort town on the southeast coast of Spain. Palomares was a fishing village nearby. Alicante was the nearest city. The Spanish Air Force Academy was located near San Javier. Not much happened there during the winter, but in season, the San Javier Hotel was a lively spot, with music and dancing, good crowds, and great booze. That hotel had an old-world feel: Moorish architecture, high ceilings, and fans. It was Rick's Café Americaine all over again.

THE RENDEZVOUS

On the morning of January 17, 1966, Tea-16 and Troubadour-14 were aligned for refueling at 30,500 feet over Palomares, Spain. The boom operator started to hook up, but for some reason, the refueling boom from the tanker missed the B-52's refueling port and crushed the aircraft's longeron (backbone) instead. Fuel was everywhere. A spark set it off, and in a moment the tanker and its crew of four were gone in a ball of fire. The B-52 began to break up. Captain Wendorf, Major Messinger, and two other crew members were able to escape the burning aircraft with successful parachute deployments bringing them back to earth.

At the same time, four other passengers began their return: the Mk-28 H-bombs loaded aboard Tea-16. As they broke free from their clip, one emerged from the flaming debris unscathed. It deployed its chute and landed as it was designed to do. Since it received no arming signal, bomb number one just plunged to earth and sat there, waiting for a ride home, a silent testimonial to the care of those who designed, engineered, and built those U.S. nukes. Two more weapons were damaged on exiting the aircraft. Their chutes did not deploy, and thus they fell to earth at high velocity. The shock of impact set off the high explosives in each, but they were one point safe. There was no nuclear yield. The explosions blew open the cases, however, scattering perceptible amounts of plutonium over a square mile of Spanish countryside. Plutonium is not particularly radioactive, but it is a toxic metal. Inhalation of plutonium dust can be fatal.

Bomb number four fell into the Mediterranean Sea. As was learned much later, it landed five and a half miles off shore in 2,250 feet of water, but on January 17, 1966, no one had the slightest idea where it was. A lot of people and a lot of governments wanted to know.

The explosion over southern Spain was noticed by other aircraft and seen by a number of villagers on the ground in and around Palomares. Within minutes the American military telecommunications system was flooded. Four Mk-28s had fallen on southern Spain, but no one knew where. By sundown the four surviving B-52 crew members were rescued by local citizens, and the first Americans arrived by helicopter from Morón AFB, home of the destroyed tanker aircraft. On January 18 the Americans found the fallen and undamaged bomb as well as the remains of two more. The B-52's combat mission folder was found in a black leather satchel near the wreckage of the plane's cockpit. There was great relief upon receipt of this news in Omaha, since the folder contained penetration routes, targets, and codes. By January 22 it seemed unlikely that the fourth nuclear weapon was on land. The Navy and a 510 Detachment were called in. Once again Lieutenant Cochran got the word, this time in France. He was just completing his orientation, settling into the peace and quiet of the French countryside.

On January 25, Cochran arrived in Spain, happy to relieve a pilot assigned there on temporary duty during the first few days of crisis. The next day he began to operate his H-43 as an airborne pickup truck. From dawn to dusk Cochran carried search parties and VIPs to and fro. Cochran's life was heaven on earth, a stark contrast to the ghastly memories of Vietnam. No one was shooting at him, nothing was on fire, no charred bodies, just wonderful flying weather, a great beach, and lots of live, vivacious people. When the sun went down, the San Javier Hotel began to rock and roll. It was there that Cochran shared a room with another H-43 pilot. They could not stay at the Air Force

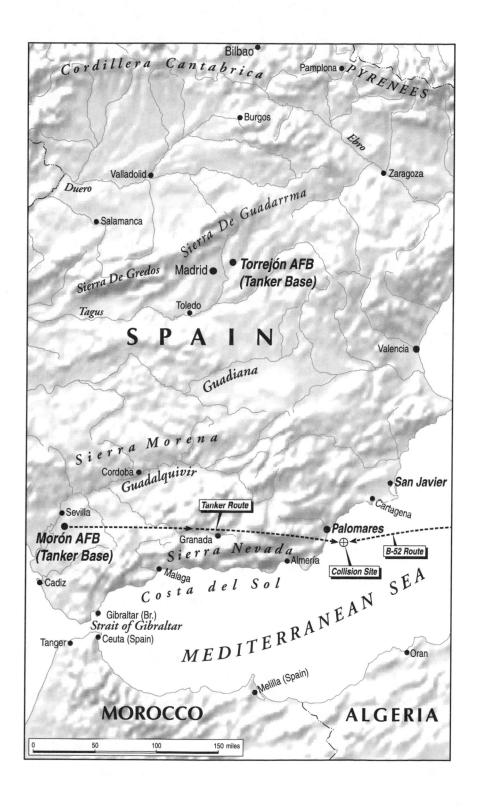

tent city on the beach at Palomares, for they needed to be near their chopper.

On February 4 the Americans came across Señor Francisco Simo, a professional fisherman who had seen objects falling from the fireball and noted where they fell. At the same time, the hated Soviet intelligence-gathering trawlers began to show up. A week later the Navy's Task Force 65 arrived to start the underwater search. Its flagship was a cruiser, the *Albany*. The flotilla included the *Alvin*, a submersible nominally from Woods Hole Oceanographic Institute. It was operated by two civilians. On February 14 the *Alvin* made its first dive. The *Washington Post* and every other arm of the international media was catatonic over the lost nuke. The Navy was ignoring the publicity, trying to focus on the difficult job at hand. Rear Admiral William Guest, the task force commander, and his staff stayed on the *Albany*. The frustrated press descended on the San Javier Hotel in growing numbers. It was clear that one of the fallen Mk-28s was in the water offshore.

By the end of February the tourist season was about to begin, but Europeans were cancelling their seaside reservations en masse, fearing plutonium in the water. The press was of no help. To deal with this threat to the local economy, a talented American ambassador, Angier Biddle Duke, and his family, arrived at Palomares for a well-publicized swim. Cochran ferried the reporters around while the ambassador hit the beach. "Damn cold, but nice water," he said. The Europeans decided the water was safe and started to reinstate their hotel reservations.

On March 15 the *Alvin*, looking where Señor Simo suggested, made first contact with the missing H-bomb. It was still in one piece. During that same week, "Marianne" and "Brunhilde" arrived in San Javier. They rented a secluded two bedroom condo down the beach from the hotel. Once ensconced, they headed off to join the bomb groupies. Everyone was at the San Javier Hotel: newsmen, peace activists, topless dancers, and bureaucrats, the curious of every stripe and the peddlers of every needed service.

Well, almost everyone was there. The exception was the American servicemen. The Navy boys were all aboard their ships. The Air Force types were confined to Camp Wilson, a tent city on the beach at Palomares. Only the two Air Force helicopter pilots were left in town. They were required to return their helicopter to the hangar at the Spanish Air Force Academy every night. They were cut off from their senior officers and armed only with a rental car to get one of them to work; the duty pilot had to be at the hangar by dawn. Cochran's roommate was a dedicated married man, a straight arrow trying to get a good night's sleep amidst all the din. Cochran, thankful to be alive and out of Vietnam, was living life to the fullest. He was the prime and easy target for Marianne.

THE GIRL

Marianne was an attractive blue-eyed blonde in her mid thirties, about five feet eight inches tall and very bright. She spoke excellent English and Spanish as well as her native German, and she was very well-connected. She claimed to have a cousin in the West German Luftwaffe who had trained in the United States. She knew all about Williams and Luke Air Force Bases, the holy temples of American fighter pilots. She liked classical music and whistled it while walking, usually Bach. The odd thing was, she wore terribly dowdy clothes. Although she was attractive to the point of glamour, she dressed more like Nina Kruscheva than Jackie Kennedy. She said her name was Marianne Ritterodt. Everyone assumed she was a "good German" because of her Luftwaffe connection and her familiarity with American ways. Marianne claimed to be vacationing in southern Spain, although winter is an odd time to hit the beaches there. She was accompanied by her "mother" or older friend, a woman well past forty years and eighty kilos. The boys gave her the name Brunhilde.

Marianne and Ted met at the bar of the San Javier Hotel, and they hit it off at once. As the days and nights progressed, the happy couple would meet at the San Javier to dance and dine. Then they would hitch a ride to Marianne's condo. Brunhilde would discreetly disappear. Marianne was great company, a terrific listener, so interested in Ted's work.

Then one day in late March, Cochran received an invitation from the lieutenant commander who was Task Force 65's Chief of Intelligence: "Fly out to the *Albany* for lunch." Not good; they must have discovered that along with the daily groceries Cochran's helicopter was delivering illicit gin to the ship's crew. But after a pleasant repast, the Navy officer brought up a different subject. "It's a tough and dirty job, Lieutenant, but somebody's got to do it. Keep sleeping with the KGB lady who picked you up at the San Javier, but keep your ears open and your mouth shut. Get your script from us every morning."

In retrospect it's clear that "Marianne" was a swallow—an agent of the Stasi, the East German security service. We must surmise that she was sent to San Javier to make contact with Americans, to find out what she could about the search patterns and prospects for recovery of the missing Mk-28. Brunhilde undoubtedly was Marianne's controller, the agent assigned to see that Marianne kept her mind on her job and off any bourgeois thoughts of defecting. To Cochran, the announcement was a bombshell; he was in love with the girl. Getting his H-43 off the deck of the *Albany* that afternoon was one of the most difficult liftoffs of his career. The rest of the week was as chaotic in his mind as it was to the crew of the *Alvin*, entangled as they were in the shrouds of the Mk-28 underwater.

At the end of March the *Alvin* tried to hook the missing weapon, which had been located on a steep underwater slope. The submersible was briefly ensnared by the billowing chute still attached to the weapon. When the excitement was over, the Mk-28 had run away, sliding down the slope and out of sight. On April 2 the *Alvin* found the chute and weapon again, this time at 2,800 feet. The attachment of lifting gear proceeded with greater care. At 8:45 A.M. on April 7, eleven weeks after the collision at 30,000 feet, the lost Mk-28 was pulled aboard the USS *Petrel*. Its nose was crushed, but it was otherwise safe and inert. Once again the AEC's attention to weapon safety paid off. There was a big press conference. The Navy declared victory and immediately weighed anchor.

THE DEPARTURES

It was all over. Thanks to the public relations skills of Ambassador Duke, the tourists wanted to get back to the beach, and the bars, hotels, and locals wanted them back. The Americans packed up with great speed and were soon gone. As "tangible evidence of our appreciation to the community," the U.S. left behind the promise of a new water desalinization plant for the citizens of Palomares. It took nine years and $150 million to build, but the citizens were appreciative. They renamed one of their streets "Calle Las Bombardas." The wreckage of the B-52 was collected from all over the countryside and the pieces were loaded onto a barge and taken out to sea for dumping—an offering to King Neptune, one might suppose, as a payback for his grudging surrender of the fourth Mk-28. About a thousand tons of Spanish soil, 4,827 barrels, contaminated with plutonium, were loaded onto ships and taken to the U.S. Atomic Energy Commission facility at Savannah River, Georgia, for burial. The intact H-bomb number one was returned to the U.S. AEC. The casing is now on display at the National Atomic Museum in Albuquerque.

In the weeks that followed, the Spanish government made known its displeasure with nuclear-armed overflights of its territory, and the United States promptly agreed to discontinue such flights over Spain. Two weeks after recovery of the Mk-28, Secretary of Defense Robert McNamara ordered the frequency of all Chrome Dome flights cut from a dozen at a time to four sorties per day. Two years later, with most of the U.S. nuclear deterrent moved to missiles underground or at sea, and with U.S. satellite technology able to provide much better warning of Soviet rocket launches, the need for such airborne alerts ended. The procedure was discontinued; one more Cold War hair trigger was disconnected.

On April 10, 1966, three days after the Mk-28 recovery at sea, Cochran was told to report to the San Javier airstrip, bag in hand. There was no chance for a farewell with Marianne. She had no phone. Marianne Ritterodt probably was not even her name. He remembers thinking, "This is just a bad Hemingway book." He never saw or heard from Marianne again.

CHAPTER 12

Dawn of the Information Age

"THINGS FALL APART; the center cannot hold."

Yeats was concerned about the disintegration of Europe when he wrote those lines, but the rough beast he feared in the 1920s was a teddy bear when compared to the nuclear monster straining its leash a generation later. As the Soviets achieved nuclear parity with the West, as those weapons metastasized to the extremities of the superpowers, the maintenance of nuclear control from the political center almost slipped away. It was advances in communication technology that kept the nuclear weapons of the United States, its adversaries, and its allies under tight control during those most dangerous of times.

But communication technology did more than that. The advent of digital, high-speed, and global communications allowed the U.S. to decentralize control of its forces, replace armor with information, and shift the military odds by orders of magnitude. In earlier times, military theory held that a well-entrenched defender, enjoying internal lines of communication, held a three-to-one advantage over any attacker besieging his position. That is what Saddam Hussein thought as he viewed the world from his palaces in Baghdad. But the information revolution changed all that. With instant access to an unlimited supply of real-time information, the odds have shifted to favor the information-advantaged. They now favor an attacker who holds the high ground of information superiority by more than a hundred to one.

The information revolution had a third even more profound impact on the Cold War—it destabilized the Soviet system. Copying machines, facsimiles, personal computers, and the Internet incapacitated the iron hand of the communist state. As the West began to speak directly to the Soviet people, and as those people spoke more freely among themselves, the Soviet government simply drowned in a flood of uncontrolled information. The Soviet general staff might keep control of its nukes, but the *nomenklatura* could not retain its hold on political power.

LOOSE NUKES IN EUROPE

By the end of the 1960s, in preparing to defend NATO from the overwhelming armor and artillery of the Red Army, the U.S. had forward-based *thousands* of nuclear weapons throughout Western Europe. Some were kept in bunkers, adjacent to the NATO–Warsaw Pact borders and along the expected routes of Soviet advance. Others were held within air bases belonging to our NATO allies. Many of these were subkiloton atomic demolition munitions, known as "backpack bombs," for placement near bridges and other chokepoints. There were nuclear artillery shells and missile warheads, ready for bombardment of the Soviet front lines. And at the NATO airbases, there were mini-H-bombs, for delivery to the Soviet invader's rear by tactical aircraft.

Each weapon was capable of inflicting the horrors of Hiroshima on every crossroad in Europe. Together they could stop any Soviet rush into Western Europe. Never mind that the residue would be a glowing wasteland, or that the Soviets were armed with similar nukes, gases, and bacteriological weapons of unimagined horror. These NATO nuclear miniweapons were to be delivered by the jeeps, guns, rockets, and airplanes of allied host countries. The nukes themselves were kept under U.S. lock and key. In theory, they were to be released only upon the say-so of the American President.

All that seemed like a sound arrangement until the spring of 1974, when an armed quarrel broke out between some of our partners. Only their common fear of the Soviet threat had brought them into the NATO alliance in the first place. With the outbreak of those hostilities, it occurred to the American Secretary of Defense, James Schlesinger, to ask the obvious questions: The U.S. stores nuclear weapons within NATO countries, does it not? Who guards them? How well? What if those people decide they want to go nuclear in their quarrel, to seize and use the weapons we have stored there? What if . . . ?

Earlier that year I joined the staff of the Secretary of Defense as his Director of Telecommunications and Command and Control Systems. That title was cumbersome and new, as the Pentagon was only reluctantly entering the information age. *Telstar,* the first experimental communications satellite, was launched only six years before. The new global communications links, such as the Defense Satellite Communication System, were held suspect by overseas military commanders who did not want microscopic supervision from their superiors in Washington. Digital computers were still large boxes of transistors, stand-alone monuments to modern technology. Their purchase and operation within the Department of Defense was funded and supervised by the Pentagon's chief financial officer, since all were deemed to be glorified bookkeeping machines. "Voice message systems" were analog telephones, generally unencrypted and operated by the individual services for their own needs. Only with great effort had a Defense Communications Agency been created and imposed on the services as a systems engineer. Signals intelligence was the province of the National Security Agency, with oversight provided by an Assistant Secretary of Defense for Intelligence. An envisioned World Wide Military Command and Control System existed only in the minds of a few.

I was to lay out a road map for assembling all of these pieces into an integrated system. It was in that capacity that Secretary Schlesinger turned to me, asking if he could talk to the U.S. officers holding the keys to our nukes within the NATO countries. Were they safe and secure? It seemed a reasonable question, but the answer opened a lot of eyes. I found that many of the NATO-based U.S. nuclear weapons were stored in locked bunkers further protected by double rings of barbed wire. A junior U.S. officer on site, often a newly minted lieutenant from West Point, held the keys and the passwords. At each such site that officer was supported by a handful of enlisted men equipped with small arms. At the major air bases there was some defense in depth; a more senior U.S. officer, usually a USAF major, was in charge of nuclear weapons security. But outside all the barbed wire, at all the bases large and small, the serious guarding was done by the locals. They were the ones ready for a serious firefight with Soviet invaders or infiltrated *Spetsnatz* teams. But given the sudden eruption of hostilities within the alliance, this arrangement gave us pause. What if our guards became our assailants?

To talk to the U.S. officer in charge of any such overseas enclosure, the Secretary of Defense could not simply dial 1-800-USNUKES. In 1974 the command link to the U.S. nuclear bunkers in Europe ran from the Pentagon via submarine cable to the U.S. commander in Europe, located outside Brussels. From there, communication was via the Cemetery Net, an unencrypted high frequency ("short wave") voice link of dubious quality, operating at the mercy of atmospheric and man-made disturbances. It was not designed to accommodate a Secretary of Defense in Washington inquiring of a junior officer in the mountains of a NATO ally about his well-being. It was there to deliver the President's release authority—to go to war.

The conversations with remote bunkers were difficult, but they confirmed that the lieutenants were there, on duty. They still had their keys. The guards were still facing outward, guarding, not attacking. At an Air Force base things got a little dicier, however. The local Army troops outside the fence wanted in. Their Air Force countrymen inside wanted them kept out. The nukes on alert aircraft were hastily returned to bunkers as the opposing commanders parleyed under a white flag. Soon both sides went off to dinner, but through it all we held our breath.

Within a few weeks the crisis passed, but back in the United States the lessons were unmistakable. The U.S. government began to take the deployment of mobile satellite ground terminals seriously. The National Security Agency moved to exploit the new digital technology, devising encryption schemes and compact hardware to accommodate secure communications worldwide. The atomic energy people improved the safety and lockout systems on our nuclear weapons. By the end of 1976 all U.S. tactical nuclear weapons were equipped with PALs.★ But while these changes were in process, the control of nukes remained a dicey game. It was the integrity of the troops on both sides of the Iron Curtain that held things together.

★ Permissive Action Links, devised by Johnny Foster at Livermore (see Chapter 8). These devices would render any nuclear device inoperable unless an outside set of digits, originating with the President, was punched into the weapon's arming controls.

LIMITED NUCLEAR OPTIONS

James Schlesinger was, and is, a most remarkable man. He is arrogant, with a great deal to be arrogant about. He is bright, with an open and inquiring mind, but any proponent of new ideas had best be prepared for a maelstrom of questions. As the nation's twelfth Secretary of Defense, Schlesinger spent little time introspecting on the nature of the enemy. To him, communism was a treacherous, cruel, and implacable world movement that needed to be defeated, not accommodated.

Secretary Schlesinger was uniquely qualified for his job, having served at RAND, a military think tank in California, and then in the new Nixon administration's Office of Management and Budget. From there he moved to the chairmanship of the Atomic Energy Commission; became Director of Central Intelligence; then moved to Defense when the man nominated and confirmed as Secretary of Defense for Nixon's second term, Eliot Richardson, moved on to the Justice Department and the Watergate sinkhole.

With his arrival at Defense in the spring of 1973, Schlesinger inherited Deputy Secretary Bill Clements. A drilling contractor from Texas who served on the Defense Blue Ribbon panel during the first Nixon term, Clements was as structured and business-oriented as Schlesinger was disorganized and academic. They came to detest each other, but in my opinion, they formed the best Secretary and Deputy Secretary team in the history of the Pentagon.

Schlesinger dealt with the big picture, rebuilding America's post-Vietnam defense policies with clarity and focus. Clements was a straight shooter from Texas who ran the Pentagon with an iron hand. He introduced reforms into the acquisition of weapons; the modern cruise missile was his personal creation. He overhauled the education and training of young officers, and welcomed women into the military academies. He imposed order on the World Wide Military Command and Control System, and through it all, he conserved resources starkly limited by the post–Vietnam Watergate Congress.

Schlesinger was not as orderly, nor was he straightforward. He liked to freelance. One of his most bizarre statements, in the aftermath of Nixon's presidential resignation, was a claim that he, Schlesinger, had instructed the military to make no unusual moves at the request of the President (and Commander in Chief) as his days in office drew to a forced close. The implication was clear: a potential coup was in the air. General George Brown, Chairman of the Joint Chiefs of Staff at the time, confirmed to me that he received no such instructions, and that if he had, he would have laughed them off. He repeated that denial in October 1974 at a public appearance at Duke University.

Air Force General Brown was a unique and capable chairman. He paid his dues over Ploesti during World War II. His career progressed through the operational Air Force, culminating in his command of the U.S. Air Forces in Vietnam. He brought the lessons learned home to the Air Force Systems Command, where the post–Vietnam generation of aircraft were just taking shape. He became Chief of Staff of the USAF in 1973, the first officer with major weapons system acquisition experience to make that grade. Brown became Chairman of the Joint Chiefs on July 1, 1974, just as the final scenes from Watergate were being played out. As July turned into August, he called his senior commanders to confirm that they would tell him of any unusual back-channel orders from the civilian leadership, but there was never any evidence of irrational presidential behavior, nor did Schlesinger ever give Brown warnings of such. During the Ford years, Chairman Brown built a unique and solid relationship with Deputy Defense Secretary Clements. Together, these two men guided—and if necessary dragged—the armed services of the United States into the information age.

Gerald Ford could not deal with Schlesinger's arrogance. He sent Donald Rumsfeld to replace him at the Pentagon once he'd settled into the presidency. But during the dark Watergate and early post–Vietnam years, Jim Schlesinger and his indispensable military assistant, Major General John Wickham, held the Pentagon fort with tenacity.

At the beginning of his tour, Schlesinger faced a serious and dangerous challenge to American security. Distracted by Vietnam, the United States had allowed the Soviet Union to move into a position of strategic nuclear superiority, at least as measured by deliverable nuclear payload. With the massive deployment of SS-18 rockets, and with their nuclear-powered submarine fleet finally reaching numerical, though not technical, parity, the Soviets were turning their attention to Western Europe.

In that theater of operations, the U.S. had deployed massive nuclear firepower. Its purpose was to offset those components of the Red Army still in place throughout Eastern Germany, Poland, and Czechoslovakia since the end of World War II. The American weapons, known as

Forward Based Systems, were mainly USAF fighter-bombers carrying nuclear weapons. These aircraft were taken seriously by the Soviets, especially after their impressive performance in Vietnam, defending the Marine outpost at Khe Sanh, fourteen miles south of the DMZ, during a February 1968 siege. The Soviets had not modernized their initial European deployment of medium range rockets in twenty years. Those now-antique SS-4s and SS-5s were liquid-fueled and slow to react, stored out in the open on unprotected launch pads in groups of four. They were sitting ducks for American airpower. As the U.S. Forward Based Systems continued to multiply, they were augmented by the introduction of a British and French nuclear capability in the air and at sea.

At the time of the first Strategic Arms Limitation agreement, signed in 1972, Soviet negotiators tried to include within the treaty the American Forward Based Systems, but they failed to do so. After the signing of those accords, the Soviets began testing a whole new family of rockets, such as the SS-16. Intelligence sources indicated that the upper two stages of that system were being readied for use as a mobile 2,400-mile intermediate range system. Flight testing of the resulting SS-20 (RSD-10) began in 1974.

As Soviet strategic nuclear firepower grew, coming to match the U.S. in the early 1970s, our NATO allies were growing nervous about the matter of "decoupling." In the event of a conventional war in Europe, would the U.S. *really* come to the defense of its NATO allies with a full nuclear broadside? Would Americans *really* risk New York and Washington in order to save Bonn and Paris? Skeptics had their doubts. It was the view of previous administrations, Secretary of Defense McNamara in particular, that there could be no "limited" use of nuclear weapons; first use of a nuke would uncork the genie's bottle. Escalation would be instantaneous because, as in the old Wild West, the price of being the last to shoot was too high. In McNamara's eyes, planning for limited nuclear use was of dubious value, although "Flexible Response" might offer one last firebreak before the cataclysm.

The administration that followed took Flexible Response to a different conclusion. Given the growth in numbers and the catastrophic implications of a full nuclear exchange, Nixon, Kissinger, and Schlesinger concluded that the United States had to at least *try* to keep any nuclear conflict localized. Such efforts might not succeed, but it would be irresponsible not to try. The U.S. had to be able to respond to a Soviet invasion of Europe with less than a full, civilization-ending salvo.

In 1973 the Nixon administration developed the doctrine of Limited

Nuclear Options (LNOs). These plans were to be subsets of the overall nuclear war plan, designed to provide a limited nuclear response without degrading overall U.S. military capabilities. This reordering of nuclear war plans was dictated by the politics of Europe, but it was made possible by advances in U.S. technology. The introduction of multiple independently targetable reentery vehicles (MIRVs) into the missile forces gave the targeteers more options, easing the problem of allocating scarce resources among many targets. The advent of reliable computers made real-time retargeting a possibility. Not only could the strategic nuclear forces reallocate assets after an LNO, they could update the master plan daily as specific targets moved and new ones were discovered.

LNOs would give the United States the ability to strike only a few (or a few hundred) military targets far from Moscow. Or the U.S. could attack the electrical power grid or the transportation system of the Soviet Union without destroying its nerve center in Moscow. Protection of the latter was important if we were to negotiate an end to a fast-moving nuclear crisis. Although some LNO targets were civil in nature, these became known as "counterforce" attacks. The civilian/industrial "countervalue" targets—the nation's cities and lesser population centers—were to await developments, perhaps to be struck a day or two later if things were not working out.

These plans for Limited Nuclear Options were formalized in President Nixon's NSDD-242, signed in January 1974. They became known as the Schlesinger Doctrine. This targeting scheme was a laudable effort to control the nuclear genie, but the thought of "just a few hundred" nuclear strikes boggles the mind of anyone who has seen a nuclear device go off. And the concept imposed incredible demands on the nation's emergency communications systems. It is one thing for the President to authorize an all-out response as a nuclear attack on the U.S. unfolds. For that purpose a few dedicated telephone and radio links will do. It is quite another thing to try to operate amidst a "limited" nuclear war, for one must assume the Soviets would not sit idly by while the U.S. bombarded the edges of their empire. Directing the operations of our remaining submarines at sea, a few surviving bombers, and the civil recovery of a burning U.S.—all from an orbiting aircraft after big pieces of the American infrastructure have been blown away—imposed staggering requirements on any communication system. And the leadership needed the ability to stop an LNO already under way if negotiations stabilized the crisis or brought it to an end.

A fleet of airborne relays, a network of buried communication lines, a galaxy of hardened communications satellites and secure communication protocols would be needed if the U.S. was to keep its remaining nuclear weapons on a tight leash. That was the job put before me in 1974 as I assumed responsibility for defense telecommunications.

TALKING TO SAIGON

Events in Saigon and then the Gulf of Thailand during the late spring of 1975 brought America's clashing communications cultures into sharp focus. The military was stuck with, and enamored of, old-world, point-to-point "telephone" communications. Thousands of civilians in Saigon and dozens of airmen and marines in southern Cambodia paid the price. When those crises were over, a clear-eyed Deputy Secretary of Defense directed a resentful military to enter the satellite age without delay.

It all started in 1973, when the U.S. withdrew its forces from Vietnam. We promised to look after our friends there if the residual Republic of South Vietnam were to collapse, but that collapse came too fast. In April 1975 the North began its spring offensive. The South Vietnamese forces in the central highlands collapsed and fled. On April 29, Saigon's Tan Son Nhut airport came under attack. Over 150 North Vietnamese rockets smashed into the facility, killing, among others, two U.S. Marines and destroying several U.S. aircraft.

Tan Son Nhut was gone; the American ambassador had dallied while it was still serviceable. He had not allowed an efficient evacuation of America's friends and supporters while he had the chance. Now a sea of humanity began to implode onto the American embassy in downtown Saigon. The only evacuation, for a lucky few, would be aboard the airborne lifeboats operated by the U.S. Marines. As the Pentagon's Director of Telecommunications, I listened in on the events of April 30, 1975, from my vantage point in the National Military Command Center.

The Marine helicopters were directed from a command post aboard a flagship offshore. They communicated with each other by HF (short-wave) radio. We could only listen in horror as the sergeant in charge of the embassy rooftop described the mob. They were battering at the embassy compound's gates as he loaded one helicopter after another with desperate Vietnamese officers, CIA informers, and U.S. civilians fortunate enough to have made it into the embassy. The numbers never added up; additional refugees seemed to make it to the rooftop by unknown routes.

"Fourteen loaded and lifting off, thirty-seven to go," the sergeant would report. Then, "Another fourteen away, twenty-eight to go." He described the North Vietnamese tanks rolling down the boulevards toward him. He asked permission to drop grenades down the embassy stairwell, to keep the mobs away from his helipad. In so doing, he would be killing families who had risked their all to support the U.S. in Vietnam.

And then a voice from the command post offshore: "This had better be your last load, Sergeant. Pull your men out."

With one last burst of grenades and gunfire, a dozen Marines left the embassy's rooftop, and the U.S. presence in Vietnam ended.

President Gerald Ford was listening to the same conversations in the Roosevelt Room of the White House. He later told me of his grief as that sad chapter of American history came to an end.

We in Washington were but bystanders to that evacuation. There were two flagships in the South China Sea off Saigon that day. For whatever reason, the Navy brass responsible for the evacuation gathered on the ship with no satellite terminal. Captains at sea and admirals commanding fleets have a long tradition of operating on their own once they leave port. A ship with a satellite terminal might be seen as a break from that tradition. The officers evacuating Saigon in April 1975 might not have wanted much more "help" from Washington. Perhaps they had received enough during the previous decade.

Deputy Secretary of Defense Bill Clements was outraged by the lack of full-bandwidth communication with those officers, and he was willing to take action. Within days of the evacuation from Saigon, Clements signed a Program Decision Memorandum calling for the purchase and installation of satellite terminals throughout the U.S. Navy.

The price of telephonic parochialism became more focused two weeks later when the *Mayaguez*, a U.S.-registered freighter, was seized by Cambodians off the coast of Koh Tang Island. As this crisis unfolded, U.S. Navy "back-channel" communications gave the Chief of Naval Operations in Washington a somewhat benign view of what was going on. That was because his ships were on the wrong side of the island. The Acting Chairman of the JCS, an Air Force general, was getting a more garbled view from his airborne command posts and helicopters; they were under attack. A rescue plan was adopted that left eighteen American servicemen dead, fifty wounded.

The events at Koh Tang Island made it clear that instantaneous, global, and secure satellite communication was essential. To assure connectivity to the highest levels of government, we directed the Air Force to put satellite terminals on the National Emergency Airborne Command Post, the Boeing 747s then being purchased and outfitted for use by the President or his designated successor in time of crisis. Henceforth, be it evacuations or nuclear confrontations, the White House could be fully involved if it so desired.

DIGITAL TECHNOLOGY, SECURE COMMUNICATIONS, AND THE INTERNET

Governments have found it possible to encrypt teletype communications. At their core, such schemes involve replacing one letter or word in a message with some other, a process known as encoding, then scrambling the recipe that effects this conversion (encryption). Sometimes those encryptions are broken, the most famous example being the British cracking of Germany's Enigma system during World War II. With the use of onetime pads,★ however, teletype communications can be protected. Even so, the slow speed and extensive support needed made teletype communication useful principally between embassies and capitals, between headquarters and command posts, and with ships at sea. It is not feasible for troops in combat to use teletype. They must communicate in real time, with the opportunity for conversational give-and-take, under adverse circumstances, with equipment they can put in their pockets or on their backs. Voice circuits are the only practical choice. In earlier wars, when such voice communication was done by means of analog field radios, it was virtually impossible to encrypt those communications. Intercepts by an enemy often led to ambush, or worse.

Some point-to-point telephone users at one time employed voice "scramblers." These devices chop the original analog voice signal into

---

★ A pair of notebooks, one held by the sender, the other by the receiver. The encryption recipe changes for every word or letter. Once used, an encoding page is discarded, i.e., used but once. In the digital age, the parties use preplanned digital key streams instead of notepads.

time-segmented pieces, then rearrange them for transmission out of order. The signal is reassembled by a receiver holding the reassembly recipe. The resulting voice quality is terrible, and scramblers can be defeated within seconds by a sophisticated computational eavesdropper. At best, scramblers remain useful only in civilian life for those wanting a modest degree of privacy in their personal and business affairs.

Another approach to analog encryption was the use of Native American Indians as radiomen during World War II. Their Navaho and other tongues baffled the Japanese in the Pacific, but by the time of Vietnam, we needed more modern and secure voice communications.

The problem got worse when individual communication links were bundled together into microwave channels. At the end of World War II, "retail" communications were carried out predominantly by copper wires and HF radio links. All that changed with the advent of microwave (upper megahertz) communications. With microwave, voice or teletype channels could be bundled, then transmitted for long distance at high speed. The reader has seen these microwave towers and dishes atop buildings in most big cities. With the coming of microwave in the U.S. and USSR, huge amounts of information could be shipped around town or across the country efficiently. But the open broadcast nature of such systems offered an appetizing target to the Soviet KGB.

When I arrived at the Pentagon, I found a first-class microwave collection scheme at work on the rooftop of the Soviet Embassy on Sixteenth Street in Washington. The Soviets were listening in to the local telephone traffic in D.C., for microwave had become the most efficient way for the Chesapeake and Potomac Telephone Company to expand its local service. The Soviets sorted the significant calls from the trivia by identifying the number called and the instrument doing the calling. While our high government officials were careful not to discuss classified material over the phone, the mere fact that the Secretary of Defense and his staff were working all night, and on what, was a significant indicator to the Soviet intelligence service.

The solution was the immediate rerouting of all critical circuits in Washington, New York, and San Francisco, the three cities where the Soviet Union had embassies or consulates, to underground coaxial cable. This protection included defense contractor and scientific laboratory circuits as well as government lines. When our work was done, the Soviets probably had to go back to their old collection system, already employed in London: sending out an agent every few hours to see which office lights were on in Whitehall.

Coaxial cables were only a patch on the challenge of secure communications, however. The seeds of a real solution had germinated a few years before. In 1968, Robert Noyce left Fairchild Semiconductor to cofound a firm to be known as Intel. At the same time, Jack Kirby, a scientist at Texas Instruments, was working on small, handheld computers. In 1969, Noyce and Kirby, working independently, hit upon the idea of putting a molecular transistor onto a wafer of silicon. Thus was born the monolithic integrated circuit, in time to be known simply as the "microchip." Within a few years this technology formed the basis of the first microcomputers. High-speed digital operations were now possible.

Microchips came to revolutionize defense, consumer electronics, and eventually the entire world's economy. One of the first uses of microcomputers, however, was to encode the human voice into a digital stream. Once digitized, those signals could then be encrypted. During the mid-1970s, I oversaw deployment of the first secure voice telephone systems to key offices. They were huge, bulky cabinets, and someone had to come change the encryption scheme manually every day. But by the time of the Cold War's denouement, commanders could speak with their troops, ships could talk to shore, and bureaucrats could talk to their counterparts overseas without fear of eavesdropping. Today, American STU-3 secure phone sets are everywhere. Secure cell phones carry an encryption package that looks like a long-life battery.

And as this new high-speed digital technology began to spread, a handful of creative minds hit upon the idea of using it to link together the large, mainframe computers then standing alone at the leading universities and research centers in the United States. Since the original system architecture was funded by the Defense Advanced Research Projects Agency, the resulting scheme came to be known as the ARPANET. It was first publicly demonstrated in 1972 at a computer conference. While the net's ability to share research files at widely separated institutions was impressive, it was the introduction of electronic mail that stole the show. The concepts of packet switching, transmission protocols, and an overall architecture, matched to the emerging microchip and minicomputer hardware, gave birth to a whole new world: the Internet.

INTELLIGENCE SATELLITES

In August 1960, America's first photoreconnaissance satellite achieved orbit, took some pictures, and returned the film negatives to earth by means of a reentry capsule. That system, known as *Corona*, was archaic by today's standards, but at the time, it constituted a real breakthrough. On its first operational flight, *Corona* provided about half as much photographic coverage of the Soviet Union as all the previous U-2 flights put together. With the success of subsequent flights, President Eisenhower and his key advisers, who earlier knew there was no bomber gap, could see that there was no missile gap either. They could plan the nation's defense based on facts, not fear.

The development of that first reconnaissance satellite was complicated not only by technology, but by politics and management challenges as well. The CIA provided the cameras and directed the project, while the Air Force provided, launched, operated, and recovered the satellite. In 1961 a most secret organization was created to manage all of the American overhead reconnaissance programs. It was to be known as the National Reconnaissance Office (NRO), and at first it was led by Richard Bissell, the CIA Deputy Director for Plans, and by Joe Charyk, Undersecretary of the Air Force. In their management of the NRO, Bissell and Charyk reported to the Deputy Secretary of Defense in connection with operations and to the Director of Central Intelligence for targeting requirements. This management scheme was cumbersome, and for a while it got worse, but in time a single Director of the NRO, usually the Undersecretary of the Air Force, with a CIA Deputy Director, managed the NRO under the guidance of a joint DoD-CIA executive committee.

For many years the NRO operated that way, with streamlined management and appropriations flowing directly from Congress, its money "fenced" so the services and other defense agencies could not poach on the NRO's turf. The very existence of this organization was classified because of the sensibilities of the nations overflown and photographed by its reconnaissance spacecraft.

As the 1950s drew to a close, there was no clear international law or precedent as to the height limits on national sovereignty. Under international aerial navigation treaties, each nation claimed the airspace over its lands. The shootdown of America's U-2, flying at 70,000 feet over

Russia, underscored that nation's rights to the edges of the atmosphere. But how about outer space? Surely each nation's sovereignty did not extend all the way to the moon.

Nikita Khrushchev, fortunately, and perhaps inadvertently, established the precedent for "Freedom of Space" in October 1957 with the launch of Sputnik I. Although he had railed at the Americans about the U-2's overflights of Russia, he felt free to fly his satellites over the U.S. and numerous other states.

The precedent made sense, of course, because satellites must orbit the earth in the grip of gravity; they do not maneuver within its atmosphere. Even so, the early U.S. and Soviet reconnaissance satellite flights triggered concerns about overflight rights in space. The fact that the United States was conducting such flights, the name of the territories they overflew, and the privacies thus invaded, were to be kept as dark secrets for decades.

During the years that followed, *Corona* gave way to more sophisticated optical systems and better recovery techniques. Resolution improved to the point where one could see the stripes on the Pentagon's parking lot. The U.S. government felt comfortable with early Strategic Arms Limitation agreements because our reconnaissance satellites could check the facts. We knew what the Soviets were doing; we could tell if they were complying with the terms of previous treaties. Satellites also came to be used for electronic surveillance: eavesdropping and establishing an electronic order of battle. These systems remain shrouded in the darkest of secrecy even today, because we do not want the bad guys, whoever they now may be, to know how well we can hear them. And the political sensibilities still persist. Today, national leaders know we orbit over their countries, but at times they do not like having to admit it.

In 1976, I assumed responsibility for the NRO as its sixth director at a time when I also was serving as Secretary of the Air Force. My achievements were not flashy; they were to keep the operational systems on track during the post-Vietnam years and to keep delivering the imaging and signals intelligence product as we negotiated follow-up treaties. But I also was to initiate service from a fundamentally new type of electro-optical reconnaissance satellite.

Early in the decade the wise men of science had asked why we continued to recover photographic film. Why could we not transmit images directly from space in near real time? This would be important in times of crisis. The answer lay in the arcane fields of optics, sensors, and satellite communications. Massive light-sensitive diodes capable of producing electro-optical digital images with exceptional resolution were developed for this spacecraft. The resulting data would be distributed rapidly to earth via wide bandwidth channels and relay satellites. The resulting images would be printed out, using laser beams and huge rolls of film.

All of this came to fruition on my watch as Director of the NRO. The process came to be known as "near real time imaging," *near* real time because it took a few minutes to collect the images from space and to display them on earth. Not quite instant TV from space, but close. All of this technology was packaged in a satellite the size of a Greyhound bus.

The first launch of the electro-optical imaging satellite took place on December 19, 1976. The flight was a complete success. Crystal-clear images were delivered to President Carter on his first day in the White House, in January 1977. In connection with that event, we honored Dr. Edwin Land, an original advocate of this system and many other breakthroughs in U.S. intelligence collection, at an awards ceremony in the Pentagon. "Din" Land was a remarkable man whose foresight, over and over again, brought increased security to the United States and the free world.

Now, a generation later, the NRO is housed in spacious and visible offices near Dulles Airport outside Washington. The organization and the name of its director are listed on Defense Department organization charts. The imaging product is still developed and stored on film, but it is also shipped electronically, in digital form, directly to field commanders in Bosnia, Afghanistan, and Iraq for their use in planning and conducting military operations in real time.

TALKING TO SUBMARINES

In 1960, America's first ballistic-missile-firing submarine, the *George Washington*, put to sea.★ By 1975 over half of our strategic nuclear warheads were aboard a fleet of nuclear-powered Poseidon boats on patrol

---

★ The frantic effort by the Soviets to stay abreast of this development led to the premature sea trials, in 1961, of an early nuclear-powered, missile-firing submarine, the *K-19*. The result was a horror story of fires, reactor malfunctions, and death at sea only recently disclosed and now set forth in the motion picture *K-19, the Widowmaker*.

throughout the North Atlantic and Pacific Oceans as well as the Mediterranean Sea. That development was a great step toward stability in times of crisis. These warships were virtually undetectable while submerged, and thus virtually immune to surprise attack.

The Soviets did not enjoy a similar immunity. Their early submarines were noisy and thus easy for American technology to track. Throughout much of the 1960s most Soviet SSBNs heading out on patrol were identified by underwater sensors, by silent U.S. Navy attack submarines, and by airborne P-3 aircraft dropping sonobuoys. This tracking capability became more difficult to maintain in the 1970s when the Walkers, Navy radiomen father and son, gave away the game to the Soviets. At the same time, the Japanese sold the Soviets the technology to mill much quieter submarine propellers.

A quiet underwater fleet may be a good thing in some respects, but if one cannot detect or track a submarine, neither can one communicate with it. Keeping control of the submarine fleet, especially when it acquired nuclear arms, became a serious challenge.

Saltwater is a good conductor of electricity; it readily absorbs electromagnetic radiation. The degree of that absorption is a function of the incoming radiation's frequency; very high frequency radar and radio signals cannot penetrate seawater at all. As a result, the submarines of World War II and immediately thereafter had to surface if they were to communicate. Those diesel-powered boats would deploy their HF (shortwave) antennae at night, from the surface or from snorkel depth, while recharging their batteries. But with the advent of more sophisticated adversaries, sitting atop the water or deploying a snorkel was too risky. Besides, HF transmission could easily be intercepted, would give away a submarine's location, and was too unreliable.

The coming of nuclear power rendered the need to surface obsolete. To communicate with submarines only a few feet below the surface, but invisible to radar or an observer's eye, the nuclear navies turned to Very Low Frequency communication systems. These transmitters operated in the three to thirty kilohertz range, resulting in a low data rate and requiring long receiving antennae at sea,★ but those VLF signals

---

★ Antennae are best sized when they are one-fourth of the transmitted signal's wavelength. Wavelength is inversely proportional to frequency. Thus megahertz frequencies (cell phones) require small antennae. VLF (the Navy) requires antennae over a mile long.

could penetrate a few feet of seawater half a world away. VLF became the standard for both Soviet and U.S. Navy communication with their nuclear submarines.

As Soviet search technology became better, however, the Navy wanted to patrol at greater depths. Studies showed that transmitters operating at Extremely Low Frequencies (ELF, forty to eighty hertz) could communicate with deeply submerged boats. The data rate would be very slow and the required antenna huge, but the game was worth the candle. Using an ELF communication system, the nation's strategic deterrent could remain truly undetectable, yet its payload of nuclear death and destruction would stay under the continuous and effective control of the National Command Authorities. Arranging for the capability to transmit such ELF signals was the catch. The required antenna would be miles long and needed to lie atop low conductivity rock. The best U.S. geology for such transmitters lay in northern Wisconsin and Michigan's Upper Peninsula.

Funding and constructing these ELF antennae involved the worst, most protracted, and most nonsensical environmental fight of my career. The ELF ground-based antennae were essentially power lines. There were some who thought the electromagnetic signals given off by such lines were bad for living creatures. Subsequent studies by the National Institutes for Health as well as the International Agency for Research on Cancer found the claimed evidence to be "weak" or "inadequate." The magnetic fields under a power line correspond to those a foot away from a kitchen microwave or a TV set. They are far less than those generated by a hair dryer. Nonetheless, I spent much of my tour as Director of Telecommunications arguing the case for ELF with the scientific community and members of Congress. For years we weighed the nation's security, keeping tight control of those nukes at sea, against concerns about the jobs of Michiganders and their environment.

My chance to lobby the most important Michigander of all came on a summer evening in July 1975. Gerald Ford had been President less than a year. We knew each other from earlier days, and he knew of my track record as a political manager. He wanted to talk. You may be important; you think you're cool. But everyone's first visit to the Oval Office is a fright. The majesty of the White House itself is overwhelming. Entry through the gates and guards, passing the Marine at the entry to the West Wing, walking down the narrow hallways, cramped for space but reeking of power, and standing in the President's outer office, all burn themselves into your memory. They leave the visitor inarticulate, barely able to hear the soothing sounds from the President's secretary. And then those fateful words: "The President will see you now." Seven o'clock on the hot summer evening of July 17, 1975, was that moment for me. I was going to meet with President Ford, alone in the Oval Office, to discuss his political future.

A short eleven months before, Gerald Ford had succeeded to the presidency when Richard Nixon resigned. Upon taking the oath of office, Ford declared that our national nightmare was over, but in time he would have to endure many more nightmares of his own. In addition to abuse from the Watergate Congress and the fall of Saigon, Ford now had to deal with his own floundering campaign for election to the presidency. In our meeting, he came immediately to the point. He asked if I would join his campaign as its deputy campaign manager, its "political director." The campaign manager at the time was resort developer and former Army Secretary Bo Callaway, who was soon to be engulfed in a public debate over the validity of his land-use permits. Callaway would be cleared of any wrongdoing, but he chose to resign.

I had run major political campaigns before and would again, all of them successful and some against immense odds. But like *Shane*, I did not want my talents as a political gunslinger known or recognized. I had gone straight. I was a physicist and businessman. At that time, I was working in the Pentagon as a high-tech bureaucrat. I liked what I was doing; I told Mr. Ford that the continuing recruitment of political helpers from the Pentagon was a poor idea and that my growing expertise in nuclear control was more important to the nation's security. I argued that moving me to a campaign job would set the wrong tone as our nation tried to recover from Vietnam and Watergate. I recommended the services of a real political pro, Stuart Spencer (whom the President had never met, but subsequently hired), and then, as quickly as I could, diverted the conversation from presidential politics to the ELF project in Upper Michigan.

You can take the President out of Congress, but you cannot take the congressman out of a President. In a flash Ford was deep into the complaints he had heard from his former constituents, about radio waves sterilizing the cattle, about miles of ditches to be dug and filled by dozens of contractors and hundreds of workers, about the vulnerability of such a system to Soviet attack, and how the bucolic Upper Peninsula of Michigan would become a prime target. He weighed all of this against the need to stay in touch with his submarines. When I left in the gathering dusk of that summer evening, the President agreed to pass the word to his Michigan allies and constituents: support construction of the ELF antenna; it is important. A few weeks later he nominated me to serve as Secretary of the Air Force during the rest of his term.

THROUGH THE LOOKING GLASS

The world's passage from the industrial to the information age was as transforming as Alice in Wonderland's trip through the looking glass. On the far side, everything looked different. A citizen of the old order once wrote that Joseph Stalin was Genghis Khan with a telephone. That was true in more ways than one. The point-to-point nature of the telephone lets the leader decide who gets what information. It leads to compartmented, isolated systems. The dictator can have his way, everywhere, quickly and efficiently. On the battlefield, a defender relying on telephonic and point-to-point radios can rest on his internal lines of communication. He can impose burdensome losses on any attacker.

I once visited the Novodevichi Cemetery outside Moscow, where the remains of many Soviet military heroes lay buried. On their headstones one finds the usual vital statistics and a bust of the great man. The astonishing thing is that many of those statues show the general not on horseback, but with a telephone to his ear. That was the symbol of real power in the Stalin era.

The problem is, when a military situation gets fluid, the man with the phone may not know who needs the information he has. He may not know who can act on it most efficiently. The advent of satellites and the associated rapid dissemination of information on the ground ended that Stalinist dilemma. It marked the beginning of the broadcast era, the Gorbachev age, when the receiver, not the sender, would decide what information he or she gets. The old world was turned upside down.

In military affairs, the commander in chief or an aircraft over the battlefield now can broadcast his instructions or his observations without knowing who needs the information he has. Everyone on the secure net gets it. The platoon leader, the pilots of other aircraft, can decide what information they want as they extract it from the broadcast flood. The attacker, if he enjoys information superiority, can draw detailed maps from satellites overhead in real time. He can identify tanks that cannot see him, and destroy them before they know they are under attack. He can watch an artillery piece fire, and return that fire while the outgoing round is still in the air.

In politics, the President in Washington or aboard his airborne command post can listen in to whatever and whomever he wants. He can query the JCS at the Pentagon or a platoon leader in the desert. He can speak directly to his commanders, his own people, or the people on the other side. It was this ability to be heard worldwide that made President Reagan's Westminster speech—demanding democracy worldwide—and his evil empire speech (serving notice on the Soviet people that they had not been abandoned) so important. The ability of the Great Communicator—as Reagan was dubbed—to wage public diplomacy, to illuminate the illegitimacy of Stalin's telephone-age empire, was a product of the broadcast age.

The problem with this new age is that the receiver has been overwhelmed by information. We can all now receive hundreds of channels on our home TV. But in the military, the receiver does not have time to sort through all the incoming data. He often misses vital pieces of his puzzle.

The Internet is changing that. Satellites no longer flood every receiver with more information than it wants. They now load that material into data banks, waiting for the military commander or patrol leader to call for the information he needs. AWACS and JSTARS aircraft can track virtually any equipment that moves, adding that information to the data base. Then a commander leading a tank column can ask his computer screen whether a convoy that suddenly appears is friend or foe. Within the life-or-death window of a few seconds, he can initiate or withhold his fire. In 1991, and even more so in 2003, the Coalition attackers had these advantages, imposing casualties of well over a hundred to one on the defending Iraqis. In the battle for Baghdad, Iraqi tanks played no meaningful role.

We have moved to the age of network-centric warfare. The general no longer need sit atop a hill, on his horse, overseeing the battle on the vast plain below. He can sit in his command center, half a world away, surrounded by screens, maps, and terminals that give him a far more complete picture of the battle, in real time.

The Internet-enabled twenty-first-century American deployments around Kabul and Baghdad made the 1991 battlefields of southern Iraq look archaic, but as the Cold War drew to its close, those 1991 examples were good enough to change history. Officers of the Red Army watched Desert Storm from the sidelines. They saw their equipment trashed, their doctrine overrun. They could only advise their political masters in the Kremlin that the game was up. The Great Communicator had delivered the same message to the people of Russia through different channels.

CHAPTER 13

The Air Force Recovers from Vietnam

*"Who understands the secret of the reaping of the grain? . . .
Or why we all must die a bit before we grow again?"*
—The Fantasticks

THAT IS THE WAY IT WAS for the United States Air Force during the
middle Cold War years. In the 1950s, America's fighter jocks dominated the skies over Korea. They ran up a ten-to-one score against the
offending North Korean MiGs. Forty years later the Yanks again ruled
the skies. USAF pilots popped laser and video-guided bombs down the
air shafts of Iraqi intelligence centers with impunity. But in between lay
winter's laboring pain. We all had to die a bit, in Vietnam, before we
grew again.

A TRAIN WRECK IN THE SKY

Americans have come to accept the loss of a dozen or so aircraft during any given modern-day struggle. During the war in Korea, the UN Command (principally the U.S.) lost 139 aircraft. But during the years of its involvement in Southeast Asia (1962-73), the losses of the United States Air Force alone totalled 2,257 aircraft. The Navy, Marines, and Army suffered proportional losses.

Eighty-three percent of the USAF combat losses were to ground fire; that is, antiaircraft artillery and small arms. Only 6 percent were lost to SAMs. The pilots of most aircraft hit by SAMs never saw the missiles coming, for if a pilot saw a SAM, he could usually outmaneuver it.

Only 4 percent of the losses came as a result of air-to-air combat. The air-to-air exchange ratio was only 1.85 to one in favor of the U.S. It was only 1.21 to one against the most common airborne enemy, MiG-21s. In comparing these kill ratios to other wars, however, one must bear in mind that in the skies over Vietnam, the U.S. combatants were often fighter-bombers heavily laden with ground-attack ordnance en route to other targets. Over half of the losers in air-to-air combat never knew they were under attack until they were hit. How could all of this have happened?

In the aftermath of Korea, Eisenhower's "new look" placed the nation's bets on nuclear deterrence. There was to be no buildup for conventional war. It was assumed that if war broke out in Europe, it would soon go nuclear. Aircraft such as the F-100 and F-105 were developed to deliver tactical nuclear weapons onto enemy positions at low altitudes and high speed. The F-102 and F-104 were developed to intercept Soviet bombers. Fighting in the sky was neglected and support of troops on the ground was ignored. Attacks on enemy infrastructure were to be effected with nukes, so repeated sorties would not be needed. Any ground war in Asia was thought to be foolish and was assumed away. As a result, a well-meant but misguided allocation of resources soon left the U.S. Air Force focused on nuclear war, to the exclusion of its other duties.

The early 1960s brought a fresh and more realistic look at nuclear matters. The Kennedy administration recognized that the Soviet Union was a major thermonuclear power, and that the USSR would soon have the ability to deliver nuclear weapons to U.S. soil. Thus, any American use of nukes could only trigger a broader exchange that would be lethal to both sides. "Assured Destruction" was the term used by Secretary of Defense Robert McNamara to describe our planned ability to respond decisively, even in the event of a surprise nuclear attack. Pundits quickly amended this expression to *Mutual* Assured Destruction, with the acronym, MAD, reflecting their view of McNamara's policies. The Kennedy administration, awash with youthful exuberance, turned to a theory of Flexible Response to deal with the threat of Soviet nuclear attacks, to an enthusiasm for Special Forces to deal with conventional threats, and to systems analysis to deal with the ever-recurrent budget crunch.

One casualty of fiscal analysis was the C-5, a large transport aircraft that fell victim to the concept of "package procurement." Under this theory, a contractor was to develop and produce a fleet of aircraft at a fixed price, set in advance. Lockheed accepted a fixed price contract for the package procurement of the C-5, a radically new concept in air transport. When the design was complete, the aircraft, on paper, was overweight. Lockheed cut back on wing structure to meet the weight specification, but as a result, wing life was shortened by over 75 percent. The ultimate replacement of the C-5's wings cost $1 billion and untold grief with the U.S. Congress.

Another marginal idea was the "one size fits all" approach to aircraft procurement. This led to the TFX disaster. This tactical fighter, later to be known as the F-111, was to be a common aircraft for Navy and Air Force use, but operating and landing an aircraft at sea is very different from flying and fighting over mountainous terrain. The result was a difficult aircraft, initially lethal to its crews. The Navy never bought any, but in time the F-111 became popular with the Air Force as a medium-range bomber with excellent low-altitude penetration abilities. As an EF-111, it also served well as an electronics warfare platform. When it was time to go to war in Vietnam, however, the Air Force had to turn to a Navy airplane, the F-4, if it was to have any air-to-air capability at all. It purchased 2,712 of those aircraft during that war.

With the advent of the Johnson administration and the escalation of the war in Vietnam, "Gradualism" was adopted as a strategy. Inexperienced civilian leadership and a few misguided generals believed that an enemy's actions could be controlled by the application of force, increased gradually so as to minimize the risk of Soviet or Chinese intervention. U.S. leaders felt gradualism was important, given the lessons of Korea and the dangers of the nuclear threshold; China had just entered the nuclear club. Under this theory, each U.S. air raid was to send a message. Attacks on North Vietnam were punctuated by nine cease-fires and ten bombing halts, each followed by pleas for negotiations, all ignored by the North Vietnamese.

Targets were picked or withheld by the President, his Secretary of Defense, National Security Adviser, and Joint Chiefs chairman at White House working luncheons. Those targeting decisions were not made by operational commanders in the field. The resulting air war abandoned the principles of surprise, massed force, and timely execution, all fundamental to military success.

The foolishness of these policies became obvious to Lieutenant Joe Ralston one day in 1967 as he flew his F-105 into North Vietnam, en route to targets in Route Package 6B. Looking down, he saw enemy MiG-21s taxiing for take off from the Phuc Yen airfield. In a few moments they would be airborne; a few moments after that, they would be trying to kill his buddies in the following wave of F-105s. At that moment those MiG-21s were very vulnerable, taxiing ducks. In earlier wars, Ralston and his wingman would have pounced, destroying a whole flight of MiG-21s on the ground, but on that day Phuc Yen was not an approved target. Those MiGs could prepare for battle unmolested. The aircraft themselves were not to be attacked until they were airborne. Ralston had to fly on; the pilots in the next wave paid the price.

A CHANGING OF THE GUARD

As the war in Vietnam dragged on, the morale of many sent there to fight sank through the floor. The men who flew executed their missions with pride, but many were resentful of Washington's naiveté, and the U.S. Air Force was learning lessons that would change its entire culture.

This process of recovery and change started as the sixties ended. The Nixon and Ford administrations brought a new generation of civilian technocrats to the Pentagon, men and women willing to listen to the lessons learned in Vietnam, willing to bring a political consistency to their work, and willing to promote those with serious Vietnam experience into positions of responsibility. My predecessor as Secretary of the Air Force, myself, and the Director of Defense Research and Engineering in the succeeding Carter administration, were the civilian leaders who presided over this transition from the Air Force of Vietnam to the powerhouse of Desert Storm. Our Secretaries of Defense—James Schlesinger, Donald Rumsfeld, and Harold Brown—provided the leadership; thousands of men and women in the ranks did the hard work.

The Pentagon is a surprisingly efficient and well-run enterprise, even though its basic mission—war—is an inherently wasteful product that no one wants. The way it works is, the service secretaries, in partnership with their service chiefs of staff, build the forces. They recruit and train people, develop and purchase equipment, see to the maintenance of that equipment throughout its life cycle, and manage the bases and network of benefits that support the whole system. The service secretaries seek appropriations from Congress and oversee the prudent expenditure of those funds. As such, they are the primary civilian advocates for their services' case to the American public. The secretaries manage selection, promotion, and assignment of most general officers, all of whom serve at the pleasure of the President with the advice and consent of the Senate. They do these things in accordance with policies laid down by the Secretary of Defense and his under and assistant secretaries. The Director of Defense Research and Engineering oversees the military investment in cutting-edge technology. When their job is done and the forces assembled, the service secretaries and their chiefs then turn the forces they have developed over to the Secretary of Defense. The services do not run wars; the Secretary of Defense does that, deploying forces and operating them through the unified theater commanders as directed by the President.

As America's involvement in Vietnam drew to a close, a most remarkable technocrat took charge as Secretary of the Air Force. John McLucas, fifty-two at the time, had a strong background in military electronics and government service. In 1969 he came to the Pentagon to serve as Undersecretary of the Air Force and Director of the National Reconnaissance Office. McLucas watched the end of the war in Vietnam from the front row, absorbing the lessons of that conflict at every turn. In July 1973 he became the tenth Secretary of the Air Force.

McLucas led the Air Force away from the mentality of package procurement and into an era of prototypes. "Fly before you buy" became his watchword. He guided the Air Force's transition to post-Vietnam tactical aircraft and supported those who were trying to apply the lessons learned in that war. But despite these achievements, John McLucas's Air Force career was cut short, and mine was created, by the President's decision to send him off to run the Federal Aviation Administration.

At the time, I was serving as Director of Telecommunications for the Secretary of Defense. As McLucas left, I was tapped to succeed him, confirmed by the U.S. Senate without much trouble and, on January 2, 1976, sworn in as the eleventh Secretary of the Air Force. I remained in office through the end of the Ford administration and beyond. President-elect Jimmy Carter designated Harold Brown to be his Secretary of Defense. Brown, in turn, asked that I stay in place through the first hundred days of the new administration. I did so, overseeing the transition budget and the reassignment of most of the Air Force four-star general officers to their Carter-era responsibilities.

Secretary Brown chose Bill Perry to serve as his Director of Defense Research and Engineering. Perry had founded and run an electronics intelligence firm in Silicon Valley and was attuned to the possibilities of smart munitions. The nation owes its greatest thanks to Brown and Perry for pursuing those possibilities and for initiating key developments in the area of stealthy aircraft.

In his final year in office, President Carter came to appreciate the perfidy of the Soviet leadership. He proposed a defense budget, shaped by Brown and Perry, that laid the technical groundwork for the Reagan era to follow. From 1973 through 1980, the years of the McLucas/ Reed/Perry tenure, the lessons of Vietnam were absorbed by an Air Force eager to enter a new era.

LESSONS LEARNED

The first lesson learned in the skies over Vietnam, one that must never be forgotten, is that the primary mission of an air force is to fly and fight in the sky. If it cannot do that, if it cannot gain control of the skies over the battlefield and over the enemy's infrastructure, then it has failed, for it will never be able to move on to the destruction of those enemy assets.

To gain control of the skies, an air force needs an air superiority fighter. Such an aircraft must be fast and highly maneuverable. It must be hard to see, by the human eye, radar, or infrared sensors. The pilot must have near perfect visual access to the skies around him and must have a radar that will let him look and shoot down as well as up, to discriminate a moving target from the background earth. He must be armed with air-to-air missiles that are as maneuverable as the enemy's aircraft, and he must have good old-fashioned guns at his disposal. Last, but not least, an air superiority fighter must be affordable, for numbers do count. An air force that is to prevail must put a large number of its aircraft into the fight. The F-4 failed most of these criteria. It was a jack-of-all-trades, master of none. Much larger than its MiG-21 adversary, the F-4 was made even more visible by its smoky engine.

The Operational Requirement for the needed new fighter was written and approved by the Air Staff in the autumn of 1965, but it took two years for the bureaucracy to settle on the specifics, sort out the tradeoffs, and forecast the technology. Two more years passed until McDonnell Douglas was selected as the contractor to build this air superiority fighter, now known as the F-15.

In one of his first moves as Secretary of the Air Force, John McLucas approved the F-15 for production. It first flew at Edwards Air Force Base in July 1972, and the first deliveries began in November 1974. The first squadron went operational in September 1975, half a year after the last American was evacuated from the rooftops of Saigon.

Two new technology Pratt & Whitney F-100 turbofan engines give the F-15 incredible power, enough to accelerate to Mach 2.5 in a flash, enough to stand the aircraft on its tail. The F-15 is the first fighter with more engine thrust than weight. It carries a pulse Doppler radar that lets the pilot look down and shoot down. His elevated seating, surrounded by a bubble canopy, gives him 360 degrees of vision as well as the ability to look over the side and thus below his aircraft. The F-15 is not as small as some would have liked, but its size was the price of its immense power and maneuverability, the latter arising from twin rudders and large horizontal surfaces. The plane can turn on a dime and can outmaneuver any foreign fighter in the world. The horizontal tail surfaces alone are as big as the wings of a MiG-21. One very lucky pilot, involved in a midair collision that sheared off a large portion of one wing, discovered that his F-15 still had enough lift to get him home safely. Size also makes room for some formidable armament: four Sidewinder AIM-9 heat-seeking missiles, four Sparrow AIM-7 radar guided missiles, and a powerful 20mm cannon. The F-15, in conjunction with the later developed F-16, now patrols the skies over U.S. cities. As of this writing, the F-15s flown in combat by U.S. and Israeli pilots have racked up a kill ratio of 104 to zero.

THE LESSON OF THE THANH HOA BRIDGE

Once an air force has won control of the skies, it must move on to its major missions—the destruction of an enemy's infrastructure and the support of its own troops on the ground. Neither job is easy; the Thanh Hoa bridge became a prime example. The bridge, spanning the Red River south of Hanoi, was a major logistics artery for the forces of North Vietnam, and thus a prime candidate for destruction early in the war. On April 3, 1965, forty-six F-105s attacked it, to no avail. Bombs missed or bounced off the concrete abutments, while the run-in to the target was a killing field for the North Vietnamese anti-aircraft gunners. Over the next three years, 869 missions were flown against the bridge at Thanh Hoa, with no results other than the loss of eleven aircraft and their crews.

From 1968 to 1972 there was a halt to bombing in the North. During that interlude, ingenious engineers looked into the guidance of bombs and artillery shells by means of laser beams. The work paid off. On May 13, 1972, a strike force of F-4s again attacked the Thanh Hoa bridge, but this time they were better equipped. The raiders delivered two dozen laser-guided bombs in that one raid; the Thanh Hoa bridge was dropped into the river, rendered useless for the rest of the war. During the following month, laser-guided bombs dropped fourteen more bridges.

Other members of the technical community were experimenting with the use of TV cameras in the nose of air-to-surface missiles. This class of weapons was given the name Maverick; its great advantage was that the host aircraft could leave the scene after launch; no continuous illumination of the target was necessary. Later variants turned to the use of infrared images. A half-dozen versions of Maverick were developed and deployed during the 1970s, all most useful in attacking armored vehicles and heavily defended installations, since a Maverick's shaped-charge warhead can penetrate over two *feet* of steel.

In the air-to-air battle, the missile improvements on our watch related to smokeless motors and all-aspect infrared trackers. In the early dogfights over Vietnam, a pilot had to get on his adversary's tail to lock onto the heat from the target's engine. In the mid-seventies we developed "all-aspect" trackers. They can lock on from any angle, before the "merge," as adversaries initially approach each other head-on.

By the end of the seventies these smart, imaging, and laser-guided weapons were all part of the Air Force inventory. We were ready for the tanks and bunkers of Iraq. In 1991, 9 percent of the weapons dropped on Iraq were precision-guided munitions. By 2003 that figure had risen to over two-thirds.

THE LESSON OF LETHAL GROUND FIRE

The support of troops on the ground is even more difficult than blowing up bridges or buildings. Shooting up a tank or a truck convoy requires a low-altitude approach by an aircraft at speeds slow enough to lay down plenty of rocket or cannon fire. Imaging weapons may be too expensive for the job, and bombing does not work. An iron bomb must land within twenty-five feet of a truck to do much damage. A direct hit is required to kill a Russian tank. But the average miss distance for bombs dropped in Vietnam was 323 feet. To achieve the accuracy needed for a kill, a flying gunship is needed, but such low-and-slow aircraft are vulnerable to small arms fire, machine guns, and antiaircraft artillery.

As the war in Vietnam wore on, a succession of Air Force officials entered into joint agreements to do something to improve close air support for ground troops. The eventual solution was to start from scratch: design an aircraft that could carry tank-killing armament, withstand small arms fire, and loiter over ground targets at low speed.

In April 1970 the Air Staff approved a concept paper for the development of a prototype AX (Attack Experimental) aircraft; two years later the A-10 began full-scale development. It was unlike any other attack aircraft ever built. For redundancy, it had two engines, spaced far from each other, so an explosion in one was not likely to damage the other. They were low-thrust, high-bypass engines, not attractive to hotshot fighter pilots, but economical in the consumption of fuel, and hard for heat-seeking missiles to find. The A-10 would loiter over the battlefield for five hours at a time. Designed with very large, straight wings, the resulting airplane could operate from small airfields close to the front lines; 4,000-foot runways would do.

The unique and least visible feature of the A-10 was the protection afforded the pilot and his cockpit equipment. They sat in a titanium bathtub impervious to small arms and machine-gun fire. More than that, the bathtub could withstand direct hits from a 23mm antiaircraft gun. The pilot's head and shoulders were protected by a bulletproof windscreen. The fuel tanks were filled with a fire-retardant foam, akin to a sponge that would accommodate the liquid but extinguish any conflagration if tracers or cannon shells hit the tanks.

Then there was the payload, the 30mm GAU-8 Gatling-gun cannon. I fired it once at a test range and have never seen or heard anything like it. A 30mm round is over one and an eighth inches in diameter, and each round is made of depleted uranium★ and weighs three-fourths of a pound. Yet the gun can fire seventy rounds per second, each leaving the barrel at over 2,300 mph. The effect on a heavily armored tank a mile away is devastating, lethal to the occupants. The A-10 also was designed with eleven hard points under the wings and fuselage, fixtures on which to hang missiles, smart bombs, or other ordnance.

The first of these aircraft flew in February 1975. John McLucas ordered them into production on his watch, although the first squadron did not go operational until after I got there, in October 1977. The A-10s acquitted themselves well in the Persian Gulf and beyond; the real problem was to get them produced in the first place. The budgets for these unglamorous airplanes had to be shepherded and protected by the Secretaries of the Army and Air Force at every turn. All told, 713 were produced, and most experts now find them indispensable in our post–Cold War conflicts.

FLIGHT SAFETY RULES CAN BE HAZARDOUS TO A PILOT'S HEALTH

Bureaucracy can kill just as surely as bullets. The U.S. Air Force entered the war in Vietnam armed with a policy known as the Universally Assignable Pilot. The idea was that every pilot should be able to fly virtually any airplane in the Air Force inventory. The purpose of this policy was flexibility, to give the Air Force the ability to focus talent where it was most needed. The result was inexperience, disastrous during the trying moments of intense combat. When tracers are flying past, a

---

★ Uranium, because it is 67 percent denser than lead. "Depleted" refers to the removal of the fissionable U-235 isotope, to be used for weapons or reactors. What is left is the inert but very dense U-238.

SAM is rising, or the fire warning light goes on, there is little time for "universal" pilots to reflect on where the levers and buttons are in *this particular* airplane.

The other hazard to the survival of new pilots, oddly enough, was the sanctity of flight safety rules. During flight and then combat crew training, the protection of the aircraft and the safe return of the pilot became the primary criteria for judging a training unit's performance. This meant that realistic combat maneuvers, dogfights lacking only live ammunition, with gut-wrenching dives to the nap of the earth, were out of the question. The result of this risk-averse approach was some lethal on-the-job training for new fighter pilots once they got to Vietnam. The statistics were interesting: a pilot's first ten missions were his most dangerous; after that there were few losses.

Major Moody Suter was only one of many fighter pilots who noticed these facts of life in Vietnam, but he was the most persistent in doing something about them. He and his comrades badgered their superiors into doing a better job of simulating adversaries during combat training. In the early days of Vietnam, flights of F-4s would mix it up with each other in the skies over their own bases, but F-4s flown by Americans do not resemble MiG-21s flown by Russians, Chinese, or Vietnamese. The MiG-21 is significantly smaller, harder to see, and much more maneuverable than the F-4. The MiGs' tactics also were much different from our own.

In the fall of 1972 the young American pilots talked the Air Force into creating the 64th Fighter Weapons Squadron, an "Aggressor Squadron" equipped with T-38s, then F-5Es. These small, supersonic aircraft were flown by instructors who had studied MiG tactics. They flew against green F-4 pilots. The results were impressive but incomplete. A similar approach to air-to-air combat training, known as Top Gun, was initiated by the U.S. Navy in 1969.

In the spring of 1975, with the war in Vietnam over, Major Suter took his statistics and ideas to the Air Staff, to Secretary McLucas, and to General Bob Dixon, commander of the Tactical Air Command. Suter had flown 232 missions in Vietnam, so he knew what he was talking about, and he convinced Dixon. The product was Red Flag, a plan for new pilots to log their first ten combat missions in a fully realistic but hopefully nonlethal training environment. The exercises would be expensive, involving the full panoply of tankers, electronic countermeasures, aggressor squadrons, integrated missile and antiaircraft systems, as well as instrumentation to keep track of hits and thus bring home the evidence. These dangerous lessons had to be learned and committed to memory. There could be aerial collisions; distracted pilots might fly their aircraft into the ground. Accident rates were bound to go up, but the increased life expectancy in battle would be worth it.

The Red Flag range was built at Nellis Air Force Base in Nevada, and the first exercise was conducted in November 1975. Thirty-seven aircraft were involved, along with a ground environment heavy with Soviet and Chinese equipment. These exercises continued during McLucas's and my tenures. We lost twenty-four aircraft to midair collisions and ground impact over the first four years of Red Flag. During the first year alone, the all–Air Force accident rate was 2.8 crashes per 100,000 hours of flying time. At Red Flag it was eleven times that, at thirty-two accidents per 100,000 hours. The largest single problem was collision with the ground as trainees tried to fly under radar coverage or got too low when delivering weapons.

Congress was horrified, but we pressed on. The results showed in the wars that followed. Pilots returning unscathed from early missions over Iraq in 1991 agreed that the combat there was a picnic compared to the rigors of Red Flag. In time, the Iraqi Air Force fled to the dubious safety of Iran rather than continue to face the USAF. A decade later, the Iraqi Air Force was nowhere to be seen.

THE PROBLEM OF COST—THE NEED FOR NUMBERS

As the USAF began to rebuild its aircraft inventory, the matter of economics crept in. Big two-engine planes are expensive to buy, although they may be cheaper in the long run because the two engines provide more reliability, a better chance of getting home after a flameout. They have more power and thus can achieve higher speeds, and they can carry more avionics, such as the radar that allows pilots to dominate the skies. But those advantages carry a price tag, and the lessons learned in other wars made it clear that high attrition rates must be expected in future air battles. Numbers count.

In 1972, McLucas initiated the development of competing single-engine prototype lightweight fighters. After a flyoff in 1975, McLucas announced that the General Dynamics F-16 was the winner, based on its agility, acceleration, range, fuel efficiency, and lower cost. In June 1975, four of our NATO allies followed suit. The F-16 was to be produced as a NATO aircraft, with components manufactured in Norway,

Denmark, and Belgium, with some assembly to be accomplished in the Netherlands. Major production would take place at the General Dynamics plant in Fort Worth, Texas. The negotiations to make all this happen were intricate, but they succeeded, thanks to the guiding genius of Air Force Assistant Secretary Frank Shrontz.

When the first F-16 squadron became operational, in October 1980, its capabilities became obvious. It carries no long range radar, but once in a dogfight, it's unbeatable. It has also evolved into an effective carrier of smart munitions. The United States has produced 2,200 of these aircraft so far. They are a favorite of our allies and other export customers.

THE HIDDEN COSTS OF VIETNAM

Vietnam was not just a war, it was a crusade to defend those who chose freedom from the Viet Cong terrorists. But it incurred a terrible cost. Some of those costs were tangible and obvious, but others were not. Domestic needs went unmet, the dangers of inflation were ignored, and the strategic forces of the United States fell into disrepair. By 1970 the Soviet Union had achieved parity with the U.S. in many measures of strategic nuclear firepower. If those trends continued unchecked, the Soviets could achieve the power to blackmail, to operate below the nuclear threshold, with a free hand.

This disintegration started in 1961, a year of major and serious confrontation between the U.S. and USSR, when every crisis, from Vienna to Berlin to surprise nuclear tests, should have sounded the alarm. The Cuban missile crisis of 1962 made matters worse, yet that was the year when the last B-52s and B-58s were delivered to the Air Force, the proposed B-70 bomber was cancelled, and Skybolt development ended. The latter was a joint U.S.-UK effort to produce an air-launched attack missile that would extend the life of the bomber fleet. Its unilateral cancellation infuriated the Brits.

As Vietnam began to devour more of the defense budget, ICBM modernization slowed and the construction of new silos stopped. In the 1970s the new Nixon administration tried to stem the tide of Soviet advances with ABM and SALT treaties, but once those agreements were in hand, the Soviets unleashed a new series of missile tests that made clear their goal of ascension to a position of strategic nuclear superiority. It was this landscape of emerging Soviet SS-18 rockets, an aging U.S. bomber fleet, and a Brezhnev Doctrine seeking global hegemony, that cried out for attention as the war in Vietnam wound down.

The cures to the Air Force's strategic weapons problems were varied, but they began to receive my attention in 1976. The remaining B-52 fleet was to be refurbished with new wing structures, improved engines, and modern avionics. Cruise missiles were developed to allow those bombers to operate in a stand-off mode, then to challenge the entire Soviet defense system with ground-based models. A new long range bomber, the B-1, was put into production, with a radar cross section only 1 percent of the B-52's. The Commander-in-Chief of SAC was delighted to discover, in 1976, that U.S. radars could not find or track the experimental B-1 he was flying in a bombing competition. But that was only the tip of the iceberg. It turns out that stealth, the greatest challenge ever posed to the air defense systems of the Soviet Union and its client states, was conceived within the Soviet Union itself.

In 1966, Pyotr Ufimtsev, the chief scientist at the Moscow Institute of Radio Engineering, wrote a paper entitled, "Method of Edge Waves in the Physical Theory of Diffraction." In this arcane and virtually unintelligible paper, Ufimtsev applied Maxwell's equations to the reflection of electromagnetic radiation—that is, radar—from various two-dimensional geometries. Senior Soviet designers were uninterested in his work, but in 1975, upon the translation of this paper into English, an astute scientist at Lockheed's Skunk Works sat up and took notice. It became clear to Denys Overholser that Ufimtsev had shown the way to calculate, rather than just model, the radar cross section of any object. Furthermore, these calculational tools could then be used to design the specific contours of an aircraft so as to render it virtually invisible to radar of any kind.

Testing of the radar returns from competitive stealth models started in 1975; development of a stealthy aircraft started on my watch, in 1976. Bill Perry, the succeeding Director of Defense Research and Engineering, pushed the program hard. A prototype aircraft first flew on December 1, 1977, and the first production of the F-117A flew on June 18, 1981. It was deployed as a secret "silver bullet" in three squadrons, none visible until needed on the opening night of Desert Storm.

Pyotr Ufimtsev came to lecture at UCLA once the Cold War was over. Until his arrival in the United States, he was unaware of his contribution to the American stealth program, but he was not surprised. Not only were his Russian peers disinterested in his work, they did not have the computational power to utilize his gift. It took a Cray I to design the F-117L, a Cray II to move up to the rounded contours of the B-2.

In the field of ballistic missiles, we set about doubling the effectiveness of the existing Minuteman III, with improved warhead yields and guidance upgrades. Then we pursued the full-scale development of an MX missile that was to replace the 1960s' weapons with a system that would redress the Soviet's advances. To command and control these new assets, the civilian leadership of the 1970s supported Air Force visionaries trying to move into space. The Global Positioning System was a prime addition to the reconnaissance assets described in the previous chapter. The development and purchase of AWACS★ aircraft brought tremendous new capabilities to the tactical arena.

By the end of the 1970s most of these fixes had taken hold. Only the B-1 production authorization, initiated in December 1976, was cancelled, by President Carter. It was restarted by President Reagan in 1981, but the off-and-on-again costs more than doubled the aircraft's unit price. This ballooning cost for no net gain might be the most important fiscal lesson to emerge from the Vietnam era: the constant restudy of decisions already made, the regular recasting of ongoing programs, is terribly wasteful and produces little in the way of useful results.

THE TYRANNY OF LEAD TIMES

The technocrats who managed the recovery at home during those post-Vietnam years did not have an easy time. The Watergate Congress, elected in 1974, was intent on disassembling American military power, and they nearly succeeded. That would have been a disaster of unimagined proportions, because one aspect of the paradox of Vietnam is the tyranny of lead times. Consider the timeliness of the weapons systems described in the preceding pages:

★ Airborne Warning and Control System, a 707 airframe mounted by a huge disk-enclosed rotating antenna and carrying a sizable battle staff. The AWACS became indispensable in searching the coastal approaches to the United States for terrorist attackers.

WEAPON SYSTEM	F-15	A-10	F-16	MAVERICK
MONEY FIRST SPENT*	August 1967	May 1970	January 1972	July 1967
FIRST FLIGHT	July 1972	May 1972	January 1974	August 1969
START PRODUCTION	November 1974	November 1975	August 1978	1971
INITIAL OP'L CAPABILITY	September 1975	October 1977	October 1980	February 1973
ELAPSED TIME, BEGINNING OF PROGRAM TO INITIAL OP'L CAPABILITY	**8 years**	**7 1/2 years**	**8 1/2 years**	**5 1/2 years**

* The date when the bureaucracy started to spend serious money, not just talk. In the case of the three aircraft programs it refers to the first funded requests for proposals from industry, once the Air Force had thought through what it wanted. In the case of Maverick it refers to the CSAF's Paveway decision, a roadmap for smart munitions.

It took about eight years from the time the Air Force decided to invest resources in a major project until that aircraft's first squadron was operational. Add another year or two to get a major deployed force, and the lesson becomes clear: No President or administration can deal itself a stronger hand. Every President is dependent on the technology and production inserted into the pipeline by his predecessor(s). A disruption of this recovery by the 1974-78 Congresses would have precluded the Reagan buildup in the 1980s and could have stalled the Cold War victory that followed.

PEOPLE

More than anything else, Vietnam changed the people of America. It changed their attitudes, their support for the armed services, and the outlook of those who made a career of the military. In the aftermath of

Vietnam, the draft ended. The services had to rely on volunteers, kids who *wanted* to be in the military. It was not an easy transition for the Army. The Air Force had more to offer in terms of training applicable to future careers, but even so, we had to recruit.

The good news is that the post–Vietnam generation did step forward, and for the first time in history they were joined by large numbers of women. The military academies opened their doors to women, a complicated but eventually rewarding transition. The arrival of female cadets represented a great infusion of new blood into the officer corps. It has worked out well; only a few arguments remain about the role of women in combat. The daughter of a recently retired USAF chief of staff flies refueling tankers every day. The current chief has three daughters in Air Force blue.

The advent of smart munitions required the retention of smart enlisted troops to care for those weapons. Attention to the careers of the senior enlisted men and women, care for their families, became a top priority as the Air Force recovered from Vietnam. At the top of the pyramid lay the future of the Air Force itself. When the war in Vietnam started, Curtis LeMay was the chief of staff. The leadership of the Air Force was dominated by the SAC/nuclear weapons/bomber pilot culture. The fighter pilots, airlift people, logisticians, scientists, and engineers all were relegated to second-class status.

The Constitution and the law are quite clear. The selection and assignment of general officers is key to the civilian control of the military, but that control has often been abandoned to the senior officers of the uniformed services and neglected by the civilians charged with looking out for the national interest. In the mid-seventies, Deputy Secretary of Defense Bill Clements and the service secretaries decided to reassert control of this system. I wanted to see R&D program managers, information systems people, and fighter pilots promoted to the rank of general, as well as bomber men and women. It was not an easy time, but when the board cycles were over, I think the Deputy Chief of Staff for Personnel and I had become close friends. The fortunes of those who had been learning the lessons of Vietnam began to ascend. Among the first to understand the paradox of Vietnam—that we all must die a bit before we grow again—were the men who had flown there.

Those unfortunate enough to have spent reflective time in Hoa Lo prison came home to address the political issues. Many ran for, and some won and served with distinction in, the United States House and Senate. Their contribution was to make sure the United States never again entered wars gradually, with unclear aims and unfocused operations.

The men who stayed alive and kept flying brought home more specific visions. They brought their experience to the Air Staff and the secretariat, to see to it that the intellectual and financial firepower of those institutions were brought to bear on the building of a whole new Air Force. To these veterans of the skies over Vietnam, "recovery" was not just a matter of restoring the status quo. It was not simply an effort to recover the honor of a badly mauled Air Force, for that Air Force had already acquitted itself with honor far above and beyond the call of duty. These pilots were determined that their service become a pre-eminent global power, able to control the skies and, if necessary, destroy the nervous system and muscle of any power endangering the American people. They were determined that their comrades on the ground never again suffer wars of attrition, that they never again endure the horrors of Ia Drang and Khe San. They saw to it that their successors would be able to deliver a withering and accurate fire from the sky, the likes of which had never been seen before, while limiting the collateral damage to innocent civilians.

They succeeded in reshaping the U.S. Air Force, perhaps beyond their wildest dreams. In 2003 *one* air raid destroyed five hundred armored vehicles and artillery pieces in an elite Republican Guard division. Only infantry with small arms were left to fend for themselves. A surviving POW described the attack: "When the bombs hit the tanks, we ran for our cars. When we turned on the ignition, the bombs hit the cars. It was terrible."

While the new U.S. Air Force cannot win wars all by itself, it now can see to it that most American soldiers, sailors, and airmen come home safely. Iraq and Afghanistan have replaced Vietnam in the American lexicon of warfare.

Exhibit A is Joe Ralston, mentioned earlier as the pilot passing over the MiG-21s at Phuc Yen. He went on to fly more than 150 missions over Vietnam. He made it home alive, although many of his fellow F-105 pilots did not: 334 of those aircraft were lost to enemy fire. Upon his return, Ralston brought his experience to bear at the headquarters of the Tactical Air Command. By 1976 he was serving on the Air Staff, helping to define the new U.S. Air Force. Ralston went on to help with the development of stealth technology, then to assume command of tactical air forces on alert around the globe. At the culmination of his Air Force career, Joe Ralston became the four-star general serving as the Supreme Allied Commander in Europe (SACEUR).

I have no doubt that if the U.S. President and Congress decided that some European dictator or ideology threatened the safety and security of the American people, General Ralston would not let the air forces that threatened us taxi around their runways unmolested. Nor would he allow the ground troops under his protection to suffer needless deaths. He would oversee the destruction of our enemies, those who would harm our families and destroy our institutions, with a fire from the sky unimaginable when he was a young lieutenant. With Joe Ralston as SACEUR, with F-15s and F-16s patrolling the skies over Washington in the aftermath of 9/11, and given the performance of the USAF in the skies over Iraq, I think the recovery from Vietnam has turned out pretty well.

CHAPTER 14

Inefficiency Kills—Empires as Well as People

NATIONS DO NOT RISE TO EMINENCE nor do they come to power simply because their chariots (or their airplanes) are bigger, faster, and more numerous than anybody else's. Nations prevail on the world stage because they enjoy a broad spectrum of power.

President Eisenhower believed the U.S. could prevail in the Cold War not by force of arms but by the strength of its economy. To that end, he demanded good intelligence. Then, based on that intelligence, he invested a modest share of his nation's wealth in the maintenance of its security while our citizens built a prosperous, strong, and just society. Eisenhower did not try to flood the world with armaments or American troops. He entrusted the nation's security to thermonuclear technology. He worked to be sure those weapons never would be used, then turned his attention to our economic health and infrastructure. When he left office, he had set the ground rules for the decades to follow: nuclear deterrence, containment of communism abroad, and economic growth at home. He warned of what might happen if those forces got out of balance. In his often quoted farewell, he referred to the dangers of a military–industrial complex. In so doing, I believe he was urging a continued reliance on a small, focused, and well-controlled thermonuclear deterrent.

Ronald Reagan understood the need for that balance, but he also understood that the free and growing economy bequeathed to him by Eisenhower and his successors was now his ace in the hole. By playing that card against the empty Soviet hand, Reagan could end and win the Cold War. The Soviet gerentocracy tried to cling to power amidst a sea of change, but younger minds in that government decided to deal with reality. The facts they had to face were not about fallen castles or lost ships. They were the economic facts of life.

THE VIEW FROM THE WHITE HOUSE, 1982

In the 1960s, I took an interest in politics. Like many of my generation, I felt that the Johnson–McNamara approach to Vietnam was couched in naiveté and deception, leading to disaster. To me, Ronald Reagan seemed the right person to restore integrity and common sense to the nation's leadership. As a result, in 1965, I enlisted in Reagan's campaign for the governorship of California. Afterward, I worked briefly in Sacramento, then turned my attention to his 1968 on-again, off-again initial run at the presidency. I helped Reagan gain and keep control of his state legislature, in the process dethroning his likely challenger to re-election. In 1970, I assumed full responsibility for the direction and management of Reagan's gubernatorial reelection campaign.

During those years, we talked, and I listened, endlessly. I prepared some speeches, hired the key staff, and tried to measure the public's reaction to his policies and campaigns. We traveled and often lived together. In the process I came to know Ronald Reagan as well as any of my contemporary peers, and in that same process, he came to entrust me with much of his political fortune.

As the 1970s unfolded, my career turned in other directions. I went to work in Nixon's Pentagon, and then, in the aftermath of Watergate, became Gerald Ford's Secretary of the Air Force. Throughout those years, Reagan and I stayed in touch. We talked about Brezhnev's arms buildup, about President Carter's proposed SALT treaty, and about the politics of Texas.

I was not involved in either of Reagan's 1976 or 1980 presidential campaigns, and once he won the White House, his first priority was the economy, so there was little reason for us to talk. My first communication with him was in October 1981, as he turned his attention to national security affairs. At the end of that year, he restructured his National Security Council (NSC) staff along lines that perhaps only coincidentally matched my October advice. On January 21, 1982, I was drawn back into the Reagan orbit, reporting to work on the staff of Judge William Clark, Reagan's new National Security Adviser. As I began to pore over the National Intelligence Estimates, one fact jumped out at me: the Soviets were going broke.

That was not the conventional wisdom of the inbred academic-intelligence community that studied the Soviet economy for years. They were impressed by the post–World War II industrial recovery of the Soviet Union, but they could not or would not recognize the onset of diminishing returns in such a top-down system. The academics had gotten into the bad habit of accepting and using official economic data published by the Soviet government. In the early 1970s their conventional wisdom was that the Soviets were spending only 5 percent of their GDP on defense. By 1980 the consensus of the intelligence graybeards had shifted only slightly, estimating a 2 to 3 percent annual growth rate, with 15 percent of the GDP devoted to defense.

There were dissenting voices, however. Andy Marshall, the longtime Director of Net Assessment at the Pentagon and an ally of onetime economist James Schlesinger, thought differently. So did Bill Lee at the Defense Intelligence Agency. They felt there was *no* real growth in the Soviet system, that the academic estimates of Soviet defense spending were low by a factor of three or four, and that the denominator of this indicator, the real size of Soviet GDP, was badly overstated. By the beginning of the Reagan years, Marshall and his allies felt that "defense" was eating up 35 to 50 percent of the Soviet GDP.

These dissenters pointed to the size of the Soviet naval support fleet: ferries in the Baltic overdesigned to transport armored divisions; doubly redundant tankers, nominally benefiting the Soviet fishing fleet, but actually there to extend the reach of the burgeoning Soviet Navy. They pointed to the massively reinforced concrete highways between Soviet and East European villages, built to accommodate the rapid movement of tanks. They noted the huge buildup of war reserve stocks of everything from ammunition to fuel to blankets, totally unnecessary for any rationally functioning economy.* They called attention to the cost of supporting client states, like Cuba and Somalia. Where once these distant lands had been the source of plunder, in time they had become expensive socialist showcases and overstaffed intelligence-gathering stations. Marshall derided the then-current CIA "fact book," a tome that estimated the East German per capita income to be on a par with the West. In reality, the East lagged by a factor of two. These views were corroborated by Western businessmen trying to deal with the Soviets. Those travelers brought home tales of incredible inefficiency, factories still locked into pre-World War II ways of doing things.

In 1981 economist Norman Bailey joined the NSC staff. He began to collect evidence of Soviet hard currency shortages and economic failures. At the same time, Stanford's Henry Rowen accepted the chairmanship of the National Intelligence Council. That body, the meeting place for officers from the entire intelligence community, undertook a more rigorous analysis. When they were done, these men and women converged on a view of the Soviet Union very different from that espoused by the establishment for years. Their conclusion: the economic system of the USSR was broken and on the verge of collapse.

Bailey's evidence and Rowen's arguments all made sense to me. The Soviet Union was not the sort of customer to whom I would extend credit. Solid indications came from reports of Soviet asset sales. They were dumping gold into a declining market. They were taking shortcuts in their production of crude oil, ignoring the long term for the sake of immediate cash. They were penetrating and attempting to manipulate the wheat exchange and the currency markets. The evidence was fragmentary and anecdotal, but there was enough to suggest that the Soviet economic chickens were headed home to roost.

Only in the decades to come would we learn the facts. Once the CPSU lost control of the archives, once Western engineers and businessmen were free to meet with their Russian peers, only then did a true picture of the Soviet economic carnage emerge. A few snapshots of what we now know follow.

---

* In later years, retired Soviet planners reported that when the Soviet Union collapsed in 1991, these inventories of war reserve supplies cushioned the fall. Their exhaustion accelerated the economic crash of the late 1990s.

OIL

It is not widely understood that the Soviet Union was once the world's leading producer of oil and gas. The big ten producers in 1980 were as follows:

SOVIET UNION	12.0 *mbpde*★	MEXICO	2.2
USA	10.8	CHINA	2.1
SAUDI ARABIA	10.3	NIGERIA	2.1
OTHER MIDEAST †	8.8	LIBYA	1.8
VENEZUELA	2.2	CANADA	1.8

In addition, the enormous mineral wealth of the Soviet Union kept that strange economic experiment going for much of the twentieth century. The USSR was rich in gold and diamonds, in bauxite and timber. But it was black gold that paid the rent. The oil shocks of 1973-74, when the world price tripled, and then 1979-80, when it tripled again, kept breathing life back into the dying Soviet economy. The Reagan administration's interest in pushing down the world price of crude oil and in blocking the sale of natural gas to Western Europe was not simply a reflection of the need to stem inflation in the U.S. It was a conscious effort to suffocate the Soviet economy.

After those price run-ups in the seventies, the world price of crude oil dropped steadily in the eighties, falling by a factor of three, in real dollar terms, during the first half of that decade. Every one dollar drop in the world price of oil cost the Soviet Union perhaps a billion dollars in annual hard currency earnings. The creaky Politburo of Leonid Brezhnev began to panic. It demanded the immediate production of oil regardless of the long-term cost. It was this full-throttle, devil-take-the-hindmost approach to oil production that was a key indicator to us at the White House.

In 1991, when the Soviet empire died and the autopsies began, Western oil executives and engineers began their travels to the former Soviet Union. From the frozen wastes of Siberia to the desert steppes

---

★ Millions of barrels per day equivalent. At $27/bbl, one mbpde becomes $10 billion of annual revenue.

† Iraq (2.5), Kuwait (1.8), UAE (1.7), Iran (1.7), others (1.1).

of Kazakhstan, they brought home tales worthy of a Harrison Ford movie. They found real oil country: well-defined geologic structures and immense petroleum reserves. Some oil-bearing formations were thousands of feet thick. They found well-trained, top-flight mechanical, chemical, and petroleum engineers, as well as middle managers who were affable and open, eager to share their knowledge of Soviet geology. Unfortunately, they also found reluctant bureaucrats, a rigid approach to oilfield development, and little understanding of reservoir engineering.

After World War II, Stalin had seen to it that the Soviet Union did a good job of mapping its raw materials. The geophysical work was good too, although the technology lagged behind the U.S. by about ten years. There was no computer-generated 3-D mapping of underground structures, only 2-D slices along a survey line, with the results used to plot underground contour maps.

The serious problems began to show up when the Soviets moved from exploration to drilling.

By 1990 they had exploited the more obvious, shallow oilfields. They needed outside help for the deeper structures. Specifically, they needed technology, management, and money. Drilling to depths of over 10,000 feet into hot, high-pressure formations strained their capabilities. The frequent presence of corrosive and poisonous hydrogen sulfide gas made matters worse.

Soviet problems started with the drilling tool itself. The technology of making a hard rock drill bit that would stand up to the hot, high pressure and corrosive environment below 10,000 feet was difficult for them. Soviet tools could drill for only a hundred feet or so before wearing out, less than 10 percent of Western practice. When one must pull two miles of drill stem to replace a tool after drilling only a hundred feet of hole, the economics of the business go negative: it costs more to drill the hole than the recovered oil is worth. Even so, to the Soviets that was the good news. The bad news was that sometimes the drilling simply had to stop. Downhole conditions got to be impossible. In one field alone, the visiting Western engineers found dozens of wells drilled, with virtually none completed to the point of production.

For lack of spare parts and maintenance, there were more rigs idle than running. Those running, seldom, if ever, had working gauges. The observed fire protection system was a bucket of sand and a shovel. Then there were the environmental and safety problems. A Soviet tractor inadvertently plowed up a major pipeline. Oil poured out, covering hundreds of acres. There was no rush to shut off the flow, although berms were erected around the spill to contain it. When asked about vacuum pumps to suck up the spill, the Soviet engineer involved looked bewildered. He had never heard of such things. Once the flow was stopped and the berms were in place, the spilled oil was set on fire to make it go away.

Other Western oil experts, visiting the oilfields in remote Siberia, found cities built in the middle of nowhere. There were fountains and parks, usable only in the few short summer months, boulevards and paved roads, huge Stalinesque apartment buildings and hydroponic farms. The designs were grandiose, but the execution was ghastly, with utilities added as an afterthought to the outside of buildings, fully exposed to the harsh winter weather. These buildings were sized to accommodate not only the drilling crews, their families, and the support staffs, but the huge political overhead involved in any Soviet effort. No Western oilfield could have supported such monstrosities.

The drilling procedures were equally bizarre. A visiting Canadian geophysicist told of the Soviets drilling through hundreds of feet of permafrost to find oil and gas. When completing those wells, they did not bother to insulate the well casings. As a result, when the hot gases began to flow up from the reservoir, they melted the permafrost, creating an annular leak around the pipe. A trillion cubic feet of gas escaped.

But the heart of the Soviet oil problem was neither technology nor the inefficiency of their drilling teams. It was reservoir engineering: drilling the right number of wells in the right places, then adjusting the production from each well to optimize the present day value of the resulting production. There was no place in communist doctrine for the "time value of money." Thus the Soviets had no idea how to calculate discounted cash flows. They had no conceptual tools with which to optimize their production plans.

Oil is found in geologic traps. Being lighter than water, oil migrates upslope to the top of its structure, be that a fault or a dome. The purpose of geophysical surveys is to find those structures. An exploratory well confirms the location of that structure, sees if it contains any oil, determines the nature of the oil-bearing formation (porosity, permeability, etc.) and then locates the oil-water interface. After each such experiment—that is, each well—one compares the well logs with the geophysical model, revises the model, and drills again. With this data, one then plans the extraction of oil so as not to leave behind pools of oil, surrounded by water, that can never be recovered. Producing an oil well wide open, early on, can leave behind many such unrecoverable pools of oil. Choking well production down will result in more oil being produced over the long term, but will slow production to an economically unacceptable rate. In the West, the balancing of these competing considerations is the essence of good reservoir engineering.

Not so in the Soviet Union. During the days of Soviet management, a potential oilfield was outlined by geology and geophysics. Then a standard template was applied and the wells were drilled with Stakhanovite zeal, each independent of the others. The goal, the basis of each manager's perks and bonuses, was the number of wells drilled. It was not wells completed, oil produced, or budget compliance. No Soviet engineer was ever able to tell my friends what it cost to drill a well; any American oilman knows those costs to three significant figures. If a Soviet well was completed and connected to a pipeline, it was run wide open, with no choke. The damage to the reservoirs was irreparable.

And then there was the problem of turning the oil produced into money. The transmission facilities, used to get product from wellhead to market, leaked badly. When delivered to Soviet cities, the product entered the price-free Soviet system; no meters and no costs were attached to the profligate use of energy, because it was "free." Oil and gas belonged to "the people." Even when delivered to ports for export, the state had problems in getting paid. In part that was because some of the recipients were deadbeat socialist client states. In other cases, the oil was shipped by hard-to-follow trucks for the personal benefit of the oil barons. Only a small amount of the Soviet Union's oil and gas production actually made it to the ports at Rotterdam and the factories of West Germany, and thus into the world's hard-currency markets. History might have turned out differently if the management skills and petroleum engineering of the Arabian-American Oil Company had been matched to the technical competence and dedication of the Russian oilmen, but that was not to be.

THE SOVIET DEFENSE BUDGET

In the Soviet sunset years, Boris Altshuler, son of an eminent nuclear weapons physicist, began researching the cost of the mad Soviet military scramble. He now talks about hundreds of Chernobyls; rivers and lakes full of plutonium, acid, and reactor wastes; explosions at chemical warfare plants. But his most compelling numbers are economic: the data on how various nations spent their national income during the Cold War.

"National income" is a UN term that approximates Gross Domestic Product (GDP). Altshuler first published his conclusions in 1971 and has been updating them ever since. He concluded that military spending in the Soviet Union in 1969 was 41 to 51 percent of national income, not including military construction. Expenditures for the latter were deeply buried in the capital investment part of the state budget. Folding reasonable estimates for those in, Altschuler now concludes that total defense expenditures in the Soviet Union were about 50 percent of national income in 1969, rising to 73 percent in 1989. His conclusion matches a statement by former Soviet Foreign Minister Eduard Shevardnadze to the effect that the defense budget ate up as much as 50 percent of the Soviet Union's gross national product annually. At the end, Gorbachev admitted: "The Politburo had no idea of the real role of the VPK [the military-industrial complex] in the state budget."

Altshuler's estimates of national income devoted to defense seem reasonable because, using consistent criteria and methodology, his estimate of U.S. defense expenditures in the 1960s was 11 percent of national income. The official U.S. number for 1966 was 9 percent of GDP. That was during the war in Vietnam, and even that level of expenditure led to the guns-and-butter inflation of the seventies. Today the United States spends about 3 percent of its GDP on defense. Israel, a small state in mortal peril, spent about 25 percent of its GDP on defense during the 1970s. It could only afford to do so because of its U.S. subsidy. During World War II the United States spent 40 percent of its GDP on defense. We could not have done so much longer. The Politburo's misallocation of half its wealth to defense, decade after decade, rising to three-quarters by the end, was a death sentence for its empire.

COSTS

Not only did the Soviets overallocate their resources to "defense," it mismanaged those expenditures on a scale that boggles the mind. Soon after the USSR ceased to exist, various freelance organizations made their way into the scattered fragments of that country, trying to help. I was called in by the International Executive Service Corps (IESC), a nonprofit foundation started in 1964 to help agrarian economies, mainly in South America, benefit from the experience of retired U.S. executives.

When the Berlin wall came crashing down, the IESC expanded its services into the former Soviet Union. A former college friend of mine, mindful of my Livermore and high-tech business experience, called on me to go to Kharkov, an industrial city on the eastern end of then newly independent Ukraine. I was to help commercialize a once-mighty Soviet technical institute.

Ukraine is a lovely country, the pre–World War I breadbasket of Europe. Then Stalin deported the successful independent farmers, known as kulaks, starved out the peasants, and stumbled into war. I have never seen such incredible black earth as in Ukraine. But the glory days of Ukrainian agriculture are gone.

During my visits there in the 1990s I never saw an operating tractor, only elderly peasants swinging scythes. Today, Ukraine is energy-starved, still communist, and a net importer of food. Ukraine is a very diverse country. The eastern side, where Kharkov is located, is a part of Russia's "near abroad," where the people speak Russian and worship in Russian Orthodox cathedrals. When Lenin's revolution was spreading communism across the Eurasian continent, Kharkov was the temporary, communist-dominated, capital of Ukraine. In the center of the country lies the old and magnificent capital city of Kiev, always struggling to balance East against West. In the West lies true Ukraine. Once part of Poland, the people there speak Ukrainian. They are Roman Catholics and hate the Russians with a passion. Many joined General Vlasov's Russian Liberation Movement during World War II, in alliance with the Nazis, to fight against Stalin.

I was dropped into that stew in an attempt to help the Verkin Institute of Low Temperature Physics find new work. Kharkov was once a center of technical excellence, but Russian distrust and the smothering communist state reduced the place to poverty. The Verkin Institute was home to theoretical physicists, experimenters, and mathematicians who did world-class work. My two-week job was to help them reconfigure to attract Western investment, or at least Western contract research work. The sales pitch to the West would be: "You can rent the entire Verkin Institute for the cost of four engineers in Palo Alto."

After a few days of orientation, talking shop and drinking vodka with some of the nicest and most hospitable men and women in the world, I asked to visit their accounting department. I wanted to know the cost of their products and services so I could advise them on a marketing strategy. I got a blank stare. "Bookkeeping? Money?" I repeated through the interpreter. Ah yes, the place where the money was handled. The management took me to a room where elderly ladies were stuffing small stacks of rapidly inflating Ukrainian currency into dirty envelopes. These were the petty cash allocations for a few key people. And that was it. There were no accounting machines, not even clerks in green eyeshades bent over dusty ledgers. There were no stacks of papers with columns of numbers. There was nothing. So I came to understand.

Raw materials were furnished to the institute according to the plan, once promulgated by GOSPLAN (the state central planning agency) in Moscow, but now set by no one. There was no purchasing department, no flexibility, no inventory records, no accounts payable, no creditors. Thus, my question about materials costs made no sense to my hosts. Workers were "paid" directly by the state. Their housing—in minuscule, walk-up apartments—was furnished by the state. Their (virtually nonexistent) food supplies were subsidized by the state. Their health care, such as it was, came from the state. And the concept of "labor cost" was incomprehensible as well. None of those people costs were attributed to Verkin's products. At the end of the pipeline the institute furnished goods or services to other institutes, factories, or stores, again according to the plan. Verkin was not paid for anything. There were no accounts receivable, no checking accounts, no cash flow statements. Those words had no meaning. Verkin's bottom line simply was the planners' approval if Verkin met its quotas.

In the West we cannot comprehend the consequences of such a system. Since the word "cost" had no meaning other than as a synonym for "price"—as in, "What is the cost/price of that loaf of bread?"—there could be no accountability, no decision criteria. Without the discipline of cost accounting, with management decisions based solely on social theory, the Soviet economic distortions grew to monstrous size.

TITANIUM

As a modest example of what happens when there is no cost accounting, consider the legendary matter of the titanium shovels. When the Soviet empire collapsed, "defense conversion" became the watchwords. In 1991–92 several defense plants in the Urals hit upon the idea of making garden spades and work shovels as alternative products. The same presses that had been making armor plate and other weapons could stamp out the metal spades. The attachment of wooden handles would keep a lot of people busy. There would be no moving parts, so there would be no need for customer support. Shovels would be an ideal export product.

There was just one problem. The principal feedstock on hand at these arms plants was titanium, a very light metal that retains great strength at very high temperatures. Titanium is most often used for aircraft parts and turbine blades. In the free market economy it is a very expensive material, carefully conserved for only the most demanding uses, but in the Soviet system it was "free." Those arms plants in the Urals started cranking out titanium shovels at a great rate, and they were a big hit, as long as the titanium lasted. In the domestic market, the peasants welcomed the new lightweight shovel, but the principal demand came from importers in the West. They melted down all the shovels they could get in order to resell the titanium at a significant markup on the open market.

PLUTONIUM

On a grand scale, a comparison of the U.S. and Soviet systems for producing plutonium provides a different kind of example. Plutonium is the touchstone of modern power politics. Its possession is the orb and scepter that separates the nuclear haves from the second and third world have–nots. Its mere presence within the borders of a sovereign state earns respect and deters the adventurism of others.

The production of plutonium is complex, dangerous, and expensive. For those reasons, not many nations have a supply. As an element, plutonium is unstable. Its most common isotopes have half-lives of 24,000 years, quite long on the human scale but short enough in the cosmic scheme of things to assure that none of it can be found in nature. It is the most popular raw material for A-bombs because only a few pounds will go critical, producing more neutrons than consumed in the chain reaction. If the geometry, timing, and speed of assembly is right, a major explosion will result.

Plutonium is manufactured in uranium piles, known as "production reactors." A large pile of natural uranium can be made to go critical, although at worst it will melt down, not explode. In production reactors, which use slightly enriched uranium, the spare neutrons are captured by U-238 to make Pu-239. One must not leave those fuel rods in the reactor too long, however, for in time Pu-239 will capture another neutron to make Pu-240, a material that is worse than useless in A-bombs. Irradiated fuel rods are removed from the production reactor, dissolved in acid, and the plutonium is then separated out from this slurry by chemical means. The residue is highly toxic. Plutonium itself is deadly if its powders are inhaled.

In the U.S., plutonium was produced at Hanford, Washington, until the late 1980s. Even with the reasonable care and respect for human life that characterized the U.S. program, cleanup at Hanford will cost billions of dollars and will take decades. The Soviet program was not hindered by such safety constraints. The first plutonium-producing reactor was built at Mayak, near Yekaterinburg, at the close of World War II. Chemical effluent was simply thrown into Lake Kurchai. To this day children who go near that waterway soon come down with leukemia.

The problem facing the collapsed Soviet empire is that no one can or will turn off these plutonium-producing reactors. The reason is that the two reactors at Tomsk and the third at Krasnoyarsk produce not only plutonium, but heat—the only source of heat and electricity for those cities. Shut them down and those communities will freeze in the dark. As a result, the Russian Federation still runs those reactors, cranking out unneeded plutonium at the rate of one and a half tons per year.

In the mid 1990s the U.S. government initiated a series of programs to help the former Soviet Union stand down its nuclear weapons complex. There were programs to find work for the nuclear scientists and engineers (so they would not migrate to Baghdad or Tehran), to secure the nuclear weapons and materials storage sites (to preclude theft and resale to terrorists), and to close down those production facilities that seemed to be running mindlessly, tended only by the sorcerer's apprentices. It took years for my associates at the Lawrence Livermore National Laboratory to gain the confidence of their Russian peers, but by the end of the decade a few of my colleagues had broken through. It was a joint endeavor. Both sides wanted to secure this part of the Russian nuclear genie, and both sides wanted the Russian economy to stop being wasteful. What these American and Russian scientists told each other provides an interesting case study of what happens when one ignores costs.

In the U.S. the production of plutonium is a sort of mining process. Fuel rods are removed from reactors. Elsewhere the by-products of parts fabrication are separated from other scrap. The resulting materials are collected and delivered to a reprocessing facility. There, they are immersed in acid, then chemically processed to extract plutonium. When the "tails"—or the residual materials—contain less than about 2 percent plutonium, the process is stopped. It is not economically worthwhile to continue. The residue is put in containers and buried.

In the accounting-free Soviet Union, however, the process was very different. Every atom of plutonium was considered to be the fruit of socialist labor. Every gram was seen as adding to the superpower status of the empire. Cost was not a consideration. As a result, the Soviets continued their reprocessing until the tails contained only two hundred parts per million (0.02 percent) of plutonium. As a result, that whole vast reactor complex, from Mayak to Tomsk to Krasnoyarsk, was consuming billions of rubles of resources just to scrape the few last atoms of plutonium off the bottom of the barrel. There was no accounting system to say, "Stop!" Soviet plutonium ended up costing substantially more than in the U.S., and the Russian plutonium stockpile is substantially larger than we thought it was. This latter discovery has a significant impact on the negotiation of proposed strategic arms treaties and on our efforts to contain the terrorist threat. All for the lack of a set of books.

A VALUE-SUBTRACTING ECONOMIC MACHINE

Economists describe the operation of a business or similar enterprise as a "value-adding" process. A shoemaker acquires leather, adds his labor and the use of his equipment (capital) to produce shoes that (hopefully) have a value significantly in excess of the leather he started with. Unfortunately, it did not always work out that way in the Soviet Union. Most industries, operating without the benefit of any cost information or controls, turned out to be giant value-subtracting machines. They would start with perfectly good steel, rubber, and glass, and turn out refrigerators no one wanted.

The *Economist* summed up this phenomenon in 1992 when it first compared the free market value of Russia's raw materials with the country's gross national product. It found that if all the oil, gas, gold, iron, bauxite, etc., that Russia produced in 1992 had been sold on the world market, Russia would have earned about twenty-seven trillion rubles, at the then-effective conversion rate. Yet Russia's GNP in 1992 was estimated to be only fifteen trillion rubles. Thus, the Soviet system was *subtracting* almost half the value of the raw materials produced before delivering products. The Soviet Union would have been better off (economically, but not politically) if it had shut down every industry but the extractive ones, sold its produced commodities on the world market, told the workers to go home, and sent their citizens a Kuwait-like welfare check.

A specific example was the Karl Zeiss Jena camera company. The prewar Zeiss firm had been located in Berlin. At the end of World War II it was split into East and West components. Forty years later, when the Wall came down, Zeiss/West looked into reacquiring that eastern Karl Zeiss Jena piece of the business. It found that for every eight deutsche marks of marketable product coming out of Zeiss/East, thirty deutsche marks of raw materials, parts, and labor were going in. Seventy percent of the input value was being subtracted before a product came out.

In Russia itself, the diamond-cutting and polishing shops in Moscow and elsewhere were turning out finished diamonds worth about half the value of the rough diamonds first produced at the mines. (This latter value is based on the DeBeers price paid for rough diamonds worldwide.) The numbers seem to be consistent. The Soviet system *subtracted* about half the value of the raw materials and labor fed into any of its industrial processes before turning out a product.

WE CASH THE SOVIET PEACE DIVIDEND

And so it came to pass that the Soviet empire collapsed. In a farewell 1991 Christmas telephone call, Mikhail Gorbachev advised the U.S. President that he was resigning his offices of president of the Soviet Union and commander in chief of its armed forces. "You can have a very quiet Christmas evening. . . . I am saying good-bye and shaking your hands." With that, the Soviet Union was gone. In its place, the new Russian Federation began the painful reallocation of resources. The value-subtracting game stopped. Local managers began to optimize their operations based on economic reality. They also stripped their comrades of any ownership rights, but that's another story, still unfolding.

The movement of bauxite and aluminum is an interesting example of what happened. In 1987 almost all (96 percent) of the aluminum produced in the Soviet Union went to domestic use. Only 4 percent made it to the export market. At that time the world price of aluminum was around $1.60 per pound. Then, in 1992, the value-subtracting stopped. The managers of bauxite mines and aluminum smelting facilities seized control of their own fates. They refused to ship aluminum to deadbeat manufacturers of useless refrigerators and unneeded fighter planes. Instead they began to export onto the world market, for cash. By 1993 the Russian Federation was exporting about half of its aluminum production. That provided welcome cash to those managers or their bankers on Cyprus, but it had another, grander effect. By 1993 the world price of aluminum, driven down by Russian exports, had dropped to sixty cents per pound. As a result, the cost of the aluminum in every western beer can, in every engine block, fell by a factor of almost three.

In the decade that followed the end of the Cold War, economists and pundits have wondered why the U.S. has suffered so little inflation. We have enjoyed one of the greatest economic booms of all time, yet inflation remained below 3 percent. Technology in general and the computer revolution in particular are given most of the credit, but I would like to suggest another contributor. We are cashing the Soviet "peace dividend." That expression refers to the resources suddenly made available to a people when their government ends a military adventure. In the strange case of the Soviet Union, however, the reallocation of Soviet raw materials onto world markets has kept the lid on *everyone's* commodities prices. The whole world has benefited.

IN HINDSIGHT, IT ALL BECOMES CLEAR

None of the above was obvious in 1982. Churchill earlier had described Russia as a riddle wrapped in a mystery inside an enigma. Nowhere was that more true than when trying to plumb the Soviet economy during the dark years of the Cold War. As the 1980s dawned, graybeards in the West held to their view of the Soviet system as monolithic and stable, lumbering along toward eternal life on the backs of its exploited but complacent serfs. The newcomers to Washington felt differently, but they had a hard time proving their point. But they really did not have to, for one of the newest and most clear-sighted of their number was the seventy-one-year-old fortieth President of the United States. Ronald Reagan's willingness to bet against the Soviet economy became clear at a meeting of the National Security Council

in March 1982. While discussing the national security study he had entrusted to my care, the President began to ruminate about new approaches to the Soviet problem.

"Why can't we just lean on the Soviets until they go broke?"

The cabinet-level elders around the table discouraged such thinking.
It would not work. The Soviet Union was a stable monolith, etc. Henry
Rowen spoke up from a back seat, along the wall, to disagree. Rowen
and his outsider colleagues felt the Soviet economic system was on the
verge of collapse. Reagan thanked Rowen for his support and then,
with a mere nod of his head, said to me, "That's the direction we're going to go."

Two years later, in late 1984, the Politburo gathered to review an extensive GRU study of the now widening gap between the American
and Soviet economies. It was not a pretty picture. At a subsequent social gathering of the Soviet military establishment, attended and noted
by the Hungarian ambassador to the Soviet Union, one general rose to
toast "the need to push the nuclear button as soon as possible, before
the imperialists can gain superiority over us in every field." According
to the ambassador: "The others . . . received their comrade's insane
words with great ovation."

Pushing the Soviet Union to the brink of economic collapse was a
gamble not without risk.

CHAPTER 15

President Reagan
Sets Up the Checkmate

IN THE EARLY 1980s, President Reagan put the pieces in place to end
and win the Cold War. He was not the "victor" in this struggle; the
citizens of the U.S. and the USSR were the big winners. Nor was he
the closer; George Bush and Mikhail Gorbachev filled those shoes.
Ronald Reagan's contribution was to rearrange the chessboard of history in a whole new way.

The Soviet leadership did not understand the American election of
1980. Their analysis of the Carter-to-Reagan transition foresaw the arrival of "a provincial actor, a puppet manipulated by U.S. monopolies
and the American military-industrial complex." On November 17,
1980, KGB Chief Andropov and Foreign Minister Gromyko advised
their Central Committee of a plan to identify the advisers who pulled
Reagan's strings. In so doing, they joined a long list of now-vanished
American journalists and politicians who made the same mistake.

Ronald Reagan was determined that the free world prevail during his time in office, even though his rendezvous with destiny started out haltingly.

1981: A VACUUM AT THE
NATIONAL SECURITY COUNCIL

Since the passage of the National Security Act in 1947, American Presidents have used the National Security Council and its supporting staff to organize their thinking about national security matters.★ The NSC staff is headed by an Assistant to the President for National Security Affairs who is also known as the National Security Adviser. The NSC staff explores policy options by means of study memoranda, then the President articulates decisions by means of decision directives. Each President changes the acronyms and starts the numbering sequence anew, but this system of studies and decisions has by now become a White House fixture. Memoranda for the President's action are drafted by the NSC staff to make sure that all constituencies within the administration are heard and their suggestions vetted before a presidential decision is made.

At the beginning of his term, Ronald Reagan would have none of this. He had been offended by Henry Kissinger's use of the NSC to promote his visions of détente. Reagan decided he would have a National Security Adviser in name only, with that man's desk buried in the basement of the White House. Since the responsibilities would not go away, however, and since nature abhors a vacuum, two factions within the new Reagan administration struggled to fill that political void.

The first contestant was Al Haig, formerly Henry Kissinger's deputy at the NSC and now Secretary of State. Reagan found Haig to be an intelligent and articulate briefer during the presidential campaign, but he was of a different culture from Reagan. He was a structured and disciplined former general. For all practical purposes, he had run the United States during the last six months of the Nixon administration. Haig had very clear views on how the Reagan national security apparatus should work.

★ In 1981 the NSC consisted of the President, Vice-President (Bush), Secretary of State (Haig, then in 1983, Schultz), Secretary of Defense (Weinberger), U.S. Ambassador to the United Nations (Kirkpatrick), and the Director of Central Intelligence (Casey).

During their first week in office, most Presidents promulgate a directive on the mechanics of their national security apparatus. Such papers usually originate with the new National Security Adviser, if not with the President himself. Not caring to wait, however, and eager to fill the policy void at the White House, Haig rushed over on inauguration day with a proposed National Security Decision Directive Number 1 (NSDD-1). It would have moved much of the NSC's power to Haig's own office at the State Department. Haig requested a Reagan signature on the spot. He did not get it. Haig's opponents in this opening challenge were presidential assistants Jim Baker and Mike Deaver and presidential counselor Ed Meese. Richard Allen, another former Kissinger staffer, carried the title of National Security Adviser in the new administration, but Allen enjoyed neither direct access to the President nor the authority that such access would have implied; he worked for Meese. Thus, the disenfranchised NSC fell under Meese's oversight during that first Reagan year.

Meese intercepted Haig's draft NSDD-1, rewrote it, and caused it to be issued on February 15, 1981, as a bland continuation of the status quo. While domestic advisers Baker, Darman, et al. grappled with double digit inflation, budgetary deficits, and tax policy, the national security process slowed to a crawl. The NSC staff tried to prepare a few NSDDs that would dispose of or continue in force the Carter-era presidential directives, known as PDs, but those efforts went nowhere. The process came to a halt with the March 30 attempt on the President's life.

As Reagan returned to work during the summer of 1981, four NSDDs did get signed. They dealt piecemeal with certain of the Carter-era policies, directives that the new administration clearly wished to change. They involved arms transfers, nonproliferation, South Africa, and Micronesia. Beyond that, the Carter PDs stood. In the fall of 1981 four other crisis-driven NSDDs were signed. Three dealt with Libya, Egypt/Sudan, and Central America, respectively. The fourth structured a White House crisis management system. It put Vice-President Bush in charge, not Al Haig.

Meanwhile, at the Pentagon, the Reagan team was taking two months of transition time and nine months in power to think about how the U.S. strategic nuclear forces should be recast from the Carter mold. Should a more accurate and powerful Trident submarine-launched ballistic missile, capable of striking Soviet missile silos and command posts, be built and deployed? Should the B-1 bomber program, cancelled by

Jimmy Carter in July 1977, be restarted? How should the M–X ICBM be based? The arms-control theologians had devised a mobile underground "racetrack" system for the latter. It was alleged to be crisis-stable, but it was surely unaffordable—politically, financially, and environmentally. And how about strategic defenses and the information systems to tie all of this together?

Knowledgeable leaders should have settled those questions during their first winter, for it is during the first hundred days of a new President's administration that initiatives are most readily accepted, but that did not happen. As the months rolled by, the Pentagon team formed study groups and blue ribbon panels. Only by the end of September did it reach some conclusions.

That is not to say things were stagnant at Reagan's Pentagon. The new administration installed a team of hawkish policy advisers, and it requested an immediate 20 percent ($33 billion) increase in the defense budget then before Congress. These actions and other signals made it clear that change was in the air. Once Secretary of Defense Weinberger came to terms with the strategic force options before him, he was able to get those matters onto the President's agenda. Reagan signed six more NSDDs during October and November 1981. They dealt with space, nuclear weapons, and the updating of corresponding Carter policies. The first, NSDD-12, was signed on October 1,1981. It ratified the Weinberger decisions on strategic forces.

And yet, as 1981 drew to a close, only a handful of ad hoc decision directives had been executed. There were no study memoranda on any subject. The mind boggles to think of the chaos that might have unfolded if a more alert and aggressive Soviet Union had understood the extent of this vacuum.

RECONNECTING WITH REAGAN

On October 2, 1981, the President held a press conference to announce the decisions reflected in NSDD-12. Secretary of Defense Weinberger was at the President's side; the presentation was a fiasco. Reagan read a credible statement, then turned the microphone over to Weinberger, who read another prepared statement. Once the questions started, however, neither man seemed to know what he was talking about. Lou Cannon of the *Washington Post* reported it as "a sorry performance."

Reflecting on those delays in national security organization and policy-making, I wrote a personal letter to Reagan that commented on the October 2 press conference and urged him to get serious about his national security apparatus. I did not know how chaotic the situation really was, but I did know Reagan's management style. I suggested he pick and then empower a real National Security Adviser, someone he trusted from way back. Cap Weinberger, Ed Meese, and Bill Clark were my suggested candidates. A few days later, in mid-October, I received a personal reply acknowledging the merits of my advice. End of story, I thought, but there were other forces at work.

Reagan liked the cabinet-style management system he had developed in Sacramento and now used at the White House. In the autumn of 1981 he came to realize that a fully empowered National Security Adviser—one whom he trusted, and especially one familiar with his policy-making style—could be compatible with his cabinet system. In addition, he wanted to focus substantially more of his time on national security matters. He advised those managing his schedule of this, and over the Christmas holidays asked Bill Clark to come talk. Their discussions produced a meeting of the minds, as they always did between those old friends.

Clark agreed to become the Assistant to the President for National Security Affairs. Access was to be unimpeded, at any hour of day or night, alone or with others, as Clark thought best. Clark was to organize a new NSC staff. Dick Allen was to depart as a result of other problems. The decisions were confirmed in a January 4, 1982, press release and an internal memo approved by the President that same week. Everyone, from the old Sacramento hands to the Jim Baker crowd to Nancy Reagan, concurred in this decision. The following week, on January 16, 1982, my longtime friend and officemate from Sacramento, Bill Clark, called to ask me, along with Bud McFarlane and a few others, to join his new team at the NSC.

SETTLING IN

On January 21, 1982, I was issued a spacious office in the Old Executive Office Building, the ornate structure across the walkway from the West Wing of the White House. Upon my arrival I also was issued a secretary and some military assistants, including a young Marine major named Oliver North.

During the first year of the Reagan administration, Bill Clark had served as Deputy Secretary of State. Having spent most of the 1970s on the California bench, culminating with a Reagan appointment to the California Supreme Court, Judge Clark was not fully versed in the intricacies of foreign policy. On the other hand, he well understood, and shared, his President's strategic visions, his suspicions of Soviet intent, and his loyalty to proven allies.

Clark's 1981 Deputy Secretary of State confirmation hearings had bordered on harassment as the President's critics posed arcane questions about the prime and foreign ministers of various third world countries. At the end of the day, however, the newly Republican Senate accommodated their President's personnel choices. Clark's prospective job was to manage the details of diplomatic intercourse, not to make foreign policy. He was to ensure the faithful implementation of the President's vision and to keep the new Secretary of State, Alexander Haig, fully connected and responsive to Reagan, the White House staff, and the rest of the national security team.

Haig liked structure. He could not deal with Reagan's fuzzy and ill-defined relationships and agendas. Bill Clark was as well-organized as Haig, but he'd been with Reagan long enough to understand how to connect Type A overachievers into the laid-back Reagan court. During the first year of the new administration, it was hoped that Clark would provide a stabilizing connection between Foggy Bottom and the White House. It did not work out that way because Haig would not talk to Dick Allen or any of the other presidential assistants. He would speak only with the President. Unfortunately (for Haig), that's not how the Reagan system worked. Now, in January 1982, Clark was to move to the newly rejuvenated NSC. He was to serve as a modem, to connect the nation's national security apparatus into the Reagan White House. In time it would become Clark's duty to disconnect the ill-suited Haig from the administration itself.

A properly functioning NSC acts as the President's eyes and ears. More accurately, it is a settling tank into which bright ideas are dumped for a quick but thorough scrubbing before becoming national policy. Some initiatives come from the cabinet departments, some from the NSC staff, and some from the President himself. My new job was to organize the defense issues at the NSC. Others were to deal with intelligence, foreign policy, economics, etc. In time those lines fuzzed over, but for the moment I tried to give Bill Clark a crash course in how the Department of Defense worked.

We went to visit the National Military Command Center and chatted with the chiefs of staff. I prepared lists of critical issues needing attention. The military establishment took a liking to Clark, but his ace in the hole was a close, fifteen-year relationship with Secretary of Defense Cap Weinberger.

Bill Clark moved from initiate to full control of the NSC on Tuesday, January 12, 1982, when the President executed three long-overdue decision directives. The first (NSDD-2) clarified the structure of the NSC. The second (NSDD-4) rendered a full set of decisions on the Carter-era PDs. The third (NSDD-19) set the ground rules for the protection of information. The NSC staff was charged with some real responsibility, and the decisions began to flow.

REAGAN AND THE COLD WAR

When Bud McFarlane and I arrived at the White House, we found no formal plan for dealing with the Soviet Union. That was surprising, given that President Reagan had long-held views on this subject, which he thoroughly communicated over the years.

Only recently, however, have I come to appreciate the priority the new President accorded the Soviet challenge in his personal, preelection thoughts. This insight does not come from early policy advisers, nor speechwriters, nor from the man himself. It comes from Stuart Spencer, Reagan's longtime, nonideological political guru. Spencer came to discuss Reagan's thinking about the Soviet Union during the long flight from Reagan's home in Los Angeles to the Republican nominating convention in Detroit during July 1980. Spencer is not a policy wonk, but he is a smart, hard-hitting political warhorse. As the two men left Los Angeles, they compared notes on immediate practical matters: delegate counts and convention strategy. Over lunch, talk turned to possible VP choices.

In the afternoon the conversation turned philosophical. Spencer asked the question all political pros learn to ask their candidates early on. "Why are you doing this, Ron? Why do you want to be President?"

Without a moment's hesitation Reagan answered, "To end the Cold War."

Spencer: "How do you plan to do that?"

Reagan: "I'm not sure, but there has got to be a way."

Reagan went on at length about the weakness of the Soviet system, about his horror at the thought of nuclear war, and about his annoyance with the accommodating, détente-oriented posture of the incumbent and preceding Presidents. Reagan was not a hawk. He did not want to "beat" the Soviets. He simply felt that it would be in the best interests of both countries, or at least of their general citizenry, to "end this thing." If the United States was strong enough, it could capitalize on the Soviet weaknesses that Reagan knew were there.

"There has to be a way, and it's time."

Only at the end of the flight did the topics of big government, taxes, and the other shibboleths of the campaign make it into the conversation. Reagan was not worried about those. He was worried about the nation's security and the possibility of nuclear war.

In the months that followed Reagan's election and inauguration, Spencer dined often with the Reagans in the private quarters of the White House. They philosophized about the history unfolding around them, and they strategized about how best to take the President's case to the American people. Those conversations with a detached observer now provide critical benchmarks on Reagan's mind-set as he devised a strategy for the endgame *vis-à-vis* the Soviet Union.

THE PLAN TO PREVAIL: NSDD-32

On Monday, February 1, 1982, Clark, McFarlane, and I met with Reagan at our usual 9:00 A.M. hour. After tending to the business of the day, we discussed the lack of a Reagan plan for dealing with the Cold War. How did this administration view Brezhnev's Soviet Union? In previous administrations, the President would have laid a policy question like that before his staff in the form of a study memorandum. The NSC staff then would organize interagency groups, analyze sets of questions, and come back with alternatives for presidential decision. So far nothing like that had happened during the Reagan years. It was time.

Given my long association with the President and my familiarity with his thinking on this subject, it was logical that he asked me to do it. We returned to our offices to write down the terms of reference for this project. At the end of that week, on February 5, 1982, the President signed National Security *Study* Directive Number 1 (NSSD-1). Its stated purpose was to review U.S. national security objectives and the impact of Soviet power and behavior on those objectives. The result would be a decision directive that would codify the President's thinking about the Cold War. I was to chair the interagency review group preparing this study.

We first met in the White House Situation Room on February 18. After that meeting, something changed in the American government. Perhaps it was just that the President had shifted his focus from the economy to national security. Words like "containment," "détente," and "mutual assured destruction" were out. The Cold War was no longer to be viewed as some permanent condition, to be accepted with the inevitability of the sun's rising and setting. The words of Whittaker Chambers from thirty years before echoed in both my mind and the President's: "In this century it will be decided whether all mankind is to become communist or whether the whole world is to become free." We were not just going to *talk* about freedom anymore. One side in this Cold War was going to win and one was going to lose. It was time to think through the steps needed for the U.S. to crystallize its case and to bring this conflict to a peaceful close on a basis acceptable to American values.

Conducting this study was hard work,★ for the bureaucracy did not like laying out a variety of options from which the President might select. They desperately wanted to deliver a predigested consensus view of the world. I knew Reagan well enough to resist.

Toward the end of April, I began delivering regular progress briefings to the National Security Council. This was a way of laying out options informally, of taking cabinet members' temperatures and getting Presidential guidance without the preparation of contentious memoranda. It was at one such session that the President provided his ever so casual but unmistakably clear evaluation of the Soviet economy described in the previous chapter. The last such cabinet briefing was conducted on April 27.

The proposed national security strategy, spelled out in the resulting draft NSDD-32, started out with some pretty conventional objectives: to preserve our democratic institutions, to protect our citizens, to promote their economic well-being, and to foster an international order that was supportive of those purposes. But the document that followed was anything but conventional. It tabulated Soviet strengths and inventoried their growing weaknesses, forecasting confrontations and the reliability of friends and allies. And then came the bottom line: to seek

---

★ Made easier by the efforts of one of my military assistants, Colonel Allan Myer.

the dissolution of the Soviet empire. NSDD-32 listed five integrated strategies to achieve this result: economic, political (at times to include covert action), diplomatic, information (both the promotion of unfettered communication and the use of propaganda), and military (to include arms control). Even so, NSDD-32 was only a beginning, designed to serve as "the starting point for all components of our future national security strategy."

President Reagan signed the eight-page NSDD-32 on May 5, 1982. The substance of our study and the ensuing directive, along with Deputy Secretary of State Eagleburger's initiatives to counter the nuclear freeze movement and to take the political war to the Soviet Union, became the basis for Reagan's speech to the British Parliament, sitting in Westminster four weeks later, on June 8, 1982. In his remarks, Reagan proposed to "foster the infrastructure of democracy." He closed by urging movement "toward a world in which all people are at last free to determine their own destiny." To future historians, he would label that speech as one of the most important he ever gave. "What eventually flowed from it became known as the Reagan Doctrine," he said.

The details of NSDD-32 were conveyed to the public in two speeches that I wrote during that same month.* The first was delivered by National Security Adviser Bill Clark to Georgetown's Center for Strategic and International Studies on May 21. The second was my address to the national convention of the Armed Forces Communications and Electronics Association on June 16. My files include the final draft of the latter, taken to Reagan for his personal approval while traveling aboard Air Force One. It carries his trademark "OK RR." The courier to Air Force One was Oliver North. Both speeches ended with a summary of our new objectives vis-à-vis the Soviet Union: "It is our fondest hope that with an active yet prudent national security policy, we might one day convince the leadership of the Soviet Union to turn their attention inward, to seek the legitimacy that comes only from the consent of the governed, and thus to address the hopes and dreams of their own people."

That's the way it turned out, but NSDD-32 was just the beginning.

---

* The Westminster speech was written by State Department staffer John Lenczowski, then White House speechwriter Tony Dolan, and eventually Reagan himself.

BREZHNEV CHECKS OUT

In the wee small hours of the morning on November 11, 1982, Soviet Ambassador Anatoly Dobrynin called Bill Clark. The call came in on one of the three ambassadorial "hot lines" installed in Clark's office and residence.* Dobrynin wanted to advise Clark that Leonid Brezhnev, the General Secretary of the Communist Party of the Soviet Union, had just died. Dobrynin hoped Reagan would attend the funeral services in Moscow later in the week. Clark thanked the ambassador for the message, then called the President.

Leonid Brezhnev seized control of the Soviet Union in 1964, at age fifty-eight, with the support of the Red Army. He forcibly retired the erratic Nikita Khrushchev and thereafter held power for eighteen years. The expansion of Soviet power was his objective, and for a while it was his pride and joy. At the end, enfeebled by strokes and alcohol, supported only by cronies and relatives, he was oblivious to the disintegration taking place all around him.

Awakened out of a sound sleep, Reagan did not hesitate in his reaction to the news of Brezhnev's death. He did not know the man and had no affinity for that stolid icon of the Cold War. Reagan wanted his first trip to Moscow to be one of substance. He told Clark that the Dobrynin-proposed trip would be pointless. But then, as was typical, Reagan asked Clark to "round-table it with the fellows. We'll talk about it in the morning." At a more reasonable hour, Clark canvassed the National Security Council principals by phone. Crisis or no, Clark usually did that every morning, just to keep the President informed. Secretary of State Shultz, Secretary of Defense Weinberger, Director of Central Intelligence Casey, and UN Ambassador Kirkpatrick were unanimous in their views that Reagan should attend the Brezhnev funeral.

Clark and the President discussed all of this at their 9:00 A.M. meeting. Clark was directed to thank "the fellows" for their advice but to send Reagan's regrets, along with the Vice-President, to Moscow. As an afterthought, Reagan suggested a stroll to the Soviet Embassy to sign

---

* That call got Clark to thinking about those phone lines. If this particular telephone was hard-wired right to the Soviet Embassy, how did we know it was turned off just because we hung up? Clark asked that question of the National Security Agency, and a few weeks later the hot lines were removed.

the condolences book. He had never been there. The next day, the President, his wife Nancy, and Bill Clark walked the four blocks up Sixteenth Street to the Soviet fortress that was its embassy in D.C.

Clark found the visit memorable for two reasons. First of all, the Soviet Embassy was the most cheerless place any of the trio had ever seen. "Like a morgue," the President observed later. Secondly, after signing the condolences book, the President turned to Clark and in his best *sotto voce* whisper asked, "Would they mind if we just said a little prayer for the man?" And so the three of them did just that, bowing their heads in the lobby of the Soviet Embassy to ask the Lord's forgiveness for the departed Soviet party boss.

Unappreciated at the time was that the departure of Leonid Brezhnev was another mysterious death of an aging Soviet dictator, unwitnessed by any members of his family.

At 7:30 A.M. on November 10, the elderly and infirm Brezhnev took breakfast and read the morning newspaper in his private Kremlin dining room. Twenty minutes later he headed upstairs to his bedroom, accompanied by his two KGB guards. All three entered the bedroom together and closed the door behind them. Brezhnev was never again seen alive. At about 8:00 A.M. the two guards emerged and went downstairs to advise Mrs. Brezhnev that her husband had just died. She was not allowed upstairs into the bedroom, nor were any doctors called, nor was any autopsy performed. She never even saw her husband's body until the state ceremonies in the Hall of Columns two days later.

Until her dying day, Victoria Petrovna Brezhneva remained convinced that her husband met with foul play. That conclusion is understandable, given that Brezhnev's successor was KGB chief Yuri Andropov, the man who personally selected those two guards.

NSDD-75

In the aftermath of that change in Moscow, President Reagan and his NSC spent some serious hours trying to think through what it all meant. In time he would build an interesting relationship with Yuri Andropov. Reagan found the man tough but realistic, but the more immediate issue was not getting along with Andropov, it was setting up the end game, if not the checkmate itself. By November 1982, Ronald Reagan was focused on the priority objective of his life: ending the Cold War.

On November 29, 1982, in the wake of Brezhnev's death, the

President signed NSDD-66, a directive that codified a stiffened plan for economic relations with the Soviet Union. Elsewhere in the NSC a more virulent process was under way. The national security planning group★ was meeting in the White House situation room to review the economic situation in the Soviet Union. Henry Rowen, Chairman of the National Intelligence Council, reiterated his earlier views about the declining Soviet economy. He urged continuing pressure on the USSR, foreseeing an economic implosion there if we stayed the course. Director of Central Intelligence Casey was implementing a plan to spoof the entire electronic nervous system of the Soviet Union. NSC staffer Richard Pipes was preparing some thoughts on overall East-West relations. Within a few weeks they were codified into a draft NSDD that was adopted by the President on January 17, 1983. (Not without a struggle; the détente-minded members of the administration fought it.)

NSDD-75 became the blueprint for the endgame. It was a nine-page document that focused the contest on three fronts: the reversal of Soviet expansionism abroad, the promotion of a more pluralistic Soviet society at home, and the engagement of the new Soviet leadership in negotiations to protect and enhance U.S. interests. NSDD-75 was a confidential declaration of economic and political war. Contrary to Soviet fears at the time, reflected in their "Project Ryan" tasking to all KGB stations, NSDD-75 did not include any plan for initiating a nuclear attack on the USSR.

The thrust of NSDD-75 was made public eight weeks later in Reagan's "evil empire" speech, delivered on March 8, 1983, in Orlando, Florida. The tone of that oratory drew gasps from those who wished to accommodate the sinking USSR, but Reagan meant every word.

During the following week, at one of their private dinners for three, both Nancy Reagan and Stu Spencer raised their collective eyebrows at the speech. Nancy always longed for friendly summit meetings with whatever Soviet dictator was in power. Stu Spencer had no problem with the philosophy expressed in the speech. He just thought that, as a matter of practical politics, the evil empire language would scare the American people to death. The President waved them both off. "It *is* an evil empire," he said. "It's time to close it down."

★ President Reagan, Vice-President Bush, National Security Adviser Clark, Secretary of Defense Weinberger, Secretary of State Haig, and Director of Central Intelligence Casey. Bud McFarlane and Henry Rowen also attended this November 1982 meeting.

Presidents Bush and Mikhail Gorbachev at the press conference closing out the Malta Summit, December 3, 1989. *Photo: George Bush Presidential Library*

Headstone and graveside of Nikita Khrushchev, located in the Novodevichi Cemetery, outside Moscow. The white and black stones symbolize the Soviet people's conflicting views of Khrushchev's contribution to their history. Lettering at the bottom reads, "Nikia Sergeyevich Khrushchev." *Photo: Elena Ushakova*

RB-47 reconnaissance version of the B-47 bomber, first flown over the Soviet Union in covert missions in 1954. *U.S. Air Force photo (Photographer unknown)*

Left to right: Pilot Hal Austin, author Tom Reed, copilot Carl Holt at their first viewing of photos taken over northern Russia by Austin and Holt forty-seven years earlier. *Photo: Thomas C. Reed*

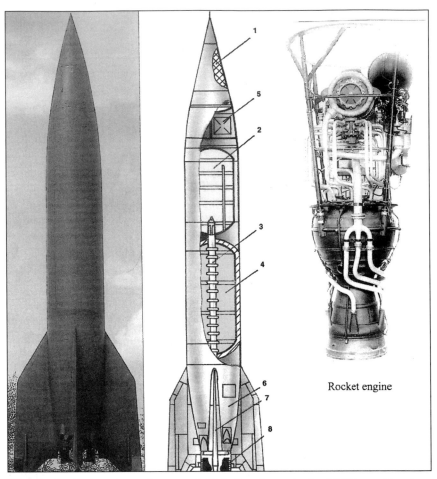

The Soviet R-1 rocket, a homemade V-2, first flown in the USSR on October 10, 1948. Components, from above sketch: 1. Warhead, 2. Fuel tank, 3. Fuel feed pipeline duct, 4. Oxidizer tank, 5. Instrumentation and guidance compartment, 6. Tail section, 7. Aerodynamic steering fin, 8. Jet vane, for propulsion vector control. *From* Russia's Arms, Vol. IV, Strategic Missile Forces, *Igor Sergeyev, Ed., 1997, Military Parade, Moscow*

The Mk-17, first operational US H-bomb. *Photo: Thomas C. Reed*

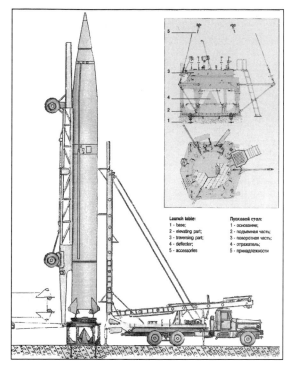

The Soviet R–5 (SS–3) rocket on its launch table. Capable of carrying a single 300 KT warhead to distances of 750 miles, the R–5 was first launched on April 2, 1953. *From* Russia's Arms, Vol. IV, Strategic Missile Forces, *Igor Sergeyev, Ed., 1997, Military Parade, Moscow*

The Russian Nuclear Weapons Museum at Sarov. *Left front:* The first "native" Soviet atomic bomb, detonated at Semipalatinsk on September 24, 1951, two years after the first Soviet test of a US Fat Man clone. All such devices had a yield of about 40 KT, but this RDS-2 had a diameter of only half, and a weight only 60% of Fat Man/RDS-1. *Second from left:* The world's first nuclear weapon, not experiment, to achieve a significant portion (15-20%) of its yield from thermonuclear burn. Fired at Semipalatinsk on August 12, 1953, it employed Sakharov's "Layer Cake" principle to achieve a yield of 400 KT. It weighed 10,000 pounds, about the size and weight of Fat Man.
Right rear: The Khrushchev super-bomb, capable of 100MT, was fired "clean" at about 50 MT, to preclude serious fallout problems and to improve the pilot's chances of escape. It was tested at Novaya Zemlya on October 30, 1961.
Russian handout at "HISAP-96" conference at Dubna, Russia, May 1996.

Shot tower still standing in Nevada, after LLNL's first attempted A-bomb test, the "Ruth" event in 1953. It did not work very well. *University of California, Lawrence Livermore National Laboratory Archives and Research Center*

President John F. Kennedy, visiting the University of California Berkeley Laboratory, March 23, 1962, to meet with the leaders of the US nuclear weapons laboratories. The purpose of the meeting was to discuss the Soviet breach of the atmospheric testing moratorium and his decision to resume US testing. *Left to right:* Norris Bradbury, Director of Los Alamos; John Foster, Director of Livermore; Edwin McMillan, Director of the Berkeley Laboratory; Glen Seaborg, Chairman of the Atomic Energy Commission; President Kennedy; Edward Teller; Robert McNamara, US Secretary of Defense; Harold Brown, Director of Defense Research and Engineering. *[Lawrence Berkeley National Laboratory]*

The PTF (Patrol Boat Fast), known as "Nasties," used to attack shipping and shore facilities along the coast of North Vietnam, 1964. Displacement: 75 tons; Length: 80 feet; Top speed: 43 knots; Powerplant: Twin 3,100 HP diesels; Armament: One 40mm and two 20mm cannon, one 81mm mortar, one .50 cal machine gun, and small arms. *Photo: www.ptfnasty.com*

Adm. James Stockdale and wife, Sybil (with umbrella), accompanied by local newsmen, tour the perimeter of the Hoa Lo prison in Hanoi, January 17, 1994. *Photo: Thomas C. Reed*

A B-52 receiving a load of fuel from a KC-135 tanker. *Photo: USAF Art Collection*

The energy-absorbing nose of the Mk-28 RI H-bomb, designed to withstand impact after low altitude delivery at high speed. *Photo: Sandia National Laboratories*

A "clip" of four Mk-28 H-bombs being readied for loading aboard a B-52.
U.S. Air Force photo (Photographer unknown)

Ted Cochran landing his H-43 rescue helicopter on the deck of the USS *Albany,* March 1966.
Cochran family photo

Casing of the Mk-28 H-bomb recovered off the coast of Spain, near Palomares on April 7, 1966. Parachute for slowing the weapon's fall is visible to the left.
Photo: Thomas C. Reed

A USAF team setting up a satellite terminal in southern Iraq, 1991. *Photo: Defense Visual Information Center*

Headstone of Red Army Marshal Ivan Peretsypkin, with telephone and telegraph in hand. Located in the Novodevichi Cemetery, outside Moscow. *Photo: Elena Ushakova*

An A-10 ground-attack aircraft rolls past the burned-out hulk of an Iraqi tank at
Talil Air Force Base, Iraq. June 22, 2003.
U.S. Air Force photo by 2nd Lt. Gerardo Gonzalez

An F-15 Eagle in flight over
Nellis AFB, Nevada. *U.S. Air
Force photo by Tech. Sgt. Robert
W. Valenca*

An F-16 Fighting Falcon
prepares to take off for a
sortie over Iraq. Note
the visibility afforded
the pilot by the bubble
canopy. *U.S. Air Force
photo by Master Sgt. Terry
L. Blevins*

General John C. Vessey being sworn in as the tenth Chairman of the Joint Chiefs of Staff on June 18, 1982. At left, President Reagan, at right, Avis Vessey, the general's wife. *White House Photo, Jack Kinglighter*

The author with a Soviet SS-20 intermediate range missile and its mobile launcher. *Photo: Thomas C. Reed*

NCS staff member Gus Weiss, exploiter of the *Farewell* dossier. *Photo: Gus Weiss*

Yuly Khariton, Chief Designer of the first Soviet atomic bomb. *From* Strategic Nuclear Forces—The 21st Century, *edited by Nikolai Spassky, 2000. Russia's Arms and Technologies, Moscow.*

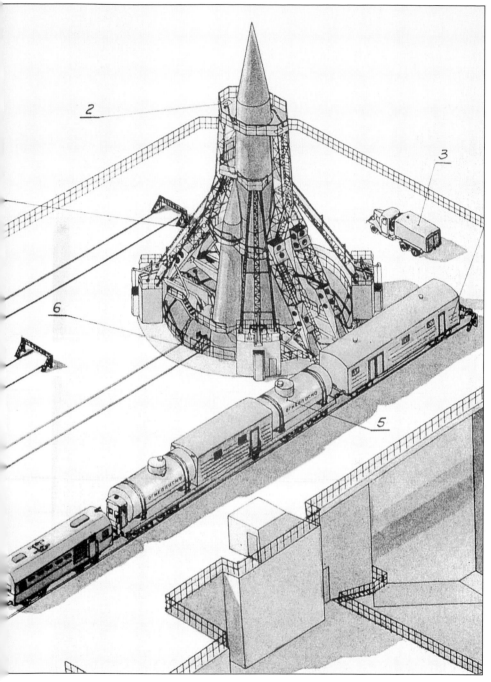

The Soviet R-7 (SS-6) rocket, erected and being readied for launch.
From Russia's Arms Catalog, Volume IV, Strategic Missile Forces, *1997, Military Parade, Moscow*

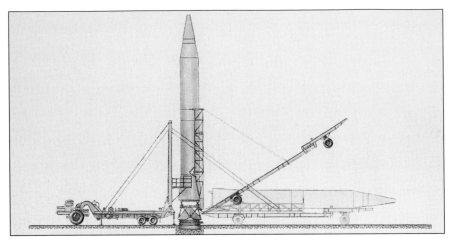

The Soviet R-14 (SS-5) medium range ballistic missile, the weapon system that never made it to Cuba—although the warheads did. *From* Russia's Arms Catalog, Volume IV, Strategic Missile Forces, *1997, Military Parade, Moscow*

Cold War hero Vladimir Petoukhov *(at right)* and author Thomas C. Reed *(second from right)* with other Russian engineers at the museum of the secret IMPULS NPO in St. Petersburg, Russia. They pose in front of an old and bulky console originally used to secure the Soviet nuclear arsenal. Reed points to its 1998 counterpart. *Photo: Thomas C. Reed*

The E4B airborne command post in the hangar at Offutt Air Force Base on the occasion of the close-down of the Strategic Air Command, May 31, 1992. *Photo: Thomas C. Reed*

CHAPTER 16

Ghost Stories from the Reagan White House

THE CENTRAL YEARS of President Reagan's first term were full of activity. Some days were happy, some were not, but the nights were less well understood. Some were haunted by ghosts waiting to be unleashed. The possibility of a nuclear detonation as a result of some terrible mistake, a terrorist statement, or an act of war, troubled Reagan in his darkest hours.

THE SIOP

Prior to every modern-day President's inauguration, the Chairman of the Joint Chiefs of Staff gives the President-elect a short briefing on the SIOP. This is the most awful briefing a senior official can receive because it lays out exactly how, and under what circumstances, the chief executive would exercise his nuclear war powers. SIOP stands for the Single Integrated Operational Plan, and as the name implies, it is the plan for uncorking the nuclear genie and all the horrors that would follow.

During the 1980–81 presidential transition, Major Kline first briefed President-elect Reagan on the "football"—the black bag containing the nuclear options notebook and communication tools that a military assistant always keeps within a few yards of the President, night and day. Then General Jones, Chairman of the Joint Chiefs of Staff, explained the contents of that notebook. He warned the President-elect that in the event of a nuclear crisis, the President might have only sketchy information and a few moments of time in which to make a fateful decision. Jones went over the procedures for releasing an Emergency Action Message, the presidential order to attack with nuclear weapons. Reagan, like most Presidents before him, did not enjoy hearing this story. He did not want to hear any more about it once he was sworn in.

Upon my arrival at the White House, after starting the ball rolling on the policy review described in the preceding chapter, I began to think about the matter of presidential communications in times of crisis. In an earlier administration, I had served as the Pentagon's command, control, and communications czar. With this new chance to look into the presidential communication system from the top down, I became alarmed.

By 1982 the World Wide Military Command and Control System had become reliable and redundant, but those virtues ended at the National Military Command Center in the Pentagon. To reach upward, to communicate with the President himself, the Pentagon relied on the White House Communications Agency.

The Wizard of Oz would have felt comfortable at the WHCA, an agency that presented a false front of security, propped up and tied together by an Eisenhower-era network of telephones, radios and hideouts, all rendered obsolete by the thermonuclear and information ages by then unfolding. It was a system designed to spirit the President out of harm's way, to keep him alive, but in these days of fast-moving crises, every President now sees it as his duty to get to the eye of the storm, not to run away from it—to defuse the crisis, not just survive it. Unfortunately, should that crisis go nuclear, the President would have put himself at ground zero; when the smoke cleared, he would be gone. The system as I found it would have been headless within minutes of an attack. Yet the institution of the presidency, the civilian control of our government, must survive. Otherwise the military would be obligated to run the country, which that is not what the Founding Fathers had in mind.

The opportunity to get the President involved in this issue was brought to my attention by young Marine Major Oliver North. In February 1982, North advised me that the military establishment and the civilian emergency agencies were about to undertake a joint command post exercise. Its purpose was to test the ability of the National Military Command Center to support the President and Secretary of Defense through a nuclear crisis and then to test procedures for retaining the continuity of civilian government after a nuclear strike on the U.S. Former senior government officials were to play the roles of President and cabinet members during this four day exercise. An effective exercise requires the participation of those who know how a President might reasonably be expected to act in times of crisis. At the same time, incumbent officeholders should not play themselves, lest they tip their hands on how they might react in a real crisis. Uncertainty about our leaders' actions is an important component of nuclear deterrence.

This exercise, known here as *Ivory Leaf*, was scheduled for March 1 to 4, 1982. It seemed like the ideal vehicle to bring the twin issues of nuclear operations and presidential survivability to Reagan's attention. Given his personal distaste for the subject, I was impressed with his prompt approval and agreement to participate.

The process started with a two-hour session on Saturday morning, February 27. Bill Clark and I, along with a few members of the White House staff, explained to the President how he would get information in times of nuclear crisis, how we would protect him personally, and how he would communicate messages back out to the forces. We described the ways in which the start of nuclear hostilities might appear, the times available for response, and the forces at his disposal for counterattack and/or withhold.★ Reagan absorbed the discussions well. From his questions, we knew he was working to understand the incredible consequences of a nuclear exchange.

The exercise itself started on a Monday morning. That afternoon both the exercise and the real President came to the Situation Room to receive the threat briefing. An intelligence officer laid out the Soviet order of battle, then the warning systems began to report simulated

---

★ A "withhold" is a concept within the SIOP wherein certain forces are withheld from an initial strike. They might be used in subsequent negotiations or follow-up attacks.

missile launches and impact predictions. The minutes flew by until a screen in that cramped basement room began to show red dots on a map of the U.S.—simulated impacts. The first ones annihilated Washington, so this briefing was assumed to be taking place in some airborne command post over the central plains.

Before the President could sip his coffee, the map was a sea of red. All the urban centers and military installations in the U.S. were gone. And then, while he looked on in stunned disbelief, he learned that the Soviet air force and the second round of missile launches were on their way in. For the next half hour more red dots wiped out the survivors and filled in the few holes in the sea of red. In less than an hour President Reagan had seen the United States of America disappear.

I have no doubt that on that Monday in March, Ronald Reagan came to understand exactly what a Soviet nuclear attack on the U.S. would be like. It was a sobering experience, and it undoubtedly stiffened his resolve to do something about a shield against such an attack.

Later that evening we met to discuss U.S. options. (In a real world crisis, such discussions would have gone on simultaneously with the attack assessment.) Again we met in the Situation Room, this time accompanied by senior Pentagon officials. I started the meeting by announcing an SIOP briefing. The President asked what SIOP stood for. I deferred to the Secretary of Defense, who did not know. He deferred to his military assistant who explained that SIOP stood for the Single Integrated Operational Plan and that in actuality it was a menu of plans from which the President must choose quickly unless he had delegated that authority to his safely hidden Vice-President or other successors.

The SIOP briefing was as scary as the earlier presentation on the Soviet attack. It made clear to Reagan that with but a nod of his head all the glories of imperial Russia, all the hopes and dreams of the peasants in Ukraine, and all the pioneering settlements in Kazakhstan would vanish. Tens of millions of women and children who had done nothing to harm American citizens would be burned to a crisp.

At a third meeting, this one attended only by Bill Clark, the President, and me, we went over the detailed procedures for keeping the President alive during such catastrophes. Then we practiced how he actually would give the order to fire. U.S. nuclear weapons are controlled by built-in Permissive Action Links, or PALs. Without a code number originating with the President or his successor, modern American nukes are just big metal cans, inert and tamper proof. To give the order to fire, the President must select an option, so advise his military assistant, then confirm his authority by inserting his authenticator code into the outgoing message. We practiced those procedures, then the exercise ended, but I have no doubt that in Reagan's mind it was not over at all. *Ivory Leaf* was something that really had happened to him. It focused his mind on the need for protection from those red dots.

PROJECT PARTRIDGE

From time immemorial societies have striven to protect their leaders. Perhaps the King, President, or Prime Minister was the embodiment of that nation's power. Or perhaps he or she was the symbol of its unity. In any case, the survival of a nation's leader has often been considered essential to the survival of that society itself. During the Eisenhower years, any threat to nation, White House, or President was to be met with an immediate evacuation. There were elaborate plans, but by the end of the fifties all were pointless. Each relocation facility was accurately targeted by the Soviet Union, and each would be gone in a flash.

At the same time, the safety of the Vice-President was ignored. Everyone assumes the Vice-President will take over if needed, but few understand how difficult such a transition can be in times of crisis; few remember the shock experienced by Harry Truman and Lyndon Johnson when they were thrust into the presidency without warning. Ronald Reagan went to great lengths to include his Vice-President in the councils of government, but in the thermonuclear age, more was needed.

In the aftermath of *Ivory Leaf*, the President agreed that we needed a system of procedures and hardware that would allow him to send his Vice-President (or some other designated constitutional successor) into cyberspace, to keep him safe from attack yet able to execute informed civilian control of the government if the President were to disappear. During the summer of 1982, Major North and I gave this matter some thought, and on September 8, I briefed my conclusions to the President. Thus was born the project we shall call *Partridge*. The details remain sensitive, but at its heart *Partridge* was a plan to support the President in the oval office while providing his successor with the ability to disappear—not just personally, but with the staff and information systems needed to conduct the nation's business in times of trouble. The resulting system was expensive in terms of bureaucratic bloodshed and money, but by the end of Reagan's term, the U.S. government did not need to fear a disabling decapitation in the midst of a crisis. The President could do his job. He could work to defuse the crisis, to negotiate an end to any confrontation, secure in the knowledge that if his efforts failed, an informed and fully supported successor was ready and able to carry on.

THE GENERAL

The Chairman of the Joint Chiefs of Staff is, by law, the President's principal military adviser. In the event of hostilities, be they local insurrections or nuclear war, this senior military officer must advise the President on the options available, and he must see to it that the President's decisions are understood and carried out by the Chiefs of Staff and the Unified Commanders. With the arrival of the Reagan administration, winning—or more accurately, prevailing—was now the only acceptable outcome of the Cold War. Reagan needed a JCS chairman to lead the charge in the coming politico-military test of wills between East and West.

At the beginning of his term, Reagan inherited Jimmy Carter's JCS Chairman: Air Force General David Jones, who served as Air Force chief of staff during my tenure as Secretary of the Air Force. Jones was in place when I assumed that position, installed by Secretary of Defense James Schlesinger two years before. A personal friend and a military officer with a distinguished record of public service to his country stretching back to the postwar occupation of Japan, Jones was my partner in rebuilding the USAF in the aftermath of Vietnam. With the coming of the Carter administration, however, that President and his new chairman came to symbolize America's humiliation at the hands of Iran's revolutionary mullahs. They also shared the view that peace with the Soviets was best achieved by good communication and forbearance.

On November 4, 1979, sixty-two Americans were taken hostage at the U.S. Embassy in Tehran. Carter wanted them back, and failure to achieve that result was corroding his stature with the American people. Thus was born the scheme to fly helicopters across the Iranian desert to a rendezvous south of Tehran, where the troops in those helicopters would descend on the American embassy, snatch the hostages, and return to the United States.

General Jones was in full charge of this operation. Legitimately concerned about secrecy, Jones did not allow adequate rehearsals or training. Eager to please all of his military constituencies, he allocated one piece of the action to the Army, another to the Marines, the Air Force, etc. The first time many of these people met was in the dusty and smoking debris of the Desert One site south of Tehran. Eight Americans were killed in this episode. One aircraft and one helocopter were destroyed, and three more helocopters were abandoned as the American forces fled the scene of the disaster. Secretary of State Cyrus Vance resigned in its aftermath, and the U.S. suffered a huge black eye. The hostages remained securely locked up in Tehran.

Most Presidents would have fired the responsible general, and perhaps his Secretary of Defense, on the spot. Carter convened a panel of generals and admirals, chaired by a former member of the JCS, to look into the matter. They found their fellow four-star officer blameless. David Jones kept his job as chairman and was in place when the Reagan team arrived.

Secretary of Defense–designate Weinberger understood this background, but he also was a veteran of Reagan's first year as governor of California. Back then, in 1967, Clark Kerr was forced out as president of the University of California in an early confrontation with Reagan over student misbehavior. Weinberger did not want another "nonpartisan" officeholder purged in the early days of this new administration. He did not consider the matter of the general's competence or his compatibility with the new administration's views of the Soviet Union to be worth the flap. And more than one retired four-star and former Secretary of Defense cautioned against breaking with the tradition of full two-year terms for Chairmen of the JCS. Thus, for the first year of the Reagan administration, JCS Chairman Jones contested the Weinberger defense buildup. His fellow chiefs, also holdovers from the Carter era, cringed as Reagan and Weinberger talked about the "decade of neglect" over which these officers had presided.

Soon after my arrival at the White House with Bill Clark, I turned my attention to this matter. It was time for Reagan to select a new Chairman of the JCS, for in reality the nuclear button would lie in that man's hands. During Governor Reagan's first hundred days in Sacramento, fifteen years before, I had come to know what kind of people he liked. I served as his personnel chief at that time, and now, as Reagan began to focus on the Cold War, he wanted the right soldier at his side. I began to talk to my peers from the Ford administration, to the young officers on my staff, and to the mid-level generals and admirals in whom I had confidence. In the process I consulted with three former

Secretaries of Defense, four Deputy or Under Secretaries, eight four-star officers from all branches, a half-dozen service secretaries or under-secretaries, and dozens of colonels. Within two weeks it was clear that General John Vessey, a four-star general in the U.S. Army, had the right credentials, that he shared Reagan's determination to push back on the Soviets, and that his personal characteristics would appeal to the President.

Jack Vessey was born into a farm community in Minnesota in 1922. His father had served as an enlisted man in World War I, and the younger Vessey enlisted in the Army as an artilleryman, fighting his way from Salerno to the Alps during World War II. He was awarded a battlefield commission at the bloody beach of Anzio. Vessey returned to the U.S. as a lieutenant, married his high school sweetheart, and settled into an Army career. He never received a formal college education, earning a degree at night school in order to meet the standards expected of an officer.

By the late 1970s, Vessy had risen to four-star rank and was Commander of the Eighth Army, the U.S. force in Korea. President Carter asked him to come to Washington to be interviewed for the job of Chief of Staff of the U.S. Army. Vessey and Carter talked alone for an hour. As Vessey put it later, "I failed my oral exams." He made it clear that, in his opinion, Carter's defense policies, from Korea to SALT II, were ill-advised. Vessey had not told the President what he wanted to hear.

A week after the interview, Carter chose Lieutenant General "Shy" Meyer to serve as Army chief of staff. Meyer asked Vessey, very much his senior, to come to Washington to serve as his vice-chief. Ever the good soldier, Vessey did so, as a last stop en route to retirement, or so he thought.

On February 26, 1982, Clark and I discussed the matter of the next JCS chairman with the President at our regular 9:00 A.M. meeting. I gave Reagan a briefing on the makeup of the JCS, confirmed that he was not comfortable with Dave Jones as chairman, then reviewed some names. Vessey was at the top of my list, although I had not yet interviewed him. Reagan liked what he heard and asked to meet him. I met with Vessey first, and thought he was the kind of soldier you want at your side when the fight begins: holder of a battlefield commission and an education grounded in reality; a man of integrity who would tell his President the truth whatever the personal cost; an officer who had seen the mud and the blood, who would not be casual about the matter of war, especially nuclear war.

At 9:30 A.M. on March 1, Vessey came to the White House, accompanied by Secretary of Defense Weinberger, to meet the President. Clark and Weinberger showed him in and then left the two to talk. Reagan and Vessey met for an hour, but Reagan did not pop the chairman question until Clark and Weinberger reappeared. When the invitation did come, Vessey thanked the President for the offer but said that he had a longstanding agreement with his wife not to do such things without consultation. Moreover, the Vesseys had already started construction of their retirement home in Minnesota. After the appropriate consultations, and with his wife's active support, Jack Vessey was sworn in as the tenth Chairman of the Joint Chiefs of Staff on June 18, 1982, a month after Reagan signed NSDD-32. The road map for winning the Cold War and the soldier to lead the charge were now both in place.

A decade later I talked to Vessey about these events and asked what his biggest contribution to prevailing in the Cold War had been. Without hesitation he answered: "The actual deployment of the intermediate range nuclear forces to Europe in 1983."

In the mid-1970s the Soviet Union decided to put Western Europe and our Pacific allies directly under the gun with the deployment of SS-20 intermediate range ballistic missiles throughout the Eastern Bloc countries and Siberia. Cooler heads in the senior ranks of the Soviet Strategic Rocket Forces demurred, reminding their government that "it would be the Caribbean Crisis all over again." But Brezhnev's Politburo turned a deaf ear, and the deployment was carried out. The Ford administration responded by adopting nuclear war fighting plans. The Carter administration concluded that some counterdeployment of medium range missiles was necessary. At the Guadaloupe summit in January 1979 the UK and West Germany agreed to accept cruise missiles and Pershing II ballistic missiles on their soil. The Soviets responded with threats and bluster, which only grew worse as other NATO allies followed suit. Soviet Defense Minister Dimitri Ustinov threatened the West European countries with "appropriate measures" if the Atlantic Alliance deployed the new weapons. Yet by the year's end, NATO had agreed on a full deployment of 572 cruise and Pershing II missiles in Western Europe.

When the Reagan administration took office, those weapons systems were undergoing their final flight tests. Production was under way. The prospect of those deployments horrified the Soviet leadership. The Pershing IIs were fast and accurate weapons.★ From their bases in West Germany, the Pershing IIs would be able to strike at Soviet command posts and party headquarters with virtually no warning. "Not even time for a trip to the bathroom," as one Russian put it to me later.

Counterdemonstrations were orchestrated all over Europe. The German elections of 1982 were fought on this issue; Chancellor Kohl's coalition won handily. In the United States the Reagan administration faced a propaganda offensive calling for a "nuclear freeze." The campaign featured a TV show, *The Day After,* which depicted in graphic detail the consequences of a nuclear laydown on the U.S. Actually, the movie was understated in its depiction of the horrors of nuclear war, but it had the unintended consequence of strengthening Reagan's determination to develop a shield against such attack. These activities, at home and overseas, were not entirely spontaneous. The archives of the Communist party of the Soviet Union, laid bare after the failed coup of August 1991, show that during the 1980s alone the CPSU distributed over $200 million in support of friendly political activities outside the Soviet Bloc.

In the midst of all this, Jack Vessey was sworn in as Chairman of the JCS. It was clear to him and the President that the Soviets would never negotiate away their SS-20s until the U.S. and NATO had demonstrated their political resolve: deploy the missiles and maintain the strategic balance. The intermediate range nuclear forces had to be deployed if they were ever to be removed from both sides of the Iron Curtain.

In 1983 the deployments started. Speed was essential, and Jack Vessey was the full-time expediter. According to Margaret Thatcher's memoirs, 108 Pershing II ballistic missiles and ninety-six cruise missiles went to West Germany. The country was awash in demonstrations. The UK took 160 cruise missiles, basing them at Molesworth and Greenham Common. The latter was the site of virulent and long-term demonstrations. Italy took 112 cruise missiles. Vessey jokes now that the Italian deployment, on Sicily, was the easiest, probably because the Mafia took a dim view of disorderly crowds in the streets. Even the tiny low countries did their part. Belgium and the Netherlands each took forty-eight cruise missiles, and the associated political abuse in the streets. The job was finished in less than a year.

★ Eight to ten minute flight times from West Germany to Moscow. Average miss distance of less than a hundred feet.

When it was over, the Soviet Union was on notice that the Reagan team had the stomach and the muscle for a fight. With luck, that fight would not turn bloody, nor would it go nuclear, but it was clear that the U.S. intended to prevail. In the process, Reagan had found his general.

THE M-X

In order to deter nuclear attack by others, the President must have strategic nuclear weapon systems that are modern, deployed under his control, and sufficiently redundant to preclude the need to shoot first in times of crisis. Reagan made the rebuilding of U.S. military strength a 1980 campaign issue. His announcements about U.S. strategic programs in October 1981 settled a lot of these issues, but they left one thorny problem unresolved: how to base the M-X missile, a new intercontinental ballistic missile needed to replace the aging Minutemen and Titan ICBMs of the sixties.

The arms control advocates in the previous administration and in Congress considered ICBMs with multiple warheads to be inherently unstable in times of crisis. So much firepower was packed into one launcher, they said, that the U.S. leadership would be faced with a "use it or lose it" dilemma upon receipt of first warning. Cooler heads did not want to have to fire based solely on radar or satellite indications of an attack, an option known as "launch on warning." They wanted confirmed detonations on U.S. soil, with the attacking nation clearly identified before being required to take action. Then and only then did they want to call on the M-X for its ghastly business.

In fact the land-based missiles are but one leg of the strategic triad. Bombers and submarine-launched ballistic missiles are the other two. The land-based missiles, by their mere existence, assure adequate warning for the bombers and submarines. If the USSR were to time its launches in order to achieve simultaneous impact of all warheads on the United States, the long missile flight times from the USSR would have given the U.S. bombers time to scramble and escape and the Navy time to alert its submarines to an imminent attack. Alternately, the USSR might fire everything simultaneously. This would result in first detonations on the coastal cities and facilities, the confirmed detonations on U.S. soil that the land-based missile crews would want. It is impossible to surprise all three legs of the strategic triad in the same attack.

If, however, one wanted *all* legs of the triad to survive a surprise attack, then the missile basing had to be unique. Some sort of mobile launcher was in order, and the arms controllers wanted them to be countable for treaty purposes. The solution to all of this, to the Carter administration, was an enormously complex underground railroad system, or "racetrack," that would have dug up much of the western desert and disemboweled the defense budget. The new Weinberger team at the Pentagon considered this to be folly, but did not come up with any better idea. Portable missiles in trucks, missiles dropped from airplanes, and all sorts of other schemes were the object of blue ribbon panel attention. At the October 1981 strategic forces press conference, the administration could only announce that it was *not* going to proceed with the racetrack. Weinberger proposed no better solution.

Republican John Tower, Chairman of the Senate Armed Services Committee, was not pleased. Tower inserted into the defense authorization bill for FY 82 language that required an M-X basing mode to be announced by December 1, 1982, if there was to be any more money for missile development. In response, the Pentagon came up with a bizarre scheme known as Closely Spaced Basing, or "Densepack." The theory was, by clustering ICBM silos within a few hundred feet of each other, the incoming Soviet warheads would destroy each other by "fratricide" and the U.S. missiles would survive. There was no preselling of this idea to Congress. A majority of the JCS did not support it, and the plan was torn to shreds in the closing days of the 1982 session of Congress. It was time to start over. ICBM basing needed to become a White House issue.

Bud McFarlane and I discussed the concept of a presidential panel to help recover from these years of Pentagon indecision. A bipartisan solution broadly vetted within the Washington establishment was needed: defense officials, arms controllers, media, think tanks, and the Congress. In late December, Bill Clark called from the California White House to ask me to take charge of this project. McFarlane and I discussed names, settling on Brent Scowcroft—Gerald Ford's National Security Adviser—as the chairman and myself as vice-chairman. The members of the President's Commission on Strategic Forces were drawn from a wide political spectrum. In addition to Scowcroft and myself, they included four individuals who had served in the Reagan, Ford, or Nixon administrations: Nick Brady, Bill Clements, Al Haig, and Richard Helms.

To assure the longevity of any commission's proposals it is best to bring on board those members of the loyal opposition who might be called upon to serve once again upon that party's return to power. Members of the Scowcroft Commission with service in the Carter administration, destined to serve again during the Clinton years, included John Deutch, Bill Perry, and Jim Woolsey. Two other commission members, John Lyons of the AFL-CIO and Vice Admiral (ret.) Levering Smith, had never held political office. The commission held its first meeting with the President in the cabinet room of the White House on January 3, 1983.

Upon the announcement of its formation, the commission was the beneficiary of extensive premortems by the establishment press. They described the Scowcroft Commission as a lifeboat that would not float. The *Washington Post*'s Evans and Novak described it as an attempted solution to "the administration's self-inflicted wounds in the dreary saga of the M-X . . ." They reported an administration source as saying, "Our duty now is to minimize further damage to the President." Surveying Capitol Hill, they found that "Defense Secretary Weinberger was being faulted by bitter grandees in Congress."

The commission began its deliberations and its back-channel negotiations with those grandees, but by the beginning of February prospects still looked dim. Melvin Laird, a former congressman and Secretary of Defense, opined that the M-X was "an absolute loser, with no chance whatsoever." Slowly, however, some common ground began to emerge from the fog of political war. After hearing from all parts of the political spectrum, dining regularly at Blair House and elsewhere with Congressional leaders and think tank gurus, and negotiating tirelessly with itself, the commission released its report on April 6.

The conclusions were threefold. First, we advised proceeding with the development of a ten warhead M-X missile, now named Peacekeeper, and to base a hundred of those missiles in existing Minuteman silos around Francis E. Warren AFB near Cheyenne, Wyoming. Second, we recommended the development of a smaller, road-mobile single warhead missile, about one-seventh the size of the M-X, easier to hide and thus more stabilizing in time of crisis. (This latter system was immediately given the sobriquet "Midgetman.") Last, the administration should undertake energetic new arms control initiatives, including the counting of warheads, not launchers, in order to reach better agreements with the Soviets. The Pentagon, although not part of the commission process, embraced the findings at once. So did the White House. Then we began the presentations and negotiations with Congress.

There ensued meetings with both freshman members, sworn in just two months before, as well as with the veterans of decades on the hill. Stitching together a majority one vote at a time, Les Aspin, Chairman of the House Armed Services Committee and a Democrat signed on. Successful committee votes followed in April, and after two months of enormous effort, the recommendations of the Scowcroft Commission were embraced by Congress. On May 24 the House of Representatives voted funds to continue the development and testing of the Peacekeeper by a vote of 239 to 186. The following day the Senate voted similar support, 59 to 39. Two days later the commission and staff met with the President in the Roosevelt Room of the White House. It was Friday, May 27, the occasion of one of the greatest TGIF parties of all time. There were very appreciative words from Reagan and photos all around. There could be no doubt then or now that a critical piece had been put in place, essential for the coming settlement with the Soviets.

Over the summer and fall the media accolades, the awards, and the congratulations poured in. More to the point, on June 9 the first Peacekeeper launch look place at Vandenberg Air Force Base. As is now required in our media-driven society, the flight was a complete success. Missile deployment started on schedule and as planned.

It was completed in December 1988, as Reagan was leaving office. Peacekeeper was there to stand guard during the final transitions, negotiations, and treaties that ended the Cold War. Reagan had swallowed the bitter pill of another nuclear deployment to once again make his point: America would stand down its fortifications only in concert with its global adversary.

THE STRATEGIC DEFENSE INITIATIVE

While the Scowcroft Commission was in session, an equally historic process was under way elsewhere in the White House: the gestation and birth of the Strategic Defense Initiative. For as long as I have known him, Ronald Reagan had a "big picture" view of nuclear weapons. He was never drawn into the intricacies of yields and accuracies, the differences between silo busting and Mutual Assured Destruction, nor the complexities of plutonium production and waste disposal. He knew that nuclear weapons had brought about an early end to World War II, that the Soviet Union possessed such weapons in profusion, and that our security lay in making sure the Soviets were not tempted to use them. At the same time, Reagan was not willing to accept the inevitability of nuclear casualties. Over and over he asked about umbrellas and defenses.

Upon assuming office, Reagan began asking these questions formally. He posed the question to a Defense Science Board panel that I chaired during the summer of 1981. He listened to Edward Teller, champion of the X-ray laser. Teller's idea was to track attacking missiles as they lifted off, to then fire a specially designed nuclear device in space, focusing the X-ray energy coming out of that device onto the attacking missile half a world away.

It is not clear whether Reagan took Teller seriously, but it is clear that a scientist of world renown had told Reagan that some sort of missile defense was technically possible. He listened to his science adviser, Jay Keyworth, who saw missile defense as a computational problem. Keyworth correctly assured the President that the 1980s would see an explosive growth in America's ability to identify, track, and intercept incoming missiles. Much of the U.S. scientific establishment disagreed, but here was support from another scientific quarter that a missile defense was possible.

By the fall of 1982 the Chairman of the JCS and the Joint Chiefs were meeting monthly with the President. The meetings were held in the Roosevelt Room rather than the more formal Cabinet Room across the hall, to promote an informal exchange of views. At the end of the December meeting, the President turned philosophical. "What if we tried to shift from Mutual Assured Destruction to a total defense?" After the meeting, Admiral Watkins, Chief of Naval Operations, called National Security Adviser Clark to ask if the President were serious. Clark confirmed that he was. During January and February 1983 the chiefs discussed this matter among themselves. They brought their conclusions to Reagan on February 11.

Chairman Vessey and Chief of Naval Operations Watkins endorsed the idea of strategic defenses, and with the President's support, the JCS began in-depth deliberations on what would become known as the Strategic Defense Initiative. This was not some bright idea that a staffer laid before the President for his initials and approval. It was Reagan's strongly held belief, reinforced by his exposure to the possible horrors of nuclear warfare during the *Ivory Leaf* exercise and his viewing of *The Day After* movie, that something must be done.

Like Admiral Watkins, Reagan never considered SDI a "bargaining chip." He wanted to get to the zero-zero option (removal of all nuclear weapons), and he saw a nuclear umbrella as both a moral imperative and as the way to get there. It was not clear to Reagan that a nuclear umbrella could be made to work, but he felt there was enough technology on the shelf to get started, and a lot of people he respected were supportive. As March dawned, most of the Joint Chiefs as well as the chairman were fully supportive of a strategic defense program; most NSC principals were strongly opposed, for all sorts of "practical and political" reasons. Reagan presented his Strategic Defense Initiative to the American public from the Oval Office on March 23.

The Soviets saw SDI as a technical challenge they could not match. At the beginning, in 1983, they spent large sums trying, but by the time of the Reykjavik Summit in October 1986, they knew such a competition was hopeless. The Soviet economy was collapsing, and, as we shall see, Reagan had an insight into that collapse that even his counterpart, Mikhail Gorbachev, did not have. Most observers now think the SDI competition was a key contributor to the Soviet collapse.

THE GHOSTS RETURN TO THEIR CHURCHYARDS

During all of these unfolding events, not a nuclear shot had been fired, except on the briefing screens of the leaders involved. *Ivory Leaf* had just been an exercise. *Partridge* provided a stable and secure environment during the closing days of the Cold War. Our leaders were able to negotiate and to decide without fear of decapitation.

By the end of the Reagan years, Mikhail Gorbachev had come to Washington to sign the INF Treaty. That agreement called for the complete removal and destruction of all Soviet SS-20 missiles threatening Europe and Asia. The American Pershing II and cruise missiles, deployed with such effort by General Vessey, would meet a similar fate. The general could not have been more pleased. During that same decade, only fifty Peacekeepers actually made it to the missile silos. The development of a mobile Midgetman was halted. A START II treaty was signed, which counted warheads, not launchers.

The impact of SDI is for future generations to decide. It is clear that no ballistic missile defense can provide 100 percent protection against a massive strike by a superpower, and so deterrence remains a valid concept. The few dozen nuclear weapons leaking through defenses should be unacceptable to a would-be attacker. On the other hand, a sound defense could save millions of lives should a terrorist or rogue state attempt a small salvo. Whatever the result, SDI was a concept that sprang directly from Ronald Reagan's concern for the safety of his people. He stuck with it as he came to understand the price it was extracting from the crippled Soviet Union. SDI was neither a staff study run wild nor a Cold War bluff without substance.

And so, with the coming of dawn, the ghosts of nuclear war, having wandered here and there, trooped home to their churchyards. It seemed like the right time for me to go home too. The President invited my then-fifteen-year-old son Andrew and me in for some farewells. Vice-President Bush, whom I had known even longer than I had known the President, asked that we stop by his office as well. On Tuesday, June 14, 1983, I took my secretary to lunch, turned in my White House badge, and left, never to return.

CHAPTER 17

The Queen of Hearts

NANCY REAGAN WAS INDISPENSABLE to the ending of the Cold War. Without her ambition, drive, and emotional support, it is unlikely that Ronald Reagan ever would have become President of the United States. Yet once in the White House, Nancy preferred the comforts of détente to the conflicts of Soviet collapse. To maintain the tranquility and glamour of her environment, Nancy became an instigator of palace intrigue that nearly derailed her husband's rendezvous with destiny. Nancy was the Queen of Hearts, and like that playing card, she presents two faces for historians to decipher.

I first met Nancy Reagan almost forty years ago, in late 1965, as her husband was considering a run for the governorship of California. She was a gracious hostess, and she seemed like a great candidate's wife. As that campaign took shape, I became Ronald Reagan's northern California campaign chairman. Nancy's public persona continued to be charming, but backstage she was on the phone regularly with complaints about schedules, accommodations, campaign materials, and a host of other trivia. Most of those calls were directed to the headquarters staff in Los Angeles, but once we were in Sacramento, they were redirected to those of us who had become senior secretaries on the governor's staff.

Her initial target was the archaic governor's mansion, provided by the state of California and occupied by the Reagans' predecessors for decades. Nancy wanted more modern accommodations in a better neighborhood. I accepted that challenge, solving the problem with a rented chateau on Forty-fifth Street. Then, during that first year in office, Reagan's personal staff was engulfed in a scandal involving unacceptable personal behavior by a few. His chief of staff and a few others were swept away; a young staffer named Mike Deaver might have been consumed in that same firestorm, but cabinet secretary Bill Clark protected him, saving his political life in the process. In the aftermath of that crisis, Clark, then Ed Meese, became Reagan's chiefs of staff. They assigned the "Nancy account" to Deaver. He was to become her keeper; none of the rest of us would then be subject to further calls. It worked. Deaver listened to Nancy's complaints, tried to solve her problems, and kept her away from the working staff.

Deaver did well at the job, and over the decades that followed, he evolved into a faithful family retainer. He managed to avoid any serious governmental or campaign responsibility while staying close to the throne. He retained and built his influence at court, and over time he took charge of the Reagans' schedule. He became their image meister. Ronald Reagan welcomed Deaver's help and began to treat him as a son—no great honor in the dysfunctional Reagan family—but never protected him. Reagan even allowed Deaver to be removed—temporarily, as it turned out—from the 1980 presidential campaign.

During that campaign, Nancy played a role in selecting the "correct" chief of staff, should her candidate-husband make it to the White House. In Sacramento and the campaigns that followed, Nancy grew tired of what she perceived to be Ed Meese's bumbling ways. She was concerned that Meese might recapture his old chief of staff role in a new Reagan White House; she had other ideas.

As the campaign drew to a close, campaign consultant Stu Spencer met with the Reagans to discuss the matter of White House staffing. The discussions started in Dallas in late October and continued as the campaign drew to a close. Spencer gave Meese credit for being a longtime and loyal friend of the Reagans, but he criticized Meese as an ineffective manager. Spencer then extolled the virtues of campaign attorney James Baker.

Houston attorney James Baker III first migrated to Washington D.C., in the mid-1970s, to serve in the Gerald Ford administration as Under Secretary of Commerce. Baker joined Ford's unsuccessful 1976 presidential campaign, then returned to Texas to run for office in his own right. He lost the race for attorney general of that state with 44 percent of the vote. In 1979, Baker turned his attention to another campaign—fellow Texan George H. W. Bush's run for the Republican presidential nomination. That did not work out either, but when Ronald Reagan tapped Bush to be his running mate, Baker was folded into the Reagan-Bush campaign. He acquitted himself well as a campaign attorney, and in the process grew closer to his old friend Stu Spencer. The two had first met during the Ford presidential campaign of 1976.

As Spencer tried to broach the subject of future White House staffing, the candidate would hear none of it. He was superstitious and did not want to talk about such things before the vote. But Nancy did. She was fond of Jim Baker's charm and good looks; she found him to be a pleasant change from the rumpled Meese. Unconcerned about Baker's record of electoral defeats, Nancy was pleased when Spencer proposed giving him more exposure to the candidate. Much to Nancy's delight, Baker was put aboard the Reagan plane during the closing weeks of the 1980 campaign.

The Spencer plan worked. On November 5, the day after the election, the President-elect tapped Baker to serve as Chief of Staff. As always, there would have to be a consolation prize for the loser. Ed Meese would be entitled "Counselor," with cabinet rank. Thus it was that James Baker III acquired the central chair in the Reagan White House.

When they all made it to the White House, both Mike Deaver and Nancy Reagan hit their stride. Deaver took seriously the plaudits from his new friends in Georgetown, while turning on those who had saved his political life. He found Bill Clark and Ed Meese to be unsophisticates from a dark age long gone. Within two years he conspired in their fall from grace, their departure from the White House. As Harry Truman put it so well, "If you want a friend in Washington, get a dog."

THE GROUP

When I first came to know the Reagans, Nancy's friends were the wives of a few prominent Hollywood agents and a lot of Los Angeles businessmen. As the Reagans grew more glamorous and powerful, her following changed. By the end of the 1970s, as Reagan's run for the presidency took on gravitas, Nancy's collection of friends morphed into "the Group," women with blond bouffant hairdos, full-length sable coats, and new, very rich, husbands. These ladies came to constitute her window onto the world, the voice of the people. With the ascendancy of the Group, the wives of the auto dealers and truck-line operators, people who lived in the real world, disappeared as surely as if they had been airbrushed away.

Once in the White House, openings for distinguished men and women to represent the President in foreign capitals presented a great opportunity for the Group, and Nancy weighed in. The appointment of ambassadors to fun, English-speaking places became her personal province, and the White House personnel office did not put up much of a fight. When there were no vacancies, Nancy would help create them by undercutting the incumbents in the eyes of the President and his advisers.

Reagan tolerated this, for his mind was on other things. Besides, he was not above using an embassy or two as a consolation prize for unsuccessful candidates for cabinet or near-cabinet positions. Presidents often do that. Leaders of the Group soon found their husbands posted to the great watering holes of Europe. The lesser acolytes were sent to charming Caribbean and Pacific beach towns. Only a few had to be recalled: one after a scandal involving young girls and porno films; another after he established his own, unauthorized back-channel communications with Libya's Muàmmar al-Gadhafi. The rest served their time harmlessly, some even beneficially, given their direct access to the President's household.

CAMELOT II

Nancy arrived at the White House without a philosophical compass. Social standing was her guiding star. "Peace," as expressed by the Soviet word "mir" (the peace of the graveyard), was her mantra. She preferred getting along to confrontation. I do not know her views on the proper role of government, on women's liberation, on environment-development conflicts. I have no idea how she envisioned an end to the Cold War, but I am sure winning it was not on her agenda. And yet she provided the ambition that propelled her husband to his rendezvous with destiny. Even their son, Ron Jr., confirms that observation; Ronald Reagan was not an ambitious man.

Upon her arrival in Washington, Nancy had a clean slate. With Frank Sinatra and his Hollywood entourage on one arm, a handsome landslide-empowered President on the other, and the enormous wealth of the Group to back her up, Nancy could have become the new Jackie Kennedy, the founding queen of a conservative Camelot. Eva Peron pulled it off a generation before. In a few short post–World War II months, with her political-personal glamour and her dictator-husband's power, Evita swept the British quasioccupation of Argentina into the dustbin of history. Nancy could have done the same to the liberal salons of Georgetown, but that was not to be. Rather than replace the entrenched liberal establishment, she sought to join it, or at least to seek its approval.

The leaders of permanent Washington are very good at cultivating the court of whatever new ruler arrives from outside the Beltway. That establishment bends the wills of senators and congressmen with their sophistication. They urge new appointees to the Supreme Court to reorient their moral compasses to the mother lode of Washington wisdom. They welcome new Presidents and their assistants with open arms, buffet tables, and bars.

The dean of this establishment was Katharine Graham, a personally delightful lady who was publisher of the *Washington Post*. Rather than attempting to dethrone her, Nancy spent enormous time and effort cultivating Mrs. Graham, and vice versa. On December 11, 1980, even before the Reagan inauguration, the first-family-to-be were guests at Mrs. Graham's home for dinner; that, despite the deadly opposition of the *Post* and the rest of the mainstream media to virtually everything Ronald Reagan stood for. Nancy had selected her route to glory. It ran through Georgetown, not across the icy tundra of the Cold War.

CONTENDING FORCES

Ronald Reagan seldom took the initiative when it came to the management of his staff. He sized people up well, but found it hard to act, or to resist the personnel actions of others on his staff. Reagan was a man capable of dealing with only one subordinate, a chief of staff who would run everything else. The events of November and December 1980 had violated that principle. James Baker, installed as Chief of Staff, was nominally in charge of administration. Ed Meese, entitled "Counselor," was in charge of ideas and policy. Assistant Mike Deaver was to handle the Nancy account. This triumvirate was complicated enough, but in January 1982 a National Security Adviser, Bill Clark, was added to the mix. Therein lay the seeds of warfare that in time would seriously discredit Reagan's entire administration.

In the autumn of 1982, Bill Safire ran a column in the *New York Times* reflecting on "this chasm that divides the White House." Safire correctly identified one Reagan White House as being run by James Baker and Michael Deaver, supported by Nancy Reagan. In time this group came to be known as the Pragmatists, since they seemed to favor form over substance. Safire identified the other faction as the "Old Shoes" from Sacramento. They were led by Bill Clark, Ed Meese, and myself. Safire forecast a fight for control of the White House.

What were the differences between these two groups? One was cosmetic. Nancy loved nice clothes, and both she and her husband appreciated those who dressed properly for their parts. The trim and handsome twosome of Baker and Deaver scored well on these counts, while the Old Shoes did not. Bill Clark was presentable, if not fashionable, in business suit and cowboy boots, but the rest of us were overweight and underdressed. Campaign press secretary Lyn Nofziger, who chose not to join the administration, gave definitive meaning to the word "sloth."

On a deeper level, these two groups of White House players were separated by their confidence, or lack thereof, in Ronald Reagan's ability to think through and give direction to his government. The Baker-Deaver axis, with their supporting cast of Pragmatists, viewed Reagan as the Great Communicator. To them, Reagan was a President of limited intellectual power whose role was to approve predigested position papers, documents that delivered a consensus solution to any given problem. He was then to sell that course of action to Congress and the American people. Among the President's staff, only Mike Deaver had any ability to read the man. The other Pragmatists could not break the code; their supporting staffs had no idea what Reagan was thinking, nor did they seem to care.

The Old Shoes were cut from different cloth, and we were far less sophisticated. We had no interest in the approval of the Georgetown set. Embassy dinners were to be avoided at all costs. Talking to the media was anathema to all but the Communications director; that was his job. We understood Reagan's core beliefs, and we had total confidence in his ability to think through where he was going. We believed he had uncanny foresight, a vision on how things would turn out, and we were comfortable with that. We knew how to read him, how each facial grimace or movie reference applied to the issue then under discussion. Our job was to scrub the alternatives, including those Reagan came up with himself, and to present them as a menu for his decision. We had full confidence in his ability to lead and to decide. Our shorthand expression was, "Let Reagan be Reagan."

A third difference between these contending forces was far more visible to the outside world. It had to do with subservience to the media. The Pragmatists were masters of public relations, having cultivated the Washington press corps and the Georgetown establishment at every turn. Approval by them, an evening at Katharine Graham's, was the ultimate high. Nancy lived by the morning headlines and the evening news. She required that the staff make the President look good in the eyes of the media and the Washington establishment every day.

Bill Clark and the Old Shoes did not, could not, meet that test, because we understood the media to be a pivotal battleground in the Cold War; it had been for decades. The Algerians and the Vietminh understood where they would win their wars with France: not on the sand dunes of the Sahara or the jungles of Vietnam, but in the streets of Paris. Soviet political manipulation had successfully headed off European deployment of neutron-generating nuclear weapons during the Carter years. A similar, broader campaign was now under way, both in the United States and Europe, to preclude the European deployment of ground-launched cruise missiles and Pershing II ballistic missiles in response to the Soviet SS-20 deployments.

But in the 1980s the Soviets were dealing with a tougher President. Ronald Reagan would not back down in the face of such an attack; on the contrary, he knew how to fight on the media battlefield. He was carrying that fight to the enemy. Under the heading of "public diplomacy," he was speaking to the captive peoples of Eastern Europe as well as to the Soviet people themselves. He talked about the illegitimacy of the occupying Soviet armies and the unelected Soviet government. He showed that the Soviets were *not* invincible, that communism was *not* the wave of the future, that a strong and free system of democracy *would* stand up to attempted Soviet encroachment. It was Clark's role in spreading these messages that drove Nancy and the Pragmatists wild.

This was the crux of the difference between these forces, contending as they were for control of the White House: their differing views of the Soviet Union and the best American policy for dealing with that apparent superpower. The Nancy-Baker-Deaver axis remained caught in the grip of the past, entranced by dreams of détente and peaceful co-existence. An immediate Nobel Peace Prize was their daily goal. In her own post–White House memoirs, Nancy spells out her nonconfrontational "let's all get along" views of the Soviet Union very clearly: "I just felt here were these two superpowers sitting there, and it was silly not to get together."★

Fortunately, her husband did not agree. At his first presidential press conferences, during the week following his inauguration,† Reagan made clear his views: "The only morality [the Soviets] recognize is what will further their cause. . . . They reserve unto themselves the right to commit any crime, to lie, to cheat in order to attain [their goals.]" Two years later, in March 1983, he urged evangelicals gathered in Orlando to beware of "the aggressive impulses of an evil empire. . . ."

We Old Shoes shared Reagan's views of the Soviet Union as an illegitimate dictatorship led by thugs and murderers. Détente with such leaders, having failed to slow the expansion of the Soviet empire in the seventies, surely would be counterproductive in the eighties. Resistance to Soviet expansionism, the pursuit of peaceful change in the Soviet Union, was our goal.

The President paid little attention to Nancy's lobbying on policies or people. The Old Shoes regularly witnessed his disapproval when she expounded in front of us, which she never did in public. Reagan made it clear by gesture or look that he was the President, that she should cool it. Thus, to work her ways, Nancy had to operate through the staff, promoting the cause of the Pragmatists when she could and denigrating the Old Shoes whenever they made the President "look bad." Her verdict on such image transgressions was vintage Queen of Hearts from *Alice in Wonderland*: "Off with their heads."

The problem with this regular pronunciamento was that she gave no thought to who might capably replace her target. Recruiting good peo-

---

★ Nancy Reagan with William Novak. *My Turn: The Memoirs of Nancy Reagan.* Random House, 1989.

† President's news conference, January 29, 1981.

ple was not Nancy's strong suit. She allied herself with the Baker-Deaver Pragmatists because she was comfortable with them and because they saw Nancy as the key to their ambitions. And thus it was that Bill Safire included a prescient line in his November 1982 article on the coming crisis in the White House. In forecasting a victory by the Old Shoes, he added a hedge: "Firing Nancy will be the hard part." How true.

THE FAREWELL DOSSIER

There could be no clearer delineation between the Old Shoes and the Pragmatists than the matter of the *Farewell* dossier.★

In the early 1970s the Nixon administration put forth the idea of détente. Henry Kissinger's hopes were that "over time, trade and investment may leaven the autarkic tendency of the Soviet system." He believed that détente might "invite the gradual association of the Soviet economy with that of the world economy and thereby foster interdependence that adds an element of stability to the political relationship."†

Leonid Brezhnev did not quite see it the same way. In 1972 he told a group of senior party officials: "We communists have to string along with the capitalists for a while. We need their credits, their agriculture, and their technology. But we are going to continue massive military programs, and by the mid-1980s we will be in a position to return to an aggressive foreign policy designed to gain the upper hand with the West."‡

Reagan was inclined to ignore Kissinger's theories of détente and to take Chairman Brezhnev at his word, but all doubt was swept away on July 19, 1981, when the new American President met with President François Mitterand of France at an economic summit meeting in Ottawa. In a side conversation, Mitterand told Reagan of his intelligence service's success in recruiting a KGB agent in Moscow Center. The man was part of a section evaluating the take from Soviet efforts to ac-

---

★ The tale that follows is extracted, and in some cases quoted, from unpublished notes by Gus Weiss: "The Farewell Dossier: Strategic Deception and Economic Warfare in the Cold War," 2003.

† *Kissinger on Detente.* Harcourt-Brace, 1994.

‡ Revealed by the Department of Defense in hearings before the House Committee on Banking and Currency, 1974.

quire, and if necessary steal, Western technology. The source, Colonel Vladimir I. Vetrov, was designated *"Farewell"* by the French DST. He enjoyed an ideal port for viewing the work of the "Line X" collection apparatus within the KGB's Technology Directorate.

Reagan expressed great interest in Mitterand's sensitive revelations and was grateful for his offer to make the material available to the U.S. administration. The dossier, added to the "KUDO" intelligence compartment, arrived at the CIA in August 1981. It immediately caused a storm. The files were incredibly explicit. They set forth the extent of Soviet penetration into U.S. and other Western laboratories, factories, and government agencies. They made clear that the Soviets had been running their R&D on the back of the West for years. Given the massive transfer of technology in radars, computers, machine tools, and semiconductors from U.S. to USSR, the Pentagon had been in an arms race with itself.

The *Farewell* dossier also identified hundreds of case officers, agents in place, and other suppliers of information and parts throughout the West and Japan. During the early years of détente, the U.S. and the USSR had set up working groups in agriculture, civil aviation, nuclear energy, oceanography, computers, and the environment. The purpose was to start construction of "peaceful bridges" between the superpowers. Working group members were to exchange home-and-home visits. The Soviets thoroughly corrupted this process by inserting intelligence officers into those delegations dealing with technology of interest to them. *Farewell* made the extent of this subterfuge glaringly apparent. Even one of the Soviet cosmonauts, participating in the joint U.S.-USSR Apollo-Soyuz space flight, was a KGB science officer.★

Aside from agent identification, the most useful information in the *Farewell* dossier was the KGB's shopping list: its targets for technology acquisition and theft during the coming few years. When the *Farewell* dossier arrived in Washington, Reagan asked Director of Central Intelligence Bill Casey to come up with a clandestine operational use for the material.

During the fall of 1981, one of my NSC associates, Dr. Gus Weiss, was cleared to read the material. He devised a remarkable plan: "Why not help the Soviets with their shopping? Now that we know what

---

★ Even today, a decade after the end of the Cold War, the U.S. does not allow intelligence operatives to participate in any similar trade, cultural, scientific, or other group visiting the former Soviet Union.

they want, we can help them get it." There would be just one catch: the CIA would add "extra ingredients" to the software and hardware on the KGB's shopping list. Weiss presented the plan to Casey in December 1981 and Casey took it to the President in January 1982. Notably absent from their meeting were any of the White House's strong believers in détente.

Reagan received the plan enthusiastically; Casey was given a "go." There are no written memoranda reflecting that meeting, or for that matter, the whole project, for many in the intelligence community were concerned about the security of the new, computerized, internal NSC communication system.

Within a few months the shipments began. The Weiss project targeted the Soviet military-industrial needs as set forth in the *Farewell* dossier. "Improved"—that is to say, erratic—computer chips were designed to pass quality acceptance tests before entry into Soviet service. Only later would they sporadically fail, frazzling the nerves of harried users. Pseudosoftware disrupted factory output. Flawed but convincing ideas on stealth, attack aircraft, and space defense made their way into Soviet ministries.

The production and transportation of oil and gas was at the top of the Soviet wish list. A new trans-Siberian pipeline was to deliver natural gas from the Urengoi gas fields in Siberia across Kazakhstan, Russia, and Eastern Europe, into the hard currency markets of the West. To automate the operation of valves, compressors, and storage facilities in such an immense undertaking, the Soviets needed sophisticated control systems. They bought early model computers on the open market, but when Russian pipeline authorities approached the U.S. for the necessary software, they were turned down. Undaunted, the Soviets looked elsewhere; a KGB operative was sent to penetrate a Canadian software supplier in an attempt to steal the needed codes. U.S. Intelligence, tipped by *Farewell*, responded and—in cooperation with some outraged Canadians—"improved" the software before sending it on.

Once in the Soviet Union, computers and software, working together, ran the pipeline beautifully—for a while. But that tranquility was deceptive. Buried in the stolen Canadian goods—the software operating this whole new pipeline system—was a Trojan horse.★ In order to

---

★ An expression describing a few lines of software, buried in the normal operating system, that will cause that system to go berserk at some future date (Halloween?) or upon the receipt of some outside message.

disrupt the Soviet gas supply, its hard currency earnings from the West, and the internal Russian economy, the pipeline software that was to run the pumps, turbines, and valves was programmed to go haywire, after a decent interval, to reset pump speeds and valve settings to produce pressures far beyond those acceptable to the pipeline joints and welds.

The result was the most monumental non-nuclear explosion and fire ever seen from space. At the White House, we received warning from our infrared satellites of some bizarre event out in the middle of Soviet nowhere. NORAD feared a missile liftoff from a place where no rockets were known to be based. Or perhaps it was the detonation of a small nuclear device. The Air Force chief of intelligence rated it at three kilotons, but he was puzzled by the silence of the Vela satellites. They had detected no electromagnetic pulse, characteristic of nuclear detonations. Before these conflicting indicators could turn into an international crisis, Gus Weiss came down the hall to tell his fellow NSC staffers not to worry. It took him another twenty years to tell me why.

The *Farewell* countermeasures campaign was cold-eyed economic warfare, put in place to inflict a price on the Soviet Union for corrupting the lofty ideals of détente. While there were no physical casualties from the pipeline explosion, there was significant damage to the Soviet economy. Its ultimate bankruptcy, not a bloody battle or nuclear exchange, is what brought the Cold War to an end. In time the Soviets came to understand that they had been stealing bogus technology, but now what were they to do? By implication, every cell of the Soviet technical leviathan might be infected. They had no way of knowing which equipment was sound, which was bogus. All was suspect, which was the intended endgame for the entire operation.

As a grand finale, in 1984–85 the U.S. and its NATO allies rolled up the entire Line X collection network, both in the U.S. and overseas. This effectively extinguished the KGB's technology collection capabilities at a time when Moscow was being sandwiched between a failing economy on one hand and an American President—intent on prevailing and ending the Cold War—on the other.

Gorbachev was infuriated at his agents' arrests and deportations, for he had no idea that American intelligence agencies had access to the *Farewell* dossier. At a meeting of the Politburo on October 22, 1986, called to debrief his associates on the Reykjavik summit, he ranted that the Americans were "acting very rudely and behaving like bandits." While presenting a soothing face in public, Gorbachev privately referred to Reagan as "a liar." During the final days of the former Soviet Union, the General Secretary of the CPSU had to operate in the dark. Gorbachev had little idea of what was going on in the American laboratories and high-tech industries; he could not tell if, or how badly, his own had been corrupted.

Through all of this, the White House Pragmatists also remained in the dark. If Nancy Reagan, Jim Baker, or Mike Deaver had known that the U.S. government was blowing up Soviet pipelines, infiltrating Soviet computers, bollixing their software, or spoofing electronic equipment—even though done with the President's approval—they would have had a fit. As it was, they remained ignorant while the President played his trump card: SDI/Star Wars. He knew the Soviets could not compete in that league because he knew the Soviet electronics industry was infected with bugs, viruses, and Trojan horses placed there by the U.S. intelligence community.

THE 1983 STRUGGLE FOR CONTROL
OF THE WHITE HOUSE

Bill Safire forecast a victory by the "Bill Clark combo" in the coming struggle for power. In Safire's scenario, Clark would succeed Baker as chief of staff, Meese would move to the cabinet, and the NSC job would be open. After reviewing the candidates on the horizon—John Lehman, Richard Perle, Fred Ikle, David Abshire, Jeanne Kirkpatrick, et al.—Safire concluded that "the man with the inside track to head a rejuvenated NSC" would be me.

Baker responded to that article in December with a different proposal to the President. His White House reorganization would have removed Clark and Meese (and all other Sacramento players) from the White House, installing himself as the National Security Adviser and Mike Deaver as the chief of staff. Reagan, in his inimitably open way, showed this plan to Clark. He asked what Clark thought of it, and suggested that Baker and Clark "work things out." It was the classic case of dropping two scorpions—or more accurately, one scorpion and one grasshopper—into a bottle.

Within days of the President's return to Washington after the 1982 year-end holidays, Baker, Deaver, and their allies unleashed the furies of the media on all the Old Shoes. The Pragmatists had courted that media assiduously for two years. Leaks of the most sensitive inside information had been laid onto favored journalists in anticipation of paybacks when the time came. The Old Shoes were hopelessly outgunned; one by one we drifted away.

CLARK MOVES ON

Bill Clark's departure from the White House was triggered by the success of another covert operation, this one using assets that were not formally Clark's to command.

During the 1980s, the Soviet Union was pushing into Central America at every turn. They were trying to do the same in South America if they could find the right toehold. From their primary political base in Cuba, the Soviets were making inroads, from Nicaragua to Grenada. A prime target was Suriname, one of the three former Guiana colonies of France, Holland, and Britain on the northeast coast of South America. U.S. intelligence confirmed a Soviet presence in its capital, Paramaribo. A Soviet embassy was planned, and a very secret deal with the local dictator, Desi Bouterese, was in the works. It would welcome Cuban troops and Libyan support into the country. The latter would take the form of arms and very sophisticated communications gear. If the Soviet initiative was successful, it would give them their first base in South America and an important anchor across the Caribbean Sea from Cuba.

Bill Casey, director of Reagan's CIA, and Bill Clark devised another unique top secret operation: a scheme to get Suriname's neighbors, Venezuela and Brazil, to clean up their own neighborhood without obvious U.S. involvement. Under Casey and Clark's direction, the Pentagon prepared an elaborate plan for an air and sea invasion of Suriname. In theory, it was to be done by U.S. forces in Panama with the support of ships already in the North Atlantic; in practice, the administration had no intention of carrying it out. Clark, his NSC staffers, and their associates from the CIA, were to fly to Caracas and Brasilia to brief the presidents of Venezuela and Brazil on the "impending U.S. action." The objective was to spur those big-time governments into action on their own, to kill off the imminent Soviet expansion into South America by themselves.

Reagan loved the plan. Clark was going to use a nondescript Air Force plane to make his rounds, but the President directed him to use

Air Force One. He felt it would lend real credibility to what would be one of America's greatest politicomilitary scams targeted at the Soviet bear.

During the third week of April 1983, Clark and his entourage pulled off this very secret trip unnoticed by the U.S. press corps. They made detailed nocturnal presentations, complete with the Pentagon's best graphics, to the presidents and defense ministers of Venezuela and Brazil. The meetings were conducted aboard Air Force One, parked at the end of deserted runways in those nations' capitals. The impact was as desired. Clark's hosts were horrified at the prospect of another gringo invasion of Latin America, but the prospect of an expanded Soviet presence next door was even worse. They were appreciative of the "heads-up" and the choices laid before them. They wanted to keep this challenge local, and Clark respectfully deferred to their wishes. The Brazilians promptly applied both carrot and stick to their tiny neighbor to the north, bringing a peace and prosperity to Suriname's quarter million people that the Soviets could never match.

When Clark got home, however, Jim Baker went ballistic. As chief of the White House staff, Baker nominally controlled the President's special aircraft, and Clark had used the plane without Baker's knowledge or permission. This affront was the last straw. Baker unleashed a torrent of leaks and innuendo about Clark's perceived usurpation of power, the implication being that Clark's lone ranger antics would tip the country into war. This internal struggle came to a head with a *Time* magazine cover story on Bill Clark. UPROAR OVER COVERT AID, was the caption, and a White House loss of trust was the underlying theme. *Newsweek* joined the chorus. Such cover stories usually are the death knell for any Washington career.

In September 1983, Clark met with Reagan at Camp David to discuss these attacks, arguing that they were damaging national security and corroding the President's image. Clark was ready to leave the public glare, to return to his ranch in California, but Reagan wanted him to stay on his team. Clark was an outdoorsman, so the two men settled on a plan for him to move to the relative tranquility of the Interior Department, serving as its secretary through the end of Reagan's first term.

DENOUEMENT

As Safire had predicted, "Firing Nancy would be the hard part." She sided with the Pragmatists in their struggle for power, and they won, but her shortsighted attitude toward any who offended her began the descent into Iran-Contra and the fiascos of the second term. By the time that second term unfolded, no one was left standing between the President and the action officers—the young staffers, both military and civilian—whose job it was to execute policies originated elsewhere. The absence of graybeards, those who might say "Wait a minute" or "What the President means" resulted in a White House operated by younger men and women who were most eager to carry out the President's wishes, even if those expressed desires made no sense. General Jack Vessey, Chairman of the Joint Chiefs of Staff and the epitome of integrity, was specifically excluded from the National Security Working Group meeting in the summer of 1985, which first considered the sale of arms to the Iranians for the benefit of the Contras. On the other hand, Oliver North, the supreme action officer, was there.

This constant decapitation produced a succession of staff chiefs who had no insight into Ronald Reagan's mind. As the White House ricocheted from crisis to scandal, James Baker was succeeded by Don Regan, then by Howard Baker, then Ken Duberstein. They were all good men, but they had no ability to read and thus interpret the wishes and the policies of an increasingly confused President. The results showed. In time even Secretary of Defense Caspar Weinberger was indicted for perjury (lying to Congress), saved only by a last minute pardon from the succeeding President, George H. W. Bush.

While Jim Baker professed great loyalty to Reagan, it is interesting to note that in his memoirs, Baker praises that President only once.★

WHO WAS RONALD REAGAN?

As the Old Shoes now gather in twos and threes, some truths become clear. One is that Ronald Reagan had *no* deep and lasting friend, as most of us understand that word. He had a few close associates and companions. One might call them segmented friends, because some were close to Reagan on spiritual matters, others on politics, and still others on a personal level. His wife had friends, and they had husbands with whom Ronald Reagan would socialize. He had longtime acquaintances,

---

★ James A. Baker III and Thomas M. DeFrank. *The Politics of Diplomacy.* Putnam, 1995, page 562.

like Holmes Tuttle, who first sold Reagan a Ford coupe in 1946 and stuck with him ever after.★ But Reagan had no friends with whom he shared complete openness, trust, and confidences as most of us do with a few other human beings. Either Reagan did not need friends because of his rock-solid faith and his self-confidence in his own beliefs, or he could not handle having any.

Nancy was his wife, his lover, his closest companion, but she was not his friend. Her close confidants have confirmed that she was not the person to whom Ronald Reagan bared his soul. Nor was anyone else. Yet if Reagan was a good President, if he laid the groundwork for ending the Cold War, it could not have happened without Nancy. She provided not only the personal care; she supplied the ambition and the focus.

As I said earlier, Ronald Reagan was not an ambitious man. He had confidence in his personal beliefs, but he was not a zealot, possessed by the need to impose his vision on others. He believed in leaving people alone to seek their own fortunes and fates. He accepted and supported the Nixon presidency, probably far longer than he should have, out of a sense of loyalty to a legitimate, anticommunist President. He saw himself as Nixon's heir, in terms of primogeniture, not ambition. Then, after Watergate, there was Gerald Ford, deposited into the line of succession by an accident of history. Reagan did not think Ford deserved to be President, but neither did Reagan burn for the job himself. It was Nancy's ambition that took over after the couple left Sacramento. Like many a wife whose husband starts coming home for lunch, she prodded him into a useless but damaging race against Gerald Ford in 1976, even though by then Ford was the incumbent Republican President.

Then Reagan's competitive instincts took over. That is one of the many conundrums of his persona. Though not ambitious, Reagan was a fierce and unstoppable competitor. Once in—whether it was his first race for governor in 1966, his run for the presidency in 1980, or his ongoing contest with communism—he was uncompromising and unstoppable. Second prizes were simply out of the question. In the late 1970s it was Nancy who harnessed her ambition alongside his driven sense of mission to pull the Reagan chariot into the coliseum of history.

★ Even so, Nancy had the Tuttles deleted from the White House guest lists by the middle of the second term, replaced by détente activist Armand Hammer, a now-documented Soviet agent. (See Edward Jay Epstein. *Dossier.* Random House, 1996.)

Now, in their golden years, Nancy is still there. Others began to note her husband's decline along the way. In 1983, Bill Clark questioned Reagan on the wisdom of a second term. As that second term unfolded, National Security Adviser John Poindexter felt sure Reagan was losing his mental grip. I last saw Reagan in the summer of 1992. He joined a group of us at a northern California resort. He was charming, but he had no idea who I was. In the summer of 1993, Reagan was diagnosed with Alzheimer's disease. In November 1994 he hand-wrote his touching farewell to the American people, then disappeared from view.

A decade later he still hangs in there, with Nancy at his side. Whether she is the queen as seen by Alice or the queen of a Camelot that never came to be, Nancy was, and continues to be, Ronald Reagan's Queen of Hearts. Despite a personality that disturbed, damaged, or destroyed so many, the fact remains that she gave Ronald Reagan's life direction and protection. If Reagan was good for the country, as I believe he was, then, in net, the country and the world are better places for Nancy having been here.

CHAPTER 18

Cheney, Powell, and the Nuclear Genie

AS THE COLD WAR DREW TO A CLOSE, the major antagonists each held around 20,000 nuclear weapons, many of them cocked and ready to fire, sitting quietly in bunkers and on a variety of platforms around the world. Then, as the Soviet empire began to implode, the American nuclear firepower once deployed to deter an ambitious Politburo began to take on a life of its own. Our nuclear genie needed to be told to back off, to accept our thanks, and to enjoy his retirement. But who could, or would, deliver that message? A powerful genie, once unleashed, does not look kindly on a return to his bottle. Two unusual Americans did pull it off. In so doing, they wrote the early chapters of life stories still unfolding.

THE WEAPONS CAME IN EVERY SHAPE AND SIZE

There were multimegaton bombs, loaded onto aircraft and stored nearby at airstrips around the world. There were megaton warheads atop thousands of missiles and rockets deployed in the empty quarters of the Dakotas and Siberia and under every ocean and sea. There were multi-kiloton weapons on short-range rockets aboard aircraft, surface ships, and other submarines. There were kiloton-size artillery shells stacked on both sides of the Iron Curtain. And there were backpack and suitcase-size fractional kiloton bombs, awaiting delivery to the critical infrastructure of the other side by SEAL and *Spetznatz* teams of the highest professionalism. The allies of the United States and the Soviet Union possessed a similar although smaller and less sophisticated nuclear inventory, and the independent players like Israel and India stood on the sidelines with nuclear arms of their own with which to protect their interests.

As the 1960s began to unfold, the strategic nuclear forces of the United States were being deployed on land, sea, and air, and that diversity was about to bring chaos. The B-52s and later the FB-111s and B-1s of the Strategic Air Command stood guard for almost half a century. Their crews lived in various stages of alert, depending on world tensions at any given time. In the 1960s some B-52s always were en route to the Soviet Union, loaded for bear, only to turn back at the no-go line if they did not receive a presidential order to proceed. More bombers were ready to take off within fifteen minutes of warning, the time interval afforded by U.S. radar and satellite capabilities. The bombers carried a big payload, but it would take them a while to reach their targets.

The second, more accurate, and immediately responsive leg of the strategic nuclear triad were the Atlas, Titan, and Minuteman intercontinental ballistic missiles, based in the heartland of the United States. These weapons were also targeted and operated by the Strategic Air Command. Since they could launch within seconds of receiving the order to do so, their operations would not conflict with the slow-flying bombers. It takes only half an hour for an ICBM to reach its target half a world away.

The third and most invulnerable delivery system was the fleet of Polaris missile-firing submarines, later augmented by Poseidon and Trident boats. The initial Polaris boats were to patrol in the Mediterranean, Norwegian, and China Seas, since their early A-1 missiles did not have the range to reach their targets from the open oceans. The impending deployment of these sea-launched ballistic missiles, from boats operated by the U.S. Navy, brought the matter of unified control of strategic nuclear weapons to the attention of Thomas Gates, a most thoughtful U.S. Secretary of Defense.★

ORGANIZING THE NUCLEAR APOCALYPSE

In 1960 there was no unified nuclear war plan. Identifying the enemy and authorizing weapons release was the President's decision, but beyond that, the services had their own plans for the actual placement of those weapons onto targets. The Atlantic and Pacific commands of the U.S. Navy had plans for attacking Soviet and Warsaw Pact targets with carrier-based aircraft. The Strategic Air Command of the U.S. Air Force had separate plans for utilizing the land-based bombers, both those on alert and those that could be generated on short order, to attack similar targets. The addition of sea- and land-based ballistic missiles to this mix was leading to chaos. Overlapping U.S. nuclear operations could have squandered U.S. airmen's lives and rendered countless sorties useless.

As this problem took on substance, the Air Force proposed a solution: the creation of a unified (all services) joint command. The Navy saw that as a power grab and objected. Secretary of Defense Gates discussed these conflicting proposals with President Eisenhower and concluded that a new joint staff was the solution. The organization, to be known as the Joint Strategic Target Planning Staff (JSTPS), would commence operations in August 1960, developing a Single Integrated Operational Plan (the SIOP) before the first Polaris boats went to sea.

Executing those plans would remain an individual service responsibility. Organizationally, the JSTPS would belong to the Joint Chiefs of

---

★ Gates served throughout the Eisenhower administration as Secretary of the Navy and then as Deputy Secretary of Defense. He was sworn in as the seventh Secretary of Defense on December 2, 1959. Gates enjoyed the President's confidence, and he brought a reasoned understanding of the Pentagon to its top job. He was the first of a new breed of Defense secretaries, men who were more than just captains of industry. Gates left behind a reputation as one of America's best Secretaries of Defense.

Staff. Physically, it would be located at the headquarters of the Strategic Air Command in Omaha. The director of this new agency would be the Air Force general also serving as Commander in Chief of the Strategic Air Command. The Vice-Director of the JSTPS would be a Navy admiral, selected by the Chief of Naval Operations and formally appointed by the Chairman of the JCS. He would be the full-time manager of this joint planning effort. The JSTPS would consist of several hundred officers drawn principally from the Air Force and Navy, but with a smattering of Army and Marine representatives as well. It was a complex arrangement, but it worked.

To assist in his war-planning duties, the Director of the JSTPS appointed a Scientific Advisory Group (SAG). These sixteen men and women were the cream of the scientific crop, specialists from Los Alamos, Livermore, Sandia, the National Security Agency, and the Central Intelligence Agency. There were a few active duty military officers of flag rank, and there were some very talented people from academia and the think tanks. For decades to come, the JSTPS and its scientific advisers would plan the deployment of American nuclear technology and might.

JOINING THE JSTPS TEAM

As the 1980s dawned, President Reagan began a massive rebuilding of U.S. military power. As part of that process, in November 1981, I was asked to join that most distinguished Scientific Advisory Group of the JSTPS. I had a solid background in nuclear weapons and military planning, but I also brought a policy approach to the table. I served on that JSTPS SAG for two years, until leaving the White House in the summer of 1983. Let me tell you how that system—the targeting of nuclear weapons—actually worked.

It starts with the President of the United States, through his Secretary of Defense, deciding who the "bad guys" are. Whom does he wish to target, under what circumstances? Next the Joint Strategic Target Planning Staff builds a data base of potential targets in those nations and adopts a targeting scheme based on our national objectives. What part of an enemy's industrial base do we wish to attack? Which military targets? Are we to attack hardened targets more than once? Are we to attack an opponent's leadership, thereby killing those with whom we might negotiate an end to the firefight? How far down the leadership chain do we wish to attack? Once the targets are identified, the staff then picks aim points (Designated Ground Zeroes, or DGZs). Many targets lie in close proximity to each other, so a weapon delivered to one aim point could well destroy several targets at the same time. What size weapon is needed on each DGZ, delivered with what accuracy and when?

A different part of the JSTPS builds attack options. In a future crisis, might the President decide on a single strike against one offending hot spot? Will he wish to attack only certain targets far removed from the offending nation's capital in hopes of negotiating an end to hostilities with that government before the firefight escalates out of control? Or if it comes to the final showdown, will he be forced to order a massive re-taliation, one that would end civilization? The alternatives can get very complicated. Limiting those choices to a reasonable number of military options was the subject of annual debate between military planners and the political leadership of our country.

Last comes sortie planning; again, not simple. Which weapons are to be used to attack which targets? There must be mission purity, as all the weapons on a bomber or ballistic missile must be part of the same op-tion. Timing is critical; first things first, defense suppression early on, full target coverage before attack conditions deteriorate. Then there is deconfliction; bombers must not be asked to fly through the radioactive debris from earlier attacks. Missile warheads must not arrive simultane-ously. Bombers must be routed carefully, since air defenses will be wait-ing if they're not already destroyed.

For years, I was part of this arcane targeting process. It was very interesting, but it all seemed like paperwork to me, just academic stud-ies of cities, maps, and route lines, until one day in the summer of 1996, when the Cold War was over. On that day, my youngest son and I found ourselves on the steps of the Peterhof, one of the Czar's gor-geous summer palaces fifty miles west of St. Petersburg, a city known as Leningrad when it was a target. We looked out over the Gulf of Fin-land, an arm of the Baltic Sea. It was summertime. The skies were blue, the sun shone brightly, a small brass quartet was playing softly in the forest a hundred yards away. The mountains and fjords of Scandinavia lay just over the horizon. How lovely was God's handiwork. And then my mind turned to how awful it might have been if something had gone wrong. If, ten years before, some quarrel had gotten out of hand, much of the United States Air Force would have come booming over this spot, passing in review en route to Armageddon.

An hour earlier, those aircraft would have refueled over the Norwegian Sea, then dropped down to treetop level to enter the fjords and forests of that lovely land. They would have risen to avoid the Trondelag Mountains, dropped down as they crossed into Sweden, then poured on the coal as they passed over Uppsala and Stockholm to enter the airspace over the Baltic. Flying at wavetop to avoid Soviet radar, they would have roared past the burning ruins of Tallinn and the other Soviet air defense sites, long since smoked by incoming submarine-launched warheads. Right where we sat, this swarm of aircraft would have begun its penetration into the Soviet Union.

It is one thing to look at a map on the wall in Omaha. It is quite another to sit there with your son looking at the place where the battle would have started. It was a virtual trip to Normandy for my nuclear generation. I sat there thinking about our frail efforts to spare the treasures of St. Petersburg. Just as the U.S. Air Corps had exempted Japan's imperial capital of Kyoto from attack during World War II, so we Cold War targeteers had tried to spare the Hermitage. But with dozens of weapons raining down all around, it would not have made much difference.

THE ARRIVAL OF DICK CHENEY

By 1989 the Soviet Union was in turmoil, heading down a slippery slope to . . . what? There was a new U.S. President, George Bush Sr., a careful man and a talented closer. He would act with cautious courage as the U.S.-Soviet endgame began to unfold, so those with responsibility for the U.S. nuclear arsenal had their work cut out for them. The rules were changing every week.

I had known Dick Cheney since the post-Watergate cleanup days fifteen years before. At that time, he had been President Ford's chief of staff, and I was working in the Office of the Secretary of Defense. With my experience in California's politics, I often was called upon, after hours, to help the new President thread his way through the thickets of political uncertainty in that state. Dick Cheney's judgment was flawless, his up-front integrity beyond doubt. He was key to ending America's "long national nightmare."

When he left Washington in 1977, Cheney returned to Wyoming to win a seat in the U.S. House of Representatives. He earned the immediate respect of his peers; within the decade he was elected to the position of minority whip. The U.S. Senate would have been the logical next step, but fate intervened. In 1989, newly elected President Bush chose his fellow Texan and longtime friend Senator John Tower to serve as his Secretary of Defense, but that nomination was devoured in the confirmation process. As a fall-back, Bush turned to then–Congressman Cheney. It was a brilliant choice. The United States Senate confirmed him in less than a week.

Dick Cheney was sworn in as the seventeenth Secretary of Defense on March 21, 1989. Without missing a beat, he began his Pentagon days with an immediate review of U.S. defense strategy. Cheney had been given no transition time, and events in the USSR were running out of control. The Red Army was leaving Hungary. Refugees were beginning to leak through the Iron Curtain, into Austria. The Baltic States were declaring their sovereignty. Only in September of 1989 did Cheney have a moment of time to look into nuclear matters before the Berlin wall came crashing down. It was then that the annual update of the Single Integrated Operational Plan was brought to his attention.

Every autumn the JSTPS director briefs the Joint Chiefs of Staff on proposed updates to the nuclear war plan, known as the SIOP. If the Joint Chiefs approve, the matter is routinely briefed to the Secretary of Defense for his sign–off prior to its transfer to the computers in Omaha. In September 1989, even as the Soviet satellite states in Eastern Europe were spinning out of Moscow's control, the Joint Chiefs received and gave their standard blessing to that year's routine revisions to the SIOP. A new target here, a changed package there, but with no substantial changes from the year before. Only when the briefing got to Secretary Cheney did the questions start. It was to have been a half hour pro forma review, but it dragged on all day. Discussions were continued after hours, and they reconvened again the following week.

By the end of September, Cheney had explored every nook and cranny of the SIOP in a fashion never before undertaken by a Secretary of Defense. He asked why we were targeting the military infrastructure of nations no longer embracing communist doctrine nor tied to the collapsing Soviet empire. He asked why we were hitting certain targets over and over again. Was not one nuke enough? After a lot of interrogation of the Joint Chiefs, Cheney accepted the immediate SIOP amendments, but he knew it was time for a fresh look at the whole question of nuclear doctrine. He directed a comprehensive review of

U.S. strategic★ nuclear weapons targeting, and he made it clear that such a review was to be done by his staff, not by the brass of the established military commands.

At that time, over 10,000 strategic nuclear weapons were targeted on the disintegrating Soviet Union. The details remain top secret even today, but it is general knowledge that in 1989 hundreds of such weapons were targeted at the greater Moscow area alone. There were reasons for that. The Soviets had deployed an antiballistic missile system around Moscow that had to be defeated one launcher at a time. Their deeply buried underground command posts and leadership bunkers had to be dug out with repeated attacks. There was a redundancy built into the U.S. attack plan to assure a sound thrashing of the Soviet capital even if they fired first and took us by surprise. But even so, *hundreds* of nuclear weapons on Moscow? I have seen a kiloton-size nuke go off dozens of miles away. I never want to see another, certainly not any bigger or any closer. The concept of such a massive laydown on Moscow was incomprehensible to Cheney.

The Vice-Chairman of the JCS, Air Force General Robert Herres, had been asking similar questions for some time. He was a bright, able young officer who flew in Vietnam and was involved in nuclear war planning for years. On October 1, 1989, Army General Colin Powell was named to serve as the new Chairman of the JCS. Together, the Secretary of Defense, the new chairman, and the vice-chairman formed an alliance to pose the hard questions never before asked. By what criteria do we settle on a nuclear force structure? What are we attacking and why, and with how much redundancy? What does it mean when our "targets" disassociate themselves from the Soviet Union? If we could achieve a strategic arms reduction treaty with the Soviets, would that make many of those targets disappear? How much nuclear firepower is enough? It was during this new era, in the summer of 1989, that I was asked by the new Bush administration to rejoin the JSTPS SAG. I was honored to do so because for the first time we were considering a *reduction* in the strategic nuclear forces of the United States.

The bureaucracy resisted Cheney's line of questions, but as the

---

★ "Strategic" in Pentagon lingo refers to the weapons carried on the strategic or intercontinental forces, i.e., the ICBMs, SLBMs, and long range bombers. Nuclear weapons fired by artillery, carried in tactical aircraft, or launched on short range missiles do not fit in this category. They are not part of the SIOP.

queries turned into close-hold studies, then policy decisions, then new SIOPs, he prevailed. He was able to drive down the nuclear weapons required in the SIOP by over 10 percent every year. The U.S. Secretary of Defense was drawing the long nuclear winter to a close. But then, just as we were beginning to reconcile the cascading events of 1989 with our obsolete defense plans, an old client of the Soviet Union went on a rampage. On August 2, 1990, Saddam Hussein, the dictator of Iraq, invaded Kuwait. His completion of that move, the occupation of Kuwait in one day, put his forces on the northern border of Saudi Arabia. By August 3 he seemed ready for another strike. If successful in an invasion of Saudi Arabia, Saddam would control half the world's oil supplies.

A DIVERSION IN THE PERSIAN GULF?

The world economy teetered on the brink of chaos as Saddam's tanks refueled and rearmed on August 3. The events that followed were not simply a local dust-up; the 1991 war in the Persian Gulf was integral to winding down the East-West conflicts of the previous forty-five years.

In August 1990, George Bush Sr. was serving as the forty-first President of the United States, but a generation before, he had served in World War II as a naval aviator. He was shot down, recovered at sea by a submarine, and lived to fly again. He understood the awful imperatives of war. Between those two stints of government service, Bush earned his living as an oil man. He did not need CIA briefings to explain the consequences of an anti-American dictator taking control of half the world's supply of oil. Around the world, agitators would demonstrate against "the trading of blood for oil," but that is what it came down to. The industrial world runs on oil; its citizens move about freely because of gasoline. Saddam's control of half the world's supply would be disastrous. The plan, however, would be to spill the invading Iraqis' blood, not that of Americans.

Bush's National Security Adviser was Brent Scowcroft, a former Air Force officer and a White House veteran. He knew international affairs like the back of his hand, but he did not brag about it. Unlike some National Security Advisers, Scowcroft was all substance and no ego. For over a decade, I had known him to be a careful but decisive man.

Dick Cheney, as a former congressman, knew how to deal. In addition to his courage and foresight in nuclear matters, he is bright, competent, fair, and tough as nails. When the Iraqis invaded Kuwait on August 2, both the U.S. and the UN immediately condemned that action. It seemed likely that Saudi Arabia would be the next target. While that nation's feudal king was interested in help, he wanted to impose all sorts of conditions on his rescuers; among them, no female troops on Saudi soil and no soldiers of Jewish faith. Cheney was dispatched to the capital of Saudi Arabia to explain things to King Fahd. This was not a diplomatic mission. It was a fire drill. The Iraqis were revving up their engines on the Saudi border. The choices put to King Fahd were simple: follow our lead and get out of the way, or flee to Switzerland while the getting is good. Fahd and Cheney settled on the first alternative, and the deal was made. The defense of Saudi Arabia and the liberation of Kuwait was on. The next day the first squadrons of F-15s began to deploy from Langley Air Force Base to Riyadh.

JCS Chairman Colin Powell was a man I had watched and admired since 1977 when, as a colonel in the U.S. Army, he served as the military assistant to the new Deputy Secretary of Defense in the Carter administration. Powell was smart and careful; he knew what he was talking about. He had paid his dues in Vietnam, had nearly been killed twice, and was the embodiment of the Vietnamese lesson: if the United States is to put its troops into harm's way, it must do so with the full support of its government and people, deploy overwhelming force, and act with immediate victory as the unambiguous objective.

These four men—Bush, Scowcroft, Cheney, and Powell—were knowledgeable and decisive wartime leaders. The war in the Persian Gulf welded them into a friction-free team that was able to bring the Cold War to a peaceful end on terms acceptable to the U.S. The events of 1990–91 also gave them and their younger staffers, including Condoleezza Rice, the experience needed to deal with the events of 9/11, the invasion of Afghanistan, and the ensuing full-scale liberation of Iraq a decade later.

In the late summer of 1991, however, Saddam made the mistake of allowing the U.S. to build up an enormous force around his borders. Included were the forces reflecting the lessons learned in Vietnam: sleek new aircraft sitting on the tarmac and shiny satellites orbiting overhead, voracious in their appetite for information. When F-15s and F-16s took control of the skies, when cruise missiles mingled with the traffic on Baghdad's streets, and when smart weapons flew down ventilator shafts, we could all take great pride in the efforts of a decade before.

When the pilots of the F-117 stealth fighter-bomber squadrons were suiting up on the night of January 17, they knew they would be flying aircraft with no defensive armament into the teeth of Soviet-produced air defenses and a French-built command and control system that would be several orders of magnitude more effective than those defending Hanoi during the war in Vietnam. With some concern, one young pilot observed to his wing commander: "I sure hope this stealth [stuff] works."

He need not have worried. Only F-117 aircraft flew against downtown Baghdad on opening night. They knocked out Iraq's integrated air defense system without any losses. During the war, F-117s flew only 2 percent of the coalition's sorties, but they struck 40 percent of the strategic targets, without the loss of a single aircraft during the entire war. Stealth worked.

The Air Force's once-unwanted A-10 turned into a deadly tank killer. "Tank plinking" came to be the sobriquet for A-10 missions up and down the Highway of Death, as the route out of Basra came to be known. And if the A-10s did not get those Iraqi tanks, the Army's sophisticated antitank weapons did. Postwar analyses showed that very few Iraqi tanks were destroyed by a head-on hit, the sort that characterized the tank-to-tank slugfests of World War II.

The World Wide Military Command and Control System laid out in the mid-seventies led to overwhelming information coherence and superiority by 1991. A complex of space, airborne, and ground sensors found and targeted the Iraqi tanks before they knew they were under attack. Not only were they sitting ducks, they were *blind* sitting ducks. Iraqi artillerymen got the same message early on: fire one round and you're dead. The first outgoing Iraqi projectile would be picked up by U.S. sensors, its trajectory calculated back to its point of origin by a microcomputer in some remote weapon. A counterstrike would be calculated and the launch point targeted. Accurate return fire was in the air before that first Iraqi round completed its flight. "Shoot one and run," became the only formula for an Iraqi artilleryman's longevity.

The U.S. military was appalled at President Bush's humanitarian decision to halt the war after a hundred hours. The agreed-upon military objective was to evict the Iraqis from Kuwait *and* to destroy Saddam Hussein's elite military forces. In particular, the plan was to destroy enough Iraqi power to deny Saddam any protection from domestic insurrection while leaving enough troops in place to preclude an invasion by Iran or Syria. The expectation was that an unprotected Saddam would be done in, replaced by his surviving coterie. But as it was, the early cessation of hostilities allowed Saddam's Republican Guard to extricate itself from the war in reasonable shape. Saddam's senior officials in Baghdad were faced with Shiite insurrections in the south, a Kurd revolt in the north, and a viable Republican Guard en route home. They decided to stick with the devil they knew. And so Saddam kept his job for another decade.

When the war was over, senior Iraqi officers, debriefed before their release, expressed surprise that the U.S. actually came to the aid of Kuwait. They thought after our experience in Vietnam, we would back down. U.S. airpower was frightening. Those officers reported desertion rates approaching 50 percent during the early, bombing phase of the war alone.

The view from Moscow was more sophisticated. Discussions in later years make it clear that the Soviets followed Desert Storm very closely. Iraq was a longtime client of the Soviet military. On the plus side, allied inability to find and target Iraq's mobile Scud missiles gave encouragement to those Soviets urging more emphasis on mobile, land-based ICBMs★ at home. On the other hand most other Soviet equipment and doctrine had been soundly thrashed. Senior officers blamed this loss on inept Iraq leadership. As one senior Soviet officer put it later: "They were neither skilled nor courageous. It would have been a more sporting match against us." The Soviet junior officers were more wary. They were well-attuned to the role of high-precision weapons under dynamic (real-time) control, and were impressed with how well the Americans made it all work.

Most important, however, was the skepticism that began to grow in the minds of the Soviet political leaders in both the Kremlin and the Duma. They suspected that the Red Army was not worth much anymore. In the nineties things had changed. Soviet arms could no longer threaten the West, nor were those armed forces a credible glue for holding together the Soviet empire, an important conclusion, as Gorbachev and Yeltsin began to formulate their own endgame.

NEW THINKING IN THE BUNKERS OF OMAHA

Lee Butler received his fourth star and assumed command of the Strategic Air Command on January 25, 1991. He was different from previous

---

★ Truck-mounted SS-25s and rail-mobile SS-24s and SS-27s.

SAC commanders. He had spent a few months in Vietnam, in the cockpit of an F-4 and at Tan Son Nhut headquarters, but at his core, Butler was an intellectual. He was a graduate of the Air Force Academy in Colorado Springs, and he went on to earn a master's degree in international affairs from the University of Paris. He served most of his junior Air Force years on the faculty of the Air Force Academy or in the Pentagon.

In the aftermath of Vietnam, the Air Force wanted to rethink how the Soviets might attack Western Europe and how the U.S. Air Force should respond. Lee Butler was manager of that effort. It was brilliantly done, and it brought his skills to the attention of the generals. When he finished that study, Butler served for three years as a B-52 bomb wing commander, then as Inspector General of SAC. Then he returned to the Pentagon.

In 1989, Butler was posted to the J-5 (plans and policy) directorate of the Joint Chiefs of Staff. It was there that he became one of Colin Powell's bright young generals during the run-up to the Persian Gulf War. Then, as Cheney was taking a new look at the role of nuclear weapons, and as the preceding Commander in Chief of SAC was preparing to retire, Butler was posted to Omaha as the new man for the nineties, also to serve as the new director of the Joint Strategic Target Planning Staff.

The year 1991 was not the time for another Curtis LeMay, the first and most truculent Commander in Chief of SAC. Lee Butler was not a cigar-smoking terror, nor was he a hell-for-leather fighter pilot. He was a compact, athletic officer whose diminutive body made the cockpit of an F-4 seem roomy and whose mind had similar room for new ideas. Unlike LeMay, Butler did not think that nuking any nation "back into the stone age" was a great idea. In time, Butler decided that he did not believe in nukes at all, although he would enunciate those views only after his retirement.

Butler's predecessor at SAC *was* a cultural descendent of Curtis LeMay. General Jack Chain was a handsome, tall, lanky combat-oriented general with years of experience in the cockpit. He usually wore combat fatigues, ready for the dash to the airborne command post upon the klaxon's first call. Chain was an excellent general, a straight arrow, and a good human being. He referred to himself and his men as "warriors," and he meant it. He ran SAC with great care and absolute readiness during the very critical decompression years of 1988-90. He did a great job in bringing the Soviets to the table.

So when General Lee Butler took over, it raised a lot of eyebrows. They were not looks of disapproval, just wonderment. Undoubtedly, Butler had the brains to lead SAC through the transition now under way. The question was, how would he do it? Butler decided to change the name of our advisory group from the Scientific to the *Strategic* Advisory Group. That was a reflection of his desire to think through the whole purpose of his nuclear forces. He, JCS Chairman Powell, and Secretary Cheney all wanted a detached look at *why* we had nuclear weapons. What was their purpose in this new post–Cold War era? To answer these questions Butler empaneled a special committee of his advisory group. It was to be known as the Policy Committee; I was to serve as its chairman.

On May 23, Butler gave us our three-page assignment. We were to think through the future of deterrence, then to advise on what deployment of nuclear weapons would be adequate to protect the national interests of the United States. One strength of democracies is their ability to sort through such fateful questions by open debate. Only dictatorships decide such things in windowless palace chambers, and when they do so, they often make ghastly mistakes.

My committee consisted of a half-dozen members of the SAG. We built on the lessons learned from the success of the Scowcroft Commission by welcoming into our deliberations a group of "advisers" and "senior representatives," elders of past administrations and the potential players in future regimes. There were five grand old men, former Secretaries of Defense, undersecretaries, and JCS Chairmen from the Nixon, Ford, Carter, and Reagan administrations. There were another six rising stars, people who would come to serve as CIA directors, Defense secretaries and assistant secretaries in the Clinton years. There were a half-dozen men and women who had or would in the future shoulder major responsibilities in the field of nuclear policy, including Condoleezza Rice. We reached out to the academics at RAND, Harvard, Stanford, and the nuclear weapons labs, for I wanted to hear all sides of the debate.

We began our deliberations in late May 1991, in the aftermath of Desert Storm and as declarations of independence were sweeping the Soviet republics. We met again in June as Boris Yeltsin was being elected president of the new Russia. During July we met in smaller groups to debate specialized topics just as the Supreme Soviet began to debate an all-union treaty, the poison pill of the Soviet empire. And then, with the most amazing timing of all, we gathered in late August as the abortive coup in Moscow died a-borning. By the time of our September meeting, we were helping the leaders at Pentagon and State make nuclear policy in real time.

The senior President Bush then in office wished to take advantage of the fluidity in Russia. He wanted to present a basket of major, denu-clearizing initiatives to the reformers in Moscow, whoever they might be. Our Policy Committee was being called on to vet those ideas. They were daring for their time; I shuttled between our conference room and the secure phone in the command center to give Secretary Cheney our considered views.

On September 29, President Bush made his unilateral offers★ in a major TV address. The proposals made sense, and we knew they would enjoy broad support; the U.S. President was trying to stuff the nuclear genie back into the bottle. Within a week Mikhail Gorbachev recipro-cated with a broad and parallel array of initiatives that pushed the cork in over the genie's head.

On October 10 we delivered our conclusions to General Butler, his staff of warriors, and my academic peers. They might be summarized as follows:

1. The role of nuclear weapons would continue to be deterrence, but whom were they to deter, from doing what? We concluded that the central strategic nuclear forces of the U.S. would continue to be needed to deter successors-in-control of the Soviet nuclear forces from any irrational attacks on the U.S. or our allies, and that they would continue to be needed to deter other adversaries from the similar use of not only nuclear, but of biological or chemical weapons against us.

2. Because nuclear weapons had played such a central role in the Cold War, and because the technology cannot be uninvented, they were not going to go away. Nuclear weapons and concerns about their use would maintain a central, though muted, dimension in the post–Cold War world.

3. More states with nuclear weapons were likely to emerge, and still others would develop chemical and biological weapons of terror. Proliferation would be the new threat. Even so, the U.S.

★ Take bombers off alert, remove tactical nuclear weapons from surface ships and SSNs, withdraw nuclear warheads from overseas, significantly reduce the number of strategic nuclear warheads, remove MIRVs from the inventories, terminate development of the new small ICBM, and cancel development of the new airborne attack missile, among others.

had an opportunity to reduce the size and characteristics of nuclear weapon inventories around the world.

4. Successor states to the Soviet Union might not be democratic, but we should work with them to achieve smaller, more stable, safer, and more secure nuclear postures on both sides. On the other hand, the U.S. must maintain some substantial deterrent to possibly hostile or erratic successor governments.

5. If the U.S. did not continue to provide a "nuclear umbrella" to the major industrial powers of the West—from Germany and Japan to Sweden and South Korea—those nations could and surely would develop their own nuclear capability in short order.

6. Thus, the U.S. nuclear arsenal should be smaller, maintaining parity with a shrinking Russian inventory while maintaining a substantial margin over other world nuclear powers. We should strive to make our nukes even safer and more secure. That would require a sound nuclear weapons industrial and scientific complex. Our nuclear arsenal should be credible; it should be more flexible, able to deal with surprises while remaining under ironclad control.

The briefing was well-received, and its text was then circulated to the senior reviewers for final comment. The advantage of developing policy in such an open fashion has already been described, but there is a downside. One cannot limit discussion to the privileged elite. In my case, the matter was soon under public scrutiny, from the *Washington Post* to various insider newsletters.

Within days of the leaks, Secretary Cheney had General Butler on the carpet. Nuclear policy was under negotiation with the new president of Russia. Cheney et al. did not want to read about our bottom-line negotiating position in the press. He did not object to the conclusions, just their leakage. After some stern discussion, those gentlemen decided, by a 2–0 vote, that the leaks were my fault. (That is what consultants are for, after all.) There followed a wonderful telephone discussion between old friends Cheney and Reed. I regretted the leaks, but I pointed out that the *Washington Post* had just editorially endorsed the findings of our committee.

When our discussion was over, Cheney had calmed down, I had not been fired, and we agreed that a sensible new approach to the role of nuclear weapons had been explained to, and accepted by, the Washington establishment. We both were able to move on.

When Presidents Bush and Yeltsin shook hands on the White House lawn a few months later, in June 1992, they were agreeing to a 50 percent reduction in the inventory of strategic nuclear weapons on alert. I was terribly proud. Dick Cheney and Colin Powell had coaxed the nuclear genie back into the bottle; perhaps my small role had been to hold the jar. I am delighted both of those men have found further government work.

CHAPTER 19

The Closers

DICTATORSHIPS SELDOM COME AND GO on little cat's feet. They are born when angry mobs topple the old order, dispatch the ancien régime on a tide of blood, then abandon power to one man or his political party. At the end, the aging dictator either dies, is toppled by new mobs, or his capital is reduced to rubble by an avenging army. He and his cronies seldom go quietly. So it is astonishing that the dictatorship of the Soviet proletariat, armed with perhaps 20,000 nuclear weapons and supported by a fearful police state, simply closed itself down. The world of the Communist Party of the Soviet Union (CPSU) ended not with a bang, but with a whimper—delivered on television and followed by a "Merry Christmas and good night" to the Western world. How could mankind have been so lucky? It all came down to two men: the Closers.

Every big deal needs a closer, for it is one thing to marshal one's arguments, money, votes, or armies for battle, and quite another to pull the camel through the eye of the needle, to assemble all of those pieces into a peaceful settlement. Ronald Reagan put the assets in place for the American people, and a string of aging dictators did the same for the Soviet Union. But then, in 1985, history cast up two intelligent, self-effacing men to bring the Cold War to a peaceful end. In that year, George H. W. Bush was inaugurated into a second term as Vice-President of the U.S. By so doing, he became the heir apparent to an aging leader. At the same time, Mikhail Gorbachev took over as General Secretary of the Communist Party of the Soviet Union.

The two first met in March of that year, in Moscow, at the funeral of Gorbachev's predecessor. Yet as these two men proceeded to make political love, not war, each also gave birth to his own Nemesis, the death star that would in time draw him into the darkness of political outer space. It is an odd story that did not turn out the way Vladimir Lenin or Whittaker Chambers thought it would.

THE PASSING OF THE SOVIET OLD GUARD

As noted earlier, Leonid Brezhnev died under mysterious circumstances on the morning of November 10, 1982. When he came to power, twenty-one years before, Brezhnev put the Soviet Union on a regimen of nuclear steroids; by the 1970s it was the world's preeminent nuclear power. He thought he sat atop the globe like a mighty colossus. In early 1973, Brezhnev presided over a secret meeting of East European communist rulers gathered in Prague. He gave his audience a *tour d'horizon*, his vision of the final stages of the Cold War. He observed: "We are achieving with détente what our predecessors have been unable to achieve using the mailed fist. . . . By 1985 . . . we will have achieved most of our objectives in Western Europe. . . . Come 1985 we will be able to extend our will wherever we need to."★

Brezhnev was right about 1985 being the turning point, but not in the way he intended. By then he would be dead. His wasteful ways would have bankrupted the Soviet system. The Politburo, having turned to a series of elderly hard-liners in an attempt to preserve the status quo, would finally give in to *glasnost*, *perestroika*, and a different world order.

★ Within weeks British Intelligence had a transcript of this meeting. They rated it as important as Khrushchev's 1956 denunciation of Stalin, but it was not a story the Nixon administration wanted to hear, committed as it was to détente. Only the *Boston Globe* ran the story, on February 11, 1973.

First came Yuri Andropov, selected to serve as General Secretary of the CPSU the day after Brezhnev died. He was sixty-eight years old at the time, and had served as Chairman of the KGB for the prior fifteen years. Earlier in his career, Andropov was their man in Budapest, on hand to oversee the brutal suppression of the Hungarian uprising of 1956. These are not the credentials of a great libertarian or reformer, but that misses a key point. The KGB was the custodian of information—real-world information—and never was that real world more visible than from Andropov's Soviet Embassy window in 1956 as he watched members of the Hungarian security service, the AVH, being strung up by the revolutionaries in the streets below. As keeper of the facts, Andropov knew, even in 1982, that the game was up. The Soviet Union could no longer compete with the United States. In every sphere that mattered—military, technical, or economic—the U.S. was on a roll and the USSR was falling farther behind with every passing day.

Reagan and Andropov started to exchange handwritten letters. It was an interesting process: the Soviet Embassy called National Security Adviser Bill Clark's office to advise there was a message waiting. Clark confirmed his readiness to receive it, telling that embassy of the preferred delivery point, home or office. A courier would then make the delivery. This short-circuiting of the State Department system drove Secretary of State Schultz wild, but by the end of 1982 this did not bother Clark. Nixon warned Clark that Shultz was a "cafeteria cabinet member," a man who would pick and choose the crises he would touch. Clark and Schultz had strongly differing views on how to deal with the Soviet Union.

The Andropov-Reagan letters began to exchange ideas on the zero-zero option—the disposal of all nuclear weapons held by each side. This exchange of correspondence is remarkable in light of Andropov's paranoia about a possible U.S. surprise nuclear attack on the Soviet Union. In May 1981, as Chairman of the KGB, Andropov had initiated Project Ryan,★ a coordinated collection of intelligence on a presumed, but nonexistent, Reagan plan to launch a nuclear first strike. The Andropov-Reagan correspondence survived NATO exercise *Able Archer 83*, which practiced nuclear release procedures and which the KGB thought might be a mask for the feared nuclear attack. It survived their confrontations over the KAL 007 shoot-down in August 1983, as well as the deployment of U.S. Pershing II missiles to Europe during

---

★ Acronym for *Raketno-Yadernoye Napadenie*, or "Missile Surprise Attack."

that same year. Shortly afterward, however, the correspondence came to an end.

In late 1983, Reagan showed Clark the most recently received Andropov note, personally handwritten in Russian. It was the scrawl of a very sick man. CIA analysts confirmed their joint view: "He'll be dead in a few weeks."

He was. On February 9, 1984, Yuri Andropov died of kidney failure in a Moscow hospital. Attempting to postpone the inevitable, the Politburo turned to one last representative of the gerentocracy, seventy-three-year-old Konstantin Chernenko. He lasted for a year, his presence barely noted. Then, on March 11, 1985, the Politburo knew it had to face reality. It turned to its youngest member to save the Soviet system.

MIKHAIL GORBACHEV

Mikhail Gorbachev was born and raised in the town of Privolye, near Stavropol in southern Russia. He was not yet a teenager during the war years, and since Privolye is well east of the Volga, he was spared the grisly wartime experiences of so many of his peers. No Russian escaped the loss of family or the horror stories from the front. Fifty million Soviet citizens perished during what they call the Great Patriotic War, but Gorbachev fought his war at the state farm, producing food for the troops and factories. By the time he headed off to Moscow State University Law School in 1952, Gorbachev was a fully qualified combine harvester operator. He became First Secretary of the Stavropol regional Communist party committee in 1970, was elected to probationary membership in the Politburo in 1979, then graduated to full membership in 1980; he was only forty-nine years old at the time.

Gorbachev had already been discussing the disastrous condition of the Soviet Union in private conversations with others. When elected to the post of General Secretary at age fifty-four, Gorbachev believed he could save communism, that only its management was in disrepair. He erroneously believed the foundation was sound. Gorbachev came to power on a platform of *glasnost* and *perestroika*,★ bringing with him a new wave of bureaucrats. One of the new hands was Boris Yeltsin.

★ "Openness" or "transparency," and "restructuring" or "reconstruction," respectively.

Yeltsin was born in Sverdlovsk and trained as an engineer. He avoided the Communist party until the age of thirty. In 1985, upon his accession to power, Gorbachev brought Yeltsin into the inner circle of the Soviet establishment, using him to replace a hard-line old-timer as First Secretary of the Moscow party committee. During those early Gorbachev years, Yeltsin built a reputation for effective administration, a disdain for communist dogma, an earthy political style, and a growing network of followers. In October 1987 he created a stir by resigning his posts on the party central committee, citing the slow pace of economic reform and the incompetence of his superiors. In March 1989, the Gorbachev government allowed the first truly free elections in the USSR. The legislative body up for grabs was the national Congress of Peoples Deputies as well as some local offices. Boris Yeltsin was elected mayor of Moscow, with five million voters supporting him. He now had a base of his own, and he would use it.

NUMBER FORTY-ONE

George H. W. Bush was a Yankee by birth. At the start of World War II, fresh out of high school, he enlisted in the Navy to become an aviator. In the war that followed, he was on his fifty-eighth mission when he was shot down. He was rescued at sea by a U.S. Navy submarine, but his two crew members were killed. As the Navy's youngest pilot, he came to understand duty-honor-country better than most politicians. With the end of the war, George Bush came home, married Barbara Pierce, attended Yale, then moved to Odessa, in West Texas, to learn the oil business. In 1954 he started his own oil and gas exploration company. As the company grew, Barbara and George moved to Houston. Upon their arrival, they stayed with my aunt and uncle, Sally and Lawrence Reed, until they were established in a home of their own.

As the 1960s began, Peter O'Donnell was building a Republican Party from scratch in Texas. He started with the election of his neighbor, Bruce Alger, to the U.S. House of Representatives from their home town of Dallas. In 1961 Texas, which had once been part of the Confederacy, elected the first Republican senator from the South since the end of Reconstruction. With the help of the solid O'Donnell organization and conservative Texas money, John Tower won the seat vacated when Lyndon Johnson became Vice-President. In 1962 there were more GOP Congressional victories, and the Republicans took aim at the other U.S. Senate seat in Texas.

In 1963, O'Donnell talked with Bush about that seat, which was held by liberal Democrat Ralph Yarborough. Conservatives in both parties disliked Yarborough intensely, so O'Donnell had the senator in his sights. George Bush was to be the silver bullet that would knock Yarborough off. O'Donnell urged Bush to enter the race and promised him organizational support. The O'Donnell machine already was functioning reasonably well in the major cities, and Bill Clements of Dallas had agreed to serve as the Bush finance chairman.

George's father, Prescott Bush, had represented the state of Connecticut in the U.S. Senate for a decade, leaving it only the year before. George knew the ways of that august body and felt he could make a contribution. He was already part of the conservative political resurgence boiling around the country, so when O'Donnell made him an offer he could not refuse, the young oilman put his business on hold and entered the race. I was living in Houston at the time, running a high-tech company, but I spent substantial time on the Bush primary campaign. It was the first of a long string of such political endeavors. On May 2, Bush won that primary with 44 percent of the minuscule Texas Republican vote against a handful of other contenders.

In the summer of that year, 1964, I returned to California, attended the Republican convention in San Francisco, and moved out of George Bush's orbit. But I left Texas having met and worked for a most unusual man. George Bush was one of the nicest, most genuine men I ever would have the good fortune to know. He exuded integrity. He had that self-confidence that comes from being part of the establishment—born to it in Connecticut, then validated by his own efforts in Texas. As a result, he was not haunted by self-doubts, nor by the need to prove himself at every turn. He had done that in the skies over the Pacific.

On the other hand, Bush was not a "man of the people." He did not have that intuitive feel for those to whom fate has been less kind. Other wealthy political heirs such as John Kennedy and Franklin Roosevelt had it. George Bush did not. Thus, his advisers were drawn from the ranks of people just like himself, a dangerous political practice in our pluralistic society. George Bush just wanted to do what was right. He did not have a burning lust for power, just a gentlemanly desire to serve.

Nor was Bush a true Texan. He may have moved there, raised a family there, and built a business. He may have been a legal resident, but he was not a boot-wearing, odd-talking, truth-expanding, egomaniac with roots two generations deep. He was not Lyndon Johnson or Ross Perot. What's more, the 1964 general election was not kind to Republicans in Texas. With Lyndon Johnson at the head of their ticket, the Democrats swept the election and swept George Bush back into private life.

He did not stay there for long. In 1966 he returned to the campaign trail, this time to run for a House seat from Houston. He won handily, and was reelected in 1968. In 1970, Bush was enticed into taking another run at Yarborough's Senate seat. Unfortunately for Bush, the Democrats were beginning to break away from their post–Civil War tradition of absolute loyalty to Democratic incumbents. Ralph Yarborough was beaten in the Democratic primary by a conservative businessman from South Texas, Lloyd Bentsen, whom Bush now faced in his race for the Senate. Bentsen won and went on to serve four terms. It took eighteen years for Bush to even up the score; in 1988 he defeated Michael Dukakis and Lloyd Bentsen, the Democratic candidates for President and Vice-President, in his race for the presidency.

After Bush's 1970 loss, Nixon put him to work at the UN, then as the first U.S. emissary to Mao's China. President Ford moved George Bush to the CIA, a new and trustworthy broom badly needed there in the aftermath of Watergate. At the end of the decade, Bush was ready to run for the presidency. He was no match for Reagan, the Great Communicator, but he did finish a respectable second. Reagan tapped him as his running mate, and in January 1981, Reagan and Bush entered the White House together.

Reagan accorded Bush every courtesy, including important office space in the West Wing, just down the hall from the President. Bush was involved in virtually every meeting and significant piece of business that involved the President. He was almost always present at our morning national security meeting with Reagan, but he never debated the President in front of others. Bush held his advice for private discussions, but he now confirms that those discussions never turned philosophical. He discovered, as did many others, that Reagan was a man of clearly defined beliefs with no interest in discussing their ramifications.

As Vice-President, Bush handled the usual veep assignments, state funerals and Republican events, but he got some hot potatoes too. One of these was the matter of Ross Perot. That highly focused Texan had taken a renewed interest in POWs and MIAs, specifically those said to be left behind in Southeast Asia in the aftermath of Vietnam.

ROSS PEROT AND THE POWS

Some people think of Ross Perot as a great American; others view him as a hustler. Whatever his personal makeup, Perot, in the late 1980s, became irrational on the matter of POWs. In the process, he developed a resentment of the Bush family that would change the course of post–Cold War history.

Perot was born in Texarkana, Texas, to a family of modest means. He worked at odd jobs during his boyhood, earned an appointment to the U.S. Naval Academy at Annapolis, then served in the Navy for the required four years. He went to sea on a Destroyer, the USS *Sigourney*, but Perot clashed with his newly assigned skipper and was reassigned. Navies around the world have a quaint view of the infallibility of their captains at sea. Perot was soon reassigned to the aircraft carrier *Leyte*, where he was but a face in the crowd.

In 1957, Perot completed his mandatory Navy tour and started work at IBM. Five years later he left that firm to found Electronic Data Systems, a company that would specialize in the complexities of the new and big number-crunching computer systems. The enactment of Medicare in 1965 was manna from heaven for Ross Perot. Every state's Medicare contractor was overwhelmed by government inefficiency on one hand and provider fraud on the other. In Texas, Perot began to run data processing centers. He never invented novel electronic hardware in his garage, nor did he write trail-blazing software in graduate school. He was a Medicare hustler. In a 1971 report, *Ramparts* magazine described him as "the world's first welfare billionaire."

In 1969, Richard Nixon asked Perot to front a POW/MIA committee as part of the new administration's peace-in-Vietnam initiatives. Perot accepted the challenge, chartering an aircraft to take some POW families to Paris to confront the negotiators. He chartered another, filled it with Christmas gifts for the POWs, and had it flown to Vientiane, Laos. The aircraft never made it to Hanoi, but his efforts won him the undying appreciation of the POWs and their families, a Medal for Distinguished Public Service from the Pentagon, and some less than visible benefits flowing to EDS.* Perot's generosity to the returning POWs and to the families of those still missing became legendary. He hosted every POW reunion, built memorials, and funded the education of any POW/MIA child in need.

In 1979, when the Shah of Iran fell from power, two EDS employees were trapped in Tehran, imprisoned by the revolutionary regime. Perot organized an armed, covert incursion to get them out. The story of that rescue made headlines and became a best-selling Ken Follett book, *On Wings of Eagles*. By 1980, Perot considered himself an expert on the rescue of POWs.

Two years and a change of administration later, the issue of American MIAs resurfaced. PFC Robert Garwood, a turncoat during the war in Vietnam, returned to the United States. He was hardly a prisoner in the usual sense of the word, but he was walking, talking evidence that there were live Americans still in Indochina. Ross Perot decided there were prisoners being held in southeast Asia, and he decided to do something about it. He funded a totally unsuccessful mercenary incursion into Laos, but a flood of soldier-of-fortune movies followed. *Rambo* was the capstone; Ross Perot saw that the POW/MIA story had legs.

As the years passed, Perot was named to various federal POW/MIA review committees. He was not always in good company, as the families of missing personnel often were deluged with discredited rumors and phony evidence by scam artists in pursuit of ransom money. "Direct mail fund-raising by MIA organizations, claiming to represent veterans and their families was increasing. A number of these relied on 'false reporting . . . false evidence, pictures, and fingerprints.' "† In 1986, tired of the bureaucracy, Perot decided to conduct his own personal investigation of the POW/MIA matter. He traveled to Hanoi on his own, met with government officials there, and in the process, seriously disrupted

---

* By the end of Nixon's first term, EDS was processing 90 percent of the Medicare claims in the United States. Perot's campaign to maintain that base is evident from his 1974 conversation with HEW Secretary Cap Weinberger. Perot: "I gave five million bucks to Nixon [in '72], and I want that [Medicare] contract now." Weinberger was neither amused nor impressed, but he remembers the conversation well.

† According to testimony given by Col. Richard Childress, USA, on August 12, 1992, to the U.S. Senate Committee on POW/MIA Matters.

U.S. negotiations on this delicate subject. When he returned to the United States he demanded a private meeting with President Reagan.

The meeting took place in the Oval Office on May 6, 1987. It was not private. Chief of Staff Howard Baker was there, as was Deputy Defense Secretary Frank Carlucci and National Security Adviser Colin Powell. During those discussions, Perot told the President of his "findings" in Vietnam, and he gave Reagan a seven page written report.

Immediate analysis by one of my associates on the NSC staff, Colonel Richard Childress, found the Perot report to be utterly useless. It contained no new facts, a lot of manufactured evidence, a full dose of unsubstantiated rumor, and plenty of political polemic. Vice-President Bush was given the job of telling his fellow Texan about the NSC's analysis, thanking him for his time, and telling him to go away.

"That's it," Perot said. "I've given you [White House people] my advice for the last time." He went home to sulk. When the nobility does that, it usually bodes ill for the king's heirs.

1989

The year 1989 brought the tangible and audible beginning of the end. I will never forget hearing of that first crack in the Iron Curtain. It was a short news bulletin from a remote village along the Austro-Hungarian border. The Hungarians had grown tired of monitoring and enforcing their sector of the Iron Curtain, a simple fence between communist Hungary and free Austria. The Red army had left, and the Hungarians started taking down the barbed wire. Handfuls of others from elsewhere in Eastern Europe were showing up to help. How odd, I thought. I knew that the Soviet system could not coexist with a mobile population. If the Iron Curtain was beginning to leak near the village of Nicklesdorf, surely it would spring leaks elsewhere. With those leaks, the dam surely would burst.

These were small events in a small village half a world away, but they had incredible implications. As I listened to that radio bulletin in August, other minds were decompressing in Paris after a rigorous meeting of the G-7. George H. W. Bush and his closest advisers were brainstorming the matter of "what next." His administration had been the target of growing criticism, both at home and abroad. The complaint was inaction. The new Bush team had been studying its Soviet options for months, but no new initiatives were forthcoming. Events were beginning to run ahead of the studies. In conversations with his National Security Adviser, Brent Scowcroft, and his Secretary of State, James Baker, Bush suggested that it might be time for a summit meeting with his Soviet counterpart.

Gorbachev and Bush had first met at Konstantin Chernenko's funeral four years before. Their paths crossed again in Washington after a Reagan-Gorbachev summit meeting in December 1987, then again in New York a year later. During all of these encounters, George Bush carried only the title of Vice-President, although by December 1988 he also was President-elect. Now that both were heads of their respective governments, Bush felt it was time for a brief and informal meeting with no agenda and minimum staff. He wanted a get-acquainted session in a remote location during December 1989.

Bush hates news leaks and loves to surprise the press, so he conveyed his suggestion to Gorbachev via the latter's military adviser, Marshal Sergei Akromeyev, then visiting the United States. He did not want the State Department bureaucrats involved. It was an odd choice of channel, and annoyed the Soviet Foreign Ministry as well as Foggy Bottom, but Gorbachev responded positively. The men started negotiations, now with their staffs involved, and settled on Malta as the meeting site. They chose that small island nation to avoid the protocol issues associated with visits to world-power capitals, deciding to meet aboard each other's warships to simplify logistics and security. No one told them about the miserable winter weather in the Mediterranean. With arrangements made for what they thought would be a simple, pro forma meeting, these two men returned their attention to the accelerating events in Eastern Europe.

The Baltic republics were declaring their sovereignty and hoisting long-unseen flags. Solidarity, the anticommunist coalition in Poland, won a major victory in that nation's first free election in half a century. The government of Hungary formalized its open-borders policy. Large anticommunist demonstrations began to break out in East Germany, and on October 11, 1989, Erich Honecker, the longtime communist boss, quit. Chaos was beginning to descend. On October 23, Hungary declared itself to be a free republic. An East German government, now led by Egon Krenz, was in turmoil. At the end of the month he sought guidance in Moscow, but all he got was confirmation that the use of force was out of the question. On the evening of November 9, Krenz's spokesman, Gunter Schabowski, made an announcement on state TV. Schabowski said that effective immediately, "East Germans were free to travel without meeting special provisions."

Lieutenant Colonel Harald Jaeger nearly choked on his sandwich when he heard that. For twenty-eight years he had defended the east side of the Berlin wall. Over 450 people were killed trying to get through, over, or around it. That evening, Jaeger was in charge of the Bornholm Strasse crossing between East and West. He had no idea what the Schabowski statement meant, but he could see the crowds beginning to gather and had received the "no use of force" directive earlier in the week. Jaeger called his boss, Colonel Rudi Zeigenhorn, asking for instructions. On the third call, Zeigenhorn admitted that there were no orders from above, that Jaeger was on his own.

Jaeger vacillated for another half hour as the crowds grew into an angry mob. Then, at 11:00 P.M. on November 9, 1989, he gave the order to open the gates at Bornholm Strasse. The Berlin wall was breached. Within an hour crowds were dancing on its top, people with sledgehammers were demolishing it for souvenirs, and TV cameras were out in droves. As he watched all of this unfold, Jaeger once again called his boss, Colonel Zeigenhorn, to report what he had done. The resigned response: "You did right, young man."★

George Bush received the reports of this historic event in the White House. It was still afternoon in Washington. His instincts told him this was no time to gloat. He called an impromptu press conference, holding it in the Oval Office to keep it low key. His comments were cautious, supporting peaceful change, in order to avoid any precipitous Soviet military action.

The press wanted a bigger show. In their stories that evening, they alleged that Bush either "did not grasp or did not care" about the events unfolding in Berlin. Senate Majority Leader Mitchell, who to this day Bush identifies as the most partisan man ever seen in that body, urged Bush to "go dance on the wall." House Majority Leader Gephart echoed those thoughts. The media taunted Bush for his stay-at-home attitude, but the President was firm in his convictions. To this day George Bush views that proposed activism as "pure foolishness." The Soviets were alarmed; it was a time for tranquility, and it was time for the closers to meet in person.

As fate would have it, the long-scheduled meeting in Malta was now only three weeks away. During those intervening weeks, the avalanche would continue. The day after the wall was breached, the old-time

---

★ This description of Colonel Jaeger's role in history comes from Roger Cohen's wonderful account in the November 9, 1999, edition of the *New York Times*.

communist strong man of Bulgaria, Todor Zhivkov, headed for the door. Then the Soviet Republic of Georgia, Stalin's home, declared its sovereignty. Crowds growing to 200,000 appeared nightly in Prague's Wenceslas Square. In Washington and Moscow national leaders realized something historic was afoot. George Bush was getting his act together by phone with the leaders of the Free World. Margaret Thatcher came to Camp David for a chat in person.

Many in Congress, in the press, and even in his administration wanted the President to lean on Gorbachev. They felt it was time to topple the whole house of cards. Bush felt otherwise. He and his small retinue, which included NSC staffer Condoleezza Rice, arrived in Malta on the morning of December 1, 1989, planning to extend a helping hand, not a clenched fist.

THE MALTA SUMMIT

Countless memoirs have been written about this meeting, held in the midst of a terrible storm on December 2-3, 1989, aboard the Soviet cruise ship *Maxim Gorky*. My visual memories come only from TV. They are of a seaworthy U.S. President, born in New England, braving the ghastly weather aboard a small U.S. Navy tender to rendezvous with the Chairman of the Supreme Soviet. Gorbachev would not travel to his own warship, the *Slava*. He remained aboard the *Gorky*, tied up dockside in Valetta harbor. Bush was headquartered aboard the USS *Belknap*, flagship of the Sixth Fleet. The weather was so foul that the *Belknap* had to be anchored fore and aft, and it was from the *Belknap* that the President of the United States sallied forth by tender to end the Cold War.

Neither chief of state really understood that they were about to cross the Rubicon, but they both had forthright things to say. To paraphrase many a memoir, as well as my recent conversations with George Bush, the President decided the time had come to put away horse trading. From the beginning, he laid out all of his cards, saying, in effect: "You have terrible economic problems. The U.S. is prepared to help on a massive scale. Let us start trade negotiations at once so that the U.S. can waive Jackson-Vanik★ as soon as possible. Let's wrap up an agreement at

---

★ A Congressional edict that precluded most favored nation trade status for the Soviet Union so long as it interfered with emigration.

a summit in June. Credits will be forthcoming." They discussed other U.S. concerns: human rights, Central America, arms control. Then they discussed areas of possible cooperation: the environment, science, and student exchanges. But the core issue stood out: "You are bankrupt. We will help you."

Gorbachev was taken aback but pleased. In their meetings the next day, still aboard the *Maxim Gorky*, he expressed appreciation for the American restraint as the Berlin wall fell. He responded to the issues Bush raised. Then he spoke the words a generation had waited to hear: The Soviet Union would never start a war, it no longer regarded the U.S. as an adversary, and if there was trouble in the Soviet republics, he [Gorbachev] would not use force to put it down. Brent Scowcroft described Gorbachev's language as "elliptical in places," but he felt that it confirmed the commitment; there would be "no coercive measures to deal with unrest."

When the heirs of Joseph Stalin renounced the use of terror and force, the game was over. Only the mopping up remained. At the Malta summit, Gorbachev and Bush established a whole new relationship. It would guide them through the denouement—the collapse of the Soviet empire, which was to unfold over the next two years—but when they left Malta, the Cold War was over. Did George Bush understand that? Not at the time, he says, but in retrospect, absolutely. Gorbachev writes that it took him a while, perhaps several months, to appreciate the significance of what had happened. He feels that things might have turned out differently in the Baltics—meaning there could have been bloodshed—if those two men had not met in December 1989.

As it was, they built the relationship that would let them work together as the old order melted away. George Bush's contribution to history was to extract a peaceful surrender from Mikhail Gorbachev, leader of the Soviet empire, without anyone ever using that word nor firing a nuclear shot.

THE DEATH STARS STRIKE BACK

Mikhail Gorbachev wanted to save communism, but not by treading anywhere near the nuclear thresholds or Stalin's Gulags. His restraint won him the Nobel Peace Prize in 1990 just as the USSR was falling apart. The breach of the wall and the Malta summit were followed by the formation of a noncommunist government in Czechoslovakia, the bloody overthrow of the Romanian dictators Ceausescu and wife, the reunification of East and West Germany, the admission of Soviet guilt in the Katyn Forest and at the Ribbentrop-Molotov negotiations, and the growing disintegration of ties between Russia and the major republics.

Aside from a brief relapse in Lithuania, Gorbachev stood by his pledge to forswear the use of force. Political freedom came to Russia. Gorbachev was booed at the 1990 May Day celebrations in Moscow but no one was shot. Boris Yeltsin resigned from the Communist party and won election in his own right as president of Russia, with 57.3 percent of the vote. The Soviet government supported the U.S. in the Persian Gulf, and Mikhail Gorbachev survived an attempted coup.

Yet in the year following American victory in the deserts of Iraq and Gorbachev's survival of the abortive coup attempt in Moscow, both George Bush and Mikhail Gorbachev were peacefully removed from power by political opposition from within. That often happens in the aftermath of historic struggles. Winston Churchill learned that lesson in 1945.

As George Bush was orchestrating victory in the Persian Gulf and standing down the nuclear arsenal of the U.S., Ross Perot was fulminating in Dallas. Close friends of Ross Perot agree that his deep resentment of the wealthy and well-connected Bush family, with roots in New England, not Texas, flamed into uncontrolled hatred when Bush told Perot to take his POW/MIA crusade home to Texas.

Perot used his unlimited wealth and organizational skills to found a new political party, the Reform party. It achieved ballot status in every state. Perot caused himself to be nominated by that party, then named the most heroic of all POW's, Jim Stockdale, to be his running mate. During the campaign that followed Perot exploited the POW/MIA families and organizations to the fullest. He won 19 percent of the popular presidential vote in 1992. He won no electoral votes, but with his sequestration of basically Republican, conservative voters, he gave Bill Clinton the big industrial states of New Jersey, Pennsylvania, Ohio, and Michigan by the narrowest of margins.* He helped Clinton win Georgia and Louisiana. Even in the mountain states Perot took his toll. By winning more than a quarter of the vote in Montana and Colorado, he delivered those states to Clinton. Taken together, those victories

---

* If only two-thirds of the Perot votes in those states had gone to Bush, the then-President would have carried them.

were more than enough. Clinton claimed the presidency with only 43 percent of the popular vote. Thus the nineties became the "Clinton Years." Perot's egomania set the course for post–Cold War America, arranging a rerun of the post–World War I years. The 1990s, like the 1920s, would be a fun-filled decade, untroubled by the fate of our fallen enemy, ignorant of the malevolent dictators taking root all about, and capped by a bursting bubble at its end.

In Moscow the communist old-timers tried to stem the tide of history. Vice-President Vanayev, Interior Minister Pugo, KGB Chairman Kryuchkov, and others initiated the August 1991 coup. They confined Gorbachev to his dacha in the Crimea, but they failed to capture or kill the greater threat, Yeltsin. He stood atop a defecting tank outside the parliamentary offices, and he worked the phones inside. The plotters did not properly organize their coup, and for that reason it collapsed within days. Gorbachev was returned safely to Moscow, but the balance of power would never be the same. Gorbachev talked about "saving" communism. Yeltsin outlawed it after forcing Gorbachev to read out loud, to the Russian parliament, documents incriminating his own colleagues.

In December, Yeltsin orchestrated the disassembly of the former Soviet Union. On Christmas Day in 1991, Mikhail Gorbachev resigned as president of a country that no longer existed. The flags at the Kremlin changed as he spoke. He was not allowed to return to his official apartment, and he was locked out of his office by Yeltsin the next day. He called George Bush to wish him "a very quiet Christmas evening. . . . I am saying good-bye and shaking your hands."

George H. W. Bush rode into office on the coattails of the Great Communicator. Once there, he found the cards already dealt, the pieces in place, for the last round in the great struggle of the twentieth century. A careless remark, a flamboyant gesture, or an arrogant speech by a man of lesser self-confidence could have destroyed the momentum. The American eagle flapping out of control might have driven the Soviet coup plotters of 1991 to greater cohesion, a more careful conspiracy, or a full-blown holocaust, but George Bush knew better. "No fingers in their eyes, no claims of victory, no ego trips," were his guidelines. We are lucky God rolled these men out of history's dice cup in 1985.

Former President Bush now lives in Houston, exhausted from watching the strange election of his son to succeed Bill Clinton in the White House and elated by his son's leadership through the challenging events of the new century. Mikhail Gorbachev attempted a political comeback in 1996. He won only 1.5 percent of the presidential vote in Russia. Lieutenant Colonel Harald Jaeger is now retired, running a newsstand in Berlin. All three men are alive; none are in prison. In the context of the tumultuous twentieth century, that is no small achievement.

CHAPTER 20

The Soviet Solstice

FOR MILLENNIA, MAN HAS NOTICED that one day in December things finally take a turn for the better. On that day the sun rises a little earlier than it did the day before. Winter still lies ahead, but that earlier sunrise on December 22 of every year gives proof that spring is on its way, that glorious summer surely will follow.

So it was in Moscow in December 1991. For seventy-four years the icy ghost of Vladimir Lenin crushed the soul and froze the hearts of most Russians. Then, during the winter solstice, the General Secretary of the Communist Party of the Soviet Union stepped to a microphone to announce the end of that union, his job, and that seemingly endless political winter.

Some Russians thought that day would be the end of their world, but most realized it would not. While the darkness of a lawless winter would hover for a decade, while the economic freeze brought on by the Marxist experiment would be hard to endure, most citizens felt the glory that once was theirs would one day return. Late December of

1991 was the winter solstice for twentieth century Russia. The buildup to that incredible week was spread throughout an incredible year. Events in the Pentagon, the Iraqi desert, the bunkers of Omaha, and even in the halls of the Kremlin itself, were hard to believe. But when the year was over, the winter solstice celebrations in those Kremlin halls and beyond will never be forgotten.

RINGING OUT THE OLD, RINGING IN THE NEW

George Sheldon and Gavril Popov first met in the early autumn of 1991. Sheldon was president of the World Presidents Organization, a group of semiretired, very successful, mostly American, independent business executives. They liked to travel, but at the highest levels. Sheldon was in charge of planning their 1991 winter outing.

Popov was the mayor of Moscow. He began his career at Moscow State University, where he was active in politics, as a hard-line communist. He joined the Soviet bureaucracy, where he proved to be adaptable. His friends now refer to him as a "Russian Greek." When the tide began to turn, with Gorbachev's ascension to power, Popov became an equally ardent democrat. In the spring of 1991 he was appointed to the largely ceremonial post of Moscow's mayor. Economic change was in the air, and Mayor Popov was in the forefront. He was a deal-making hustler, a man who would have felt right at home in the council chambers of most big U.S. cities. He was looking for investment in Moscow's new economy. Sheldon's coterie of successful entrepreneurs were prime targets.

The two men met at a World Presidents conference in Brussels during the summer of 1991. They fell to talking about the ferment cooking in Russia. "How about a New Year's celebration in Moscow?" Popov asked. He was proposing a four day round of private dinners, business meetings, and opulent parties to be held in the new Moscow. A hundred business executives and their spouses were to be invited. The festivities would be capped by a grand ball at the Kremlin on New Year's Eve. The men shook hands on the deal. Sheldon was to line up one hundred prosperous businessmen with an interest in Russian investment and to deposit $100,000 with a "travel agent" in New York. Popov was to organize the festivities. They would next meet at Moscow's Octoberskaya Hotel three months later.

Boris Yeltsin, the new kingpin of Russia, took control of the Kremlin on December 25, 1991. Gorbachev's former office was immediately put to a more functional use. Having dumped the Communist party into the dustbin of history, Yeltsin and his buddies decided it was time for a drink. What better place to celebrate than on the green baize conference tables so often photographed with dour General Secretaries glowering across at visiting Western supplicants? Yeltsin's big problem was neither security nor visitor control—it was finding the Kremlin's stash of vodka and caviar. Into that vacuum rode Sheldon's hundred businessmen and their spouses. There was vodka to the left of them, caviar to the right of them. They landed at Sheremetyevo on the morning of December 29, four days after Gorbachev had been driven from the Kremlin. Popov's man was there at the airport to meet them.

They rode into town past toppled statues and empty pedestals. The guests could not read the Cyrillic inscriptions, but the words might well have been written by Shelley: " 'Look on my works ye mighty and despair!' Round the decay of [this] colossal wreck, boundless and bare, the lone and level [snows] stretch far away." The two hundred were taken to the Octoberskaya Hotel, a former haven for Soviet bigwigs in the Arbat section of Moscow. The rooms were huge; every one had a TV, although the movie offerings were a little unique. They included *An Englishman Abroad*, the story of Guy Burgess's life in Russia,★ or *Riley, Ace of Spies*, a story of the KGB's brightest and best at work.

During the two days that followed, Sheldon's one hundred business people and their spouses were treated to a fashion show at the huge Rossiya Hotel, across Red Square from the Kremlin. The models were awash in furs, sable, and mink from all over Russia. They were gorgeous, both furs and girls. There was a reception at the residence of the Russian foreign minister, rides on Russian troikas (traditional Russian three-horse sleighs) through the cold and snowy Moscow night air, and private dinners for each of the visiting couples, hosted by scientists and "bizessmen" trying for a new start.

And then it was time for the grand ball. At 8:00 P.M. on December 31, a flotilla of black Zil limousines arrived at the Octoberskaya to ferry the two hundred across Moscow and through the Kremlin's historic Spassky Gate. Once inside, cautious optimism was everywhere. This new nation was celebrating its rebirth, arm in arm with its former adversary. The people were looking forward to the sunny days that

---

★ Guy Burgess, with the British Foreign Office, spied for the USSR for years before fleeing to Russia one step ahead of MI-5.

peace and a free economy would bring. "Moscow could be like Los Angeles," the mayor whispered to Sheldon. The crowd circulated freely through the great halls of the Kremlin, from St. George's to St. Catherine's. Sheldon had his picture taken at the dais of the Supreme Soviet. The Americans drank toasts to their Russian hosts in the quarters of Ivan the Terrible.

At 10:30 P.M. the crowd moved into the Congress Hall for dinner. The head of the Russian Orthodox Church said the blessing, in rooms he had never before entered. The food, wine, and vodka were magnificent and in unending supply, but that was only the beginning. At 11:00 P.M. the Moscow Symphony Orchestra began to play Tchaikovsky. Then, at 11:30, the Red Army Band and Chorus took the stage. After a few introductory Russian folk tunes they turned their attention to an American repertoire. The band played "Stars and Stripes Forever"; the marble walls shook. To close out the show, the evening, and the year of 1991, the Red Army Chorus broke into a stunning rendition of "God Bless America." It was a shocker; there was not a single, solitary dry eye in the house. As the two hundred headed for home, fireworks and happy crowds filled Red Square.

THE MEN FROM THE SECRET CITIES

I came to celebrate the Soviet solstice with two Russians named Vladimir. The date was February 9, 1992, six weeks after Gorbachev's departure from power. The place was the Wente winery in Livermore. That town hosts an American nuclear weapons laboratory as well as some lovely vineyards. Vladimir Belugin was head of Arzamas-16, the senior Soviet nuclear weapons design institute.★ Vladimir Nechai ran Chelyabinsk-70, the junior Soviet lab. We all came to be there because, as the winter solstice came and went, the directors of the Soviet and American nuclear weapons institutes felt the need to reach out and touch one another.

It all started when early travelers Danny Stillman and Nerses Krikorian, of Los Alamos, first connected with their Russian peers. Soviet

---

★ Russians use the word "institute" where we use "laboratory," meaning a very large organization, employing thousands of people and devoted to pushing a specific envelope of technology. A "laboratory" is also a room filled with glass tubes and Bunsen burners. That's what the Russians mean when they use the word. In this text "lab" and "laboratory" are taken to mean "institute."

nuclear scientists had never been allowed to publish their work in the open literature, yet they were intellectual giants. They wanted to join E. O. Lawrence, J. Robert Oppenheimer, and Edward Teller in the pantheon of physics history. They were also concerned about the safety and security of their handiwork—the nuclear weapons of the Soviet Union—and about their economic survival as their empire collapsed.

Jim Watkins, the U.S. Secretary of Energy, had been thinking about how to connect with those secret labs. Here was his chance. With the connections established by the Los Alamos travelers, Watkins made arrangements for the leaders of Arzamas-16 and Chelyabinsk-70 to visit their American counterparts at Los Alamos and Livermore. In late 1991 the crumbling Soviet government did not know how to say no to this proposal, and in January 1992 the new Russian government, awash in euphoria, wanted to open its archives to public view. Within a month of the collapse of the Soviet Union, Vladimir Belugin and one of his brightest research deputies, Alexander Pavlovski, along with Vladimir Nechai and his deputy scientific director, Boris Litvinov, all came to small, candlelit tables in the Wente winery.

Their host was John Nuckolls, director of the Lawrence Livermore National Laboratory, along with a few of his associates, including myself. Words cannot do justice to that evening and the meetings that followed. There was an atmosphere of elation, of quiet celebration. Everyone in that room, except the interpreters, had *seen* megaton-scale nuclear explosions. They understood the scale of the disaster we had avoided. The atmosphere was too heavy with history to allow a celebration that opening night, but the air of thankful relief was thick enough to cut with a knife.

That Sunday evening marked the beginning of an historic week. On the morrow, the group would visit the Livermore Laboratory for two days. Then there would be a day of travel, by special aircraft directly to the mesa at Los Alamos. Once there, Sig Hecker, director of the Los Alamos National Laboratory, would host the same group for two more days. On Saturday the visitors would return home, to prepare for a return engagement by the Americans one week later.

On February 22 the American lab directors and two of their associates headed out for Russia. They were accorded reciprocal hospitality, two days each at Arzamas-16 and Chelyabinsk-70, that again defied description. First of all, there were welcoming discussions with Yuli Khariton, the J. Robert Oppenheimer of the Soviet nuclear program. Khariton, eighty-eight years old at the time, has since passed away. But during the visit, his English was fluent, his mind clear, his manners impeccable.

Khariton was open about the early Soviet weapons program. He was unequivocal in stating that Klaus Fuchs, a British scientist working at Los Alamos, was of enormous technical help in developing the first Soviet A-bomb. The Rosenbergs and their associates were his couriers, and the first Soviet bomb, detonated on August 29, 1949, was an exact copy of the Nagasaki Fat Man. He said it would have been foolish to improvise when the plans for a known success were available and the penalty for failure in Stalin's Soviet Union was death. Khariton's guests were flabbergasted at this sudden confirmation of all we had suspected.

Khariton was proud of his scientific staff. He assured his guests they would see virtually everything in his domain, but that there were problems. Clouds of uncertainty now hung over both Russian scientific centers. When the visitors toured Arzamas-16, they found a completely closed city. The same was true of Chelyabinsk-70. The institutes were responsible for the development of nuclear weapons, but they also had to run the schools and hospitals, plow and maintain the roads, keep everyone fed, and secure the perimeter. No one was allowed into either town without a pass. With the collapse of the empire where was the money to come from? The institutes were "borrowing" hundreds of millions of rubles from the central bank every month just to keep people fed. How long could they keep that up?

The American visitors listened to a recitation of nifty technologic achievements, some truly spectacular. But they also found a lot of sandboxes—pet projects of distinguished academicians that were never turned off—for there was no Congressional committee, no peer reviewers, to ask, "What are you doing and why?" This explained a lot of intelligence mysteries from the Cold War. In days gone by we saw, from satellite photography, bizarre excavations or pieces of equipment which made no sense but whose ongoing construction worried us for years. It turns out these projects did *not* make any sense, but in the Soviet Union there was no way to kill them off.

The Soviets were well aware of nuclear weapon safety issues. Even though that subject touches on the internals of weapon design, they were willing to talk and seek advice. They discussed the merits of their transportation containers, which they felt to be superior to U.S. models, and they confirmed that their weapons were "disabled" when in storage, whatever that meant. On the other hand, security (preventing theft or misuse) was a new subject to them. Throughout the Soviet system nuclear weapons had been secured by operational means: people watching people who watched still other people. The Soviets confirmed that there were no electronic or mechanical locking devices on their weapons (as there are in the U.S.), a subject that grew to be of enormous concern as the KGB disappeared, the army disintegrated, and well-financed terrorists infiltrated the country.

Underlying all of this technology was a deep concern about the future. The closed cities were disintegrating too. Those scientific temples and their cousins with other numbers—Tomsk-7, Krasnoyarsk-26, etc.—were on a death spiral. What were they to do? The Soviet hosts implored their new American friends for help; not with handouts, but with cooperative ventures that would utilize the talent, keep it at home, and give it the recognition it deserved.

It was a tall order. The American government devised a series of slow-moving programs that immediately fell afoul of jurisdictional disputes within Russia. Who controlled the money? The Academy of Science or the Ministry of Atomic Energy? Within a few years, Vladimir Nechai, the director of Chelyabinsk-70 and one of our guests at Livermore, would give up. He took his own life in despair.

In time some American-funded programs would be created to pay for Soviet weapons dismantlement, help safeguard Russian nuclear materials, provide pure-science work for some of those Russians, open parts of the secret cities to joint industrial ventures, and grant academic recognition to those who labored in the Soviet darkness for so long. A decade later these programs are beginning to pay off, but it has been a long, dark winter for the nuclear community of Russia.

BOB GATES RETURNS AN OVERDUE VIDEO

In the autumn of 1973 a couple of well-dressed civilians came to my office in the Pentagon to tell me a story. Known as the Office of the Special Assistant, it was directly across the hall from the office of the Secretary and Deputy Secretary of Defense. Martin Hoffmann and I tended to the odd jobs: politics (which we fought to keep out of the Pentagon), executive recruiting (it was the beginning of the second Nixon term, and there were a lot of vacancies in the presidentially appointed ranks), and sensitive intelligence. It was this last that brought those two gentlemen to see me. The Secretary of Defense wanted us to keep track of Project Jennifer. The tale that unfolded still boggles my mind.

In April 1968 the Soviet diesel-powered, ballistic-missile-firing submarine *Red Star* left its home port of Vladivostok to go on patrol. This was a Golf II class boat, an interim response to the American fleet of nuclear-powered Polaris submarines that first went operational in 1960. Diesel submarines run underwater on battery power. They must surface daily, or at least come to snorkel depth, to run their diesels and recharge those batteries.

In April 1968, *Red Star* apparently suffered an explosion while recharging its batteries, probably from the hydrogen gas given off in the process. The explosion tore a ten-foot hole in the hull, flooded the ship, and sent it to the bottom. There was no time to send off a distress message to fleet headquarters. Within days the Soviet Pacific fleet was going bonkers looking for *Red Star*, just as they were said to do in *The Hunt for Red October*. The U.S. Navy took note of all this activity, and while the Soviets never were able to find *Red Star*, by midsummer the U.S. Navy's technology had given it a pretty good idea of where to look: 1,700 miles northwest of Hawaii.

In August 1968 our Navy found it, under 16,580 feet of water, and started taking pictures by means of a remote submersible. On September 9 those photos made their way back to Washington. Naval Intelligence was intrigued. If they could reach down those three miles into the dark and rushing currents of the north Pacific, they might be able to recover a Soviet nuclear warhead, cryptographic equipment, and some mysterious radio transmitters that had defied all U.S. efforts at decoding.

The White House was interested too, but a presidential election was under way, and transition was in the air. When the new Nixon team took over, Henry Kissinger's military assistant, Al Haig, was fascinated by the intelligence possibilities. He showed the photos to his bosses, and they authorized an attempt at recovery. The new Deputy at OMB for National Security, James Schlesinger, was told to find the funds and to assure the continued support of the project, code name Jennifer.

There ensued a bureaucratic struggle between the Navy and the CIA, with the latter winning control of the project and probably making the recovery more complicated than it needed to be. In any event, Schlesinger moved from OMB to become Chairman of the Atomic Energy Commission in 1971, then Director of Central Intelligence. In both jobs, he continued to be godfather to the program. The CIA hit upon the idea of recruiting Howard Hughes to front the construction of a new, mammoth ship that nominally was to mine for manganese nodules on the ocean floor. Hughes's well-known eccentricity, secrecy, and wealth made all this credible.

In February 1973, Schlesinger moved again, this time to become Secretary of Defense. He wanted to keep an eye on Jennifer, which is why Hoffmann and I heard this tale. At the time of those conversations, the Hughes ship had a name, the *Glomar Explorer*. It was being outfitted with lifting rigs, a recovery bay, and even a morgue for the remains of any Soviet seamen who might be found in the *Red Star*'s hull. I thanked my visitors for the briefing. They reminded me of the absolute secrecy required, for the *Glomar Explorer* would put to sea within a few months and any leakage of information would be disastrous. The Soviet Union might still claim legal ownership of the wreck.

The *Glomar Explorer* started its sea trials in early 1974, and by March it was making serious but random-looking runs all over the North Pacific. By August it was on station and the recovery attempt began. Claws and a steel net went over the *Red Star*, and the ascent began at the rate of 300 feet per hour. But then, about a third of the way up, the old hull just fell apart. Most of the *Red Star* settled back to its permanent resting place on the ocean floor. The *Glomar Explorer* recovered only a quarter of the *Red Star*'s hull—no nukes, crypto gear, or transmitters. When pieces of the hull were hauled into the recovery bay of the mother ship, however, the remains of six Soviet sailors were aboard.

On September 4, 1974, after getting more urgent matters settled, these remains were given a proper burial at sea. The full-honors ceremony took place in the hold of the *Glomar Explorer*, with American and Soviet flags on display. Traditional services were conducted in both English and Russian. The Soviet anthem was played, the caskets were closed, then lifted to deck level. After further appropriate words about honorable men who served their country well, the caskets were lowered over the side and the men were returned to their watery graves.

All of this was videotaped. The records and souvenirs of that episode were brought home and shown to the appropriate CIA officials. Then they were consigned to the vaults, just as if they had been recovered by the *Raiders of the Lost Ark*. Fast forward to 1992. The Cold War was over. Boris Yeltsin and George Bush were presidents of their countries. Robert Gates was the latter's Director of Central Intelligence. His counterpart in Russia, Yevgeny Primakov, decided to invite Gates to Moscow for a visit—not just to the city, but to the headquarters of the once-arch enemy, the KGB, and to the Kremlin. No CIA director had ever done any of that.

The visit took place in October 1992, a mind-boggling event for both sides. Gates was accorded full honors everywhere he went. He was driven in a Zil limousine that had once ferried the Moscow party boss about town. They went to KGB headquarters, where every window had a head protruding, all watching Gates's arrival with stunned disbelief. Then the delegation moved on to the Kremlin. In planning the trip, Gates told his Russian hosts that he would be bringing a gift for President Yeltsin, one of "historic significance." Gates was accompanied to the meeting by U.S. Ambassador Strauss, two CIA officials, and their interpreter. They were escorted through Moscow and into the Kremlin by efficient Russian police.

The Americans were welcomed to the president's office by Yeltsin, Foreign Minister Kozyrev, and the heads of the two successor organizations to the KGB, Yevgeny Primakov of the FSB and Viktor Barannikov of the FSS. The meeting started with a discussion of the new age then dawning. The Soviet solstice had come and gone. There was great opportunity for cooperation. Yeltsin talked about history. Gates then said, "We are here to write finis to all that." To the astonishment of all, he unfurled a Soviet flag that had covered one of the sailors' caskets at the time of the funeral services aboard the *Glomar Explorer* eighteen years before. He then handed Yeltsin a videotape of those services. Gates repeated his point: even at the height of the Cold War, America respected the courage of, and accorded full honors to, the men who did their duty and gave their all for the Soviet Union. The video was only fifteen minutes long, but Yeltsin wept. So did every one of us who have seen it.

WHEN WORLD WARS END

The last time a global conflict ended, in 1945, the losers enjoyed nothing but the hatred and scorn of world opinion. Not only were they brutal warriors, they had inflicted unspeakable atrocities on helpless prisoners and innocent civilians from Auschwitz to Nanking. The losers of World War II pulled down the pillars of their own temples, leaving their national capitals in fiery ruin. Their once-elite armaments industries were gutted shells. The corpses of defeated leaders were burned by their aides or vilified by angry mobs.

In 1991 it was different. Communist governments were unconcerned about human life, but for the most part it was their own people who suffered in the Gulags and dungeons. When defeat was clearly written on the wind, most communist leaders went away quietly, into peaceful retirement. When the end came, Moscow was not aflame, like Berlin or Tokyo. The city was alight with parties as its citizens welcomed the victors in hopes of replicating their success. The nuclear weapons laboratories at Arzamas-16 and Chelyabinsk-70 were not empty halls. They were crowded but confused cities, welcoming their American peers to a quiet celebration of the fact that their ghastly products had never been used. The men in Moscow were alive to welcome those from Washington. Both sides shed a tear in memory of the fallen heroes on both sides, for there had been such heroes, and we both knew it.

CHAPTER 21

The Heroes

ON SEPTEMBER 14, 1954, the Soviet Army fired off a twenty-kiloton A-bomb only a thousand feet over a mock battlefield near the town of Totskoe. Seven minutes later "attack troops" in protective clothing moved into the area, "taking" the target at ground zero. The fact that there were no immediate adverse effects on the troops encouraged the Soviet leadership, all the way up to Khrushchev, to decide that nuclear weapons were just better artillery. Marshal Sokolovsky, chief of the general staff, wrote as much in *Military Strategy*, the prime military text of the time.

By the mid 1950s the leaders of the Soviet Union had come to believe that nuclear war was a reasonable military and political option. Leaders of the U.S. Strategic Air Command may have felt the same way, but in reality it was not. The real heroes of the Cold War were the officers and civilians who stood their ground between the red meat of nuclear weapons and the hungry dogs of political war. There were many such heroes, but the tales of a typical four follow: two engineers from Leningrad and two sailors from Annapolis. Only because of their steady hands and good judgment are we all here today.

THE SOVIET MONSTER ROCKETS

By 1957 the Soviet Union had begun testing intercontinental ballistic missiles; within three years the first large and cumbersome R-7 rockets were being deployed. These were the same boosters that put Sputnik into orbit, a kluge of monster parts, fueled immediately prior to launch from railroad tank cars nearby. Only six R-7s were ever deployed, despite Khrushchev's threats to "crank them out like sausages." By 1961 a more sophisticated two-stage rocket, the R-16, was making its appearance. This weapon system also used a storable liquid fuel and oxidizer, delivered from movable tanks on trucks or railroad cars. The rockets were stored horizontally, without fuel, until made ready for use. According to Russian nuclear scientists visiting the United States in 2002, both of these rocket systems—R-7 and R-16—carried 2.8-megaton thermonuclear warheads, tested twice in the Soviet nuclear test series of 1958.

Orders to fire these R-7 and R-16 rockets were to come from Moscow over very bad telephone lines, by hard-wired telegraph, by Morse code over a shortwave radio link, and/or by couriers. When received, the orders were to be authenticated by comparison with a code sealed inside a paper envelope and held by a regimental commander. He was to acknowledge receipt of the valid order back to Moscow over the same archaic phone lines. There would ensue the hours needed to erect, fuel, and launch those rockets. While any such launch was supposed to be authorized by Moscow, the launch crews could have fired without such permission. There was no centrally controlled lockout key, only the discipline of the Red Army. This was the system in place in October 1962 when the Cuban missile crisis erupted.

In Russia, those days are known as the Caribbean Crisis. Valery Yarynich remembers them well. As a staff officer from rocket corps headquarters, he was on a business trip to the Urals, driving between regiments, when he saw tank trucks filled with rocket fuel heading toward the rocket launch platforms. What is going on? he wondered.

Yarynich raced to the telegraph desk at the Nizhny Tagil division command post. Picking up the tape, he saw the instructions from

Moscow: the rocket forces were to go to "Combat Mode." In combat mode, weapons are loaded, communications frequencies changed, and operational documents distributed. That had never happened before in the Strategic Rocket Force (SRF), but everyone knew about the confrontation building up in Cuba. The regimental commander tried to open the secret package containing the authenticator. His hands were shaking so badly that he could not do it. The paper envelope was to be cut open with scissors or knife, but the officer cut himself instead. Yarynich still can see the faces of those officers, showing three feelings at once: alarm but not fear; shock, because the SRF had never before gone to combat mode; and determination, a legacy of the Great Patriotic War (World War II). Those troops would do whatever had to be done, at whatever personal cost, to protect Mother Russia.

In July of that year, prior to his departure for Cuba, General Issa Pliyev, the Soviet commander-designate in Cuba, met with Khrushchev to receive his instructions. If, in the heat of combat, he could not contact Moscow, Pliyev was given the authority to use his tactical nuclear weapons. During the closing weeks of October 1962 there were ninety-eight such weapons in Cuba, with another twenty-four slated for attachment to the intermediate range ballistic missiles (IRBMs) that never arrived.★

On October 28, Khrushchev and Kennedy came to an understanding that defused the crisis. The Soviet ships bearing IRBMs turned around and returned to the Soviet Union. The Americans would forswear an armed attack on Cuba and, in time, would remove their IRBMs from Turkey. General Pliyev never fired a rocket. The launch order never came to Nizhny Tagil. But the events of those six days, in October 1962, opened a lot of Soviet and American eyes.

★ USAF General W. Y. Smith and Red Army General A. I. Gribkov first met at a Cold War history conference in Havana in January 1992. Two years later they published their joint findings on Soviet Project Anadyr. This was the secret shipment of Soviet missiles into Cuba, triggering the missile crisis of October 1962. In their book they reported that General Pliyev had control of twelve two-kiloton warheads for his Luna tactical rockets, eighty ten-kiloton warheads for his FKR cruise missiles, and six six-kiloton bombs for carriage by IL-28 bombers. The IRBM warheads, with yields of around a half a megaton each, were still aboard the *Alexandrovsk* in the port of La Isabella, not available to Pliyev. In subsequent private discussions, other retired Soviet generals have confirmed these numbers.

CONSEQUENCES OF A MISTAKE

Things could have gone wrong. In Cuba, General Pliyev could have lost contact with Moscow during an American naval maneuver. Back in the Soviet Union, a confused regimental commander could have misunderstood an order sent over those primitive telephones. Any of those commanders could have lost communication with higher head-quarters and feared the worst. Any officer could have taken foreign policy into his own hands, as young men sometimes do. By any number of routes, Soviet rockets could have been launched without the approval of Moscow.

An attack on the U.S. heartland in October 1962 might have started with an attack on a few key military bases. The submarine base in New London and the Electric Boat Company shipyard in Groton across the river would be one candidate. A 2.8-megaton warhead landing there would have burned and destroyed much of central Connecticut. The naval and air facilities in and around Norfolk, Virginia, might have been another target. A multimegaton warhead there would have oblit-erated everything in the Hampton Roads estuary of the James River.

Whatever the military targets, a 1962 Soviet war plan certainly would have focused on the political centers of the United States. A 2.8-megaton weapon targeted on the White House would have killed virtually everyone inside the Beltway. The firestorms would have reached as far as Dulles Airport and halfway to Baltimore. The core of the U.S. federal government would have ceased to exist. One weapon allocated to New York City, the heart of "capitalist imperialism," would have left few survivors on the island of Manhattan, in Queens, Brook-lyn, the Bronx, or Jersey City. Firestorms would have devoured Staten Island, Kennedy Airport, New Rochelle, Yonkers, and the stately homes of Great Neck, Long Island.

One Soviet regiment, acting on its own, could have killed almost everyone on the island of Manhattan and within the Washington Belt-way while incapacitating key parts of the U.S. military establishment. The United States, of course, would have struck back. The President might have been reluctant to order a retaliatory launch based on a few electronic signals from radars and HF transmitter screens, but once nu-clear detonations in Greenland and in the northern U.S. had been de-tected by the Vela Hotel satellites orbiting overhead, he would have known that this was the real thing. Every bomber already in the air, submarine hidden at sea, and missile silo not yet destroyed would have wrought its ghastly havoc.

As the 1960s began to unfold, such scenarios could have come to pass. Those regimental commanders in the Soviet SRF and that general in Cuba really were out there on their own, at the far ends of the world's worst telephone system. With the support of only a few fellow officers, those commanders could have fired.

Such a launch was improbable. There was, first of all, the discipline of the Communist Party of the Soviet Union. On top of that lay the professionalism of the SRF officer corps. Then there was the practical consideration of time. The half-dozen hours it took to fuel and fire an R-16 left a lot of time for the staff to ask questions. And there was the omnipresent surveillance by the KGB. These considerations, taken together, made an unauthorized launch unlikely. But to cooler heads in the SRF, "unlikely" was not good enough. Besides, the Soviet military-industrial complex was making things worse. Soviet design bureaus were spawning new generations of ballistic missiles, with individual, uncoordinated schemes for the control and launch of those weapons. A nuclear Tower of Babel was in the making.

As the Cuban missile crisis unfolded, reality was injected into the thinking of the Soviet general staff. In my conversations with senior Russian officers today, most point to October 1962 as the time when reality dawned. That week of watching and waiting on full nuclear alert while Kennedy and Khrushchev faced off, gave officers up and down the line on both sides time to think about their families. Most military officers expect to come into harm's way. That is their job. But that week of forced reflection made Americans and Soviets realize that their families, their children, and millions of other innocents, would be consumed by the fires of hell if things went wrong. During those six days in October the possibility of nuclear war changed from a policy option to a dreaded disaster.

THE ENGINEERS OF LENINGRAD

Although they did not know each other then, Vladimir Petoukhov and Valery Yarynich grew up together in Leningrad. Petoukhov was born there in 1936, the son of a communications engineer. Yarynich was born nearby on Kronstadt Island in 1937, the son of a naval officer. Theirs was not to be an innocent childhood. Hitler invaded the Soviet

Union in June 1941, expecting as easy a trip across the Slavic flatlands as he had enjoyed in Poland the previous fall. His troops did not bother with equipment for the Russian winter, and he already had chosen the historic Astoria Hotel in Leningrad for his victory banquet. Hitler did not understand the tenacity of the Russian people or the harshness of their winters. By September 8, 1941, the Wehrmacht had fought its way to the outskirts of Leningrad, where it was stopped.

At age five, as the Germans approached Leningrad, young Vladimir Petoukhov was evacuated to Omsk. He and his mother got there by barge across Lake Ladoga, then by railroad freight car across Russia, all the while under German aerial bombardment. They went to live with Vladimir's uncle, a kind man who loved his sister. But she cried a lot during those years, for there was little or no food for young Vladimir. He still remembers the big treat: powdered eggs and sausage from America. Valery Yarynich, a boy of four, was sent to Kirov by train. When he got there, the village was devoid of men and food. The winters were bitterly cold. The summer brought only the opportunity to subsist on tree roots.

Both boys' fathers stayed behind to defend the old imperial capital. For nine hundred days the Nazis besieged the city, but for nine hundred days the citizens of Leningrad held out. Under constant bombardment, workers subsisted on a few hundred grams of bread per day. In Leningrad's darkest hours that ration shrank to 250 grams. Elders and other nonproducers were only allocated half rations. This led old women and young children to work in the eight armament factories in town in order to double their food rations. A quarter of the population died, mostly from starvation and disease.

As Americans gathered around family tables for their Christmas dinner in 1941, reeling from the shock of Pearl Harbor but otherwise not inconvenienced, a top-secret KGB report was being issued to the Leningrad party leadership. During the earlier part of that month alone, about 39,000 Leningrad residents died. During the previous week, 656 Soviet citizens dropped dead in the streets. There were twenty-five *reported* cases of cannibalism; countless more in reality.

On the other hand, starvation was not a problem for the Communist party leadership in Leningrad. The archives now open at party headquarters in the Smolney Institute confirm the operation of a cafeteria during the siege serving flown-in caviar and other goodies to the elite. Photos show a roomful of tables for eight at the Smolney, an arrangement hardly needed for a once-a-day serving of bread and tea. An internal memorandum now available states: "There was no limit to [party boss Andrei] Zhdanov's buffet." Only city officials, Komsomol youth, and party regulars were welcome at that buffet.

I am a contemporary of Vladimir Pethoukov and Valery Yarynich, but I spent those war years in Washington, D.C., in reasonable comfort. My father came home every night from his job at the War Production Board to help with my homework. We always had a good dinner, and he tucked me into a warm bed at night. To me, World War II was the story of the few to whom so many owed so much in the skies over Britain, or it was the story of Admiral Spruance and the American dive bombers at Midway; but to Vladimir and Valery, it was separation from fathers and homes they might never see again, fathers left to suffer from German artillery and the arctic cold.

Vladimir's father, Efrem Ivanovich Petoukhov, is the sort of man who has made Russian history for generations. On June 22, 1941, he was already thirty-five years old, a technical instructor working on an automatic machine for delivering forage to farm animals. He was living peacefully in Leningrad with his family. Two days later he was a junior lieutenant in the Soviet Army. As his wife and son disappeared into the east, Efrem stayed behind to build communications equipment for the troops.

His masterpiece was a six-railroad-car mobile command post. To get it out of Leningrad, to the forces in need, he drove it across frozen Lake Ladoga on tracks laid on the ice. Calculations said the ice would not crack under that load, but there was not a lot of supporting evidence. Valery Yarynich's father was already a naval officer when war broke out. Yevgeny Andreevich Yarynich stayed behind, in Leningrad, to help repair ships. He traveled back and forth, under fire, to the shipyard on Kronstadt.

During the long years of the Cold War, we Americans often would say to each other, "The Russians are just like us," but that is not true. Americans cannot possibly comprehend the horrors of the Great Patriotic War in Russia nor the impact it left on that younger generation.

When World War II was over, young Petoukhov returned to Leningrad to find his father still alive. Vladimir was a bright child. He returned to school, graduating from the Leningrad Polytechnic Institute in 1959. In 1960 he began work there with Professor Taras Sokolov, an expert in automatic control. Valery Yarynich also made it home to Leningrad, and he too found his father alive and well. Valery entered the Leningrad Military Communications Academy in 1954. In October

1957 the U.S.SR launched Sputnik, the first man-made satellite. It was an exciting time for both young men. To Petoukhov, the young scientist, it was tangible evidence of the role technology would play in postwar Russia. To Yarynich , the young soldier, Sputnik foretold the coming of the SRF.

By the time Yarynich graduated from the communications academy, in 1959, those forces were in formation. As a new lieutenant, Yarynich was assigned to the first Soviet ICBM division. He was sent to Yuriya, near Kirov, where he served for a year at a construction site. His first combat operations were pretty simple, shooting the bears and wolves trying to attack the construction workers to steal their food. At the end of 1960, Yarynich moved up to the corps headquarters in Kirov where five new missile divisions were being formed. In America, John Kennedy was decrying the "missile gap." Subsequent history would show there was no such gap, but there certainly was a race. Yarynich was there when the starting gate opened.

THE RACE TO RELIABILITY: *KAZBECK* AND *SIGNAL*

In the 1950s, while Vladimir Petoukhov was still a student at the Leningrad Polytechnic Institute, Professor Sokolov was beginning to think about computers. But it was only after the Cuban crisis that Sokolov got serious about the challenge of reliable and fail-safe communications to the new SRF. The Soviet general staff got serious too. Once the lessons of that crisis had sunk in, and faced with the proliferation of different rocket programs, the general staff initiated a design competition for a standardized command and control system for their nuclear forces.

Two design teams were asked for proposals. The design group in Moscow, led by future academician Vladimir Semenikhin, and known as the Institute of Automatic Apparatus, proposed an approach using new digital computers and software. Given the state of Soviet computer technology in the early 1960s, most Soviet analysts thought components of the resulting system would be huge and that the system itself would be unreliable.

The Leningrad Polytechnic Institute proposal, developed by Professor Sokolov, called for a hard-wired system based on ferromagnetic cores. Logic elements were to be plated onto a substrate, then covered with a plastic compound to assure reliability and security. This system was not flexible, nor was it capable of executing many commands, but unlike the Moscow approach, it would be reliable. The Leningrad Polytechnic Institute won the competition, and their first prototype was built in 1964. Young Vladimir Petoukhov was part of the design team.

At the same time, Yarynich was reassigned from SRF corps headquarters in Kirov to the Soviet Army communications school at Stavropol. Once there, he became part of the control system evaluation team. He returned to Leningrad, posted to work with the Leningrad Polytechnic Institute, where he met up with Vladimir Petoukhov. Thus began a thirty year partnership to secure the strategic nuclear weapons of the Soviet Union. When the design competition was settled, Yarynich was assigned to the central office for the SRF in Vlasikha, fifteen miles west of downtown Moscow. In due course he moved to the general staff, all the while retaining his focus on the need for careful and foolproof control of nuclear weapons. During this same period, the Leningrad Polytechnic Institute spun off its strategic nuclear controls work to a new design bureau, known today as NPO Impuls.

Over the next twenty-five years the scientists (like Petoukhov) and the soldiers (like Yarynich) developed and built an integrated system that would absolutely control their strategic nuclear forces. It ended up as a true Soviet system: rigid, hard-wired, with every box checking up on every other box. Deviant behavior, be it electrical or human, was to be reported to higher headquarters, with the deviant elements disconnected at once. The oddity of the design was the disconnect between the political leadership and the military general staff.

The presidential part of this system is now known as *Kazbek*. It pulls in warning and attack assessment information from the data fusion center at Solnechnogorsk (*Krokus*); it displays the data and offers up options on the president's terminal (the *Cheget*); and it then disseminates decisions to the general staff. The *Cheget* is a standard, hard-shell briefcase containing a laptop computer with a "special program" on its hard disk. It stays plugged into the *Kavkaz* communications net via cable, radio, and satellite antenna. *Kavkaz* maintains continuous communications between the president, the minister of defense, and the general staff, whether they were at the poolside, dacha, or office.

In theory, the president of Russia can sit down at his *Cheget*, punch in his password, and find out what's going on. In practical fact, the *Cheget* is operated by a "special officer" who carries it around and stays close to the president. By these means, the president of Russia is to sanction the use of nuclear weapons. The *Cheget* does not contain a

"Red Button." There is no electrical connection between the president's *Cheget* and the operational communication systems or the rockets. The presidential system can only deliver the "Permission Command," which includes the authenticating *Goschislo*, or "state number," to the military headquarters. In Brezhnev's time the *Goschislo* was thought to be his birthday so he could remember it.

This Permission Command from the president does become the basis for the "Direct Command" flowing from the general staff to the troops, but the general staff can shoot (or not shoot) regardless of any physical action taken by the president. Yarynich reports, and several other retired officers confirm, that at the time of the attempted coup in August 1991, as the American government worried about Soviet nuclear anarchy, the Soviet nuclear force commanders took matters into their own hands. They agreed to conduct no nuclear operations without mutual agreement among themselves as to the rationality of such orders. In effect, the Soviet general staff disconnected the presidential *Cheget*, and they are proud of that fact.

Once the staffs of the SRF, air force, and navy decide to commence operations, they prepare the Direct Command, which is pumped out to the forces via two different systems. It gets to the SRF via *Signal*, traversing the whole system automatically in about fifteen seconds. The air force bases and navy communication facilities receive the Direct Command through the *KSBU* system. These Direct Commands unblock the weapons and identify which war plan is to be executed.

Signal is at the heart of the Russian strategic nuclear security system. It consists of reliable and redundant communications nets, keyboards, and screens all organized to send the Direct Command down and to receive acknowledgments back up at great speed. At every level these orders are compared with numbers located inside hard-wired authenticators. These authenticators, known as "code blocking devices," are the size of egg cartons and are delivered directly to, and are installed into, the machines at corps, division, and regimental headquarters by couriers from the general staff and the main staff of the SRF. If the electronic orders coming down match the authenticator, they are passed along. If not, there is an immediate report-back, delivered all the way up to SRF headquarters and the general staff, and the system will shut down. In the event of tampering, there are algorithms which feed back reports to the SRF main staff and the general staff in real time. If a marauder or hacker tries to access *Signal* to read an incoming message, the system will erase that message, send a notification back up the chain of command, then block all downward messages.

In the thirty-five years since the Cuban missile crisis, the scientists at NPO Impuls and the soldiers of the Soviet Army have continually modernized that system. *Signal* gave way to *Signal-M*, then *Signal-A*. *Vyuga* radio and satellite links have been added. *Perimetr* relieves the need for hair-trigger response to a perceived attack, an action sometimes known as "launch on warning." *Perimetr* allows the military commanders to wait until there is unambiguous evidence of nuclear detonations on Russian soil before being required to act.

These and other assurances built into the electronics, hardware, and rocket force procedures have made an accidental, unauthorized, or irrational Russian launch a virtual impossibility. Things are now beginning to fall apart, but for the duration of the Cold War the scientists and soldiers, like Vladimir Petoukhov and Valery Yarynich, dedicated their lives to preventing the escape of the nuclear genie. They did their job well.

AMERICAN SSBN OPERATIONS

On the other side of the world, most of America's nuclear firepower is carried aboard its fleet of ballistic-missile-firing submarines, known as SSBNs. In theory, the decision to unleash that nuclear deterrent can only be made by the President of the United States. That may be the individual elected a few years earlier, or it may be his Vice-President or another successor who escaped the destruction of the White House in some awful confrontation or terrorist surprise.

He communicates with his nuclear forces—the submarines, bombers, and land-based missiles—through the communications system organized and managed by the Joint Chiefs of Staff. The President selects a nuclear option, conveys that decision to the military representative always at his side with the nuclear briefcase known as "the football," and the decision is pumped through the World Wide Military Command and Control System directly to the unit commanders, the boat skippers, bomber pilots, and launch control officers. The transmission is known as an Emergency Action Message, or EAM.

The validity of the EAM is confirmed by an authentication code, carried by the President and his constitutional successors. Copies of the authenticators are carried in the submarines, on the bombers, and in vaults of the missile launch control centers, with no one person ever having sole access to them. EAMs are not chatty newsgrams as depicted in the movies. They are a string of letters and numbers, which, taken together, tell the boat commander that it is truly the President speaking, that he wishes to execute option X (a total retaliation against a nuclear superpower or a single weapon against an aggressor), and that he wishes the attack to commence at a certain E-hour. The latter is important because nuclear war plans constitute an intricate ballet of complimentary forces.

Aboard the SSBNs it is not likely that an EAM would be received out of the blue. As world crises develop, the Department of Defense raises its forces to higher levels of alert, or DEFCON levels. Submarines are in continuous contact with their naval communications stations, receiving messages over the Very Low Frequency (VLF) or Extra Low Frequency (ELF) net. If communication is lost, the submarines will come to periscope depth to listen for messages, including the awful EAM, from satellites or standard shortwave. An EAM is first received in the radioroom aboard an SSBN. Upon receipt, the radioman immediately announces that fact: "We have an EAM." Another communicator confirms the message. When hearing the alarm, the officer of the deck brings the boat to launch depth and begins readiness procedures. At the same time, the communicators bring the EAM to the captain. He and his executive officer proceed to the captain's cabin, where there is a red safe within a gray safe, each with its own combination dial. The exec opens the first or outer vault door with the memorized combination known only to him, then the captain opens the inner door with his different combination. In the vault they find the sealed authenticator card, known as "the cookie" and the "Permission to Fire" key. Together, the captain and exec break open the cookie and compare the string of letters on the card inside with those on the EAM received. If they match it's a "go."

As Director of Telecommunications in the Office of the Secretary of Defense, I oversaw the manufacture and the very closely guarded distribution of those plastic laminated cards by the National Security Agency. For all the power it reflects, the nuclear authenticator looks just like a bank ATM card, carefully sealed in plastic. Upon confirmation of the valid EAM, the captain orders the weapons officer and his assistant to start the countdowns, for execution at the E-hour specified in the EAM. These two men ready the launchers, pressurize the launch tubes, spin up the gyros, and do all the things necessary to launch. The two weapons officers retrieve their firing key from their own separate safe within a safe, and in practical fact they must agree that the orders they have received from the captain and the executive officer make sense. Those officers are located on a different level of the ship from the control room.

The captain now holds the Permission to Fire key which he took from the two-door safe. If he inserts it into the lock and turns it, he can give the Permission to Fire order. The computers give the actual orders to each missile once the launch sequence is started, the Permission to Fire key has been inserted and turned, and the firing key is held closed by the weapons officer.

In the 1960s some options available to the President would have resulted in the launch of only one or a few of the sixteen missiles aboard a *Polaris* submarine, perhaps because a war in Europe had "gone nuclear," or a terrorist state made good on a threat to attack New York. The Navy in general, and submarine skippers in particular, do not like such options because they give away the boat's location. Today, in a world constantly orbited by surveillance satellites, the skipper of a boat launching missiles or anything else must anticipate an immediate counterattack. For that reason, the *Polaris* boats could have fired their entire load of sixteen missiles in less than four minutes.

The boat skippers do not know at which targets they are shooting, although they could figure it out from the target tapes if they wanted to. The target coordinates for various options are installed while in port, with the capability to change them at sea if so directed. A Polaris skipper in the 1960s, executing a legitimate EAM, would be sending sixteen nuclear warheads on their way. The keys to such an Armageddon lay in the hands of America's submariners. They were supposed to open their vaults and extract the Permission to Fire key only upon receipt of authentic instructions from the President, but the skipper and his exec had the physical ability to do so any time they jointly decided that the world situation merited such action.

KEN CARR AND BOB AUSTIN

Long ago and far away, during World War II, submarines crept into Purvis Bay only at night. There were no lights and no docks to welcome them. But neither were there Japanese aircraft or destroyers to bother them. Purvis Bay was a deserted cove in the Florida Islands, around the coast from Tulagi and across the sound from Guadalcanal. Since snorkels and nuclear power had not been invented, the American submarine skippers had to surface to run their diesels and recharge their batteries. They could do so safely in Purvis Bay.

KEN CARR was then an eighteen-year-old seaman first class. He too was technically a skipper, coxswain of an LCVP (Landing Craft, Vehicle and Personnel). At thirty-six feet in length, the LCVP could carry a jeep or three dozen fully equipped men. Carr's crew consisted of an engineer, who operated the ramp and one of the .50 caliber machine guns, and one other deckhand. During those dark nights of 1943, Carr watched the American submarines come in from patrol. He watched them disappear again into the darkness of night and sea, and he knew then that those skippers had a real advantage. Only later would he hear the submariners' mantra: "There are only two kinds of ships: submarines and targets."

When the war ended, Carr came home to pursue his naval career via Annapolis. He graduated from the U.S. Naval Academy in 1949 with honors. He spent some time aboard a submarine during his Annapolis summers, but assignment to submarine duty required first qualifying as an officer of the deck underway on a surface ship. He served his first year as an ensign aboard the destroyer *Eversole* as the assistant gunnery officer. In the process, he earned his certification, so in June 1950 he was off to submarine school in New London. As part of the curriculum, a visionary young Navy captain named Hyman Rickover came to talk about the possibility of nuclear power plants driving submarines. Such boats could travel around the world unrefueled, staying underwater for months at a time. They would have power to spare, enough to manufacture oxygen out of seawater. There would be no need to surface, to expose oneself to the enemy, until returning to home port. It all sounded like Jules Verne and his fictional *Nautilus*, which traveled for 20,000 leagues under the sea, but Rickover made it sound real.

From school, Carr went to sea aboard the diesel submarine *Blackfin*. In 1953 he was selected for nuclear submarine duty. After three months of training ashore, he reported to Rickover's first nuclear-powered boat. It was aptly named the *Nautilus*. Carr served on the *Nautilus* for six years, with duty at sea interspersed with nuclear power training ashore. During those years, he built a reputation for calm leadership, the first requirement for command of a submarine. In 1960 he was posted to the *Scorpion*, another SSN, as its executive officer, the second in command.

With the arrival of the 1960s, another type of submarine appeared. The technology of nuclear power plants, sonar, and undersea navigation was married to the technology of ballistic missiles. The result was the Polaris missile-firing submarine. The first such SSBN, the *George Washington*, went on patrol in December 1960. On leaving the *Scorpion*, Carr was assigned to serve as the executive officer of the *James Monroe*, the fourteenth SSBN to be commissioned. One stunning legacy of the 1950s was the commissioning of one American SSBN every two months; forty-one such boats were built between 1960 and 1967.

Nuclear-powered hunter-killer submarines, known as SSNs, carry only torpedoes as their major weapon. They are hot rods, fighting ships designed to hunt down and destroy their quarry, be it surface or submarine. Their skippers are fighter pilots. SSBNs are different. Their objective is to remain unfindable at sea but always ready to launch their terrible payload. Their skippers are like B-2 aircraft commanders: methodical, smart, and highly focused. The SSBNs carry torpedoes for defense, but their role is to patrol quietly and undetected until receiving an order to fire. SSBNs typically run at 20 percent power. The early Polaris boats carried sixteen ballistic missiles. They would patrol in the Norwegian or Mediterranean Seas within striking range of the Soviet Union. By the mid-sixties the new A2 Polaris missiles could carry a thermonuclear warhead to a range of 1,500 nautical miles. The Polaris fleet was becoming a key part of America's nuclear deterrent.

Command of such arsenals was, and continues to be, an enormous responsibility, so the Navy applies the most stringent standards in selecting commanding officers for the SSBNs. A candidate has usually served as the skipper of something else, displaying the cool under pressure that is only evident when one has the responsibility of command at sea. He must have spent time on an SSBN, so there will be no novelty to the procedures. He must have been recommended by former SSBN skippers, and that recommendation approved by the Navy's Bureau of Personnel, with full access to all the candidate's files, and by the commander of the submarines in his proposed theater of operations (Atlantic or Pacific). There are some detail training requirements (computers, sonar, missile technology), and in those days the candidate had to have written an acceptable thesis on some aspect of submarine warfare. To complete his qualifications to command an SSBN, Carr was assigned to the new SSN *Flasher* as its prospective commanding officer. In 1966 he earned his first command as skipper of that boat.

Having passed through all of the gates, Commander Carr flew to

Spain in September 1967 to take command of the *John Adams*, SSBN 620. Submarines of the Atlantic Fleet were home-ported in New London, Connecticut, and Charleston, South Carolina, but they were forward-deployed to bases in Holy Loch, Scotland, and Rota, Spain, for more efficient access to their respective operating areas in the Norwegian and Mediterranean Seas. The *John Adams* was a new boat, huge by any standards. At 400 feet long, displacing 8,000 tons, it was larger than some World War II cruisers. It carried a crew of thirteen officers and 133 enlisted men. It also carried sixteen Polaris A2 missiles. When he took command, Carr found an experienced executive officer, Lieutenant Commander Robert Austin, already on board. It was the first time they had met.

BOB AUSTIN was five years younger than Carr. Austin's grandfather was a naval officer, one of the first to fly. He was the Navy's first test pilot, and he piloted an NC-3 aircraft on its first transatlantic flight. He educated young Bob about the challenges of life at sea with visits to the Smithsonian Museum. In high school, Bob thought about Annapolis, but his math teacher was not supportive. Family finances were not compatible with such ambition, and connections to nominating members of Congress were nonexistent. So Bob Austin enlisted. He was sent to electronics school, and while there, saw the notice about examinations for admission to the U.S. Naval Academy. The Secretary of the Navy holds seventy-five nominations for use in the selection of enlisted men. Bob did well on the entrance exams, entered the Naval Academy in 1950, and graduated four years later with distinction.

From there his career progressed up the same steps as Ken Carr's. In 1965, Austin was posted to the newly commissioned *John Adams* as its executive officer. He had been aboard two years by the time Carr assumed command. Entrusted with awesome responsibility for the security of Americans and the safety of all mankind, Carr and Austin formed a close team. For two patrols they would lurk beneath the sea, their fingers on the nuclear trigger that could unleash sixteen enormous nuclear weapons on the Soviet homeland.

If ever they had decided to shoot, with or without authority to do so, the target package for a U.S. Polaris A2 boat, operating in the eastern end of the Mediterranean Sea, might have included the early warning radars on Crimea; the headquarters of the Odessa Military District, an interceptor base in Southern Ukraine, the headquarters of the Black Sea Fleet in Sevastopol, the shipyards of Nikolayev, the military industries in Dnepropetrovsk, the rail and industrial center of Kharkov, and the Ukrainian capital city of Kiev. Having expended half of its war-heads on Ukraine, the *John Adams* target package could then have moved on to Belarus and Russia itself: Pervomaysk, Minsk, some inter-ceptor base on the ingress route in southern Russia, and the general staff headquarters at Chekov, fifty miles south of Moscow. The Soviet capital would be on every boat's hit list. Perhaps the *John Adams* would have been responsible for one shot at the city center and another at the ABM system defending Moscow. Lastly, one weapon might be assigned to the old monastery at Sarov. Stalin had assigned the mysterious name Arzamas-16 to that town when putting his first nuclear weapons design bureau there in 1945.

As a result of that one turn of the key, dozens of Russian and Ukrainian cities and towns could lie in ruins. Tens of millions of Soviet citizens would have died terrible deaths, and tens of millions more would be on the radioactive slide to a similar fate. The children would be gone. The heart of Mother Russia would be gone. The museums and icons, the great gate at Kiev, and the onion domes of St. Basil's all would have disappeared with the bunkers, airfields, docks, and power plants. And as he watched the incoming warheads on his *Krokus* warn-ing system, the General Secretary of the Communist Party of the So-viet Union would have reacted in kind.

The first evidence of a launch from the *John Adams* would have shown up on the Soviet radar at Mukachevo in Ukraine. These indica-tions would have been passed to the general staff in Moscow. Without asking for political approval, the general staff immediately would have passed the Preliminary Command to the nuclear forces; they would at once go to Combat Mode. At the same time, this indication of an American launch would have brought Brezhnev's military aide to his side with the *Cheget*. Faced with unambiguous evidence of an Ameri-can SSBN launching its entire load of *Polaris* missiles, with a significant number of them headed toward Moscow, and with only minutes to de-cide how best to protect the Soviet Union, Brezhnev might well have ordered a full retaliatory strike against the U.S. and its NATO allies. Those orders would have flashed through the Soviet military commu-nications network in seconds. Within half an hour of Brezhnev's Per-mission Command, much of the United States would lie in ruins.

All of this might have been, and the power to do it all lay in the red safe in Ken Carr's cabin aboard the *John Adams*. Ken Carr and Bob Austin to this day have no doubt they would have fired if they had re-ceived an authenticated EAM. Implied in their answers is the assumption that DEFCON levels or other world events would have made such an order credible. On the other hand, they never, ever, even thought about opening that red safe, to access its enclosed authentication card, on their own. They could have done it. They had the combinations in their heads, and with some forethought they might possibly have co-opted the communicators and the launch officers aboard ship. But they didn't. And neither did the officers aboard any other American SSBN at any time during any of the darkest days of the Cold War.

While at sea, Bob Austin often lay awake at night reflecting on how this whole system could go wrong. He could not conceive of any way. Austin had no doubt that if the President so ordered, he would shoot, but he could not conceive of how such a shot would be fired without presidential orders, and he was dedicated to keeping it that way.

Men and women like Ken Carr and Bob Austin, Vladimir Petoukhov and Valery Yarynich, were the real heroes of the Cold War. They kept their cool and they promoted or tolerated the collapse of the Soviet empire without a holocaust sweeping over the planet. People make mistakes, human beings get confused, and dictatorships usually don't give up without a bloodbath, but these men stood their ground be-tween thousands of nuclear weapons on one hand and the chaos of the Cold War everywhere else. They could have triggered the end of civili-zation, but they did not. They allowed the politicians time to coax the camel through the eye of the needle.

ON THE BEACH

The scary book of that title was written by Nevil Shute in 1957. Two years later it was made into a movie, starring Gregory Peck. It de-scribed the aftermath of a nuclear war that left only an American sub-marine and its crew to patrol the world, looking for signs of life. I thought about that title forty years later when I sat on the beach in La Jolla, California, with Petoukhov and Yarynich.

The three of us are in our sixties now, and we have become good friends. As we sat there with our feet in the Pacific Ocean, watching the sun go down and waiting for the green flash, I congratulated those two Russians on keeping the Soviet nuclear dogs of war on a very tight leash. They expressed similar sentiments about the submarines still out there somewhere. We toasted each other with California wine and Russian vodka, and we passed around pictures of our grandchildren.

CHAPTER 22

Closing Down

AMERICA'S STRATEGIC AIR COMMAND was the talisman of the Cold War. SAC was born at the time of Churchill's "Iron Curtain" speech. During the Cuban missile crisis and others to follow it was the B-47s and B-52s on alert that represented American nuclear muscle. Those alert facilities were the kennels where the dogs of nuclear war were fed and housed, chained but ever ready. The Cold War could not really be over until those kennels were closed down. That is what happened at Offutt Air Force Base on May 31, 1992.

THE STRATEGIC AIR COMMAND

Winston Churchill was the first to give the Soviet challenge a name. On March 5, 1946, he warned that "an iron curtain has descended across the continent" of Europe. A year later it was referred to as the "Cold War" during Congressional testimony by Bernard Baruch. On

June 24, 1948, it nearly became a hot war when the Soviet Union imposed a blockade on the western sectors of Berlin. The fledgling U.S. Air Force was called on to resupply that beleaguered city, and within a month the Soviets had moved forty divisions into eastern Germany. In response, the United States moved three air bombardment groups to Britain, allegedly accompanied by a significant portion of the U.S. A-bomb inventory. Managing this resupply of Berlin as well as the nuclear deployment was the Commander of the U.S. Air Forces in Europe, forty-two-year-old Lieutenant General Curtis LeMay.

LeMay spent the early part of World War II as a bomb group commander in the Pacific, but when early raids on the Japanese homeland produced only minimal results, he was installed as Commander of the XXI Bomber Command. By the end of the war he was Chief of Staff of the 20th Air Force, with primary responsibility for the destruction of the military and industrial power of Japan from the air. LeMay devised the firebomb raids that first destroyed Tokyo and then the other cities of Japan as a prelude to the A-bombing of Hiroshima and Nagasaki.

The Berlin airlift went on for a year before the Soviets folded, but by the end of 1948, LeMay had been recalled to the U.S. for a higher assignment. The events of 1948 made it clear that nuclear retaliation against the Soviet Union might become necessary, and that the Strategic Air Command must be the instrument of that threat. LeMay assumed command of SAC in November 1948. While the command had been in administrative existence for two years, he was appalled at its laxity. In later years he observed that, in 1948, "We didn't have one crew, *not one crew,* in the entire command who could do a professional job." During his nine years as Commander in Chief of SAC, LeMay instilled discipline and a sense of readiness in his men and developed a set of war plans that forged SAC into America's nuclear sword and shield.

Some historians say the Cold War ended when Gorbachev came to power in 1985, when the Berlin wall came down in 1989, or when the four allied powers signed the German reunification treaty in 1990. Some say it came with the events of 1991, when Boris Yeltsin was elected directly by his people as president of Russia, or when the coup failed, or when the white, blue, and red flag of Russia replaced the red hammer and sickle over the Kremlin. Those events were the death throes of the Soviet empire, but the war truly ended on May 31, 1992. On that rainy night in Omaha, Nebraska, the Strategic Air Command furled its colors, and that supreme symbol of the Cold War ceased to exist.

THE LAST DAYS OF THE CPSU

The Communist Party of the Soviet Union lost control with the abortive coup of August 1991. Boris Yeltsin, the politically born-again child of communism, moved in to fill the vacuum. Yeltsin enjoyed something new in Russia: political legitimacy. In June 1991 he was elected president of Russia in a free and open election. Armed with this mandate, Yeltsin met with his fellow (also freely elected) presidents of Ukraine and Belarus in a hunting lodge outside Minsk. On December 7 and 8, 1991, they declared their countries to be no longer part of the Soviet Union. They invented a political fig leaf called the Confederation of Independent States to cover their departure. Within two weeks eleven other Republics of the Soviet Union (all but Stalin's Georgia) met in Alma Ata to sign the Commonwealth Declaration. By doing so, they ended the Union of Soviet Socialist Republics. Gorbachev made it official on Christmas Day, December 25, 1991, as he turned over the nuclear *Cheget* to the president of Russia.

Newly empowered, President Yeltsin authorized an even faster reverse arms race by agreeing to a whole package of arms reductions that were to become the START II treaty. It became clear to U.S. political leaders that the Cold War really was drawing to a close. There was no longer a need for its principal instrumentality, the Strategic Air Command. In April 1992, Secretary of Defense Cheney signed the orders that would transfer planning and management of America's nuclear deterrent to a new triservice Strategic Command. A Navy admiral would soon take over, and the bombers would be returned to the operational Air Force. The closedown of SAC was set for May 31, 1992, forty-six years after its birth.

THE END OF SAC

The events of May 31 drew quite a crowd. SAC headquarters were moved from the Washington area to Omaha, Nebraska, in 1948 when LeMay first took over. Nebraska was equidistant from the two American coasts. Fort Crook, an old cavalry post and then a World War II airplane factory, was chosen for SAC's headquarters perhaps because of its geography or perhaps because of the enthusiasm of that town's citizens.

Their clout in Washington may have diverted the headquarters from its intended move to Colorado. The record is not clear.

In any case, the 1948 Host Committee wanted SAC in Omaha, and some of its members were still around in May 1992 to celebrate the American victory. They were the people who had raised the money to restore the historic buildings and build the local amenities. They were proud of their Air Force. Military retirees were there, reminiscing about the good old days. Young warriors now on duty were all around: the pilots, navigators, electronic systems operators, ground crews, and supporting staff who kept those planes in the air, armed and safe. And the retired generals were on hand, including several former Commanders in Chief of SAC. One of them was General Richard Ellis.

Ellis had graduated from college in the summer of 1941 and entered the Army Air Corps as an aviation cadet. In April 1942 he received his wings and his commission and was off to the South Pacific. Once there, he flew over two hundred missions, night and day, with the Third Bombardment Group from bases in Australia, New Guinea, and then the Philippines. Two and a half years after earning his wings and gold bars, he assumed command of the Third Bombardment Group with the rank of Lieutenant Colonel, at age twenty-four. In April 1945 he was promoted to Colonel and became Deputy Chief of Staff of the Far East Air Force, at age twenty-five. When the war was over he came home, married, completed law school, and settled down to the quiet practice of law in Wilmington, Delaware. But not for long.

Korea changed life for a lot of reservists. An America that had blindly disarmed after World War II now had to scramble for planes and pilots. Dick Ellis was recalled to active duty, to take charge of training bomber crews for the Tactical Air Command. When the smoke cleared, he decided to stay in the Air Force, spending his time in Europe and Washington. He spent seventeen years in the grade of Colonel, not earning his first general's star until 1962. When I became Secretary of the Air Force in 1976, Dick Ellis was Commander in Chief of U.S. Air Forces in Europe. At the end of my tour I had the opportunity to reassign the general officers. I chose Dick Ellis to be Commander in Chief of the Strategic Air Command.

That was neither a routine nor a conventional decision, for SAC was more than just another Air Force command. It was a culture, actually a religion, worshiping the legacy of Curtis LeMay. SAC's commanders always had come from within that culture, with years in the cockpits of

B-47s or B-52s. Despite that precedent, I chose Ellis, a B-26 pilot from the Tactical Air Command, because he had been in a real war, flying real missions, dropping real bombs on real enemy troops who fired back with real bullets, and he had done all that with distinction.

The active duty officer presiding that evening was the then-current Commander in Chief of SAC, General Lee Butler, who had been assigned to Omaha a year before. He arrived with enough vision to recognize the end of the Cold War, enough courage to stand down the no-longer-needed SAC, and enough sense to provide this closure for the men, women, and families who had given their all for SAC, their Air Force, and their country.

There was brass from Washington in attendance. General Merrill McPeak, the Air Force chief of staff, spoke, but America's most visible general of the day, Colin Powell, stole the show. "No gloating" had been the elder President Bush's guideline as the Cold War wound down. He knew that deference to the defeated foe was the key to a peaceful surrender from the Soviet empire. But in the privacy of Omaha, as the Cold War ended, Powell could tell it like it was. The general was Chairman of the Joint Chiefs of Staff at the time. He came to Omaha on that historic day to pronounce a benediction on the Strategic Air Command:

> *"The long bitter years of the Cold War are over. America and her allies have won; totally, decisively, and overwhelmingly. . . . So thank you SAC. Job well done. Enjoy your retirement."*

The crowd included the civilian defense leadership. The men and women who serve as the secretaries and the assistant secretaries of the Air Force provide that unique American link in the chain of command that leads up from the warriors to the elected President and Congress and thus to the people themselves. I was one such observer in Omaha that night. I was enormously proud of all those people on the tarmac: the old men and women huddled under umbrellas, the generals to whom terrible responsibility had been entrusted, and the young men and women now on parade. The ceremonies began around 11:00 P.M., and the rain started about the same time. That was just as well, because the tears flowing down the cheeks of so many grown men and women would have been unseemly had they been noticed.

THE AIRBORNE COMMAND POST

The band, the stage, and the huge airplane all were inside the E-4 hangar, a maintenance building that swallowed up the immaculately white Boeing 747 with blue Air Force trim and insignia. It made a stunning and appropriate backdrop for the show to come.

That aircraft was known formally as the National Emergency Airborne Command Post, or NEACP. It was built during Cold War days to serve as the final message center for Armageddon, the "office" that could unleash the holocaust. Lifting off from a dispersed airfield when warning was received, the NEACP was to orbit in the central United States, collecting authority from the President or sheltering his successor on board. Its size was used to accommodate offices, conference rooms, message centers, sleeping accommodations, and dining facilities for the politicians as they struggled to contain whatever crisis was crushing down on mankind. Communications gear of every type tied the entire U.S. government into one movable and hopefully safe nerve center. The NEACP could stay airborne for days with in-flight refueling.

If all those political efforts failed and the awful decision to fire nuclear weapons had been made, then the NEACP was to distribute the Emergency Action Message, over and over, to every missile silo, every bomber, and every ship at sea. Hundreds of millions of deaths and the dark of nuclear winter would have followed from that string of digits leaving the aircraft through the little satellite antenna on the roof and the mile-long Very Low Frequency (VLF) antenna trailing behind.

With the end of the Cold War, the NEACP changed its name. That fleet of aircraft became known as the National Airborne Operations Center. One of them follows the President on his world travels, and they stand by to take charge if a terrorist blows up a key piece of the American government or infrastructure. But in 1992 it was the harbinger of Armageddon, a most fitting backdrop for the closing down of SAC. The audience stood outside, under the canopy of night that had provided a welcome cover of darkness for so many missions. We were out there so we could see the flyover of a B-1 bomber and so we would not miss the grand fireworks display at the end of the show. On cue, the band started to play. The lights went down outside and went up inside the hangar.

FIVE AIRMEN WHO GAVE THEIR ALL

As the ceremonies unfolded, five airmen walked onto a dimly lit and fog-shrouded stage. They were stand-ins in combat uniforms, there to represent five officers and enlisted who gave their all for SAC, their country, and our safety. One by one the announcer called out a name, a date of birth, and the date and circumstances of death.

The first name called was that of a U-2 pilot lost over Cuba in 1962. He represented all the men who sought out the intelligence needed by national leaders and unit commanders to plan, decide, and act in our nation's defense. In the early days, they were the RB-47 crews who often disappeared into the darkness of Russia on unannounced forays. Later, they were the U-2 pilots who flew for SAC or the CIA. They mapped the heartland of the Soviet Union and spotted the missiles in Cuba. Later still, they were the SR-71 pilots who raced across continents at altitudes and speeds that left petty tyrants wondering, What was that?

The second name was a missile-launch control officer lost in a fire at Minot Air Force Base in 1984. From the beginning of the missile age, the liquid-fueled and very dangerous Atlas and Titan missiles occasionally claimed the lives of their keepers. The underground complexity of Minuteman silos and launch control centers became fiery tombs for others.

The third name called was that of a KC-135 refueling boom operator, a sergeant lost in a fiery midair collision over California in 1985. The men who flew and operated those 30,000 gallon tanks of aviation fuel were aboard flying bombs. They risked their lives every day of the Cold War.

The fourth hero was an electronics technician, a young girl killed in Riyadh in 1990. She stood for all the men and women who served at bases thought to be secure, but that often came under attack, by Viet Cong rockets, Iraqi scuds, or terrorist truck bombs.

And lastly there was the B-52 navigator lost over Hanoi in 1972. He was honored on behalf of all the men who disappeared in fireballs over their targets or at the end of their runways.

The audience stood. The band played the "Battle Hymn of the Republic." Everyone else was silent until the theater's fog enveloped the stage and the five were gone.

By now it was pouring rain. Aides scurried about with umbrellas. I thought about my three children and why I, like so many others in so many different ways, had fought the Cold War. Those kids were babies or not yet born when America rode to the nuclear precipice over Cuba. If worse had come to worst, they would not have understood why the house was on fire. They were unruly teenagers when the Soviet Union achieved nuclear parity. To them, the Mideast war of 1973 meant gas lines, not a nuclear alert to DEFCON 3. They were busy college students when men with strange accents and ominous messages called to interrupt the family's dinner. And now they were grown adults. None of them would have to wear the uniform unless they wanted to. None of them would see their buddies disappear in those awful balls of fire. In a few years their children would ask, "What was the Cold War all about?"

What a happy ending. Just before midnight the fireworks began. The Strategic Air Command furled its colors, and at that moment that enormous symbol of American nuclear power ceased to exist. The bombers were off alert, the missiles were targeted at the open ocean. In that pouring rain this former lieutenant, now also a former Air Force secretary, stood—too proud to take refuge under an umbrella and far too proud of those men and women to drop the salute until the show was over.

On the other side of the world it was morning in Moscow. The white, blue, and red flag of the Russian Federation snapped in the breeze over a very different Kremlin.

EPILOGUE

A HALF CENTURY HAS NOW PASSED since Dwight Eisenhower set the course for America's passage through the Cold War. Upon his ascension to power, the retired general wisely forswore immediate confrontation with the Soviet Union, even though we were then at war in Korea with two Soviet client states. He opted for an immediate truce, followed by a reliance on the inherent strengths of a free and just society to pull America through to victory. To protect the economic engine that had proved so powerful during World War II, Eisenhower needed, authorized, and was willing to support an entirely new intelligence regime. The results, often purchased with the lives of dedicated airmen, sailors, and spooks, allowed the new President to limit, but allocate with precision, his nation's defense expenditures.

In making these decisions, Eisenhower turned to the scientific community for advice, the first American President to do so in such a deliberate fashion. He then developed his budgets in consonance with that advice. Some of the new technologies were lethal (thermonuclear) and some benign (space), but all represented a sharp departure from the reliance on land armies and naval power favored by the President's old comrades in arms. The resulting defense posture came to be known as the "new look." Its reliance on nuclear weapons allowed the American economy to compete with and ultimately overwhelm a highly focused but terribly inefficient police state. Along the way, we all had to live at the edge of the nuclear abyss; the possible use of nuclear weapons, as a quick fix or a last resort, was always on the table.

During the three decades and seven administrations that followed, U.S. reliance on technology continued and blossomed. At the end,

American military power, based on those investments and shaped by the lessons of Vietnam, was overwhelming. The demonstration of that power in the Gulf War of 1991 was a coup de grace to the collapsing Soviet empire.

GENERAL DVORKIN'S PERSPECTIVE

Vladimir Dvorkin was the very model of a modern Soviet officer—a stern, athletic, and well-disciplined cold warrior, dedicated to the defeat of American imperialism. He was one of our most determined adversaries, his steely dark eyes a fright to those of us across the negotiating table. At the same time, he was one of the USSR's most responsible and intellectually honest citizens, counseling his government against nuclear adventures at every opportunity. A graduate of the Soviet Naval Officers' School, Dvorkin spent his early years developing sea-launched missiles. Reassigned to the new Soviet Strategic Rocket Force at its inception in 1962, he spent the next forty years in its service, capping his career with command of the Fourth Central Research Institute of the Ministry of Defense—the systems engineering, hardware development, and production arm of the Strategic Rocket Force. Rising to the rank of major general, Dvorkin was the keeper of the nuclear muscle that had become the mainstay of Soviet military power.

In 1997, with the Cold War behind us, General Dvorkin invited me to visit the sprawling, campuslike headquarters of his command on the outskirts of Moscow. I was only the third American to enjoy that hospitality. It was an impressive day, not just for the range of hardware in the inevitable museum, nor for the intellect on display around the conference table. It was the integrity and professionalism of the staff that left its mark. The Soviet hammer and sickle were gone from the woodwork in Dvorkin's office, replaced by the double-headed eagle of the Russian Federation, now etched into the glass doors of his personal bookcase. Dvorkin had become a trusted member of the new Yeltsin team. It was from that aerie that he had watched the Gulf War unfold.

Dvorkin is now retired, running a think tank for the Russian Ministry of Defense. In reflecting upon the Gulf War and the war in Iraq twelve years later, the general recently observed, publicly: "The obsolete structure of the Russian armed forces has to be urgently changed. The gap between our capabilities and those of the Americans has been revealed, and it is vast.★ We are very lucky that Russia has no major enemies at the moment, but the future is impossible to predict, and we must be ready." Translation: the Russian bear has not gone into hibernation.

AN ISLAND IN THE ARCTIC

Vast herds of beautiful white polar bears roam the islands of Novaya Zemlya, a northern extension of Russia's Ural Mountains. My Russian friends show me pictures of those creatures peering into the windows of Red Army trucks. They tell me of Soviet GIs arriving from the mainland and losing an arm or worse to those hungry hulks, thinking them to be cuddly toys. But Novaya Zemlya is more than an Arctic zoo; it is a nuclear test range, the only one still under the control of the Russian Federation, and today it is a busy place. Although Russia is supposed to be in the grip of economic crisis, and although nuclear weapons are supposed to be passé, I am told by my Russian friends that every summer now brings a migration of scientists, from the nuclear weapons laboratories at Sarov (Arzamas-16) and Snezhinsk (Chelyabinsk-70), to the barren wastes of Novaya Zemlya. The visitors deploy dozens of trailers, miles of cabling, and thousands of workers around excavations into that Arctic tundra.

During the heady days of 1992, when U.S. and Russian nuclear weapons lab directors were exchanging visits and toasts, our Russian counterparts proposed the joint development of large spherical chambers capable of withstanding and containing thirty-ton explosions. The Russians told us their interest lay in creating artificial diamonds, but we suspected otherwise. Such spheres would be most useful in testing just barely critical nuclear assemblies, be they stand-alone primaries or energy sources for sophisticated secondary designs.

It now appears our fears were well-founded; I believe the Russians are burying such test chambers at Novaya Zemlya, using them to contain the debris from low-yield nuclear tests. Such tests might be part of a program to assure the reliability of existing stockpiled weapons, or

---

★ After the Gulf War, Russian officials or individuals exported a half dozen GPS jammers into Iraq. These systems were intended to disable the American Global Positioning Satellite system and thus degrade the performance of U.S. smart weapons. It was a nice try, but to no avail. During the 2003 war in Iraq, the Soviet GPS jammers all failed and were destroyed, one by a GPS-guided weapon.

tests of very low yield designs needed to attack the deeply buried assets of threatening powers, or they may be precursors of a nuclear technology we do not yet understand.

The United States chose to celebrate the end of the Cold War by closing down any further investigation of nuclear weapon technology; Russia may not have taken such a vow of nuclear celibacy. Could they have torn a page from Eisenhower's playbook, opting for a twenty-first century nuclear new look while rebuilding their once communist and still mismanaged economies? Nuclear-driven electromagnetic pulse or directed-energy weapons offer an interesting response to America's electronic dominance of the battlefield. The Russian nuclear bear has not gone away, nor has the duplicity that characterized the Cold War years. In Russia fear of the old KGB is back, a different class of gangster rules, and Russian scientists now commute from Sarov to Novaya Zemlya and Tehran on a regular basis.

THE OTHER NUCLEAR CANDIDATES

Iraq is one of the oil-rich states of the Middle East. That fact draws American attention, not because Western oil companies covet the production—which they do.★ Our global concern is that petrodollars, flowing to dictators with more money than sense, can fuel mischief on a scale unreachable by other third world despots. Fifty to sixty million dollars *a day*, flowing to Iraq when it restores full production, could have supported a lot of nuclear research, industrial development, and terrorist field work.

Why have we granted the petrodollar despots this control over our lives? That is a central question for this new century, and it is the reason I joined James Schlesinger in 1977 in organizing a new U.S. Department of Energy (DOE). We envisioned an energy policy that would wean the United States, if not the Western world, from its dependence

---

★ Access to Arab-world oil is no longer a windfall to the major oil companies. Big money is still involved, but terms must now be negotiated with sharp oil ministers trained in the West. The major U.S. and European oil companies are invited into the OPEC countries because those nations want, and are willing to pay for, the technology and reservoir engineering skills of the majors. These companies often suffer enormous losses when the political winds change or corrupt officials prevail. We consumers ultimately reimburse those costs.

on Middle Eastern crude. That has not happened because oil is not a commodity—it is a narcotic. Americans are neither willing to make rational choices nor to accept energy-conservation tax policies if any of those strictures interfere with their daily low-cost energy fix. Every one cent of an expanded federal gasoline tax would add a billion dollars to the annual federal revenue stream. Gasoline taxes at the European level could solve the Social Security and Medicare deficits in one stroke while encouraging energy independence within our lifetime. But Congress has no stomach for such action. The DOE has spun off into irrelevance; "pump more oil" seems to be our only energy policy. And so, in time, our children will pay the terrible price. The continuing imbalance of payments to pay for this oil will one day burn through the dollar's thick skin. The buildup of cash in the hands of nuclear wannabes could one day vaporize a major city.

This petrodollar funding of terror escalated to the big time in the 1980s. The 1974 and 1979 spikes in oil prices gave Saddam Hussein the wherewithal to start work on a nuclear capability. Central to his hopes was the Osirak reactor, built by the French (Saddam's longtime covert ally) at his atomic city of Tuwaitha. The Israelis saw this project for what it was: a plutonium producer and a threat to their survival. On June 7, 1981, they took action. Dozens of Israeli F-16s bombed Osirak into oblivion, with no Israeli losses. There was a great international outcry at the time, but in private President Reagan was unconcerned.

As a result of that raid, Saddam learned to be more discreet. By 1991 he had reconstituted his nuclear program, producing enriched uranium with outdated and energy-profligate equipment. These drawbacks were not a problem to Saddam; he had plenty of energy, and the oddity of the equipment made its purchase unnoticeable in the West. During that year's Gulf War, Tuwaitha was bombed again, this time by the Americans. Postwar inspections revealed both uranium enrichment hardware and crates of documentation, all supporting a massive nuclear weapons program. Today much of that know-how remains within the heads of the Iraqi scientific community. According to recently defecting Iraqi scientists, specific plans and key pieces of equipment still lie buried in their gardens, hidden for use another day.

The question remains, to what end all this effort? Studies conducted after the 1991 war suggested the most effective use of one Iraqi nuke would have been to attack the American port facilities in Saudi Arabia. The logistics pipeline would have been destroyed; the Americans would have been outgunned and starved in the Iraqi desert.

But I believe the most politically useful blast would have been a test in space, lofted straight up by an Iraqi Scud and detonated well above the Iraqi desert. Such a shot would have burnt out the electronics in most U.S.—and other nations'—satellites; it would have reminded our then-allies, from London to Riyadh, of their vulnerability to nuclear black-mail; and Saddam could claim to be a peaceful scientist, conducting a test over his own territory "for research purposes." An Iraq armed with even a few nuclear weapons would have changed the balance of power in the world. Nations whose capitals lay within nuclear Scud range would have lost interest in standing up to Saddam; his army's march to take over half the world's oil supply could have proceeded unopposed.

Iran is another Middle Eastern state with too many petrodollars and not enough caution. Their mullahs also learned the lesson of Osirak: when developing a nuclear capability, keep a low profile. The Iranians are pursuing a stealth weapons program, operating just inside the strictures of the Nuclear Non-Proliferation Treaty. The Iranian nuclear program, funded at a reported $800 million level, is buying technology and hardware from the Russian Federation. Most of those equipment purchases are aboveboard, and the Russian government denies any weapons intent, but other Russians visiting Iran are freelance experts, refugees from the disintegrating Soviet weapons labs. And at the same time, the Iranians are completing flight tests of their own ballistic missile (Shahab-3) with a range in excess of 800 miles, a one-ton payload, and a genealogy that runs back to North Korea, China, and Russia.

There is little to prevent the Iranians from abandoning their NNPT commitments and going nuclear on short notice. It is essential that the West not tolerate a nuclear-armed Iran; it is a healthy sign that the UN Security Council supports that view. The now-deceased Ayatollah Ruhollah Khomeini was the spiritual leader (and chief executioner) of the 1979 Iranian revolution. His heirs are the men building a nuclear state. Yet Khomeini's grandson (Sayyid Hussein Khomeini) now travels the Persian Gulf urging the formation of moderate and modern non-sectarian governments. With a little luck, these reformers in Iran will remove the anti-Western ideologues from power before irreparable harm is done. If not, a nuclear-armed Muslim theocracy in Iran will have the Middle East and much of southern Russia in its crosshairs. Should we expect the Israelis to view such a development with equanimity? Not likely.

North Korea is a stranger yet equally dangerous case. A psychotic second-generation dictator is starving his people in order to support a two-track nuclear weapons program. In the beginning, Kim Jong Il built a plutonium-producing reactor at Yongbyon. By the end of the eighties that reactor may have delivered enough metal for one or two A-bombs. In the spring of 1994, Bill Perry's Pentagon developed plans for an Osirak-like strike on Yongbyon. Such an attack would have collapsed the reactor and entombed all of the plutonium then in production without a Chernobyl-like radioactive plume downwind. That plan was not executed in part because of fears of the North Korean response: an invasion of the South, starting with a massive artillery and missile barrage aimed at Seoul. The U.S. feared casualties might reach a hundred thousand.

On the positive side, the North Koreans did agree to an eight-year nuclear truce known as the Agreed Framework. That time-out is now over; Kim Jong Il has expanded his nuclear weapons program to include a uranium enrichment facility suitable for the production of Hiroshima-type gun-assembly A-bombs. On top of that, high explosive test facilities seem to be under construction at Youngdoktong.

What is this man's objective? Perhaps he envisions North Korea as the arsenal of autocracy. Sales of crude nuclear weapons—to petrodollar-funded terrorists or to other nations holding both copious oil supplies and anti-American grudges—could fund an economic recovery in North Korea and a comfortable life for its reclusive dictator. Negotiations with that regime, in concert with its patrons and neighbors—China, Japan, South Korea, and Russia—would seem to be the first line of defense. There is much economic relief to be gained for the peasants of North Korea if such an accommodation could be reached, but the U.S. must be prepared to deal forcefully with North Korea if our partners do not. Former Secretary of Defense Perry thinks the North Koreans may soon actually test a device.

The good news is that the nuclear horizon is not all dark. Brazil and Argentina, the South American equivalents of India and Pakistan, once started down their own nuclear paths, but cooler heads prevailed. Their weapons options were buried at a presidential summit at Iguazu Falls on November 28, 1990. At that time, the presidents of Argentina and Brazil agreed to allow only peaceful uses of nuclear energy in their countries, and they established the machinery to assure the execution of that policy. Those countries are now trying to cope with the aftermath of corrupt and inefficient governments, but at least their recoveries are not burdened by nuclear paranoia.

In the early 1970s the apartheid government of South Africa was well on its way to a nuclear capability. It saw itself as a beleaguered state, surrounded by enemies; it felt a kinship with a similarly surrounded Israel, a nation with which it shared a long and mysterious nuclear relationship. Then, on July 30, 1977, a Soviet satellite passing over South Africa noticed test preparations at the Vastrap military facility in the Kalahari Desert. On August 6 another Soviet satellite made similar observations. Even though the U.S. and the USSR were locked in a life-and-death Cold War struggle, Moscow alerted Washington to its findings. The United States took its own look, then sent a strong warning to Pretoria: nuclear testing would lead to severe consequences. Paris, Bonn, and London followed suit. Within a few months the underground facilities at Vastrap were sealed shut.

Two years later, on September 22, 1979, a U.S. *Vela* satellite detected what most of us believe to have been a nuclear explosion in the South Atlantic Ocean. The politically correct explanation put forth by the Carter administration's Ruina Commission in 1980: a small meteorite had hit the satellite, triggering spurious signals in the process. But in time the truth came out:

- The U.S. Naval Research Laboratory took the position that an acoustic signal, detected on September 22, 1979, was consistent with a small nuclear explosion on, or slightly under, the ocean's surface. An underwater shot would have masked much of the fallout evidence from such a test.

- A postmark from correspondence mailed aboard the *S.A. Agulmas* operating off Gough Island, 1600 miles east of Capetown, South Africa on October 5, 1979, includes a graphic of wavy lines and the inscription, "Neutron Research."

- On April 20, 1997, the Deputy Foreign Minister of the Republic of South Africa (Aziz Pahad) officially confirmed that the flare detected by the *Vela* satellite in September 1979, was from a nuclear test, conducted by the previous government of South Africa, as part of a joint venture with Israel. The latter helped South Africa with bomb technology in exchange for 550 tons of uranium ore and "other assistance."

The lesson for today's world: governments tend to disguise and discount inconvenient intelligence.

At any rate, as the winds of change began to blow across South

Africa, the Botha government decided to disassemble and abandon its nuclear weapons program. South Africa became a signatory to the Nuclear Non-Proliferation Treaty of 1991; its stand-down from nuclear ambitions was confirmed by very intrusive UN inspectors.

Ukraine, Kazakhstan, and Belarus all inherited thousands of nuclear weapons as the Soviet Union collapsed. The end of that empire came with such speed, there was neither time nor authority for the Russian government to recall those weapons to central storage. Over 1,900 nukes lay atop rockets buried in Ukraine. There were an equivalent number of tactical weapons on the Belarus border with Poland. A full nuclear test facility with weapons in storage lay in Kazakhstan. In addition, warehouses full of weapons-grade uranium fuel disks, refined for a Soviet submarine fleet no longer operational, lay unattended around the shattered empire.

None of those newly sovereign states possessed the technical infrastructure to secure or maintain those weapons and materials, and nukes are not pieces of stone one can leave in the garage, untended for a decade. Batteries must be recharged, key materials and components monitored and replaced. On top of that, Soviet nuclear weapons were not inherently safe; enriched uranium storage was not secure. There were fears that these three republics, spun off from the former Soviet Union, might wish to keep their nukes, to join the nuclear club.

The first of these, Ukraine, initially announced plans to do just that. Their weapons would have been cared for by technical institutes in Kharkov, some of which I had a chance to visit. With carrots and sticks, the U.S. brokered a deal to return those weapons to Russia in exchange for the fuel rods needed to keep Ukraine's nuclear power plants running. Such help was desperately needed. After the collapse of the Soviet Union, Ukraine had virtually no domestic source of power other than its nuclear reactors. The deal worked; by the end of June 1996 the Russians confirmed that all the nuclear weapons in Ukraine had come home. The bad news is that the provided fuel rods kept the surviving reactors at Chernobyl on line far longer than anyone wished.

Another republic, Kazakhstan, was wealthy enough, with large oil reserves, to stand on its own two feet. For over forty-two years Kazakhstan had been the home of the principal Soviet nuclear test site at Semipalatinsk. Given the Soviet disregard for environmental matters, nuclear testing there had taken a terrible toll on the lives and health of the Kazakh people. The new government wanted all things nuclear out of the country as soon as possible. When the president of Kazakhstan found out about a stash of highly enriched uranium on his territory, he called the U.S. President to ask for help.

On November 23, 1994, a U.S. Air Force C-5 aircraft took off from the Kazakh town of Ust-Kamenogorsk in the greatest of secrecy. They were departing with over *half a ton* of weapons-grade uranium on board. That metal had been purchased by the United States; it was en route to Oak Ridge for dilution and reprocessing into fuel rods for commercial U.S. power reactors.

The third newly nuclear Soviet republic, Belarus, was so closely tied to the Russian economy that the Russians were able to remove the weapons located there without incident. As the twentieth century ended, all three former Soviet republics had renounced their nuclear dreams.

The happiest nuclear news of all is barely noticed because things have been so quiet for so long. After an immediate postwar spurt of nuclear development by Russia, then Britain, France, and China, the major industrial powers of the world signed a Nuclear Non-Proliferation Treaty in which the signatories relied on the American and Soviet nuclear umbrellas to deter others from nuclear adventure.

Today, when considering a dismantlement of the U.S. nuclear capability, or when lurching toward an estrangement from our traditional industrial allies, we must bear in mind that Germany, Japan, Sweden, and Taiwan, among others, all have the resources and the technical know-how to develop nuclear weapons on their own quickly. The fact they have not done so is one of the great triumphs of the postwar nuclear era, but it is a condition that will maintain only as long as those societies continue to trust their American protectors.

LESSONS FROM A HALF CENTURY NOW GONE

First of all, as noted earlier, preeminence is never a permanent condition. Unlike General Dvorkin's view of the Russian horizon, the United States *does* have major enemies: nations and cultures that do not wish us well, that would destroy us in a minute if they could. If we wish to protect the lives and homes of our citizens, to preserve the freedoms and the democracy we enjoy, and to save all we have worked for to pass on to our children, then our attention to the nation's security must be unrelenting. As in Eisenhower's time, it need not be profligate, but it must be focused and steadfast.

Second, as has been the case since Eisenhower's time, the nation's defense must be based on technology, on an excellence that leaves all others behind. Any attempts to ignore or stifle technology will in time be paid for with the lives of innocent young American troops. On a grander scale, I believe our society will be humbled and our freedoms curtailed if we allow the technical initiative to pass to others, such as China. This pursuit of technical supremacy sounds simple enough, but in practice the choices are hard. The decision to pursue thermonuclear technology was contested—in the United States—at the highest levels, but when pursued, it led to a more stable nuclear deterrent: submarine-launched ballistic missiles at sea. Advances in electronics have led to snooping on a massive scale, but those intercepts warned us of Soviet dangers and misrepresentations during the Cold War, and they abort the plans of terrorists today.

Third, the state must always remain the servant of the people, not the other way around. Thomas Jefferson got it just right at the founding of our republic: "All men . . . are endowed by their Creator with certain inalienable rights. To secure these rights Governments are instituted among men, deriving their just powers from the consent of the governed." This issue was at the heart of the Cold War; when the roles get reversed, when the state gets the upper hand, the Gulags, in one form or another, are sure to follow.

And finally, we continue to live at the abyss. Nuclear technology cannot be uninvented, nor should we abandon that deterrent power. Too many societies are counting on us; too many despots are seeking access to such power. We must remember that these weapons are unlike anything ever seen or experienced by most people now alive.

The aircraft crashing into the twin towers of New York on 9/11 released only about 0.1 kiloton of energy. Eight years earlier, on February 26, 1993, similarly minded terrorists parked a Ryder truck in the basement of those same buildings. It carried a 1,200-pound mixture of fuel oil and fertilizer, and the resulting explosion killed six and injured thousands. But suppose that truck had been carrying an amateur's A-bomb of the same weight, built from plans downloaded from the Web and made with materials purchased or stolen from reactors or inventory anywhere in the world? The builders of such a device might only get a few kilotons from their handiwork, versus the fifteen released at Hiroshima from much more primitive technology, but consider the possible consequences. After a five-kiloton blast at the World Trade Center most buildings south of Central Park would be destroyed. Millions

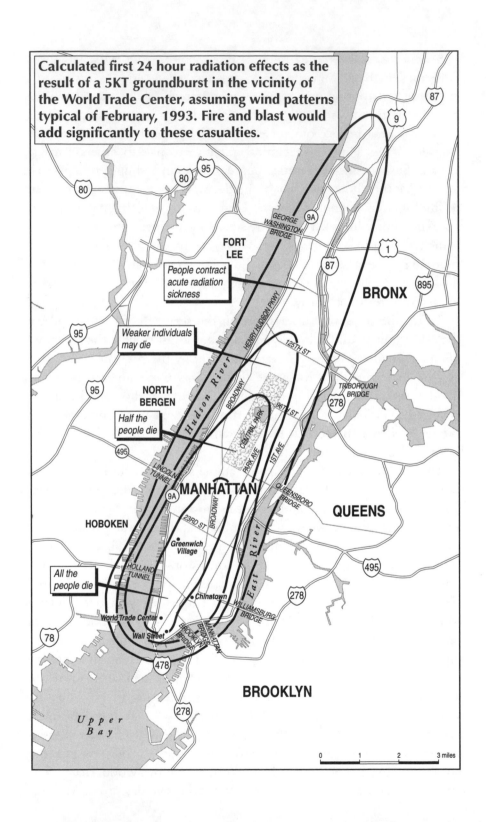

Calculated first 24 hour radiation effects as the result of a 5KT groundburst in the vicinity of the World Trade Center, assuming wind patterns typical of February, 1993. Fire and blast would add significantly to these casualties.

of New Yorkers would die; millions more would suffer acute radiation sickness. The map on the preceding page indicates the expected distribution of radiation effects from such a burst, assuming typical winter wind patterns. Fire and blast effects would add significantly to these casualties.

Or even worse, consider the consequences of a modern, compact, multimegaton thermonuclear weapon fired outside the White House gates. The blast, fires, and radiation would kill every living thing inside the Beltway. Few people now alive have seen such an explosion, heard the roar, felt the heat. I have; I hope none of my readers ever do.

We humans are very fragile creatures, living on a very fragile planet. Enrico Fermi and I share a not widely accepted view of our status here. Fermi was one of the giants of twentieth century physics, an expert on neutron behavior at the dawn of the fission age. In 1938 he fled Mussolini's Italy, in time settling into the University of Chicago's Metallurgical Laboratory. In December 1941, as the U.S. undertook an all-out effort to build an atomic bomb, he was given responsibility for the world's first chain-reacting fission pile. A year later, on December 2, 1942, with Fermi at the control rods, that first pile went critical and the world entered the nuclear age. A coded message was sent to Washington: "The Italian Navigator has entered the New World." Ironically, Fermi had not yet gained U.S. citizenship; he was still Italian, and by then the United States was at war with all of the Axis powers, including Italy. An enemy alien was at the controls of that first nuclear reactor. Today the mind boggles at the thought of such an achievement: a nuclear reactor, built in secret on a university campus in the midst of an urban area, up and running within one year, operated by a citizen of an enemy state.

In later years, in conversation with Edward Teller, Herb York, and others, Fermi casually posed what has come to be known as the Fermi paradox: "If the universe is teeming with aliens, where is everybody?" Expanded, Fermi's point is that there has been plenty of time since the universe began—the big bang fourteen billion years ago—for intelligent, communicating civilizations to colonize other galaxies. Based on human experience and expectations, any such civilization should need, at most, a hundred million years to develop the near-speed-of-light spaceships required for such colonization. We humans have been around for only three or four million years, and intergalactic travel for us cannot be more than a millennium away. Thus there has been time for hundreds of such migrations. Yet we hear and see nothing.

Fermi implied (and I believe) that we humans are alone in this universe. By "we," I mean intelligent, language-communicating living creatures. There are plenty of planets that might support life. Arthur Clarke hypothesizes sea life under the ice on Jupiter's moon Europa. Dolphins are intelligent, and they communicate by whistling within the Earth's oceans. But language communicators—people who can tell their fellow tribesmen where the food came from, how to build a radio telescope, or when history seems to be repeating itself—are unique creatures. It is a capability that came to us only 50,000 to 100,000 years ago, a frightening responsibility.

We have been entrusted with so much. At the beginning of the American experiment, in 1790, John Philpot Curran warned: "Eternal vigilance is the price of liberty." Since he composed those words, the revelation of nuclear secrets, the claims of conflicting religions (including nontheocratic religions, such as communism), and the compression of successful and failed societies into close informational proximity, have all raised the stakes and shortened the fuse. Yet the verities remain. Every citizen must attend to our nation's well-being, else we will surely topple into the waiting abyss. In so doing, we will leave behind only a spot of dark matter, a puzzle for other astronomers who may arise a long time from now in a galaxy far away.

INDEX

Abel, Rudolf, 56, 56n
Abshire, David, 270
Acton, Lord, 19
Adams, Dobree, 130
Adamskii, Victor, 102–3
Adelmann, Dick, 136
Agnew, Harold, 75
Air Force Ballistic Missile Division (BMD), 83, 85
aircraft (UK)
RAF RB-45C, 41–42
aircraft (U.S.)
A-10 (AX), 200–201, 207, 286
AWACS, 206, 206n
B-1, 205, 206, 230–31, 277
B-29, 37
B-36, 79
B-47, 44, 45, 47, 50, 343
B-52/52G, 32, 152–53, 156–58, 160, 204, 205, 277, 343, 345
B-58, 204
F-4, 198, 202
F-5E, 202
F-15, 198, 207, 285
F-16, 203–4, 207, 285
F-80 Shooting Star, 37
F-86 Sabrejets, 37–38
F-100/F-102/F-104/F-105, 193
F-117 (stealth fighter-bomber), 286
FB-111, 277
KC-97, 44, 46, 158
KC-135, 158, 160, 345
National Emergency Airborne Command Post (NEACP), 344
P-51 Mustang, 37
T-38, 202
WB-29, 105–6
Weapons System 125A, 32–33
aircraft (U.S.: reconnaissance)
F-11, 63
RB-45, 36
RB-47, 5, 36, 44–49, 50–51, 80, 345
RB-57, 36
RF-80A, 37
RF-86/RF-86F, 38, 40
SR-71 (A-12), 36, 59
U-2, 5, 33, 36, 43, 51–57, 58, 59, 80, 183–84, 345
aircraft (U.S.S.R.), 193–94
Ilyushin-28, 40
MiG-15, 37, 38, 40, 45, 46
MiG-17, 45, 46–47
MiG-19, 53
MiG-21, 195, 198, 202
Myasichev M-4, 36, 43–44, 49, 51
SA-2, 56, 57
Sukhoi Su-9, 53, 55, 56
Tupolev Tu-4, 36, 37
Akromeyev, Sergei, 303
Albright, Joe, 97–98
Alger, Bruce, 297

Allen, Richard, 230, 233
Allen, Harvey Julian, 75
Altshuler, Boris, 218–19
Alvarez, Everett, 150
Ames Laboratory, 75
Andropov, Yuri, 228, 239, 295–96
Applebaum, Anne, 12
Argentina as a nuclear threat, 353
Armed Forces Special Weapons Center (Albuquerque), 119
Armed Forces Special Weapons Project, 120
Aspin, Les, 254
Atomic Energy Commission (AEC), 79, 105, 107, 111–12, 113, 169
General Advisory Committee (GAC), 108–11
Atlee, Clement, 41
Austin, Bob, 336–38
Austin, Hal, 44–49
Avco Everett Research Laboratory, 131
Ayvazayan, Boris, 57

Baikonur Cosmodrome, 84
Baker, Howard, 273, 302
Baker, James, III, 230, 232, 260, 263, 270, 272, 273, 303
Ballistic Missile Early Warning System (BMEWS), 158–60
Bannister, Judith, 16
Barannikov, Viktor, 319
Barkovsky, Vladimir, 100–102
Baruch, Bernard, 339
Batitsky, Pavel, 27
Belarus as a nuclear threat, 355
Bell Telephone Laboratories, 77–78
Belugin, Vladimir, 313–14
Benson, Robert Louis, 10n
Bentsen, Lloyd, 299
Beria, Lavrenti, 4, 22, 23, 24–27, 100, 103
Berkeley Radiation Laboratory, 114, 137
Berle, Adolph, 9
Berlin
airlift, 340
wall, fall of, 1, 303–4, 340
Black Book of Communism, The, 14, 16, 18
Bode, Henrik, 74n
Bombshell (Albright/Kunstel), 98
Bouterese, Desi, 271
Brady, Nick, 252
Brazil as a nuclear threat, 353
Brent, Jonathan, 25
Brezhnev, Leonid, 95, 205, 215, 238–39, 266, 294
Brezhnev, Victoria Petrovna, 239
Brown, George, 175
Brown, Harold, 92, 119, 121, 123, 125, 126, 140, 141, 196, 197
Brugoni, Dino, 53n
Bulganin, Nikolai, 22, 25–27
Bush, Barbara, 297

Bush, George H. W., 1–2, 6, 228, 229n,
238, 260, 273, 294
Bush/Gorbachev Malta summit, 305–6
and the collapse of the U.S.S.R., 302–5,
308
early career, 297–300
and the Gulf War, 284–87, 348
and the media, 303
and Ross Perot, 302, 307–8
personality, 298
unilateral offers, 290, 290n, 292
as Vice President, 299–300
Bush, George W., 308–9
Bush, Prescott, 298
Butler, Lee, 287–92, 343

Callaway, Bo, 188
Cambodia, 18–19
Cannon, Lou, 231–32
Carr, Ken, 334–38
Carter, Jimmy, 125, 197, 231, 246, 247
Casey, Bill, 229n, 238, 267–68, 271
Castro, Fidel, 18
Ceausescu, Nicolae, 17–18
Chain, Jack, 288
Chambers, Whittaker, 8–11, 19, 294
Charyk, Joe, 183
Cheney, Dick, 281–84, 284–87, 289, 291,
292, 341
Chernenko, Konstantin, 296, 303
Childress, Richard, 301n, 302
China, 3, 38–40, 69
Cultural Revolution, 15–16
See also communism; Korean War; Mao
Tse-tung; Vietnam War
Churchill, Winston, 89, 226, 307, 339
CIA (Central Intelligence Agency), 107
Farewell dossier, 266–70
and the Red Star video tape, 318–19
Venona transcripts, 10, 10n, 22, 97
and Vietnam, 145–46
Clark, William (Bill), 213, 232, 233–34,
237, 238, 243, 244, 247–48, 249,
252, 255, 259–60, 263, 264, 270,
271–72, 275, 295, 296
Clements, Bill, 174, 175, 179, 208, 252,
298
Clinton, Bill, 307–8, 308
coaxial cables, 181–82
Cochran, Ted, 161–63, 164, 166–67,
167–68
Cohen, Morris and Lona, 97
communication technology, 170–91
intelligence satellites, 183–85
Internet, 182, 190
security and, 180–82
U.S.S.R., 328–31
communism, 7, 10, 11, 19
in America, 8–11
Communist Party of the Soviet Union
(CPSU), 11, 250, 293
See also Black Book of Communism, The

Contemporary Chinese Population, 16
Crabb, Lionel, 52n
Crampton, John, 42
Cuban missile crisis, 4, 18, 159–60,
322–23, 324–25
Curran, John Philpot, 360

Day After, The (TV movie), 250, 255
Deaver, Mike, 230, 259, 263, 270
Defense Advanced Research Projects
Agency, 182
Defense Communications Agency, 172
Defense Satellite Communication System,
172
Desert Storm, 284–87, 348
Deutch, John, 253
Dietrich, Noah, 62
Distant Early Warning (DEW) Line,
158–60
Diven, Ben, 75
Dixon, Bob, 202
Dobrynin, Anatoly, 238
Dodge, Colonel, 89, 91
Dodge, Jack, 83
Dolan, Tony, 237n
Doyle, Arthur Conan, 3
Draper, C. Stark "Doc," 75–76
Duberstein, Ken, 273
Duckett, Carl, 85n
Dukakis, Michael, 299
Duke, Angier Biddle, 166
Dulles, John Foster, 4, 96
Dunn, Louis, 74n
Dvorkin, Vladimir, 348–49

East Germany
Berlin wall, fall of, 1, 303–4, 340
Peenemunde, 70–71
Economist, 224
Einstein, Albert, 124–25
Eisenhower, Dwight D., 4, 5, 19, 21, 29–32,
33, 36, 51, 52, 58, 71, 96, 211, 347
Eisenhower, Mamie, 33
Electronic Data Systems (EDS), 300–301,
301n
ELF communication system, 187–89
Ellis, Richard, 342
Ericson, Bob, 53, 54, 55
espionage (UK)
Frogman Episode, 52, 52n
espionage (U.S.), 86
intelligence satellites, 183–85
at Los Alamos, 22, 97, 98, 101–2, 112,
116
and nuclear technology, 22, 96–98,
100–102, 112
Ware group, 9–11
See also CIA; reconnaissance
espionage (U.S.S.R.), 100–102, 153n
in America, 9–11, 22, 29, 274n
Farewell dossier, 266–70
and nuclear technology, 22, 96–98,
100–102, 112, 315

the Rosenbergs, 97, 315
TEA-16 affair, 166, 167–68
Venona transcripts, 10, 10n, 22, 97
See also Barkovsky, Vladimir; Fuchs,
  Klaus; Hall, Ed
Evans and Novak, 253

Fahd, King, 285
Farewell dossier, 266–70
Fermi, Enrico, 109, 359–60
First Lightning, 103, 105–8
Fletcher, Jim, 65
Ford, Gerald, 175, 179, 187–89, 195, 260,
  274, 299
Forward Based Systems, 175–76
Foster, Johnny, 117, 118–21, 122
Foster, Johnny, 173n
Frogman Episode, 52, 52n
Fuchs, Klaus, 22, 97, 101–2, 112, 116, 315

Gadhafi, Mu'ammar, 353
Gagarin, Yuri, 95
Gardner, Trevor, 73, 73–74
Gates, Robert, 318–19
Gates, Thomas, 278, 278n
General Dynamics, 203–4
Gephardt, Dick, 304
Ghiorso, Albert, 107
Gold, Harry, 102
Goldwater, Barry, 145
Goodpaster, Andrew J., 30, 32
Gorbachev, Mikhail, 2, 6, 219, 225, 228,
  256, 269–70, 287, 294, 296–97,
  305–6, 306–7, 340
Gouzenko, Igor, 10
Graham, Katherine, 262, 264
Gribkov, A. I., 323n
Gromyko, Andrei, 228
Guest, William, 166
Gulags, 11–12, 13
Gulf War, 284–87, 348

Haig, Al, 229–30, 229n, 233, 252, 317
Hall, Ed, 80, 81, 86–88, 88–91, 92, 96–98
Hall, Ted ("Mlad"), 22, 97–98, 101
Hammer, Armand, 274n
Hanford, Washington, 223
Haussmann, Carl, 121–23, 126, 129, 140, 141
Heavilin, Vance, 44–49
Hecker, Sig, 314
Helms, Richard, 252
Herres, Robert, 283
Herrick, John, 147
Hiroshima, bombing of, 4
Hiss, Alger, 9–10, 29
Ho Chi Minh, 151
Hoffmann, Martin, 316
Holt, Carl, 44–49
Honecker, Erich, 303
Hubbard, Tim, 149
Hughes, Howard, 61, 62–63, 63, 66–68, 317
Hughes Aircraft Company, 62–63, 64,
  64–66, 66–68

Hussein, Saddam, 171, 284, 287, 351–52
Hyland, Lawrence, 74n

Ikle, Fred, 270
information age, 170–91
Intelligence Panel, 51, 57–60
International Executive Service Corps
  (IESC), 219–20
Internet, 182, 190
Iraq
  French support of, 351
  the Gulf War, 284–87, 348
  liberation of, 285
  oil reserves, 350–51, 350n
  Russian GPS jammers, 349n
  weapons of mass destruction,
    351–52
Iran as a nuclear threat, 352
Ivory Leaf exercise, 243–45, 255

Jaeger, Harald, 304, 309
Jet Propulsion Laboratory (Cal Tech), 78
Johnson, Kelly, 51
Johnson, Louis, 106–7
Johnson, Lyndon B., 125, 144–45, 149,
  150, 151, 245, 297, 299
Joint Strategic Target Planning Staff
  (JSTPS), 278–79, 279–81
Jones, David C., 242, 246–47, 248

Kantrowitz, Arthur, 136
Karpenko, Victor, 136, 137
Kazakhstan as a nuclear threat, 355–56
Kazbek system, 329–30
Kennan, George, 30
Kennedy, John F., *xi,* 33, 94–95, 121, 125,
  136–37, 144
  and the Cuban missile crisis, 18,
    159–60, 322–23, 324–25
Kerr, Clark, 247
Keyworth, Jay, 255
Khariton, Yuli, 22, 24, 78, 103, 314–15
Khmer Rouge, 18–19
Khomeini, Ayatollah Ruhollah, 352
Khomeini, Sayyid Hussein, 352
Khrushchev, Nikita, *xi,* 21, 25–27, 27–28,
  28–29, 33–34, 49, 52n, 55, 86, 95,
  132, 133, 184, 238
  and the Cuban missile crisis, 18,
    159–60, 322–23, 324–25
  Stalin, denunciation of, 14, 27
Khrushchev, Sergei, 95
Khrustalev (Stalin's guard), 25, 26
Kikoin, Isaak, 23–24
Killian, James, 51
Kim Il Sung, 17, 353
Kim Jong-il, 17
Kinchloe, Ivan, 32
Kirkpatrick, Jeanne, 229n, 238, 270
Kissinger, Henry, 229, 266, 317
Kistiakowski, George, 74n
Kline, Major, 242
Kohl, Helmut, 250

Korean War, 3, 17, 19, 29, 30, 35–37,
  37–40, 40–42, 69, 106, 119
  aircraft lost during, 193
  nuclear weapons, possible use of, 7–8,
    40–42, 96
  See also North Korea
Korolev, Sergei Pavlovich, 70, 96
Kozyrev, Andrei V., 319
Kramish, Arnold, 107
Kravchuk, Leonid, 1
Krenz, Egon, 303
Krikorian, Nerses, 313
Kryuchkov, Vladimir, 308
Kunstel, Marcia, 97–98
Kurchatov, Igor, 24, 103, 105
Kurnakov, Sergei, 97

Laird, Melvin, 253
Land, Edwin, 51, 185
Lauritsen, Charles, 74n
Lawrence, E. O., 114, 314
Lawrence Livermore Laboratory. *See under*
  nuclear weapons (U.S.)
Lee, Bill, 213
Lehman, John, 270
LeMay, Curtis E., 49, 88, 145, 208, 288,
  340, 341
Lenczowski, John, 237n
Lenin, Vladimir, 12, 19, 294, 310
Leningrad Polytechnic Institute, 328–29
Life magazine, 135
Limited Nuclear Options (LNOs), 176–78
Linebacker II, 152–53
Litton, Charles, 65
Litvinov, Boris, 314
Liu Shao-qi, 15–16
Live Oak plan, 96
Los Alamos. *See under* nuclear weapons
  (U.S.)
Los Alamos Primer, The (Serber), 124
Lozgachev (Stalin's guard), 25
Luce, Henry, 9

MacArthur, Douglas, 8, 41
McCormick, James, 30
McDonnell Douglas, 198
McElroy, Neil, 88
McFarlane, Bud, 232, 234, 235, 252
McLucas, John, 196–97, 198, 201, 203
McMahon, Brien, 108
McNamara, Robert, 95, 95n, 149, 151,
  169, 176, 194
McPeak, Merrill, 343
Maenchen, George, 136
Maiman, Ted, 65
Malenkov, Georgi, 22, 25–27, 72–73
Manhattan, effects of a Nuclear attack on,
  357–59, 358
Mao Tse-tung, 15–16, 125
Mark, Carson, 75
Marshall, Andy, 213
Marshall, George, 106–7
Marxism. *See* communism

May, Mike, 130
Meese, Ed, 230, 232, 259–60, 263, 270
Messinger, Larry, 160, 163
Mettler, Rube, 65, 80, 92–93
Meyer, Edward "Shy," 248
Millikan, Clark, 74n
Minuteman program. *See under* rockets and
  missiles
missiles. *See* rockets and missiles
Mitchell, George, 304
Mitterand, François, 266
Mohr, Milt, 65
Molotov, Vyacheslav, 26
Murphy, Charles J. V., 135
Mutual Assured Destruction (MAD), 193–94
Myasnikov, A. L., 26
Myer, Allan, 236n

Nath, Vann, 18–19
National Emergency Airborne Command
  Post (NEACP), 344
National Ignition Facility, 140
National Military Command Center, 242,
  243
National Reconnaissance Office (NRO),
  183–85
National Security Council (NSC), 213,
  229–31, 229n, 233–34
  NSDD-32, 235–37
  NSDD-75, 239–40
NATO, 1, 5, 29, 29n, 171–73, 269
Naumov, Vladimir, 25
Naval Research Lab (Washington, D.C.),
  106, 107
Nechai, Vladimir, 313–14
Neddermeyer, Seth, 115
New York Times, 14
Newsweek magazine, 272
Nichols, Mary Dunham, 60
Nixon, Richard, 10, 19, 30, 33, 145, 177,
  188, 195, 274, 295, 299
Nofziger, Lyn, 263
North, Harper, 65
North, Oliver, 232, 237, 243, 245, 273
North Korea, 17
  as a nuclear threat, 17, 352–53
  See also Korean War
Novak, Robert, 8
Nuckolls, John, 22, 23, 103, 124–26, 127,
  131, 136, 140, 141, 314
nuclear weapons
  China, 194–95
  France, 107–8
  North Korea, 17
  UK, 78, 107, 130
nuclear weapons (U.S.), 4–5
  accidents involving, 119–20, 156–69
  arsenal, 277–78, 283
  command and control systems, 331–33
  as deterrents, 7–8, 40–42, 96, 111
  espionage and, 22, 96–98, 100–102, 112
  H-bomb opposition, 124–25

H-bomb technology, 22–23, 51, 75,
    78–79, 108–9, 110, 111–12,
    113–14, 114–18, 118–21, 122–23
Hiroshima bomb (Little Boy), 4, 100,
    114, 115
Lawrence Livermore Laboratory, 93,
    113–14, 117, 118, 119–21, 123,
    126–27, 128, 130, 131, 137,
    140–41, 314
Los Alamos, 22, 91, 97, 101–2, 114–18,
    124, 126, 137, 140, 313–14
Mk-28 H-bomb, 160, 160–62, 168–69
moratoriums and treaties, 90, 126, 204,
    256
Nagasaki bomb (Fat Man), 22, 110, 111
Oak Ridge, 137
Oso device, 135–36, 136–40, 141
Policy Committee conclusions, 289–92
security of, 172–73
"strategic," 283n
strategic nuclear superiority, 175–78, 204
TEA-16 affair, 160–69
testing, 78, 90, 93, 121, 132–33, 135
testing (atmospheric), 134, 136–40
Trident II warhead, 110
U.S./Russian exchanges, 313–16
war plan, 278–79, 279–81
Woods Hole conference, 117, 118–19
See also Korean War; rockets and
    missiles; Vietnam War
nuclear weapons (U.S.S.R.), 3, 4–5, 78,
    99–112, 321–22
A-bomb technology, 22–24, 41, 69,
    102–3, 105–8, 321
Arzamas-16 (Saroy), 24, 102–3, 126,
    135, 315
Chelyabinsk-70, 315
command and control systems, 328–31
and the Cuban missile crisis, 18,
    159–60, 322–23, 324–25
Energia (Eighty-eight Scientific
    Research Institute), 69–71, 71n, 73,
    79–80, 96
espionage and, 22, 96–98, 100–102, 112
First Lightning, 103, 105–8
H-bomb technology, 51, 72–73,
    110–11, 117, 134
Mayak (Chelyabinsk-70), 104–5, 107
moratoriums, 90, 121, 126
Moscow Laboratory Number 2, 114
preemptive use, threat of, 18
testing, 132–35
U.S./Russian exchanges, 313–16
O'Donnell, Peter, 297–98
oil and terrorism, 350–51
On Wings of Eagles (Follett), 301
Open Skies policy, 52
Oppenheimer, J. Robert, 97, 105, 108–9,
    114, 314
Oso device, 135–36, 136–40, 141
Overholser, Denys, 205

Pahad, Aziz, 354
PALs (Permissive Action Links), 173, 173n
Pavlovski, Alexander, 314
Peenemunde (East Germany), 70–71
Pentagon Papers, 146
Perle, Richard, 270
Perot, Ross, 300–302
    and Electronic Data Systems (EDS),
        300–301, 301n
    and the POW/MIA committee, 300–302
    and the Reform party, 307–8
Perry, Bill, 85n, 197, 353, 205, 253
Perseus (spy at Los Alamos), 102, 102n
Petoukhov, Efrem Ivanovich, 327
Petoukhov, Vladimir, 325–28, 328–31, 338
Pliyev, Issa, 5, 323, 323n, 324
plutonium, 222–24
Poe, Bryce, 37
Poindexter, John, 275
Pol Pot, 18–19
Polaris program. *See under* rockets and
    missiles (U.S.)
Popov, Gavril, 311–13
Powell, Colin, 283, 285–87, 288, 289, 292,
    302, 343
Powers, Francis Gary, 54, 55–57
Preston, Joe, 44, 49
Primakov, Yevgeny, 318, 319
Project Matterhorn (Princeton), 122
Project Q. *See under* rockets and missiles
Puckett, Allen, 65, 74n
Pugo, Boris, 308

Quarles, Donald, 81

Rabi, I. I., 109, 124
Ralston, Joe, 195, 209–10
Ramo, Si, 63–64, 64–66, 66–68, 74, 74n, 92
Ramo-Wooldridge Corporation/TRW,
    66–68, 74, 78, 81, 88–89, 92
Reagan, Nancy, 232, 258–60
    and detente, 240, 270
    as first lady, 259–60, 261, 261–62
    lifestyle, 261, 262, 274n
    personality and temperament, 258–59,
        272–73, 274n
    political involvement, 261, 261–66,
        270, 270–71, 272–73
    and Ronald, 274
Ramparts magazine, 300
Reagan, Ronald, 5–6, 117–18, 145, 190,
    299, 302
    Andropov-Reagan correspondence,
        295–96
    and the Cold War, 239–40
    and the collapse of the U.S.S.R., 212–14,
        226–27, 228–29, 293–94, 295
    Ivory Leaf exercise, 243–45, 255
    management style, 229, 234–35,
        238–39, 247–51, 263–64
    personality and temperament, 258–59,
        262, 273–75
Reagan, Ronald, Jr., 262

Reagan administration
  cabinet conflicts (Pragmatists vs Old
    Shoes), 262–66, 270, 270–71
  and the Chairman of the JCS, 247–48
  Farewell dossier, 266–70
  M-X missile program, 251–54
  media and, 231–32, 250, 253, 263,
    270–71
  military buildup, 206, 207, 212,
    230–31, 247–51, 279–81
  National Security Council, 229–31,
    229n, 233–34, 240
  NSDD-32, 235–37
  NSDD-75, 239–40
  Project *"Partridge,"* 245–46, 256
  (Scowcroft) Commission of Strategic
    Forces, 252–54
  and SIOP (Single Integrated
    Operational Plan), 241–45
  START II treaty, 256
Real, Jack, 67
Rechtin, Eb, 85n
reconnaissance (UK)
  overflights (Special Duty Flight), 36,
    41–43
reconnaissance (U.S.), 80, 82
  Home Run operation, 49–51
  last U-2 flights (1960), 54
  National Reconnaissance Office
    (NRO), 183–85
  overflights, 5, 31–32, 35–37, 38–40,
    43–49, 49–51, 51–57, 183–84
  PARPRO (Peacetime Airborne
    Reconnaissance Program), 35–36, 60
  RB-47E overflight (1954), 45
  satellites, 36–37
  Vojvodich overflight (1953), 39
  See also espionage
Red Flag, 202–3
Red Guards, 16
Red Star video tape, 316–19
Reed, Sally and Lawrence, 297
Reed, Thomas, 2, 19–20, 348
  and communication technology, 172,
    178, 181, 184–85, 187
  and the defense establishment, 83, 91,
    93–94, 113–14, 127–31, 197, 203,
    280, 332
  at Edwards Air Force Base, 32–33
  government service, 212, 342, 350
  at the NR, 184–85, 187–89
  at the NSC, 232, 234, 235, 243,
    247–48, 332
  and the *Oso* device, 135–36, 136–40,
    141
  Policy Committee conclusions,
    289–92
  and political involvement, 188–89, 212,
    258, 298
  at the Reagan White House, 263–66
  Red Star video tape, 316–19

  (Scowcroft) Commission of Strategic
    Forces, 252–54
  as speech writer, 237
Reform party, 307–8
Regan, Don, 273
Rice, Condoleezza, 285, 289
Richardson, Eliot, 174
Rickover, Hyman, 334
Rigley, Jim, 48
Ritterodt, Marianne, 166, 167–68, 169
Rockefeller, Nelson, 72
rockets and missiles, 69–83
  in France, 92
  Nazi V-1/V-2 rockets, 70-71, 84
  Scud missiles, 287
  and the UK, 80–81, 93, 204
rockets and missiles (U.S.), 73, 79–80, 204
  Atlas program, 71, 73, 76–77, 79, 81,
    85, 87, 89–90, 93, 94, 117, 277
  government financing of, 81
  Maverick program, 199–200, 207
  M-X ("Midgetman") program, 251–54,
    256
  Minuteman program (Project Q), 84,
    86–88, 88–91, 91–93, 93–94, 95,
    130, 206, 277
  missile gap, 94–95, 95n
  Peacekeeper program, 253–54, 256
  Pershing program, 249–50, 256, 264
  Polaris program, 81, 92, 93, 95, 117,
    119, 333, 335
  Poseidon program, 111
  SAMs, 193
  Thor program, 80–81, 89–90, 93, 94, 95
  Titan program, 80, 89–90, 277
  Teapot Committee, 73–79
  Woods Hole conference, 117, 118–19
rockets and missiles (U.S.S.R.), 79, 322–23
  Kapustin Yar (Cabbage Ravine), 43
  R-5/5M (SS-3), 79, 79n, 86, 94, 96
  R-7/7M (SS-6), 84–85, 84n, 85, 94,
    117, 322
  R-16 (SS-7), 55, 94, 322
  SA-2 (S-75), 53
  SS-4/SS-5/SS-16, 176
  SS-20, 176, 249, 256, 264
Romania, 17–18
Rosenberg, Julius, 86, 315
Rosengren, Jack, 92, 93, 130, 140, 141
Rowen, Henry, 214, 240
Ruina Commission, 354
Rumsfeld, Donald, 175, 196
Rusk, Dean, 151
Russian Federation
  and economic development, 311–13
  exports from, 225–26
  See also U.S.S.R.; Yeltsin, Boris

Safire, Bill, 263, 270, 272
Safronov, Sergei, 57
Saiko, Vasily, 60
Sakharov, Andrei, 110n, 111

Sandia Laboratories, 91, 120
Sather, Richard C., 150
Schabowski, Gunter, 303–4
Schlesinger, James, 172, 174–75, 196, 246, 317–18, 350
Schriever, Bernard, 74, 77, 79, 81, 83, 87–88, 89, 90, 92
Schrontz, Frank, 204
Schultz, George, 229n, 238, 295
Scientific Advisory Group (SAG), 279
Scowcroft, Brent, 252, 284–87, 303
Scud missiles, 287
Semenikhin, Vladimir, 328
Serber, Robert, 124
Severodvinsk (Soviet submarine facility), 59–60
Shakespeare, William, 3
Sheldon, George, 311–13
Shevardnadze, Eduard, 219
ships (U.S.)
    Alvin submersible, 166, 168
    PTF (Patrol Torpedo Fast), 146
    submarines, ballistic-missile-firing (SSBNs), 331–33
    submarines, communications with, 185–89
    USS *Albany*, 166
    USS *Blackfin*, 334
    USS *Constellation*, 147, 149, 150
    USS *George Washington*, 95, 185, 335
    USS *James Monroe*, 335
    USS *John Adams*, 336–37
    USS *Maddox*, 146, 147, 148, 149
    USS *Nautilus*, 334
    USS *Oriskany*, 145
    USS *Petrel*, 168
    USS *Pueblo*, 144
    USS *Scorpion*, 334
    USS *Ticonderoga*, 147, 148–49, 149–50
    USS *Turner Joy*, 147, 148, 149
ships (U.S.S.R.), 186, 187
    K-19, 185n
    Red Star submarine, 316–19
Shushchevik, Stanislav, 1
Signal system, 330–31
Simo, Francisco, 166
Sinatra, Frank, 262
Singleton, Henry, 65
SIOP (Single Integrated Operational Plan), 241–45, 281–84
Slavsky, Efim, 24
Smith, W. Y., 323n
Smyth Report *(Atomic Energy for Military Purposes)*, 105, 105n, 124
Sokhina, Liya, 104–5
Sokolov, Taras, 327, 328
Sokolovsky, V. D., 4, 321
South Africa as a nuclear threat, 353–55
Soviet Strategic Rocket Force, 85
space program (U.S.)
    Apollo program, 95

Discoverer program, 58–59
    intelligence satellites, 183–85
    satellites, 36–37, 57–60, 60
    Strategic Defense Initiative (Star Wars), 5–6, 95, 117–18, 254–56, 256–57, 270
    Weapon System 117L, 58
space program (U.S.S.R.)
    decline of, 95–96
    Sputnick, 58, 59, 85–86, 117, 327–28
Spencer, Stuart, 188, 234–35, 240, 259–60
Spruce Goose, 63, 63n
Sputnick, 58, 59, 85–86, 117, 327–28
Stalin, Joseph, 3–4, 21–27, 100, 108, 189
    death of, 25–27
    and Lenin Mausoleum, 26, 29
    purges and deaths under, 9, 12, 13–15, 21–22, 125
    and the Ukraine famine, 12–13
Stalin, Svetlana, 26
Star Wars. *See under* space program (U.S.)
START II treaty, 256
Stillman, Danny, 313
Stockdale, James, 5, 145, 147, 148–49, 152, 153–55, 307
Stockdale, Sybil, 154
Stockman, Harvey, 52
Strategic Air Command (SAC), 158–60, 277, 288–89, 340, 341–43
    Omaha as headquarters, 342
Strauss, Robert S., 319
submarines, communications with, 185–89
Suter, Moody, 202

Talbott, Harold, 73
Talent-Keyhole, 58, 58n
Tamm, Igor, 110
Tass (Soviet News agency), 26
TEA-16, flight of, 160–67
Teapot Committee, 43, 73–79
Technical Capabilities (Surprise Attack) Panel, 51
Telemetry and Beacon Analysis Committee (TABAC), 85–86
Teller, Edward, 92, 113, 114–18, 123, 136, 140, 255, 314, 359
Terhune, Charles, 88
terrorism
    oil dollars funding, 351
    Manhattan, effects of a nuclear attack on, 357–59, 358
    9/11 attack, 357
Thatcher, Margaret, 250
Thomson Products/TRW, 67, 68
Thornton, Tex, 65
Thule (Greenland), 49–50
Time magazine, 8–9, 81, 89, 272
titanium, 221–22
Tower, John, 252, 297
TracerLab Company, 106
Truman, Harry, 7–8, 23, 29, 30, 41, 106, 108, 111–12, 122, 245, 260
Tsiolkovskii, Konstantin, 70

Tu, Mary, 16
Tu, Sam, 15–16
Tukhachevsky, Mikhail, 14
Tuol Sleng prison (Phnom Penh), 18–19
Tuttle, Holmes, 274

Ukraine, 220
  famine in, 12–13
  as a nuclear threat, 355
U.S.
  containment policy, 30–32
  Cuban missile crisis, 18, 159–60,
    322–23, 324–25
  HUAC (House Committee of
    Un-American Activities), 9
  Peace Dividend, 225–26
  See also Air Force (U.S.); aircraft;
    espionage; Korean War; nuclear
    weapons; reconnaissance; rockets
    and missiles; ships
U.S.S.R., 11, 310–11
  as an ally, 9
  Battle of Leningrad, 325–26
  Bush/Gorbachev Malta summit, 305–6
  and Cental America, 271–72
  Communist Party of the Soviet Union
    (CPSU), 11, 250, 293, 341
  confrontation policy, 33–34
  collapse of, 1–2, 213–14, 226–27, 256,
    293–94, 294–96, 302–5, 306–9, 341
  defense budget, 218–19, 219–21
  Gulags and political deaths, 11–12, 13,
    13–15, 21–22
  and the Korean War, 40
  Nazi German invasion of, 9
  oil reserves of, 215–18
  Ukraine famine, 12–13
  slave labor in, 14
  See also aircraft; communism; espionage;
    Gorbachev, Mikhail; Khrushchev,
    Nikita; Korean War; nuclear weapons;
    Russian Federation; Stalin, Joseph;
    Yeltsin, Boris
Ufimtsev, Pyotr, 205–6
Ulam, Stanislaus, 113, 116–17
Universally Assignable Pilot policy, 201–3
uranium, 201, 201n
Ustinov, Dimitri, 249

Valentine, Jimmy, 46
Van Dorn, William, 125
Van Karman, Theodore, 64
Vanayev, Gennady, 308
Vance, Cyrus, 247
Venona transcripts, 10, 10n, 22, 97
Vessey, John, 248–51, 255, 256, 273
Vetrow, Vladimir I., 267
Vietnam War, 5, 19–20, 142–55, 196–97
  background, 142–45
  DeSoto patrols, 146–47
  and the domino effect, 144

Gulf of Tonkin navel action, 145–47,
  148–49, 149–50
Gulf of Tonkin resolution, 150–51
Hanoi, air campaign against, 152–53
hidden cost of, 204–6
nuclear weapons, possible use of,
  143–44, 143n, 151–52
Paris Peace Accords, 153
Saigon, fall of, 178–80
Thanh Hoa bridge, 199–200
Vito, Carmine, 52
Vlasov, Andrey, 220
Vojvodich, Mele, 38–40
  flight of, 39
von Neumann, John, 72, 74n, 115, 116
Voronov, Major, 57
Vyshinsky, Andrei, 22

Warner, Michael, 10n
Washington Post, 102, 166, 231–32, 253,
  262, 291
Watkins, James A., 255, 314
Weinberger, Casper W., 229n, 231, 232,
  238, 247, 249, 253, 273
Weiss, Gus, 267, 269
Wendorf, Charles F., 160, 163
Western Development Division (WDD),
  77, 80
Western Electric, 120
Wheeler, Earle G., 151
Wheeler, John, 122
Wheelon, Bud, 85n
White House Communications Agency,
  242
Wickham, John, 175
Wiesner, Jerome, 74n
Wigner, Eugene, 115
Wilson, Charles E., 73, 119
Witness (Chambers), 8–11
Wolfe, Marcus, 96
Wooldridge, Dean, 64–66, 66–68, 74n
Woolsey, Jim, 253
World Wide Military Command and
  Control System, 172, 174, 242,
  286
Wray, Carol, 19
Wray, Bob, 19

Yakimenko, Elena, 13
Yarborough, Ralph, 298, 299
Yarynich, Valery, 322–23, 325–28, 328–31,
  338
Yeager, Chuck, 32
Yeltsin, Boris, 1, 287, 289, 292, 296–97,
  307–8, 311–12, 341
  and the *Red Star* video tape, 318–19
York, Herbert, 114, 121, 359

Zeigenhorn, Rudi, 304
Zeldovich, Yakov, 137–38
Zhivkov, Todor, 305
Zhukov, Georgi, 26